Luso-tropicalism and Its Discontents

Luso-tropicalism and Its Discontents
The Making and Unmaking of Racial Exceptionalism

Edited by
*Warwick Anderson, Ricardo Roque,
and Ricardo Ventura Santos*

NEW YORK · OXFORD
www.berghahnbooks.com

First published in 2019 by

Berghahn Books

www.berghahnbooks.com

© 2019, 2023 Warwick Anderson, Ricardo Roque, and Ricardo Ventura Santos
First paperback edition published in 2023

All rights reserved. Except for the quotation of short passages for the purposes of criticism and review, no part of this book may be reproduced in any form or by any means, electronic or mechanical, including photocopying, recording, or any information storage and retrieval system now known or to be invented, without written permission of the publisher.

Library of Congress Cataloging-in-Publication Data

A C.I.P. cataloging record is available from the Library of Congress

Library of Congress Cataloging in Publication Control Number: 2019002287

British Library Cataloguing in Publication Data

A catalogue record for this book is available from the British Library

ISBN 978-1-78920-113-0 hardback
ISBN 978-1-80073-636-8 paperback
ISBN 978-1-78920-114-7 ebook

https://doi.org/10.3167/9781789201130

Contents

List of Maps and Illustrations   vii

Acknowledgments   viii

Introduction   1
   Warwick Anderson, Ricardo Roque, and Ricardo Ventura Santos

PART I. PICTURING AND READING FREYRE

1. Gilberto Freyre's View of Miscegenation and Its Circulation in the Portuguese Empire, 1930s–1960s   23
Cláudia Castelo

2. Gilberto Freyre: Racial Populism and Ethnic Nationalism   45
Jerry Dávila

3. Anthropology and Pan-Africanism at the Margins of the Portuguese Empire: Trajectories of Kamba Simango   68
Lorenzo Macagno

PART II. IMAGINING A MIXED-RACE NATION

4. Eugenics, Genetics, and Anthropology in Brazil: *The Masters and the Slaves*, Racial Miscegenation, and Its Discontents   89
Robert Wegner and Vanderlei Sebastião de Souza

5. Gilberto Freyre and the UNESCO Research Project on Race Relations in Brazil   112
Marcos Chor Maio

6. "An Immense Mosaic": Race Mixing and the Creation of the Genetic Nation in 1960s Brazil   135
Rosanna Dent and Ricardo Ventura Santos

PART III. THE COLONIAL SCIENCES OF RACE

7. The Racial Science of Patriotic Primitives:
   António Mendes Correia in Portuguese Timor 159
   Ricardo Roque

8. Reassessing Portuguese Exceptionalism: Racial Concepts
   and Colonial Policies toward the "Bushmen" in Southern
   Angola, 1880s–1970s 184
   Samuël Coghe

9. "Anthrobiology," Racial Miscegenation, and Body Normality:
   Comparing Biotypological Studies in Brazil and Portugal,
   1930–1940 215
   Ana Carolina Vimieiro-Gomes

PART IV. PORTUGUESENESS IN THE TROPICS

10. Luso-tropicalism Debunked, Again: Race, Racism, and
    Racialism in Three Portuguese-Speaking Societies 243
    Cristiana Bastos

11. Being Goan (Modern) in Zanzibar: Mobility, Relationality,
    and the Stitching of Race 265
    Pamila Gupta

Afterword I. Mixing the Global Color Palette 287
Nélia Dias

Afterword II. Luso-tropicalism and Mixture in the
Latin American Context 296
Peter Wade

Index 307

Maps and Illustrations

Map

Map 8.1. Distribution of non-Bantu groups in Angola.   193

Illustrations

Figure 7.1. António Mendes Correia upon his arrival at Dili in 1953.   166

Figure 7.2. António Mendes Correia and his reception at Ossu, Timor Anthropological Mission, 1953.   176

Figure 9.1. Examples of the Barbára-Berardinelli classification.   222

Figure 9.2. Biotypogram and the study of corporal proportionality in the Portuguese population.   223

Figure 10.1. Portuguese settlers from Madeira at Chibia, Huíla Plateau, Angola, circa 1890.   248

Figure 10.2. Portuguese boys in Fall River, Massachusetts, circa 1910.   250

Figure 10.3. Portuguese girls and a boy working in a sugar field, Lahaina, Maui, Hawai'i, circa 1911.   252

Figure 10.4. Picture illustrating "Portuguese ancestry" in Romanzo Adams's *Interracial Marriage in Hawaii* (1937).   254

Figure 11.1. General stores of Isidore I. Dias, circa 1950s.   274

Figure 11.2. Tailoring and outfitting, S. R. Faleiro, circa 1950s.   275

Figure 11.3. Newlyweds, Capital Art Studio, circa 1950s.   277

Figure 11.4. Wedding party, steps of St. Joseph's Cathedral, circa 1950s.   278

Figure 11.5. John Da Silva, 2012.   281

Figure 11.6. Robin Batista, 2015.   282

Acknowledgments

All the contributors to this volume join with the editors in expressing our profound gratitude to James Dunk for his intellectual guidance, his exceptional organizational and editorial skills, and his grace and efficiency in making sure these important essays could be published. Without his patience, enthusiasm, and insight, this collection would not exist.

Some of the research presented in this book was first presented and discussed within the framework of "Racial Conceptions in the Twentieth-Century: Comparisons, Connections and Circulations in the Portuguese-Speaking Global South" in Rio de Janeiro 5–7 April 2016. The contributors were able to come together thanks to the support of Warwick Anderson's "Race and Ethnicity in the Global South" Laureate Fellowship research program at the University of Sydney (Australian Research Council FL110100243), the Wellcome Trust (Medical Humanities grant 109340/Z/15/Z), and the Brazilian National Council for Scientific and Technological Development (CNPq grant 304.358/2014-2). James Dunk, Elaine Barroso, and Carlos Coimbra Jr. looked after the complicated logistics, while Ricardo Ventura Santos was a generous host. We thank Nélia Dias, Peter Fry, Sebastián Gil-Riaño, Ilana Löwy, Peter Wade, and Sarah Walsh for their stimulating comments and discussion. Sebastián and Sarah later wrote an extensive report for the 2016 *History of Anthropology Newsletter*.[1]

Gabriela Soto Laveaga, Cristiana Bastos, and Hans Pols gave helpful advice on framing the introduction to this volume. Ricardo Roque ensured the editors were able to write the introduction and arrange the collection in Lisbon. During the past year, it was a great pleasure to work with Chris Chappell, Amanda Horn, and Soyolmaa Lkhagvadorj at Berghahn.

Note

1. Sebastián Gil-Riaño and Sarah Walsh, "Racial Conceptions in the Twentieth-Century: Comparisons, Connections and Circulations in the Portuguese-Speaking Global South," *History of Anthropology Newsletter* 40 (20 June 2016), http://www.histanthro.org/racial-conceptions-in-the-twentieth-century/#more-916.

Introduction

Warwick Anderson, Ricardo Roque, and Ricardo Ventura Santos

In thinking about racial difference and race relations in the Global South, Gilberto Freyre's theories, propounded in the 1930s and formalized in the 1950s, of Portuguese (and therefore Brazilian) racial exceptionalism should immediately come to mind. Notwithstanding the ambivalence of his prose, Freyre's work fostered an appreciation that Portugal had been more benign and racially tolerant as a colonizer than had other European powers, that Brazil as a nation might one day constitute a racially mixed Arcadia, and that the vast Portuguese imperial world was ultimately a successful, if sometimes troubled, interracial experiment. Preoccupied with cultural particularism and autonomy, Freyre helped to concoct the myth of Brazilian racial democracy, arguing that peculiarities of Portuguese colonialism cultivated a convivial mixed-race society, which had incorporated Africans. His major study, *Casa-grande & senzala* (1933)—poetic and impressionistic, and bearing the imprint of his association with anthropologists at Columbia University—was largely an aversive reaction to the rigid racial regime he had experienced in the Southern United States, that other "exceptional" society.[1] In this influential tract, Freyre implicitly juxtaposed American racial segregation and Lusophone racial mixing—racial exclusion and racial "harmony"—looking back nostalgically to what he imagined to be the relatively benign patriarchal structures established under Portuguese colonialism.[2] But what was the true valence of this supposed Lusophone exceptionalism? Was it self-deceiving? Was it even distinctive compared to other racial regimes in the Global South?

In this interconnected collection, we reconsider Freyre's *Luso-tropicalismo*, testing the concept against racialized practices elsewhere in the southern remnants of the Portuguese Empire, South America, and Portugal itself. We reassess its exceptionalist argument by exploring a variety of scientific forms of racialization beyond the trope of "race mixing": from concerns with human plasticity to attitudes toward Indigenous peoples; from issues regarding race and environment to discussions of population and demography; from anxieties associated with whiteness and settlement to those tethered to control, education, and labor. We thus expand the range of theories and knowledge formations through which "race" was conceived, materialized, and put into practice across the Portuguese-speaking world in this period. Through the privileging of comparison and entanglement, we seek to revise and reevaluate Luso-tropicalist claims. Consequently, distinctiveness is imagined more as an unpremeditated outcome of contingent patterns of intellectual exchanges and connections than as a historical, cultural, or geographical ontology, or a kind of national or imperial trait. Accordingly, the volume is concerned with exploring how a variety of racial conceptions emerged in the twentieth century within the Portuguese regions of the Global South, that is, through multiple southern connections and cohabitations.

Here we use "Global South" as shorthand for the colonies of exploitation and settler societies located principally, though not exclusively, in the Southern Hemisphere. This has proved to be a useful heuristic in exploring other patterns of racial thought and practice, and for differentiating them (at least partially) from notions of racial difference prevailing along the North Atlantic littoral.[3] Accordingly, our book extends and enriches the study of "southern" racial distinctiveness. These chapters contribute, from a Lusophone point of departure, to the critical reassessment of discourse on the exceptionality of southern racial thought, as well as the broader historiography of racial sciences in the twentieth century. They unearth plural scientific fabrications and transnational or diasporic intellectual geographies; they expose conceptual fissures and interrogate essentialist logics. Importantly, our studies challenge and resituate—in a sense, "provincializing"—the standard view of twentieth-century racial thought, especially race science, upsetting the conventional North Atlantic bias.

This represents an unrivalled opportunity to interrogate exceptionalism in all its guises—whether biological, cultural, or political. To do so effectively, we are seeking to recuperate or reactivate a comparative imaginary in the Lusophone world, a vision of affinity and difference across the empire and former empire that often has been occluded. Both the earliness and lateness of decolonization in the Portuguese Empire make postcolonial and south-south comparative readings more difficult and demanding—yet also more necessary. We want to juxtapose the supposed exceptionalism of the modern nation-state with the cosmopolitanism—or at least interconnection—of an empire sharing, in part, political structure, culture, and language. This means, in effect, attempting to link racial exceptionalism to the nation-state, and then contextualizing or resituating this cognate nationalism as a "variation" on transnational and even imperial themes—thereby challenging the moral valence, the virtuous teleology, of exceptionalist assertion.[4] These essays, then, can be read together as a contribution toward the "comparative analysis of exceptionalism as a cultural phenomenon."⁵

We echo Sigmund Freud's translator in emphasizing "discontent" in our title, since we are seeking a *critical* engagement with theories of racial exceptionalism and virtue in the twentieth century—their evasions, fantasies, and bad faith.⁶ We thus reveal complex and heterogeneous patterning of racial thought across the Global South, and we trace fraught and intricate relations of human biology and state power, or nationalism. At the same time, we want to recapture here the hopefulness and generative potential of concepts of racial distinctiveness during this period: their imbrication with the nation, and uneasy connections with modernity and science. In multiple ways, we explore how such subject positioning provided a ready-made population—perhaps as much "content" as discontent—for late-colonial, national, and developmental projects.

Racial Connections in Portuguese Colonialism

In the twentieth century the Portuguese-speaking world stretched from Portugal itself to the jungles and vast cities of Brazil; it included remnant colonies such as Angola, Mozambique, Cape Verde, São Tomé, Guinea-Bissau, Goa, Macau, and Timor-Leste, as well as a widespread diaspora. Its population numbered over two hundred million. It constituted an extremely active cultural and intellectual network, particularly across the Southern Hemisphere. Hitherto, little has been said about the history of race and science in the twentieth-century Portuguese-speaking world in its own terms, let alone from a comparative global perspective, emphasizing south-south connections. While some studies of racial thought along national lines, and comparative studies of Brazilian and other Latin American racial formations, have recently been published, until now we have lacked any comparative study of racial thought and practice across the diasporic Lusophone world in the twentieth century.

Luso-tropicalism and Its Discontents builds on a set of valuable, though isolated, case studies that have treated the history of Portuguese and Brazilian nineteenth-century and early-twentieth-century racial science, anthropology, and eugenics.⁷ The history of "Latin eugenics" provides perhaps the sturdiest platform for experiments in comparison. Following on Nancy Stepan's studies, collective works have sought to address the "specificity" of eugenics and genomics in Spanish-speaking Latin America and across the so-called Latin world (including Brazil and Southern Europe) more widely.⁸ Francisco Bethencourt and Adrian Pearce's collection on "race relations" in the Portuguese empire since the 1500s is an important contribution to understanding comparatively the forms of racial prejudice and discrimination in Lusophone colonial history.⁹ However, the significance of twentieth-century racial thought in the human sciences produced in the vast Portuguese-speaking world has not been systematically assessed. Moreover, the existing literature on race and science in Latin and Luso-Brazilian contexts has not yet examined in depth the assumptions of exceptionality that underlie Latin and Lusophone racial regimes—their characterization not only as "unique" but also, in some cases, as particularly "benign."

"Race mixing" has been central to claims for telling a Latin and particularly a Lusophone-centered history of racial conceptions in contrast to Northern Hemisphere racial formations. *Luso-tropicalismo* since the 1950s has argued for the specificity of race mixing in Portuguese-speaking countries, with broad political implications in post–World War II decolonization processes in Africa and in other parts of the Southern Hemisphere. But as several chapters in this book demonstrate, Freyre's views of race mixing and sexual intimacy were hardly "consensual": they could be rejected, criticized, ignored, or at best tolerated with difficulty in some Portuguese (and even Brazilian) intellectual and political circles. Whether or not miscegenation was flagged, the extolling of the Portuguese colonies as "nonracist" was a recurrent trope in the defense of Portuguese colonialism, gaining momentum after World War II as Portugal faced growing international pressure to decolonize. Even so, assertions of the unique benignity of Portuguese colonizers, revealed in their lack of racial discrimination and an innate psycho-ethnic capacity to integrate distinct races and peoples into one single national community, might sound implausibly hollow and self-serving. Detractors found much to criticize. Thus, in the 1960s, the British historian Charles R. Boxer convincingly documented the many deceptions and obfuscations of Luso-tropical rhetoric, in work that proved profoundly influential in later rebuttals of colonial ideologies.[10] In this context, informal comparison of race relations and labor exploitation in Portugal's colonies vis-à-vis other former empires (such as the British) became more common, feeding lively international debates.[11] And yet, political claims to a uniquely Portuguese way of dealing with "race" through integration and mixing were still voiced. Many politicians, academics, social scientists, and intellectuals—sometimes in reference to Freyre—evoked either racial miscegenation per se, or the absence of racial prejudice more generally, as a trait of national character.[12]

Focusing on scientific imaginaries, *Luso-tropicalism and Its Discontents* explores specifically the making, as well as the unmaking, of *Luso-tropicalismo* and other variants of "racial exceptionalism" across Brazil, Portugal, and Portuguese-speaking countries in Africa and Asia during the twentieth century. In the past two decades, a series of important historical studies have explored the intellectual and political origins of Freyre's Luso-tropicalism, as well as its postcolonial impact on the conceptualization of nation, colonialism, popular culture, and social sciences in both Brazil and Portugal.[13] The critique of the ideological fallacies of Luso-tropicalism has also become well established in Lusophone academia since the early 2000s.[14] However, most of this critical scholarship on Luso-tropicalism remains obscure to English readers.[15] Furthermore, these studies (especially in the Brazilian context) often reveal a double tendency to concentrate on singular nation-based approaches and on circumscribed intellectual biography.

In the early twenty-first century, the broad, comparative, and critical reassessment of Luso-tropicalism is not just academically timely but also politically relevant. It is, after all, the specter that continues to haunt contemporary debates on *lusofonia* and to suborn discussions of the legacies of colonial racism in Portugal.[16] Recent implementation of multiculturalist public policies concerning race and racial disparities in Brazil stem from the perceived aftereffects of Freyre's thought, and these policies have repercussions well beyond Brazil's borders, including some African countries.[17]

Picturing and Reading Freyre

The book begins with chapters written by Jerry Dávila and Cláudia Castelo, which vividly trace Freyre's trajectory, followed by Lorenzo Macagno's fascinating study of the parallel career path of the African missionary and Pan-Africanist intellectual Kamba Simango. Dávila and Castelo take us from the early days of Freyre's life, including his birth and privileged intellectual formation in Northeast Region of Brazil, one of the poorest areas in the country, through his later peregrinations, when he was present in major centers of knowledge production in the United States and Europe. These two initial chapters help to explain how the Brazilian intellectual's work became so popular and compelling in the Lusophone world during the second half of the twentieth century. Dávila and Castelo offer analyses through which Freyre is revealed as a character deeply embedded in, and marked by, the historical, social, cultural, and political contexts that he experienced. At the same time, they unveil the figure of a social scientist constantly worried about building and cultivating his identity as a public intellectual. The chapters show Freyre's supposed debt to the anthropology of the American Franz Boas at Columbia University; the personal ties and inclinations that led him to approach and be appropriated by the repressive Salazar regime, which dominated political life in Portugal for decades during the second half of the twentieth century; and, not least, the polyphony of voices, concordant and discordant, in the expression of his ideas. Macagno's chapter sets Freyre's self-mythologized intellectual trajectory in perspective through comparison with that of the more obscure Mozambique-born Indigenous ethnographer and activist Simango, for some time also Boas's de facto collaborator.

Dávila asks how we might weigh Freyre's influence. "One way is to subtract him," he writes, "to consider the ways in which race relations and their interpretation in Brazil in the 1930s and since then would be different in the absence of his work." But as Dávila shows, "subtracting" Freyre is a difficult exercise because of the ubiquity of his personality and work, not only in the Brazilian national context but in the Lusophone world more generally. The attempt at "subtraction" can be understood as a strategy to counterbalance, or even to deconstruct, the mystique built around the persona and work of the Pernambuco sociologist—much of it fueled by him, according to Dávila. Themes that Dávila explores, which up until the present had been sparsely investigated in the extensive literature about Freyre's personality and career, include "the careful ways in which Freyre constructed an identity as a public intellectual: how he imbued that role with moral and scientific authority, and how he used that role to delegitimate the voices of Brazilians of African descent and subjects in Portuguese colonies who spoke out and resisted against the political, social, and cultural values systems to which they were subordinated."

Castelo's text, like Dávila's, offers us a window into Freyre's work and its sociopolitical implications in the Lusophone world. Essentially comparative, the chapter creates a dialogue between various perspectives regarding the Brazilian sociologist's ideas about miscegenation. In order to do so, Castelo explores the writings of intellectuals and politicians from different Portuguese-speaking countries including Portugal, Cape Verde, Angola, Mozambique, and Goa. Specifically, she addresses the debates prompted by Freyre's ideas about race and miscegenation during two periods: the 1930s through the early 1940s, and 1950 to 1960. As she puts it, during the first period, "Portuguese imperial policy was anchored in white racial superiority, and anti-miscegenation was the predominant position among physical anthropologists." After the war, though, the "Portuguese dictatorship (*Estado Novo*) was confronted with the anticolonial contestation and independence movements." Castelo reveals the varied reception of Freyre's miscegenation ideas across Portugal and its remnant empire, with responses ranging from "applause" to "rejection." Significantly, intellectuals and politicians in Portugal before World War II felt little pressure to justify the empire or decolonize, so they could afford to ignore Freyre's assertion of their racial beneficence and special tolerance, while in the 1950s, pressed to rationalize distant territorial claims, they often took up Luso-tropicalism as the rhetorical basis for "Portuguese pluricontinental national unity."

Macagno's fine-grained intellectual biography of Simango displaces and disperses Freyrean Luso-tropicalism, emphasizing instead the hidden role of African agency and voices in the intellectual and political fabric of the twentieth-century Portuguese colonial world. The later trajectory of Simango, born in the Portuguese colony of Mozambique in 1890, was utterly cosmopolitan. His travels soon exceeded the limits of the Lusophone world, connecting African American social movements and American social science with missionary work in Mozambique and non-Portuguese African colonies. Protestant missionaries sent Simango in his youth to study at Columbia University in New York City. There, he met Boas with whom he collaborated in ethnographical works on Africa, especially on his own Vandau culture. Impressed by his skills, Boas saw Simango as more than an informant; he expected him to become, upon his return to Mozambique, what we now might call a "native ethnographer," who would produce work of independent scientific worth. In the United States, Simango also became involved in the Pan-Africanist movement, a commitment that persisted on his return as a missionary to Africa. Macagno's focus on Simango—who was contemporary to Freyre at Columbia—throws critical light on Freyre's claimed connection to Boas, which was often more imagined than real. While Freyre was celebrating Boas as mentor of emerging *Luso-tropicalismo*, Boas was in fact investing his time in creating bonds not with the Brazilian but with a promising Indigenous intellectual who endorsed W. E. B. Du Bois's visions and the Pan-Africanist critique of Portuguese colonialism.

Imagining a Mixed-Race Nation

With a focus on Brazil as a "racial laboratory," the chapters by Robert Wegner and Vanderlei Sebastião de Souza, Marcos Chor Maio, and Rosanna Dent and Ricardo Ventura Santos reveal the eventual disintegration of those visions of Brazilian national exceptionalism that once coalesced as *mestiçagem*, antiracism, and racial democracy. These concepts and practices are considered within the sciences of eugenics, physical anthropology, cultural anthropology, and human population genetics. Read together, the chapters encompass the period from about 1920 to 1970, addressing complex and interconnected circulations (of knowledge, expertise, intervention projects, etc.) surrounding the issues of race relations constructed in Freyre's work. In principle, the focus is on the Brazilian national context, but the authors repeatedly emphasize that we cannot lose sight of international scenarios. In this sense, the multiple notions of Brazil as a "racial laboratory," as demonstrated by the three chapters, came saturated with framings and expectations from elsewhere, haunted by other places and other racial regimes. This is particularly evident following World War II, when the Brazilian socio-racial experience, once encapsulated in Freyre's earlier work, might serve as a monitory projection onto the rest of the world.

In their contribution, Wegner and Souza consider conditions for the production of knowledge surrounding the issues of race and miscegenation present in Brazilian scientific fields during the first decades of the twentieth century.

The 1990s witnessed the emergence of the critical history of eugenics in Latin America between the late nineteenth and early twentieth centuries. Wegner and Souza argue that Freyre's work has strongly shaped the historical understanding of eugenics in Brazilian social thought. According to them, "The immediate success of [*Casa-grande & senzala*], with its scientific underpinnings, may have had the effect, in hindsight, of making the intellectual circles immediately before its publication appear predominantly neo-Lamarckian, a view that recent studies have tended to moderate." As shown in their chapter, debates about race and eugenics in Brazil during the early twentieth century prove far more complex. The perspectives that prevailed in various intellectual and political circuits were more commonly aligned with Mendelian principles—more rigid than the presumed Lamarckian intellectual matrix—and thus supporting "negative eugenics." Wegner and Souza investigate a heterogeneous and often conflicting group of Brazilian theorists of anthropology, medicine, and genetics. They map the surprisingly difficult and complex Brazilian conceptual terrain from which *Casa-grande & senzala* emerged in the 1930s.

Taking us into the late 1940s and the 1950s, Maio examines the influence of Freyre and his work on UNESCO-sponsored race relations projects in Brazil. These studies were a crucial part of the anti-racist agenda the agency adopted after World War II. Indeed, Freyre's scholarship was one reason why UNESCO selected Brazil as a research site, hoping to find support for his views that race relations were more "benign" there. The project involved a transatlantic network of social scientists from the United States, France, and Brazil. Maio addresses the role Freyre played in the expansion of the UNESCO project in Brazil beyond the original planned research sites, resulting in the inclusion of Recife, in his home state of Pernambuco. There he could exert significant influence over the study led by the Brazilian anthropologist René Ribeiro. Additionally, Maio explains Brazilian and foreign scholars' growing criticism of Freyre's theories—reproval he tried to counter using the UNESCO research findings. Well before the 1960s, when Freyre's Luso-tropicalism came under ever more intense criticism, many scholars had questioned his views on race relations in Brazil.

In the third chapter of this part, Dent and Santos analyze an influential monograph on the genetics of human populations, published in 1967 by the Brazilian geneticists Francisco M. Salzano and Newton Freire-Maia. The English version appeared in 1970 as *Problems in Human Biology: A Study of Brazilian Populations*. Dent and Santos inquire into the dialogues in which geneticists engaged with social scientists, especially as they touch on race relations and racism in Brazil. Of particular interest is the lack of *explicit* reference to Freyre—who was perhaps nonetheless present in his absence, for the geneticists do cite frequently authors such as Florestan Fernandes, Octavio Ianni, and Fernando Henrique Cardoso, sociologists who issued decisive critiques of Freyre's interpretations of race relations in Brazil. This chapter also explores how geneticists situated Brazil as a research site on the international stage. As Salzano and Freire-Maia wrote, an "aspect which makes Brazilian populations an excellent field of research for the geneticist, the anthropologist, and the sociologist is the interracial relations which are different from those prevailing in many other countries."[18] Probing the notion of a "racial laboratory," Dent and Santos suggest that *Populações brasileiras* can be read as a defense of the specificity of Brazil, even as it refuses to enlist, or retain in any explicit way, Freyre's Luso-tropicalism. According to Dent and Santos, "echoing both Freyre's early work and his subsequent *Luso-tropicalismo,* the geneticists set Brazilian bodies and genes apart from other populations due to historical, environmental, and cultural factors, particularly *mestiçagem* (race mixing), promoting Brazil as a specific site of cognition."

The Colonial Sciences of Race

Subsequent chapters by Ricardo Roque, Samuël Coghe, and Ana Carolina Vimieiro-Gomes move beyond Freyre's emphasis on miscegenation to explore the racializing of Indigenous "primitives" within Brazil, Portugal, and the vast Portuguese colonial world. This part considers the Portuguese program of "colonial anthropology," which the physical anthropologist António Mendes Correia designed in the 1930s as a form of Lusophone racial and colonial exceptionalism in parallel to Freyre's theories. Developed and sponsored by the imperial state in the postwar years, the metropolitan visions of Portuguese colonial anthropology led to several colonial field studies, the so-called anthropological missions. In this context, these chapters examine the theories and practices of Portuguese exceptionalism accompanying the racialization of the Indigenous inhabitants of "Portuguese Timor" and the "Bushmen" (Khoisan) in Angola. Vimieiro-Gomes supplements this analysis with critical study of the creation of "biotypes" of national and colonial populations more widely. Central to the chapters is a concern with identifying intercolonial and transnational connections, with tracing the dispersive frameworks within which Lusophone racial conceptions were articulated and contested—beyond the metropole-colony nexus, beyond even self-declared claims to the "Portugueseness" of such conceptions. Coghe's contribution shows the significance of non-Lusophone south-south transits in Portuguese colonial visions of the Angolan Bushmen, particularly in relation to German Namibia and South Africa. In contrast, in Vimieiro-Gomes's chapter, similar modes of comparison and tracing of connections bring to light differences and fractures, as that revealed in Mendes Correia's and the Portuguese anthropologists' divergent approaches to Brazilian biotypology.

Roque's chapter charts the intellectual context of Mendes Correia's singular racial mind-set, paying close attention to his obsession with populations of the Portuguese colony of Timor-Leste. Addressing particularly the work of Mendes Correia and his role in the Timor Anthropological Mission from 1930 to 1960, Roque investigates the repositioning of the East Timorese—and of colonial "natives" or *indígenas* more broadly—as "patriotic primitives." While Freyre toured the Portuguese world to confirm and promote his belief in the uniqueness of Portuguese race mixing and colonization, Mendes Correia was visiting the colony of Timor-Leste. Unlike Freyre, Mendes Correia was highly skeptical of the benefits of miscegenation. Instead, he insisted on a kind of Portuguese national-colonial exceptionalism grounded on a combination of racialized visions of difference and spiritualized notions of affect. As Roque argues, "racial theories that circumvented miscegenation and emphasized biological difference were articulated in conjunction with ideas of spiritual unity and 'cross-racial' affect between Portuguese and Indigenous." Hence, this chapter demonstrates—along with Castelo's—that Freyrean celebration of interracial sexual contact was far from being the only way of imagining Portuguese national and imperial distinctiveness. In contrast, nationalist and Christian notions of interracial *spiritual* fusion—again, a unique product of Portuguese colonization—pervaded certain scientific circles concerned with the study of supposed biological "primitives." A similar conjunction between race and affect, difference and communion, appeared to structure the wider racial program of the colonial anthropological missions in the postwar years, including those launched in Portuguese Africa.

Tracing a wide chronological arch, from the late nineteenth century to the end of the empire in 1974, Coghe's chapter follows the changing racial conceptions and colonial policies regarding the "Bushmen" of Angola. The author draws out the historical nexus between administrative policies and anthropological understandings, a kind of coevolution of racial conceptions and colonial governance. By adopting a comparative and transcolonial approach, Coghe proposes a critique of the apparent distinctiveness of Portuguese ideas about Bushmen. Rather than deriving from intellectual translations between metropole and colony, or among Portuguese-speaking scholars, the making of the Bushmen—as the racialized object of anthropological reasoning and administrative intervention—was shaped by debates outside Lusophone circuits. In particular, Coghe shows how anthropological stereotypes and colonial policies concerning the Bushmen as a "dying race" at the turn of the century resembled similar postulates and programs in the British, French, and German empires. These characterizations tracked especially closely those prevailing in German Southwest Africa (Namibia) and in South Africa. After World War II, Coghe reveals, scientific and colonial administrative notions of Bushmen as doomed to extinction gave way to representations that emphasized their "capacity of cultural and socioeconomic adaptation," as far more malleable figures. Accordingly, these peoples were to become subject to demographic, physical anthropological, and nutritional considerations, among which the recommendations of the medical doctor and anthropologist António de Almeida stood out. Leader of the Angola Anthropobiological Mission, Almeida dedicated himself to the study of the Bushmen and over time developed a complex racial typological approach that questioned their relations with Bantu-speaking peoples while recognizing their biological and sociocultural plasticity and adaptation. The latter notion was key to administrative policies regarding the Bushmen in the same period, when active policies of "Bantuization" became relevant in the colonial governance of Bushmen. Throughout this period, Portuguese racial conceptions remained subordinate to pragmatic adoptions from the neighboring non-Lusophone colonies and dominions. "For Portuguese scholars and administrators," Coghe concludes, "it was much easier and more intuitive to borrow and/or adapt concepts and practices from their Germanophone and/or Anglophone (colonial) neighbors trying to manage very similar populations."

Intellectual exchange and cross-reactivity are also themes of Vimieiro-Gomes's chapter. We now shift focus from southern Africa to the Luso-Brazilian Atlantic. Vimieiro-Gomes here proposes an exercise in historical comparison between the ways in which scholars in Brazil and Portugal adapted and appropriated the tradition of racial "biotypology"—created in continental Europe—according to distinct theoretical and political agenda. Particular Lusophone variants of biotypology emerged within the authoritarian regimes in different countries. At the same time, Portuguese and Brazilian anthropologists, including Mendes Correia, were aware of the independent developments across the Atlantic. In Brazil, the concern with nation building—visible in preoccupations with the "problem" of racial heterogeneity—was expressed in a strong and strict application of Italian methods and models and in the search of "body normality." In Portugal, mostly at the University of Porto under Mendes Correia's directorship, concerns with heterogeneity and race mixing were secondary, and a more methodologically diverse form of biotypology, subsidiary to an anthropobiology of colonial populations, emerged. In the context of "anthropobiology," the issue of the "constitution" of individuals was seen as but another possible method, a complementary pathway, to address the problem of biological and racial characterization—as promoting racial classification, which prevailed in some Portuguese circles, even as Freyrean Luso-tropicalism gained ideological importance in the 1950s.

Portugueseness in the Tropics

To comprehend Lusophone racial conceptions in the twentieth century, it is necessary to consider how "Portugueseness" was fashioned, and sometimes discarded, as a mode of identity among migrant and settler communities. Freyre's fantasies of the uniqueness of the Portuguese-speaking world conjured up mixed-race communities, maybe gradually whitening, inhabiting the territories of offshoot nations and remnant empire, shaped by centuries of overseas expansion and colonization. The chapters in the final part question these assumptions and disrupt the colonial geography that underlies the Luso-tropical valorization of race mixing. They thus expand the scope of comparative analysis to reflect on the making and unmaking of racial exceptionalism beyond the imagination of empire. Cristiana Bastos and Pamila Gupta offer a critique of Freyre's theory of Luso-tropical exceptionalism through intensive studies of the multiple practices of Portuguese identity formation among diasporic communities. Both chapters consider the complex patterns of human mobility that generated vernacular perceptions of racial whiteness, within and beyond the borders of the Portuguese empire: Goans in British Zanzibar, in Gupta's chapter; and Portuguese migrant laborers in New England and Hawai'i, in Bastos's analysis. Critical to the chapters is a concern with how Lusophone communities are racialized by others (including social scientists and physical anthropologists), as well as how these communities racialize (or deracialize) themselves.

Bastos compares "racialized lives and racialist theorizations" in three distinct formations in the twentieth century: the physical anthropological studies of the Goan medical doctor and anthropologist Alberto Germano da Silva Correia on Portuguese Madeiran settlers, so-called *eurafricanos* or *lusodescendentes*, in Angola in the 1920s; the white American sociologist Donald Taft's work on the Portuguese migrants in industrial New England and the heated reactions to his work by members of the same Portuguese communities; and finally, a case study of Portuguese in the plantation economy of Hawai'i and the complexities surrounding the history of their racialized an deracialized (self-)definitions. Bastos's starting point is a critique of Luso-tropicalism and its legacies in contemporary Portugal. Thus, she describes prevailing myths of the exceptionally benign and nonracist nature of Portuguese colonization—a trope that has again gained wide significance in the Portuguese public sphere, serving to obscure past and present racisms. Instead of regarding positive valorization of race mixing as *the* essential trait of Portuguese racialization, Bastos argues, one must heed historical and contemporary "practices and theorization in Portuguese-speaking contexts that go in opposite directions." In particular, she urges us to consider the obsession with whiteness professed by both racialist scholars and Portuguese settler communities—the compulsion with the manifold social, cultural, and biological indices and categories of whiteness. The three case studies provide strong examples of the overarching and abiding significance of whiteness in diasporic communities. Correia's studies sought to bypass, or ignore, the problem of miscegenation in order to secure and celebrate the whiteness of Madeiran settlers in Angola. Countering Taft's negative and degrading view of Portuguese racial character, the Portuguese migrant communities in New England asserted their racial purity and superiority. In Hawai'i—where Portuguese migrants (against the Freyrean grain) apparently preferred to marry among themselves—a rapid process of social, cultural, and racial differentiation of the Portuguese settlers from other plantation workers took place, conferring on them a whiter racial identity. Never in these three cases, Bastos concludes, "were the tropes of Luso-tropicalism ever evoked as distinctly Portuguese traits."

In the closing chapter, Gupta, describing practices of self-representation and identity making among the Goan diaspora in Zanzibar, explains the failure of Luso-tropical racial rhetoric to take hold on diasporic communities. She contrasts the inherently essentialist views of Portuguese identity proposed in Luso-tropicalism with the heterogeneous ways in which Goans abroad perceive and articulate their own Goan Portugueseness. Moreover, the cosmopolitan world in which Goans circulated, Gupta shows, hardly coincided with the boundaries of Portugal's former empire or the so-called Lusophone world; instead, an "intercolonial world" connected different national and imperial geographies. Gupta's points are grounded on her ethnographic studies of the uses and meaning of photography among the Goans in Zanzibar. By following the history of a Goan-owned studio, she is able to trace how, through photographic image and practice, people manufacture their own historical sense of Portugueseness and Goan identity. Using the metaphor of stitching, Gupta argues that, in Zanzibar, rather than a quality prescribed by some external and abstract Luso-tropical theory, "the category of 'Goan' was always relational ... and was very much connected to the ability to harness Portugueseness (and Roman Catholicism) as signifiers of their community's civility and modernity." Portugueseness was stitched as an adornment, Gupta suggests, such that "race" was often a loose and absent marker. The self-perception of Goanness as a cultural embodiment of Europeanness, associated with certain civilizing behaviors and religious beliefs inherited from Portuguese Roman Catholic pasts, was crucial in marking and differentiating "Goans" in an African setting.

Conclusion

Taken together, these chapters should cause us to rethink what we believe about "race mixing" or "human hybridity"—not simply in Brazil and the Portuguese-speaking world but also wherever population variability and difference are perceived to matter socially, economically, and politically. Conventionally, Freyre has been extolled for describing exceptionally mixed and congenial social relations, derived from the Portuguese colonial heritage of tolerance and sympathy, and tending toward a racial democracy. But as the contributions to this collection demonstrate, this Luso-tropicalism was not limited to Brazil, Portugal, and the Portuguese Empire; indeed, it was not even particularly prevalent in Brazil, Portugal, and the Portuguese Empire, though it could often serve in these places as convenient rhetoric for purposes of self-aggrandizement and amour propre. We have shown that there was little "exceptional" about Brazilian and Portuguese racial thought in this period, for the preoccupation of nations and empire with race mixing and harmonization was commonplace, even if multifarious: everyone across the planet seemed intrigued by interracial sex, engrossed by prospects of blending and amalgamation, though rarely did such concerns fit as well with national self-fashioning as in Brazil. These chapters challenge us to question further what race mixing and human hybridity might mean: evidently, the concept of somatic mixedness had different connotations depending on the time, the place, and the political exigencies. They illuminate the useful pluripotentiality and constitutive ambiguity of concepts of race mixing, the relations of these polysemous thought styles to biological and genetic investigation, their contested and controversial political and social implications, and their occasional function as hopeful tropes for whiteness or whitening. Freyre's preoccupation with race mixing clearly did not conjure up racial democracy in Brazil, but it did at least represent the heterogeneous population as modern, thus making persons visible and amenable to the state and global capitalism in unanticipated, and often contested, ways. It was no accident that, for Freyre, race mixing took place originally on the colonial plantation. Luso-tropicalism provided a productive and lasting idiom in which imperial and national forms of governmentality could—and can still—be articulated in Portuguese-speaking countries.

We have pieced together here a mosaic of Luso-tropical knowledge and practice in the twentieth century. As William James observed, "it is as if the pieces cling together by their edges, the transitions experienced between them forming their cement. . . . Life is in the transitions as much as in the terms connected."[19] One might therefore reimagine the history of racial thought, not as concentrated in Western Europe or North America, or even in Brazil or South Africa, but rather as a series of "edge effects" scattered around the world, in this case the Lusophone world.[20] Thus, we hope to contribute critically to the global ecology of racial knowledge.

Warwick Anderson is the Janet Dora Hine Professor of Politics, Governance, and Ethics in the Department of History and the Charles Perkins Centre at the University of Sydney. From 2018 to 2019 he was the Gough Whitlam and Malcolm Fraser Chair of Australian Studies at Harvard University. He has written extensively on histories of colonial science, medicine, and racial thought.

His books include *The Cultivation of Whiteness* (Melbourne University Press, 2002; Duke University Press, 2006); *Colonial Pathologies* (Duke University Press, 2006); and *The Collectors of Lost Souls* (Johns Hopkins University Press, 2008). Among his edited collections are (with Richard Keller and Deborah Jenson) *Unconscious Dominions* (Duke University Press, 2011); (with Miranda Johnson and Barbara Brookes) *Pacific Futures* (University of Hawaii Press, 2018); and a special issue (with Ricardo Roque) of the *Journal of Southeast Asian Studies* (vo. 49, no. 3, 2018) on comparative racialization in the region.

RICARDO ROQUE is Research Fellow at the Institute of Social Sciences (ICS) in the University of Lisbon (Instituto de Ciências Sociais da Universidade de Lisboa), and Honorary Associate in the Department of History at the University of Sydney. He works in the history and anthropology of colonialism, human sciences, and cross-cultural contact in the Portuguese-speaking world, from 1800 to the twentieth century. He has published widely on the history of racial science and the anthropology of colonialism in Timor-Leste, and on the theory and ethnography of colonial archives and museum collections. He is the author of *Headhunting and Colonialism* (Palgrave, 2010) and the coeditor of *Engaging Colonial Knowledge* (Palgrave, 2012). At the ICS, he coordinates the research group Empires, Colonialism and Post-colonial Societies.

RICARDO VENTURA SANTOS is an anthropologist affiliated with the Fundação Oswaldo Cruz (Oswaldo Cruz Foundation) in Rio de Janeiro and Professor in the Department of Anthropology at the Brazilian National Museum. He received his PhD in anthropology from Indiana University, Bloomington, in 1991. He has been a visiting scholar in MIT's Program on Science, Technology, and Society (1998–1999) and at the Max Planck Institute for the History of Science (2012–2013). He is one of the authors of *The Xavante in Transition* (University of Michigan Press, 2002) and the coeditor of (with Sahra Gibbon and Monica Sans) *Racial Identities, Genetic Ancestry, and Health in South America* (Palgrave, 2011); (with Susan Lindee) *The Biological Anthropology of Living Human Populations: World Histories, National Styles, and International Networks* (special issue of the journal *Current Anthropology*, vol. 53, no. S5, 2012); and (with Peter Wade, Carlos López Beltrán, and Eduardo Restrepo) *Mestizo Genomics* (Duke University Press, 2014). He recently received a Wellcome Trust Senior Investigator Award in Humanities and Social Science (2017–2021).

Notes

1. Gilberto Freyre, *Casa-grande & senzala: Formação da família brasileira sob o regimen de economia patriarcal* (Rio de Janeiro, 1933); Gilberto Freyre, *O mundo que o português criou: Aspectos das relações sociais e de cultura do Brasil com Portugal e as colónias portuguesa* (Rio de Janeiro, 1933); Gilberto Freyre, *O luso e o trópico* (Lisbon, 1960).

See also Dorothy Ross, "Historical Consciousness in Nineteenth-Century America," *American Historical Review* 89, no. 4 (1984): 909-28; Carl Degler, *Neither Black nor White: Slavery and Race Relations in Brazil and the United States* (New York, 1971).
2. Dain Borges, "'Puffy, Ugly, Slothful, and Inert': Degeneration in Brazilian Social Thought, 1880-1940," *Journal of Latin American Studies* 25, no. 2 (1993): 235-56; Jeffrey D. Needell, "Identity, Race, Gender, and Modernity in the Origins of Gilberto Freyre's Oeuvre," *American Historical Review* 100, no. 1 (1995): 51-77.
3. Warwick Anderson, "Racial Conceptions in the Global South," *Isis* 105, no. 4 (2014): 782-92.
4. Ian Tyrrell, "American Exceptionalism in an Age of International History," *American Historical Review* 96, no. 4 (1991): 1038; Laurence Veysey, "The Autonomy of American History Reconsidered," *American Quarterly* 31, no. 4 (1979): 455-77; and George M. Fredrickson, "From Exceptionalism to Variability: Recent Developments in Cross-National and Comparative History," *Journal of American History* 82, no. 2 (1995): 587-604.
5. Michael Kammen, "The Problem of American Exceptionalism: A Reconsideration," *American Quarterly* 45, no. 1 (1993): 33.
6. Sigmund Freud, *Civilisation and Its Discontents*, trans. Joan Rivière (London, 1973), originally published as *Unbehagen in der Kultur* (Vienna, 1930).
7. Lilia Schwarcz, *The Spectacle of the Races: Scientists, Institutions, and the Race Question in Brazil, 1870-1930* (New York, 1999); Antonio Sérgio Guimarães, *Racismo e anti-racismo no Brasil* (São Paulo, 2005); Patricia Ferraz de Matos, *The Colours of Empire: Racialized Representations during Portuguese Colonialism* (Oxford, 2013); Ricardo Roque, *Antropologia e império: Fonseca Cardoso e a expedição à Índia em 1895* (Lisbon, 2001); Ricardo Roque, *Headhunting and Colonialism: Anthropology and the Circulation of Human Skulls in the Portuguese Empire, 1870-1930* (London, 2010); Omar Ribeiro Thomaz, *Ecos do Atlântico Sul: Representações sobre o Terceiro Império Português* (Rio de Janeiro, 2002); Marcos Chor Maio and Ricardo Ventura Santos, eds., *Raça, ciência e sociedade* (Rio de Janeiro, 1996); Marcos Chor Maio and Ricardo Ventura Santos, eds., *Raça como questão: História, ciência e identidades no Brasil* (Rio de Janeiro, 2010); Sahra Gibbon, Ricardo Ventura Santos, and Mónica Sans, eds., *Racial Identities, Genetic Ancestry, and Health in South America Argentina, Brazil, Colombia, and Uruguay* (New York, 2011); Vanderlei Sebastião de Souza and Ricardo Ventura Santos, ed., "Corpos, medidas e nação," special issue, *Boletim Museu Paraense Emílio Goeldi—Ciências Humanas* 7, no. 3 (2012); Richard Cleminson, *Catholicism, Race and Science: Eugenics in Portugal, 1900-1950* (Budapest, 2014).
8. See Nancy Stepan, *The Hour of Eugenics: Race, Gender, and Nation in Latin America* (Ithaca, NY, 1991); for Latin America, see Peter Wade, Carlos López Beltrán, Eduardo Restrepo, and Ricardo Ventura Santos, eds., *Mestizo Genomics: Race Mixture, Nation, and Science in Latin America* (Durham, NC, 2014); Peter Wade, Vivette García Deister, Michael Kent, María Fernanda Olarte Sierra, and Adriana Díaz del Castillo Hernández, "Nation and the Absent Presence of Race in Latin American Genomics," *Current Anthropology* 55, no. 5 (2014): 497–522; for Latin eugenics, see Marius Turda and Aaron Gillette, *Latin Eugenics in Comparative Perspective* (London, 2014); Gilberto Hochman, Nísia Trindade Lima, and Marcos Chor Maio, "The Path of Eugenics in Brazil: Dilemmas of Miscegenation," in *The Oxford Handbook of the History of Eugenics*, ed. Alison Bashford and Philippa Levine (New York, 2010), 493–510; Ana Carolina Vimieiro-Gomes, Robert Wegner, and Vanderlei Souza, eds., "Eugenia latina em contexto transnacional," special issue, *História, Ciências Saúde—Manguinhos* 23, no. 1 (2016).

9. Francisco Bethencourt and Adrian Pearce, eds., *Racism and Ethnic Relations in the Portuguese-Speaking World* (Oxford, 2012).
10. Charles R. Boxer, *Race Relations in the Portuguese Colonial Empire, 1415–1825* (Oxford, 1963). See also Alberto Luiz Schneider, "Charles Boxer (contra Gilberto Freyre): Raça e racismo no Império Português ou a erudição histórica contra o regime salazarista," *Estudos Históricos* 26, no. 52 (2013): 253–73.
11. See Marvin Harris, "Portugal's Contribution to the Underdevelopment of Africa and Brazil," in *Protest and Resistance in Angola and Brazil: Comparative Studies,* ed. Ronald H. Chilcote (Berkeley, CA, 1972), 209–23; Gerald J. Bender, *Angola under the Portuguese: The Myth and the Reality* (Berkeley, CA, 1978); Diogo Ramada Curto, "The Debate on Race Relations in the Portuguese Empire and Charles R. Boxer's Position," *E-Journal of Portuguese History* 11, no. 1 (2013): 1–42; Miguel Bandeira Jerónimo and António Costa Pinto, "A Modernizing Empire? Politics, Culture, and Economy in Portuguese Late Colonialism," in *The Ends of European Colonial Empire: Cases and Comparisons,* ed. Miguel Bandeira Jerónimo and António Costa Pinto (London, 2015), 51–80.
12. For an overview in English, see Cláudia Castelo, "Luso-tropicalism and Portuguese Late Colonialism," *Buala,* 28 May 2015, http://www.buala.org/en/to-read/luso-tropicalism-and-portuguese-late-colonialism.
13. E.g., Ricardo Benzaquen de *Araújo, Guerra e paz*: Casa-grande & senzala *e a obra de Gilberto Freyre nos anos 30* (São Paulo, 1993); Cláudia Castelo, *O modo português de estar no mundo: O luso-tropicalismo e a ideologia colonial portuguesa (1933–1961)* (Porto, 1998); Marcos Cardão, *Fado tropical: O luso-tropicalismo na cultura de massas (1960–1974)* (Lisbon, 2014); Marcos Cardão, "Allegories of Exceptionalism: Luso-tropicalism in Mass Culture (1960–74)," *Portuguese Journal of Social Science* 14, no. 3 (2016): 257–73; Joshua Lund and Malcolm McNee, eds., *Gilberto Freyre e os estudos lationoamericanos* (Pittsburgh, 2006); Alberto Luiz Schneider, "Iberismo e luso-tropicalismo na obra de Gilberto Freyre," *Revista de Historiografía* 10 (2012): 75–93; Maria Lucia Pallares-Burke, *Gilberto Freyre: Um vitoriano nos trópicos* (São Paulo, 2005).
14. Cristiana Bastos, Bela Feldman-Bianco, and Miguel Vale de Almeida, eds., *Trânsitos coloniais: Diálogos críticos luso-brasileiros* (Lisbon, 2002); Peter Fry, *A persistência da raça: Ensaios antropológicos sobre o Brasil e a África austral* (Rio de Janeiro, 2005); Cláudia Castelo and Marcos Cardão, eds., *Gilberto Freyre: Novas leituras, do outro lado do Atlântico* (São Paulo, 2015).
15. E.g., Peter Burke and Maria Lucia Pallares-Burke, *Gilberto Freyre: Social Theory in the Tropics* (Oxford, 2008).
16. On the resilience of Luso-tropicalism, cf. Jorge Vala, Diniz Lopes, and Marcus Lima, "Black Immigrants in Portugal: Luso-tropicalism and Prejudice," *Journal of Social Issues* 64, no. 2 (2008): 287–302; Margarida Calafate Ribeiro, "Between Europe and the Atlantic: The Melancholy Paths of Lusotropicalism," in *New Dangerous Liaisons: Discourses on Europe and Love in the Last Century,* ed. Luisa Passerini, Liliana Ellena, and Alexander C. T. Geppert (Oxford, 2010), 215–32; Adriano de Freixo, "Ecos do luso-tropicalismo: A presença do pensamento de Gilberto Freyre no discurso da lusofonia," *Textos e Debates* 27, no. 2 (2015): 471–84.
17. Jerry Dávila, *Diploma of Whiteness: Race and Social Policy in Brazil, 1917–1945* (Durham, NC, 2003); Jerry Dávila, *Hotel Trópico: Brazil and the Challenge of African Decolonization, 1950–1980* (Durham, NC, 2010).
18. Francisco M. Salzano and Newton Freire-Maia, *Problems in Human Biology: A Study of Brazilian Populations* (Detroit, 1970), 178.

19. William James, *Essays in Radical Empiricism* (New York, 1912), 41, 87.
20. Warwick Anderson, "Edge Effects in Science and Medicine," *Western Humanities Review* 69, no. 3 (2015): 373–84.

Bibliography

Anderson, Warwick. "Edge Effects in Science and Medicine." *Western Humanities Review* 69, no. 3 (2015): 373–84.
———. "Racial Conceptions in the Global South." *Isis* 105, no. 4 (2014): 782–92.
Araújo. Ricardo Benzaquen de. *Guerra e paz*: Casa-grande & senzala e a obra de Gilberto Freyre nos anos 30. São Paulo: Editora 34, 1993.
Bastos, Cristiana, Bela Feldman-Bianco, and Miguel Vale de Almeida, eds. *Trânsitos coloniais: Diálogos críticos luso-brasileiros*. Lisbon: Imprensa de Ciências Sociais, 2002.
Bender, Gerald J. *Angola under the Portuguese: The Myth and the Reality*. Berkeley: University of California Press, 1978.
Bethencourt, Francisco, and Adrian Pearce, eds. *Racism and Ethnic Relations in the Portuguese-Speaking World*. Oxford: Oxford University Press, 2012.
Borges, Dain. "'Puffy, Ugly, Slothful, and Inert': Degeneration in Brazilian Social Thought, 1880–1940." *Journal of Latin American Studies* 25, no. 2 (1993): 235–56.
Boxer, Charles R. *Race Relations in the Portuguese Colonial Empire, 1415–1825*. Oxford: Clarendon Press, 1963.
Burke, Peter, and Maria Lucia Pallares-Burke. *Gilberto Freyre: Social Theory in the Tropics*. Oxford: Peter Lang, 2008.
Cardão, Marcos. "Allegories of Exceptionalism: Lusotropicalism in Mass Culture (1960–74)." *Portuguese Journal of Social Science* 14, no. 3 (2016): 257–73.
———. *Fado tropical: O luso-tropicalismo na cultura de massas (1960–1974)*. Lisbon: Edições Unipop, 2014.
Castelo, Cláudia. "'Luso-tropicalism' and Portuguese Late Colonialism." *Buala*, 28 May 2015. http://www.buala.org/en/to-read/luso-tropicalism-and-portuguese-late-colonialism.
———. *O modo português de estar no mundo: O luso-tropicalismo e a ideologia colonial portuguesa (1933–1961)*. Porto: Afrontamento, 1998.
Castelo, Cláudia, and Marcos Cardão, eds. *Gilberto Freyre: Novas leituras, do outro lado do Atlântico*. São Paulo: Edusp, 2015.
Cleminson, Richard. *Catholicism, Race and Science: Eugenics in Portugal, 1900–1950*. Budapest: Central European University Press, 2014.
Curto, Diogo Ramada. "The Debate on Race Relations in the Portuguese Empire and Charles R. Boxer's Position." *E-Journal of Portuguese History* 11, no. 1 (2013): 1–42.
Dávila, Jerry. *Diploma of Whiteness: Race and Social Policy in Brazil, 1917–1945*. Durham, NC: Duke University Press, 2003.
———. *Hotel Trópico: Brazil and the Challenge of African Decolonization, 1950–1980*. Durham, NC: Duke University Press, 2010.
Degler, Carl. *Neither Black nor White: Slavery and Race Relations in Brazil and the United States*. New York: Macmillan, 1971.
Fredrickson, George M. "From Exceptionalism to Variability: Recent Developments in Cross-National and Comparative History." *Journal of American History* 82, no. 2 (1995): 587–604.
Freud, Sigmund. *Civilisation and Its Discontents*. Translated by Joan Rivière. London: Hogarth Press, 1973. Originally published as *Unbehagen in der Kultur* (Vienna: Internationaler Psychoanalytischer Verlag, 1930).

Freixo, Adriano de. "Ecos do luso-tropicalismo: A presença do pensamento de Gilberto Freyre no discurso da lusofonia." *Textos e Debates* 27, no. 2 (2015): 471–84.

Freyre, Gilberto. *Casa-grande & senzala: Formação da família brasileira sob o regimen de economia patriarchal.* Rio de Janeiro: Maia & Schmidt, 1933.

——. *O luso e o trópico.* Lisbon: Comissão Executiva do V Centenário da Morte do Infante D. Henrique, 1960.

——. *O mundo que o português criou: Aspectos das relações sociais e de cultura do Brasil com Portugal e as colónias portuguesa.* Rio de Janeiro: José Olympio, 1940.

Fry, Peter. *A persistência da raça: Ensaios antropológicos sobre o Brasil e a África austral.* Rio de Janeiro: Civilização Brasileira, 2005.

Gibbon, Sahra, Ricardo Ventura Santos, and Mónica Sans, eds. *Racial Identities, Genetic Ancestry, and Health in South America Argentina, Brazil, Colombia, and Uruguay.* New York: Palgrave Macmillan, 2011.

Guimarães, Antonio Sérgio. *Racismo e anti-racismo no Brasil.* São Paulo: Editora 34, 2005.

Harris, Marvin. "Portugal's Contribution to the Underdevelopment of Africa and Brazil." In *Protest and Resistance in Angola and Brazil: Comparative Studies,* edited by Ronald H. Chilcote, 209–23. Berkeley: University of California Press, 1972.

Hochman, Gilberto, Nísia Trindade Lima, and Marcos Chor Maio. "The Path of Eugenics in Brazil: Dilemmas of Miscegenation." In *The Oxford Handbook of the History of Eugenics,* edited by Alison Bashford and Philippa Levine, 493–510. New York: Oxford University Press, 2010.

James, William. *Essays in Radical Empiricism.* New York: Longman, Green & Co., 1912.

Jerónimo, Miguel Bandeira, and António Costa Pinto. "A Modernizing Empire? Politics, Culture, and Economy in Portuguese Late Colonialism." In *The Ends of European Colonial Empires: Cases and Comparisons,* edited by Miguel Bandeira Jerónimo and António Costa Pinto, 51–80. London: Palgrave Macmillan, 2015.

Kammen, Michael. "The Problem of American Exceptionalism: A Reconsideration." *American Quarterly* 45, no. 1 (1993): 1–43.

Lund, Joshua, and Malcolm McNee, eds. *Gilberto Freyre e os estudos lationoamericanos.* Pittsburgh, PA: International Institute of Latin American Literature, University of Pittsburgh, 2006.

Maio, Marcos Chor, and Ricardo Ventura Santos, eds. *Raça como questão: História, ciência e identidades no Brasil.* Rio de Janeiro: Editora Fiocruz, 2010.

——, eds. *Raça, ciência e sociedade.* Rio de Janeiro: Editora Fiocruz / CCBB, 1996.

Matos, Patricia Ferraz de. *The Colours of Empire: Racialized Representations during Portuguese Colonialism.* Oxford: Berghahn Books, 2013.

Needell, Jeffrey D. "Identity, Race, Gender, and Modernity in the Origins of Gilberto Freyre's Oeuvre." *American Historical Review* 100, no. 1 (1995): 51–77.

Pallares-Burke, Maria Lucia. *Gilberto Freyre: Um vitoriano nos trópicos.* São Paulo: Editora Unesp, 2005.

Ribeiro, Margarida Calafate. "Between Europe and the Atlantic: The Melancholy Paths of Lusotropicalism." In *New Dangerous Liaisons: Discourses on Europe and Love in the Last Century,* edited by Luisa Passerini, Liliana Ellena, and Alexander C. T. Geppert, 215–32. Oxford: Berghahn Books, 2010.

Roque, Ricardo. *Antropologia e império: Fonseca Cardoso e a expedição à Índia em 1895.* Lisbon: Imprensa de Ciências Sociais, 2001.

——. *Headhunting and Colonialism: Anthropology and the Circulation of Human Skulls in the Portuguese Empire, 1870–1930.* London: Palgrave Macmillan, 2010.

Ross, Dorothy. "Historical Consciousness in Nineteenth-Century America." *American Historical Review* 89, no. 4 (1984): 909–28.

Salzano, Francisco M., and Newton Freire-Maia. *Problems in Human Biology: A Study of Brazilian Populations*. Detroit: Wayne State University Press, 1970.

Schneider, Alberto Luiz. "Charles Boxer (contra Gilberto Freyre): Raça e racismo no Império Português ou a erudição histórica contra o regime salazarista." *Estudos Históricos* 26, no. 52 (2013): 253–73.

———. "Iberismo e luso-tropicalismo na obra de Gilberto Freyre." *Revista de Historiografia* 10 (2012): 75–93.

Schwarcz, Lilia. *The Spectacle of the Races: Scientists, Institutions, and the Race Question in Brazil, 1870–1930*. New York: Hill & Wang, 1999.

Souza, Vanderlei Sebastião de, and Ricardo Ventura Santos, eds. "Corpos, medidas e nação." Special issue, *Boletim Museu Paraense Emílio Goeldi—Ciências Humanas* 7, no. 3 (2012): 639–43.

Stepan, Nancy. *The Hour of Eugenics: Race, Gender, and Nation in Latin America*. Ithaca, NY: Cornell University Press, 1991.

Thomaz, Omar Ribeiro. *Ecos do Atlântico Sul: Representações sobre o Terceiro Império Português*. Rio de Janeiro: Editora da Universidade Federal do Rio de Janeiro, 2002.

Turda, Marius, and Aaron Gillette. *Latin Eugenics in Comparative Perspective*. London: Bloomsbury Academic, 2014.

Tyrrell, Ian. "American Exceptionalism in an Age of International History." *American Historical Review* 96, no. 4 (1991): 1031–55.

Vala, Jorge, Diniz Lopes, and Marcus Lima. "Black Immigrants in Portugal: Luso-tropicalism and Prejudice." *Journal of Social Issues* 64, no. 2 (2008): 287–302.

Veysey, Laurence. "The Autonomy of American History Reconsidered." *American Quarterly* 31, no. 4 (1979): 455–77.

Vimieiro-Gomes, Ana Carolina, Robert Wegner, and Vanderlei Souza, eds. "Eugenia latina em contexto transnacional." Special issue, *História, Ciências Saúde—Manguinhos* 23, no. S1 (2016).

Wade, Peter, Carlos López Beltrán, Eduardo Restrepo, and Ricardo Ventura Santos, eds. *Mestizo Genomics: Race Mixture, Nation, and Science in Latin America*. Durham, NC: Duke University Press, 2014.

Wade, Peter, Vivette García Deister, Michael Kent, María Fernanda Olarte Sierra, and Adriana Díaz del Castillo Hernández. "Nation and the Absent Presence of Race in Latin American Genomics." *Current Anthropology* 55, no. 5 (2014): 497–522.

PART I

Picturing and Reading Freyre

CHAPTER 1

Gilberto Freyre's View of Miscegenation and Its Circulation in the Portuguese Empire, 1930s–1960s

Cláudia Castelo

"Miscegenation" is a key concept in Gilberto Freyre's thought about the formation of Brazil, Portugal's "national character," and the peopling of the spaces of Portuguese colonization. Notions of biological and cultural hybridization, understood as positive processes, permeate almost all his work since *Casa-grande & senzala* (*CGS*).[1] Published in 1933, the year Nazism gained control of Germany, *CGS* also was formulated against an international tide of racial segregation in the United States and the European colonial empires. Freyre's valorization of miscegenation continued through the postwar period, the civil rights movement, and the era of decolonization. And yet, according to Nancy Stepan, if Freyre's work subverted scientific racism and negative views about race degeneration, it also provided the framework within which a form of eugenics would survive.[2]

Attempting to reconstruct "twentieth-century networks of racial thought and vision across the Global South, transiting empires and nation-states,"[3] this chapter addresses Gilberto Freyre's ideas about miscegenation and their genesis in dialogue with North American studies of race mixing. It frames the circulation of these ideas in the Portuguese colonial empire as an active and transformative process.[4] It further discusses the exchanges and debates that Freyre's racial conception provoked among scientists and politicians, in two different historical moments: the 1930s to the early 1940s, when Portuguese imperial policy was anchored in white racial superiority and anti-miscegenation was the predominant position among physical anthropologists; and the 1950s to the 1960s, when the Portuguese dictatorship (*Estado Novo*), confronted with anticolonial contestation and independence movements, adopted multiracialism as its official discourse, and pro-miscegenation stances imposed themselves in the scientific field. Finally, it argues that Almerindo Lessa's research program on the Luso-tropical *mestiço* emerged from the questioning of racial prejudices against miscegenation.

Miscegenation in Freyre's Oeuvre

Freyre's biography and intellectual networks need to be taken into account if we are to locate and understand the production of his ideas about miscegenation.[5] I begin by providing some basic coordinates of his early life, and I will highlight other relevant circumstances and relationships throughout the chapter.[6]

Gilberto Freyre (1900–1987) descended from wealthy and Catholic sugar planter families of Pernambuco (Northeast Region of Brazil) who had only recently moved to townhouses and entered the liberal professions. His father was a judge and university professor. He had private lessons at home and studied at a high school run by US Baptist missionaries in Recife. At the age of eighteen, he followed an older brother to Baylor University, a Baptist institution in Waco, Texas. After concluding his bachelor's degree, he enrolled in a master's degree at Columbia University in New York City. There, he attended courses in history, public law, anthropology, sociology, English, and arts. He became friends with a German colleague, Rüdiger Bilden, a disciple and friend of anthropologist Franz Boas, who was preparing a thesis about slavery in the Americas, especially in Brazil, and Francis Butler Simkins, who was studying the effects of abolition in South Carolina. Under the supervision of William R. Shepherd, a historian of South America, Freyre presented his MA thesis "Social Life in Brazil in the Middle of the Nineteenth Century."[7] He returned to Recife in his early twenties after a European tour, where he was secretary to the governor of Pernambuco and director of *A Província*, a state-sponsored newspaper. In the mid-1920s, Freyre became involved in the regionalist cultural movement of the Northeast and praised the Afro-Brazilian contribution to the patriarchal origins of the Brazilian culture. The Revolution of 1930 pushed Freyre into exile in Portugal, where he established an intellectual network that would grow in the following decades. At the invitation of Percy Alvin Martin, he was visiting professor at Stanford University in the spring of 1931. Afterward, he visited the "Deep South" with his former colleagues Bilden and Simkins.[8] Back in Brazil, he did research in Rio de Janeiro for his first book, *Casa-grande & senzala*. As we shall see, its publication helped him make contact with North American scholars and activists interested in comparisons between race relations in the United States and Brazil. In the next decades, Freyre would publish prolifically in Latin America, the United States, and Europe; travel often at the invitation of foreign scholars and institutions; and become an internationally recognized and controversial public intellectual.

The issue of miscegenation was not central for Freyre when he was writing his master's thesis at Columbia in the early 1920s.[9] His work was closer to the prevailing ideas on race and the merits of eugenics, far from the ideas he would express in CGS. He wrote of the "improvement" of the enslaved race then underway, and of Argentina as a good model for resolution of the race problem by whitening its population.[10] However, in the preface to the first edition of CGS, Freyre claimed:

> It was my studies in anthropology under the direction of Professor Boas that first revealed to me the Negro and the mulatto for what they are—with the effects of environment or cultural experience separated from racial characteristics. I learned to regard as fundamental the difference between *race* and *culture*, to discriminate between the effects of purely genetic relationships and those resulting from social influences, the cultural heritage and the milieu. It is upon this criterion of the basic differentiation between race and culture that the entire plan of this essay rests, as well as upon the distinction to be made between racial and family heredity.[11]

Maria Lúcia Pallares-Burke views this attempt to trace a direct affiliation with Boas and the US cultural anthropology skeptically. She establishes the contribution of several authors from diverse geographies and disciplines to the gestation of CGS, namely Edgard Roquette-Pinto, Lafcadio Hearn, G. K. Chesterton, Alfred Zimmern, Herbert Spencer, and Franklin Giddings. She also reveals the surprising role played by Bilden: Bilden was Freyre's "flesh and blood" discussion partner, who probably also introduced him to Roquette-Pinto in Rio de Janeiro in 1926 while doing research for his PhD on the role of slavery in the history of Brazil. Boas's influence on Freyre's "culturalist turn" must have also been an outcome of Freyre and Bilden's interaction.[12] In 2012, Pallares-Burke extended her arguments about the repercussion of Bilden's ideas on Brazilian miscegenation through Freyre's work.[13] In the preface to the first edition of CGS, Freyre acknowledges that he benefited from Bilden's "valuable suggestions."[14] He owed to Bilden the positive conception of miscegenation as something good, beautiful, and enriching, and the idea about the distinctive characteristics of the Portuguese colonizer, including the alleged Portuguese aptitude for miscegenation. Throughout the book, Freyre quotes or refers to Bilden's texts and manuscript in progress, to which he had first-hand access.[15] Freyre continued to value Bilden's influence in his own work into the early 1940s:

> I am indebted to Rudiger [sic] Bilden, now a contracted professor at Fisk University,[16] and, like me, a former disciple of anthropology of Professor Franz Boas, at Columbia University, to suggestions for the study of Brazil's social history, compared to other American areas; suggestions as valuable as those I owe to Professor Franz Boas himself.[17]

From this point, however, Freyre tended to forget his intellectual debt to Bilden, who never finished his PhD or produced a book from his research.[18]

It is difficult to determine whether Bilden discussed with Freyre the works that were published in English in the first decades of the twentieth century intended for a black audience—works that argued that slavery in Brazil created the conditions for cordial relations between the races that obviated the color line.[19] Bilden certainly moved in anti-racist intellectual circles, however,[20] and Freyre cited in *CGS*, among others, *The Negro in the New World* (1910), by the British colonialist and explorer Henry Johnston; *South America: Observations and Impressions* (1914, rev. ed.), by the British historian and politician James Bryce; *The Negro* (1915) by W. E. B. Du Bois (founder and president of the National Association for the Advancement of Colored People [NAACP] and director of its journal, *The Crisis*); and *The Conquest of Brazil* (1926), by Roy Nash.[21] After graduating in social sciences from Columbia University in 1908, Nash was secretary of the NAACP and worked on its anti-lynching campaign. In the early 1920s, he traveled around Brazil for three years and spent a summer in Portugal, the "old metropole," to write a book on Brazil's history. Joel Elias Spingarn—literary critic, civil rights activist, second president of the NAACP, and Nash's friend and editor—commented on the book in correspondence with Freyre.[22] Nash's book had an underlying US-Brazil comparison, presenting Brazil as a promising "social laboratory":

> Except the Portuguese colonies in Africa, Brazil is the one country in the world where fusion of Europeans and Africans is going on unchecked by law and costume. More than in any other place in the world, readmixture of the most divergent types of humanity is there injecting meaning into the "*egalité*" of Revolutionary France and the "human solidarity" of philosophers and class-conscious proletarians.[23]

CGS described the colonial condition in Brazil in the sixteenth and seventeenth centuries—more precisely, in the sugar-producing Northeast—under the plantation economy based on slavery and structured around the *casa-grande* and the patriarchal family headed by the *senhor de engenho* (sugar mill owner). According to Freyre, the specificity of Brazilian society resulted from frequent crossbreeding between white, black, and Amerindian, in both biological and cultural terms. Published when deterministic racial models were still very popular among Brazilian scientists,[24] *CGS* built a positive image of racial mixing within the patriarchal and slavery society during the colonial period, highlighting African and Amerindian contributions to Brazilian national identity. Its arguments generated wide discussion within and outside the academic world, and they exerted an enduring impact on Brazil's self-perception and its external appraisal. The new insights in *CGS* called into question ideas that were commonly accepted in the United States and Europe in the interwar years, such as the inferiority of the black people, African heritage as an obstacle to progress, and the idea of "whitening" as a solution to the problem of racial degeneration.

Freyre held that the Portuguese national character resulted from the nation's hybrid ethnic origins, location between Europe and Africa, and history of contacts with Muslims and Jews in the Iberian Peninsula during the first centuries of Portuguese statehood. The recurrent features of the Portuguese—mobility, miscibility and acclimatization—resulting from their cultural and racial "dualism" were carried to Brazil and assured the colonists' skillful adjustment to the new land. Following Nash, Freyre argued that the long Moorish domination explained the aptitude of the Portuguese for miscegenation. They were prepared by the "intimate terms of social and sexual intercourse on which they had lived with the colored races that invaded their peninsula or were close neighbors to it, one of which, of the Mohammedan faith, was technically more highly skilled and possessed an intellectual and artistic culture superior to that of the blond Christians."[25] Like Nash, Freyre noted that the Christian inhabitants of Iberia regarded the Muslims as socially superior and considered it an honor to marry their women. Moreover, the idealization of the brown Moorish woman as the supreme type of human beauty was a cultural trait of the Portuguese, and produced a preference for what Luís de Camões, the sixteenth-century Portuguese epic poet, had called the "varied color."[26]

In the two chapters of *CGS* on the Africans who were transported to Brazil from the beginning of the sixteenth to the mid-nineteenth centuries, Freyre valued their contribution to the formation of the Brazilian family and society under the slavery system. His positive view was based on his belief that there was no such thing as racial superiority or inferiority. He used Boas and one of his first-generation students, Robert Harry Lowie—an expert in North American Indians and author of *Are We Civilised? Human Culture in Perspective* (1929)—to argue that mental differences between whites and blacks did not represent innate or hereditary aptitudes but instead were the result of environment, economic, and cultural circumstances that were hard to determine.[27]

In *Conferências na Europa* (Lectures in Europe) (1938), republished as *O mundo que o português criou* (The world that the Portuguese created) (1940), Freyre enlarged his inquiry to all the areas of Portuguese colonization and reached the same conclusions. The entire "Portuguese world" shared the same feeling and culture, he argued, despite significant regional differences. Brazilians, Portuguese, and Portuguese descendants from the Portuguese colonies all belonged to a transnational community produced by miscegenation. In the early 1950s, Freyre developed from the arguments of *CGS* the concept of Lusotropicalism, the idea that the Portuguese possessed a special capacity to adapt to life in the tropics.[28] In contrast to Anglo-Saxon, Dutch, and French colonizers, the tropical vocation of the Portuguese was a product not of political or economic self-interest but rather of a creative and innate empathy. According to Freyre, the intrinsic plasticity of the Portuguese revealed itself in all areas and times of Portuguese colonization, regardless of geohistorical context.

Boas's ideas on the racial admixture and assimilation of the "natives" that were carried out by the Arabized Hamitic tribes who invaded Sudan inspired Freyre to compare the Portuguese colonization of the tropics with the Muslim one. He perceived a sociological kinship between the two: pacific conquest through intermarriage with African women, assimilation of their mestizo children, and ecological adaptation to the climate and physical environment.[29] He advanced the hypothesis that the Portuguese "followed the example and the methods of the Arab slave system—that of personal, patriarchal and family relationships between master and slave—rather than imitating the impersonal form of industrial or semi-industrial slavery mainly used by northern Europeans in their tropical ventures."[30]

In his late works on Luso-tropicalism, Freyre called for a political project within the "Luso-tropical world"—political in the sense of a cultural policy, migration policy, and ethnic democracy policy shared by every member of the Luso-tropical community, against all kinds of ethnocentrisms.[31] He envisioned that, in the areas of Portuguese influence, "hybrid forms of men and culture," a "third man or a third culture" was in the making, and what made the new civilization "symbiotically Luso-tropical" was its supplanting of the biological condition by the sociological one.[32] Freyre's ideas on miscegenation fit in the intense intellectual exchange between social scientists from the United States and Brazil who were studying race relations and race mixing in the 1930s and 1940s that involved, in combinations of variable geometry, Rüdiger Bilden, Franz Boas, Franz Frazier, Melville Herskovits, Otto Klineberg, Ruth Landes, Robert E. Park, Donald Pierson, Arthur Ramos, Guerreiro Ramos, and Edgard Roquette-Pinto.[33] The American social scientists shared a positive view of Brazil as a harmonious and successful social experiment in terms of race relations. Freyre emphasized that Bilden and Pierson had "written almost enthusiastically about social and aesthetic results of race amalgamation in Brazil."[34] Correspondence between these scholars uncovers important aspects of that circulation.[35]

Early Reception in Portugal: Applause and Rejection

Freyre's positive approach to Africans and race relations in Brazil was highlighted in the reception of *CGS* among intellectuals in Portugal, Cape Verde, and Angola.[36] José Osório de Oliveira (1900–1964), a writer, journalist, and colonial official, was the most emphatic defender of the idea of miscegenation as a distinctive Portuguese colonizing process, resulting from the Portuguese cordiality and capacity of human sympathy.[37] He had lived in Brazil in his childhood (1923–1925) and in 1933, in Mozambique (1919–1920), and in Cape Verde (1926–1928). His action in favor of the Luso-Brazilian cultural exchange was acknowledged on both sides of the Atlantic. Oliveira argued that Brazilians considered the mulatto a Portuguese creation: "When in Rio de Janeiro, passing a beautiful mulatto woman, I heard the *cariocas* say: Long live Portugal! I did not offend."[38] He predicted that a race fully adapted to the geographical environment would arise in Brazil within a few centuries: the Brazilian race. He assembled the "authorized Gilberto Freyre" specifically to contest the alleged inferiority of the *mestiço* and demonstrate the intellectual, artistic, and moral qualities of the Brazilian mulattos.[39] He thought that the Portuguese, more than any other people, should be interested in demonstrating that the idea of the inferiority of the *mestiço* was false.

In the Portuguese colony of Cape Verde, the intellectual group that would create the cultural journal *Claridade* in 1936 embraced Freyre's work. Baltasar Lopes (1907–1989), a high school teacher, publicist, and novelist, reported that he and a small group of friends had started thinking of the social formation process of Cape Verde twenty years earlier. By then, they encountered some Brazilian fiction and poetry that helped them reflect on the "problem of Cape Verde": "Meanwhile . . . the revelation occurred. A magnificent book—*Casa-grande and senzala,* from Gilberto Freyre—was greatly responsible for that revelation, along with the volumes, dense of research and interpretation, from the early deceased Artur Ramos."[40] Henrique Teixeira de Sousa (1919–2005), a doctor and writer of the following generation, has claimed that Freyre was one of the most discussed and appreciated authors when, in the mid-1930s, a group of Cape Verdean writers and artists became involved in the Brazilian cultural movement: "The enthusiasm was so great that some of them slept with *Casa-grande & senzala* on their bedside table, and handled it with the same fervor that the believers read the Holy Scriptures. It's hardly surprisingly. The historical-social and racial factors, that support the origin of the Brazilian people are, almost entirely, the same that intervened in our formation."[41]

The overwhelming reception of Freyre's work in Cape Verde has much to do with the importance it gives to miscegenation in the formation of Brazilian society. The *Claridade* group understood Cape Verde as being produced by a similar process that was quite different from the Anglo-Saxon colonization because it was able to establish an ethnic and cultural equilibrium amidst deep poverty but great human freedom.[42] Freyre was one of the first "masters" of the *Claridade* group, with whom they were able to address their own identity and from whom they borrowed a significant part of their interpretative scheme of reality.[43]

CGS also penetrated intellectual circles in Angola, namely within the Liga Nacional Africana (African National League) and the Associação dos Naturais de Angola (Association of the Angola Natives), where it was read alongside novels and poetry from the Brazilian Northeast. A couple of articles by mestizo intellectuals who criticized racial discrimination and defended natives' education and development may be found in the league's journal, *Angola: Revista de doutrina, estudo e propaganda instrutiva*.⁴⁴ Immediately after the First National Congress of Colonial Anthropology held in Porto in 1934, to which I will return, José Morgado signed an article that attacked the congress's conclusions on the degeneration of race mixing, and stressed that the idea of the inferiority of some races had already been scientifically rebutted. Mulattos were not inferior to their parents, the author argued, and were capable of creating good literary and scientific work. The problem that the *mestiço* faced in Angola was not hereditary but instead poor education and opportunities for social mobility.⁴⁵ For the younger generation of Europeanized blacks and mestizos of the Association of the Angola Natives, "the author of *Casa-grande & senzala* and *Sobrados e Mucambos* [was] a valuable and combative soldier of [their] cause—the rehabilitation of [their] black brothers and of the entire world."⁴⁶ Even if they would later repudiate his compromising attitude toward Portuguese dictatorship and colonialism,⁴⁷ the intellectuals who launched the movement "Let's Discover Angola!" warmly received Freyre's valorization of the African contribution to the formation of Brazil and its positive approach to miscegenation.

Despite these favorable reactions, many Portuguese intellectuals and scientists in the metropole and in the colonies still looked upon miscegenation with concern, and politicians still viewed it as a national problem. In the First National Congress of Colonial Anthropology, miscegenation was spoken of as an unacceptable practice. Although the scientific studies that were presented did not support the thesis of the inferiority of the *mestiços,* the congress concluded that crossbreeding was discouraged for social reasons. In the plenary session, Eusébio Tamagnini (1880–1972), a full professor of anthropology and natural history sciences from the University of Coimbra and "the most enthusiastic proponent of Germanic eugenics,"⁴⁸ said humanity was undoubtedly constituted by several races that were different from each other in somatic, physiologic, and mental terms.⁴⁹ He asserted that the Portuguese belonged to the "Mediterranean race," which "has brilliantly collaborated in the history of occidental civilization." The aptitude for miscegenation, widely seen as an ethnic characteristic of the Portuguese and used as proof of the Portuguese colonial vocation, had to be radically modified.

Alberto Germano da Silva Correia (1888–1967), a Goan physician and physical anthropologist who had been director of the Goa Medical College, presented a paper about the Euro-African of Angola and defended notions more in line with Latin eugenics. Since it was "impossible to prevent or diminish mestizos coming into the world," he asserted, anthropologists should study the better eugenic and ecological conditions for their birth, reproduction, multiplication, and education.[50] He acknowledged the convergence of the data he had collected with Roquette-Pinto's data and invoked the Brazilian anthropologist as an authority to contest the misconceived view of mestizos as sick or racially degenerate: "It is not miscegenation but disease that causes the poor appearance of some of them."[51] He had had opportunity to confirm in Angola and India the deductions of the Brazilian colleague, he added, which "are currently accepted by almost all anthropologists who don't have racial or social prejudices and have scientific true for their exclusive aim."[52] Finally, Germano Correia argued for a humanitarian and liberal colonial policy regarding the *mestiços*: a colonial policy based in science and free of prejudice; and an elite settlement, not only from the professional point of view but also from the moral one, and the state's assistance regarding education of the children of the proletarian colonists. His position reflected a more general preoccupation with the morally counterproductive effect of sending poor white settlers to African colonies.

The Congresso do Mundo Português (Congress of the Portuguese World) was held in Lisbon in 1940 within the double centenary commemorations of nationality and independence, a high moment of Portuguese imperial nationalism. At the congress, António Augusto Mendes Correia (1888–1960), a physical anthropologist at the University of Porto (later director of the Colonial School and the Colonial Research Board), claimed that the miscegenation problem in the Portuguese colonies might have been of occasional political convenience, despite "moral and social painful aspects in all times."[53] The Portuguese Crown's encouragement of mixed marriages in India and Brazil in the sixteenth century had meant that Portuguese expansion could be accomplished with few Portuguese colonialists. Indeed, for a time, miscegenation was the only way of assuring Portuguese settlement. In the present, however, Mendes Correia saw nothing to justify such a policy. He admitted that the scientific argument against miscegenation was weak, but maintained that the physical characteristics of the "half-breed" were variable and unpredictable. He advised the Portuguese government to follow the Italian colonial injunction against miscegenation in the African colonies so that "the prestige of the dominant race and the possibilities of developing the colonized lands aren't jeopardized."[54] Moreover, he proposed that mestizos should not be given access to senior posts in the state administration. Contrary to Freyre and Roquette-Pinto, Mendes Correia considered that miscegenation could not be envisaged "as the secure origin of a better humanity." He was concerned with the "defense of race," "national interest," and "Portuguese historical mission in the world"; whereas miscegenation endangered these aspirations.[55]

The physician and ethnologist Joaquim Alberto Pires de Lima (1877–1959), a medical professor and an ethnographer, contradicted several of the ideas laid out in *CGS*, namely the hybrid ethnic and cultural origin of the Portuguese and the importance of the Moors and Jews in the Portuguese people's racial tolerance. He said only three ethnic groups were fundamental in the constitution of the Portuguese: the Lusitanian, the Romans, and the Germanics. Like Tamagnini and Mendes Correia, he too opposed miscegenation in the Portuguese colonies on the grounds that the black race was "incapable of any progress and irreducibly inferior." He advocated "racial purity."[56] These were long-lasting positions. In the late 1950s, Mendes Correia would still criticize Freyre's work because it exalted the Portuguese tendency toward miscegenation, a secondary aspect of their commendable human sympathy and solidarity. According to Mendes Correia, the influx of Moorish and African slaves to the metropole and intense miscegenation at the beginning of Portuguese maritime expansion could not change the germinal purity of the Portuguese blood, at least in its fundamental qualities and skills.[57]

Portuguese politicians ignored or rejected Freyre's thought until the end of World War II. Once colonial occupation was concluded, the Portuguese state focused on asserting its empire, expanding its administrative and fiscal machine, and submitting the Indigenous people, looked upon as savages, to the superior values of a supposedly Portuguese race.[58] The "Christian Reconquest," one of the foundational myths of the nation, did not accord with Freyre's emphasis on Arabic and African roots in forming the national character. But the main reason for disagreement was Freyre's views on miscegenation. In 1944, during a top meeting of the National Union (*Estado Novo*'s single-party system), António Vicente Ferreira (1874–1953), who had been high commissioner in Angola during the military dictatorship (1926–1928) and had planned a huge project of white settlement in the Angolan plateau, expressed doubts about *CGS*'s scientific value because of its emphasis on racial mixing.[59] Miscegenation would lead, he argued, to the degeneration of psychological and moral characters, and eventually even somatic characters. Ferreira's picture of mestizos, mulattos, and creoles was charged with prejudice; he described them as "impulsive, indolent, and usually lacking in intelligence, docility, and morals."[60] He proposed the establishment of racial segregation policies in white settler areas in order to prevent miscegenation, socialization, and economic competition between white and black.[61] These measures were never realized.

The Appropriation of Freyre's Ideas in the Postwar Period

After the end of World War II, the international community condemned the project of hegemony and racial purity of Nazi Germany, and promoted freedom as a universal goal rather than a preserve of European nations. The United Nations, created in 1945, consecrated the principle of self-determination for all colonized peoples and obliged colonial powers to prepare the territories under their administration for independence. It was in this context that anticolonial movements emerged and the decolonization process began. The wide reach of *CGS* and Freyre's international prestige meant that he enjoyed "a paradoxical situation" in this period. His work on Brazil inspired UNESCO's anti-racist policy, and he was invited to participate in an experts' forum on the "Tensions That Cause Wars" (1948). The *Estado Novo* dictatorship, however, used his ideas to perpetuate the Portuguese empire.[62]

Confronted with international pressures that favored self-determination in colonial territories, Portugal presented itself in the 1951 constitutional revision as a "multi-continental nation," composed by European and overseas provinces.[63] Some months later, Freyre visited Portugal and the Portuguese "overseas provinces" as an official guest of the Portuguese government. Luso-tropicalism was a useful theory to strengthen the idea of "Portuguese pluri-continental national unity" and the Portuguese settlement program overseas. The main figures of the regime and its propaganda apparatus reproduced a nationalized version of Luso-tropicalism in service of Portuguese foreign policy and for domestic public consumption, stressing the existence of harmonious multiracial societies in Portuguese Africa.[64]

In the 1950s and 1960s, Freyre's thought was disseminated, appropriated, and reworked within the High Institute of Overseas Studies, the school for colonial officials' formation, and the Center for Political and Social Studies (Centro de Estudos Políticos e Sociais, CEPS) of the Overseas Research Board (Junta de Investigações do Ultramar, JIU) both directed by Adriano Moreira. Moreira had a major role in the dissemination of Luso-tropicalism in his course on overseas policy, in the CEPS's research agenda, and as minister of Overseas Territories (1961–1962), in key measures taken after the beginning of the liberation war in Angola. These included extending Portuguese citizenship to all inhabitants of the colonies and designing a new settlement to create multiracial communities in Portuguese Africa.[65] Moreira subscribed to Freyre's ideas on the hybrid origins of the Portuguese people and its manifestations overseas. Like the Brazilian social scientist, Moreira defended miscegenation as the natural result of a belief in human equality.[66] Family was the foundational institution in Portuguese colonized areas, and "the Portuguese mulatto was always the child of love and not the result of violence against the native woman."[67] Jorge Dias (1907–1973), who held a PhD in ethnology from the University of Munich, was a professor at the High Institute of Overseas Studies and a researcher at the CEPS (and its interim director when Moreira served as minister for overseas). He was responsible for introducing cultural anthropology, and advanced similar positions on miscegenation and its contribution to the enrichment of society. Dias highlighted the heterogeneity of the Portuguese population from its national origins and the understanding and tolerance that the cordiality with Moors and Jews bequeathed to the Portuguese character. His writing on the Portuguese national character dialogued with Freyre's work.[68]

From both sociopolitical and anthropological perspectives, Moreira and Dias wrote in positive terms about miscegenation in the areas under Portuguese colonization. Medical doctor Almerindo Lessa (1909–1995), "the most prominent figure of the Latin eugenic movement in Portugal,"[69] would develop a research program in genetic anthropology on the mestizo populations of Cape Verde and Macao that was clearly driven by Freyre's thought. Lessa had been responsible for the blood transfusion service of the Civil Hospitals of Lisbon (Hospitais Civis de Lisboa, HCL), organized the services in the Portuguese colonies (Angola, Mozambique, Portuguese India, Cape Verde), and was a regular presence in international hematology conferences.[70]

Almerindo Lessa and the Luso-tropical *Mestiço*

In June and July 1956, Lessa carried out a sero-anthropological mission to Cape Verde, sponsored by the JIU. The fieldwork was done with Jacques Ruffié (1921–2004), then the subdirector of the Blood Center of Toulouse and a geneticist of blood groups. Lessa suggested Ruffié's inclusion in the mission to take advantage of the fact that the French professor had received a government grant to do research in the HCL blood service. The mission also included Mortó Dessai, a former assistant of the Goa Medical College and an HCL biochemist analyst, and Olímpio Nobre Martins, a doctor of the Instituto de Medicina Tropical (Institute of Tropical Medicine). Lessa and Ruffié studied the genetic characters that allowed for evaluating the persistence of the two biological roots of the Cape Verdean men (the Negroid and the Caucasian) after the course of four hundred years of evolution. They argued that the most interesting observations of the study concerned blood groups. The Cape Verdean population was homogeneous as a result of random mixing, and their blood groups differed from both the Portuguese and the African populations. Although the percentage of "Caucasian genes" was only 25 percent, the Cape Verdeans were creating a regional Luso-tropical civilization with occidental traits.[71] Thus Lessa concurred with Cape Verdean intellectuals that the result of miscegenation in the archipelago was Portuguese cultural predominance.[72] The mission's results were presented in international blood congresses and in several lectures in Portugal and abroad.

In 1958, Moreira, as CEPS director, asked Lessa, arriving for a four-month stay in Rio de Janeiro at the invitation of the local university and the Instituto Oswaldo Cruz, to prepare a research project on the "Portuguese *mestiço*," which the CEPS's scientific council considered very important from scientific and political points of view.[73] The project, framed in the "modern biochemist anthropology and cultural anthropology," intended to [...] political value" of the "Portuguese *mestiços*" in all Portu[...]cial and in Brazil, where "the mestizo constitutes a third social cla[...]ries and [...] portant novelty of South American anthropology: 'the gre[...]ost im- perience ever seen,' in the expression of the philosopher Rud[...]cal ex- would give advice to the project in his field of expertise, cultur[...] Dias and Moreira in his field, political science.[...] ology,

After arriving in Rio, Lessa wrote to Freyre, sending him his [...] ect and thanking him for the kind reference he had made in a new [...] sero-anthropological mission to Cape Verde. He explained that [...] the to collect in Brazil materials to continue his sero-anthropological [...] ded deepen the questions already raised about the Cape Verdean mestiz[...] laboratory of genetics and sociology":

> I have been in Rio for 8 days and I have already begun to analyze the doc[...]
> mentioned in some books that I did not know—by Guerreiro Ramos, Fern[...]
> Azevedo, Castro Barreto, Carneiro Leão and Artur Ramos. I do not speak of [...]
> own books, because I know them by heart. They have lived with me, for many year[...]
> the older ones and at all times those that keep coming out.[75]

During his stay in Rio, Lessa presented on "The Roots of The New Man" at two conferences at the Museu Nacional, discussing the results of the [s]ero-anthropological mission to Cape Verde and the ecological and human [sim]ilarities between the Brazilian Northeast and those African islands. He gave other presentations in Rio, São Paulo, and Baía and took the opportunity to expose "the social and nonracial discrimination bases of our overseas policy." In 1960, Lessa conducted a "tropical anthropology mission to Macao" aimed at evaluating the mestizo element in biological and psychological terms, the intensity of the hybridization process, and the relative importance of the two original branches—the Portuguese and the Chinese—in the origin of the actual population:

> Given the rapid political evolution that is taking place in Asian and African populations, this analysis of the biological formation of Macao will certainly have repercussions, as it will demonstrate the scientific attention that we continue to provide to overseas provinces which in the balance of material interests do not represent much, but which we are bound by imperatives of historical consciousness. At the national level this work . . . will contribute to the analysis of the extremely original contribution that the Portuguese people brought to the modern world. Since the formation of the Portuguese mestizo—the new tropical man—has no equivalent in the world.[76]

The initial project was more ambitious and expensive because it included fieldwork in Portuguese Timor. President of the JIU Executive Committee of JIU

Costa, a professor and geologist, gave an unfavorable opinion, [ci]ting a lack of funds and the absence of immediate social utility [and] reproducibility in Lessa's research, in contrast with the overseas [re]search mission and the geological brigade to Portuguese India [al]so awaiting funding.⁷⁷

[Lessa be]nefited from the collaboration of Dias and the Brazilian Luiz Costa [in p]reparing the cultural and social surveys. Along with Ruffié (by now [a key] figure of French hemotypology,"⁷⁸ or blood grouping), Fernando [Bio] (HCL biochemist and researcher), Leopoldo Mayor (director of the [C]enter of Luanda), and Clóvis Junqueira (from the Brazilian Society [of Hem]atology and Hemotherapy) accompanied him in the field. The results [of the] Macao mission were presented by Lessa and Ruffié at the National [Acad]emy of Medicine in Paris and by Lessa in a course delivered at the Uni[vers]ity of Brasília. The positive feedback encouraged Lessa approach JIU once [aga]in for funding and support for launching a bioanthropological mission [to] Portuguese Timor.⁷⁹ He would have Ruffié help in the fieldwork for a [m]onth, and the French National Center for Scientific Research's hemotypology center and the University of Toulouse's hematological clinic would also contribute funds. His request, however, was not granted, probably because of António de Almeida's ongoing research on the Portuguese Timor ethnolinguistic map.

Over several decades, Lessa, "against biased opponents, some of whom assume themselves as wise men," extolled the "eugenic and civilizing possibilities of the Luso-tropical *mestiço*."⁸⁰ Through his field missions, he tried to ensure that Cape Verde and Macao would no longer be, from the biological angle, scientific terra incognita regarding race mixture. On several occasions, he reproduced Freyre's main ideas about the Portuguese character, colonization, and integration in the tropics. Being a biologist, Lessa praised in Freyre's thought the anthropological understanding of the behavior of the Portuguese outside Europe and the evolution of the mestizo societies.⁸¹ After the end of Portuguese Empire, Lessa gave courses on the "Portuguese Occupation of the Tropics" in the Collège de France. As a professor at the University of Évora in southern Portugal, he organized a postgraduate course on human ecology and founded the Research Center of the Global Ecology of the Men from Alentejo (south of the Tagus River) that intended to study from the biological, social, and historical points of view "the Portuguese region where men and civilizations from other parts (from the Oriental Mediterranean to the north and central Africa) met along centuries, leaving varied physical and cultural genes."⁸² Until his death, Lessa continued his research agenda based in the belief that Portugal created in half a millennium, by "human graft," a psychocultural and biological novelty: "the Luso-mestizo of the tropics," a "universal man."⁸³

Conclusion

Gilberto Freyre's views on miscegenation resulted largely from intense intellectual exchanges between Brazilian and American scholars, especially around their obsession with making comparisons between the United States and Brazil in the management of slavery and racial relations. The favorable reception of his ideas among Portuguese, Cape Verdean, and Angolan intellectuals, despite the prominence of anti-miscegenation positions in some scientific and political circles, reveals the diversity of racial thought in Portugal and the Portuguese Empire in the 1930s. In the 1950s and 1960s, the *Estado Novo* appropriated and manipulated Freyre's ideas to legitimize the Portuguese presence outside Europe. Later, Luso-tropicalism was used to justify the national project of constitution of multiracial societies in Portuguese Africa in the era of decolonization. It also orientated the social and political research agenda of CEPS, committed as it was to the defense of the national interest and unity. Curiously, Adriano Moreira and Jorge Dias, who had approached race mixing through social and cultural anthropology, supported Lessa's anti-racist perspective on miscegenation in the Portuguese colonies, which was based on the new genetic anthropology perspective that gained preponderance in the postwar period—an alternative to the out-of-date racist physical anthropology of António Augusto Mendes Correia and António de Almeida. The new Luso-tropical man whose existence Freyre attributed to biological and cultural miscegenation was for Lessa—also influenced by Pierre Teilhard de Chardin's beliefs about the unity of humankind and the convergence of civilizations—a perfect achievement of both human evolution and transcendence.

CLÁUDIA CASTELO is Research Fellow at the Interuniversity Center for the History of Science and Technology in the University of Lisbon. Her research interests focus on the history of modern imperialism and colonialism. She has worked on the reception and appropriation of Luso-tropicalism in Portugal and on colonial settlement in Angola and Mozambique. She is currently coordinating a Fundação para a Ciência e a Tecnologia project on field scientists in the late Portuguese Empire. She is the author of *O modo português de estar no mundo* (1998) and the coeditor of *Gilberto Freyre: Novas leituras do outro lado do Atlântico* (2015).

Notes

1. *Casa-grande & senzala* if taken literally would be in English *The Big House and the Slave Quarters*. Gilberto Freyre, *Casa-grande & senzala: Formação da família brasileira sob o regímen de economia patriarchal* (Rio de Janeiro, 1933), trans. Samuel Putnam as

The Masters and the Slaves: A Study in the Development of Brazilian Civilization (New York, 1946). Whenever there is an English translation of Freyre's books, the quotations will be from the translation. All other translations in this chapter are my own unless otherwise noted.
2. Nancy Stepan, *The Hour of Eugenics: Race, Gender, and Nation in Latin America* (Ithaca, NY, 1991), 167–68.
3. Warwick Anderson, "Racial Conceptions in the Global South," *Isis* 105, no. 4 (2014): 791.
4. I have borrowed this insight from Kapil Raj, "Beyond Postcolonialism . . . and Postpositivism: Circulation and the Global History of Science," *Isis* 104, no. 2 (2013): 343.
5. "We need further geographical and institutional specificity in locating ideas about race," as pointed out by Anderson, "Racial Conceptions in the Global South," 786. Biography has the virtue of accounting for the local, the personal, and the institutional dimensions.
6. For this purpose, I resorted in particular to Jeffrey D. Needell, "Identity, Race, Gender, and Modernity in the Origins of Gilberto Freyre's Oeuvre," *American Historical Review* 100, no. 1 (1995): 51–77; Maria Lúcia Pallares-Burke, *Gilberto Freyre: Um vitoriano nos trópicos* (São Paulo, 2005).
7. It was published as Gilberto Freyre, "Social Life in Brazil in the Middle of the Nineteenth Century," *Hispanic American Historical Review* 5, no. 4 (1922): 597–630.
8. Freyre, *The Masters and the Slaves*, xx.
9. Needell, "Identity, Race, Gender, and Modernity," 65–66, cited in Pallares-Burke, *Gilberto Freyre*, 264.
10. Pallares-Burke, *Gilberto Freyre*, 266. Pallares-Burke has shown that Freyre added in the 1980s much data on the miscegenation in Brazil to the Portuguese version of his MA thesis.
11. Freyre, *The Masters and the Slaves*, xxi.
12. Pallares-Burke, *Gilberto Freyre*, 378, 400.
13. Maria Lúcia Garcia Pallares-Burke, *O triunfo do fracasso: Rüdiger Bilden, o amigo esquecido de Gilberto Freyre* (São Paulo, 2012).
14. Freyre, *The Masters and the Slaves*, xx.
15. Rüdiger Bilden, "Brazil, a Laboratory of Civilization," *Nation* 128, no. 3315 (1929): 71–76; Rüdiger Bilden, "Race Relations in Latin America with Special Reference to the Development of Indigenous Cultures," Round Table on Latin American Relations, Institute of Public Affairs, University of Virginia, 1 July 1931, cited in Freyre, *The Masters and the Slaves*, 12, 26, 82, 141, 322, 328, and 368.
16. Fisk was a black university in Nashville (Tennessee) whose social sciences department was chaired by Charles S. Johnson. Robert E. Park joined the department after his retirement from the University of Chicago in 1936. In 1937, after returning from his fieldwork in Bahia, Brazil, Donald Pierson directed at Fisk a seminar on race and culture with the collaboration of Bilden, Ruth Landes, and Robert Park. Pallares-Burke, *O triunfo do fracasso*, 231.
17. Gilberto Freyre, *O mundo que o português criou: Aspectos das relações sociais e de cultura do Brasil com Portugal e as colónias portuguesa* (São Paulo, 2010), 60, 79–80. In fact, Boas himself had acknowledged that Bilden described to him the relations between blacks, Indians, and whites in Brazil. Franz Boas, *Anthropology of Modern Life* (New York, 1928), 65.
18. Pallares-Burke, *O triunfo do fracasso*, 348–55.
19. Zita Nunes, *Cannibal Democracy: Race and Representation in the Literature of the Americas* (Minneapolis, MN, 2008), 89–90.

20. Pallares-Burke, *O triunfo do fracasso*, 244–54.
21. Freyre considered Nash's book "one of the best ever written on Brazil from a sociological standpoint." Gilberto Freyre, *Brazil: An Interpretation* (New York, 1945), 20.
22. Guillermo Guicci and Enrique Rodriguéz Larreta, *Gilberto Freyre, uma biografia cultural: A formação de um intelectual brasileiro, 1900–1936* (Rio de Janeiro, 2007), 127.
23. Roy Nash, *The Conquest of Brazil* (New York, 1926), 166. Seigel has drawn our attention to the fact that Nash was paraphrasing without attribution Du Bois's 1915 citation of Bryce's 1912 travelogue. Micol Seigel, "Beyond Compare: Comparative Method after the Transnational Turn," *Radical History Review* 91 (2005): 72.
24. Lilia Moritz Schwarcz, *O espetáculo das raças: Cientistas, instituições e questão racial no Brasil, 1870–1930* (São Paulo, 1993), 248.
25. Freyre, *The Masters and the Slaves*, 11. Freyre cites Nash, *The Conquest of Brazil*, in *The Masters and the Slaves*, 66.
26. Gilberto Freyre, *The Portuguese and the Tropics: Suggestions Inspired by the Portuguese Methods of Integrating Autochthonous Peoples and Cultures Differing from the European in a New, or Luso-tropical Complex of Civilization*, trans. Helen M. D'O. Matthew and Fernando de Mello Moser (Lisbon, 1961), 59, 125.
27. Freyre, *The Masters and the Slaves*, 297–98.
28. Gilberto Freyre, *Um brasileiro em terras portuguesas: Introdução a uma possível luso-tropicologia, acompanhada de conferências e discursos proferidos em Portugal e em terras lusitanas e ex-lusitanas da Ásia, da África e do Atlântico* (São Paulo, 2010). In addition to a long introduction, in which Freyre presents a synthesis of Luso-tropicalism, this book includes two lectures he delivered during his official visit to Portugal and the Portuguese colonies—"Uma cultura moderna: A luso-tropical" [A modern culture: The Luso-tropical] (Goa, November 1951) and "Em torno de um novo conceito de tropicalismo" [About a new concept of tropicalism] (Coimbra, January 1952)—where one finds already the formulation of Luso-tropicalism.
29. Freyre, *Um brasileiro em terras portuguesas*, 52–53, 59.
30. Freyre, *The Portuguese and the Tropics*, 88.
31. Gilberto Freyre, *Integração portuguesa nos trópicos / Portuguese Integration in the Tropics* (Lisbon, 1958), 64.
32. Freyre, *The Portuguese and the Tropics*, 80.
33. Important aspects of that transnational circulation were discussed in Seigel, "Beyond Compare"; Vanderlei Sebastião de Sousa, "Ciência e miscigenação racial no início do século XX: Debates e controvérsias de Edgard Roquette-Pinto com a antropologia física norte-americana," *História, Ciências, Saúde—Manguinhos* 23, no. 3 (2016): 597–614; Marcos Chor Maio and Thiago da Costa Lopes, "Entre Chicago e Salvador: Donald Pierson e o Estudo das Relações Raciais," *Estudos Históricos* 30, no. 60 (2017): 115–40; Marcos Chor Maio, "A crítica de Otto Klineberg aos testes de inteligência: O Brasil como laboratório racial," *Varia Historia* 33, no. 61 (2017): 145–46.
34. Freyre, *Brazil*, 133.
35. Arquivo Documental Gilberto Freyre (ADGF), Fundação Gilberto Freyre, Recife, Brazil; Arquivo Pessoal Roquette-Pinto, Centro de Memória da Academia Brasileira de Letras, Rio de Janeiro; Arquivo Arthur Ramos, Biblioteca Nacional do Brasil, Rio de Janeiro; Melville Herskovits Papers, Northwestern University Archives, Evanston, IL.
36. Cláudia Castelo, *"O Modo Português de Estar no Mundo": O Luso-tropicalismo e a Ideologia Colonial Portuguesa* (Porto, 1999), 69–80.
37. José Osório de Oliveira, "A mestiçagem: Esboço duma opinião favorável," *O Mundo Português* 1, no. 11 (1934): 367–68.
38. Ibid., 369.

39. José Osório de Oliveira, "A suposta inferioridade do Mestiço," *O Mundo Português* 6, no. 62 (1939): 57–60.
40. Baltasar Lopes, *Cabo Verde visto por Gilberto Freyre: Apontamentos lidos ao microfone de Rádio Barlavento* (Praia, 1956), 5–6.
41. Henrique Teixeira de Sousa, "Uma visita desejada," *Cabo Verde: Boletim de Propaganda e Informação* 27 (1951): 31.
42. João Lopes, "Apontamento," *Claridade* 1 (1936): 9.
43. Mário António de Oliveira, "Influência da literatura brasileira sobre as literaturas portuguesas do Atlântico tropical," in *Reler África* (Coimbra, 1990), 249–50.
44. On the African National League, see Eugénia Rodrigues, *A geração silenciada: A Liga Nacional Africana e a representação do branco em Angola na década de 30* (Porto, 2003).
45. José Morgado, "Verdades científicas ou pataratas de um pseudo-científico," *Angola: Revista Mensal de Doutrina, Estudo e Propaganda Instrutiva* 11 (1934): 5.
46. Letter from Mário de Alcântara Monteiro to Gilberto Freyre, 22 September 1951, ADGF.
47. Buanga Fele [Mário Pinto de Andrade], "Qu'est-ce que le 'lusotropicalismo'?" *Présence Africaine* 4 (1955): 24–35.
48. Richard Cleminson, "Between Germanic and Latin Eugenics: Portugal, 1930–1960," *História, Ciências, Saúde—Manguinhos* 23, no. 1 (2016): 82.
49. Eusébio Tamagnini, *Os problemas da mestiçagem: Conferência proferida na sessão plenária do I Congresso Nacional de Antropologia Colonial* (Porto, 1934), 16.
50. Alberto C. Germano da Silva Correia, *Os euro-africanos de Angola: Comunicação ao I Congresso Nacional de Antropologia Colonial* (Porto, 1934), 8.
51. Edgard Roquette-Pinto, *Ensaios de antrolopogia brasiliana* (Rio de Janeiro, 1934), 147, cited in Silva Correia, *Os euro-africanos de Angola*, 19.
52. Silva Correia, *Os euro-africanos de Angola*, 19.
53. António Augusto Mendes Correia, "O mestiçamento nas colónias portuguesas," in *Congresso do Mundo Portuguê*, vol. 14, book 1 (Lisbon, 1940), 122.
54. Ibid., 128.
55. Ibid., 130–32.
56. Joaquim Alberto Pires de Lima, "Influência dos mouros, judeus e negros na etnografia portuguesa," in *Congresso do Mundo Português*, vol. 18, book 2 (Lisbon, 1940), 64.
57. António Augusto Mendes Correia, "Factores de Independência Nacional," in *Portugal: Oito séculos de história ao serviço da valorização do homem e da aproximação dos povos* (Lisbon, 1958), 58.
58. Valentim Alexandre, *Origens do colonialismo português moderno* (Lisbon, 1979), 7.
59. Vicente Ferreira, *Colonização étnica na África portuguesa: Estudo apresentado ao II Congresso da União Nacional* (Lisbon, 1944), 41.
60. Ibid., 40.
61. Ibid., 78.
62. Marcos Chor Maio, "Tempo controverso: Gilberto Freyre e o projecto UNESCO," *Tempo Social* 11, no. 1 (1999): 112.
63. Law no. 2048, 11 June 1951.
64. Castelo, "*O Modo Português de Estar no Mundo*," 96–101.
65. Only in 1962 did the Estado Novo permit the free movement of Portuguese people in the Portuguese Empire and the free settlement of Portuguese colonists in Portuguese Africa. Until then, the state had controlled the entrance of poor or unqualified migrants.

66. Adriano Moreira, *Política Ultramarina* (Lisbon, 1956), 138–39.
67. Adriano Moreira, "O pensamento do Infante D. Henrique e a actual política ultramarina de África," *Boletim da Sociedade de Geografia de Lisboa* 78, nos. 4–6 (1960): 139.
68. Omar Ribeiro Thomaz, "'The Good-Hearted Portuguese People': Anthropology of Nation, Anthropology of Empire," in *Empires, Nations, and Natives: Anthropology and State-Making*, ed. Benoît de L'Estoile, Federico Neiburg, abd Lygia Maria Sigaud (Durham, NC, 2005), 78–81.
69. Richard Cleminson, *Catholicism, Race and Empire: Eugenics in Portugal, 1900–1950* (Budapest, 2014), 137–46, Cleminson, "Between Germanic and Latin Eugenics," 77–82.
70. Almerindo Lessa, *Meridianos brasileiros: Metas políticas e sociais, fundamentos da administração, organização da ciência, presença de Portugal, posição do Brasil no espaço luso-tropical* (Lisbon, 1960); Almerindo Lessa, "O homem cabo-verdiano: Suas raízes, sua multiplicação, suas doenças (linha vertebral de um ensaio demográfico, com uma análise crítica dos métodos para o estudo do mestiço luso-tropical)," in *Seroantropologia das Ilhas de Cabo Verde: Mesa redonda sobre o homem cabo-verdiano*, 2nd ed., ed. Almerindo Lessa and Jacques Ruffié (Lisbon, 1960), 115–30.
71. Almerindo Lessa and Jacques Ruffié, eds., *Seroantropologia das Ilhas de Cabo Verde: Mesa redonda sobre o homem cabo-verdiano* (Lisbon, 1957), 61–62.
72. An insightful analysis of this discussion in Miguel Vale de Almeida, "Projecto crioulo: Cabo Verde, colonialismo e crioulidade," in *Outros destinos: Ensaios de Antropologia e Cidadania* (Porto, 2004), 255–74.
73. Proc. 260—Centro de Estudos Políticos e Sociais, vol. 2, doc. no. 242, Arquivo Histórico, Instituto Investigação Cientfífica Tropical (IICT), Universidade de Lisboa.
74. Research project attached to doc. no. 242, Arquivo Histórico, IICT.
75. Letter from Almerindo Lessa to Gilberto Freyre [Rio de Janeiro, 1958], ADGF.
76. Proposal from Almerindo Lessa to the president of the JIU Executive Committee, 15 June 1960, for a "Tropical Anthropology Mission to Macao," proc. 831—Missão de Estudos de Antropologia Tropical em Macau (1960–1966), Arquivo Histórico, IICT.
77. Information no. 831/60 of JIU, 5 February 1960. Proc. 831—Missão de Estudos de Antropologia Tropical em Macau (1960–1966), Arquivo Histórico, IICT.
78. Claude-Olivier Doron, "Metamorphosis of the Concept of 'Race' in French Hemotypology (1950's–1980's): Between Europe and South-America," in *25th International Congress for the History of Science and Technology: Book of Abstracts* (Rio de Janeiro, 2017), 296.
79. Letter from Almerindo Lessa to the president of the Executive Committee of JIU, 18 May 1966. Proc. 831—Missão de Estudos de Antropologia Tropical em Macau (1960–1966), Arquivo Histórico, IICT.
80. Almerindo Lessa, "A vocação ardente dos portugueses," in *Mesas redondas internacionais: Realizadas em 1960 nos hospitais civis e do ultramar de Lisboa* (Lisbon, 1961), 295–303.
81. Lessa, *Meridianos brasileiros*, 177.
82. Letter from Almerindo Lessa to Gilberto Freyre, Évora, 29 June 1977, Archives of the Fundação Gilberto Freyre.
83. Almerindo Lessa, "Expansão bio-social do homem português: Uma linha vertebral e dois exemplos de ocupação por 'exteria de homem'—Antropologia genética de Cabo Verde e de Macau," in *Convergência de raças e culturas: Biologia e sociologia da Mestiçagem* (Évora, 1983), 33.

Bibliography

Alexandre, Valentim. *Origens do colonialismo português moderno.* Lisbon: Livraria Sá da Costa Editora, 1979.

Almeida, Miguel Vale de. "Projecto crioulo: Cabo Verde, colonialismo e crioulidade." In *Outros destinos: Ensaios de Antropologia e Cidadania,* 255–305. Porto: Companhia das Letras, 2004.

Anderson, Warwick. "Racial Conceptions in the Global South." *Isis* 105, no. 4 (2014): 782–92.

Bilden, Rüdiger. "Brazil, a Laboratory of Civilization." *Nation* 128, no. 3315 (1929): 71–76.

———. "Race Relations in Latin America with Special Reference to the Development of Indigenous Cultures." Round Table on Latin American Relations, Institute of Public Affairs, University of Virginia, 1 July 1931.

Boas, Franz. *Anthropology of Modern Life.* New York: Norton, 1928.

Castelo, Cláudia. *"O Modo Português de Estar no Mundo": O luso-tropicalismo e a ideologia colonial portuguesa, 1933–1961.* Porto: Afrontamento, 1999.

Cleminson, Richard. "Between Germanic and Latin Eugenics: Portugal, 1930–1960." *História, Ciências, Saúde—Manguinhos* 23, no. S1 (2016): 73–92.

———. *Catholicism, Race and Empire: Eugenics in Portugal, 1900–1950.* Budapest: Central European University Press, 2014.

Correia, António Augusto Mendes. "Factores de Independência Nacional." In *Portugal: Oito séculos de história ao serviço da valorização do homem e da aproximação dos povos,* by AAVV, 45–59. Lisbon: Comissariado da Exposição Universal de Bruxelas, 1958.

———. "O mestiçamento nas colónias portuguesas." In *Congresso do Mundo Português,* vol. 14, book 1, 113–33. Lisbon: Comissão Executiva dos Centenários, 1940.

Doron, Claude-Olivier. "Metamorphosis of the Concept of 'Race' in French Hemotypology (1950's–1980's): Between Europe and South-America." In *25th International Congress for the History of Science and Technology: Book of Abstracts,* 296. Rio de Janeiro: ICHST, 2017.

Ferreira, Vicente. *Colonização étnica na África portuguesa: Estudo apresentado ao II Congresso da União Nacional.* Lisbon: Ferreira, 1944.

Fele, Buanga [Mário Pinto de Andrade]. "Qu'est-ce que le 'lusotropicalismo'?" *Presènce Africaine* 4 (1955): 24–35.

Freyre, Gilberto. *Brazil: An Interpretation.* New York: Knopf, 1945.

———. *Casa-grande & senzala: Formação da família brasileira sob o regímen de economia patriarchal.* Rio de Janeiro: Editora Maia & Schmidt, 1933. Translated by Samuel Putnam as *The Masters and the Slaves: A Study in the Development of Brazilian Civilization* (Knopf: New York, 1946).

———. *Integração portuguesa nos trópicos / Portuguese Integration in the Tropics.* Lisbon: Junta de Investigações do Ultramar, 1958.

———. *O mundo que o português criou: Aspectos das relações sociais e de cultura do Brasil com Portugal e as colónias portuguesa.* São Paulo: É Realizações, 2010. First published 1940 by José Olympio (Rio de Janeiro).

———. "Social Life in Brazil in the Middle of the Nineteenth Century." *Hispanic American Historical Review* 5, no. 4 (1922): 597–630.

———. *The Portuguese and the Tropics: Suggestions Inspired by the Portuguese Methods of Integrating Autochthonous Peoples and Cultures Differing from the European in a New, or Luso-tropical Complex of Civilization.* Translated by Helen M. D'O. Matthew and Fernando de Mello Moser. Lisbon: Executive Committee for the Commemoration of the 5th Centenary of the Death of Prince Henry the Navigator, 1961.

———. *Um brasileiro em terras portuguesas: Introdução a uma possível luso-tropicologia, acompanhada de conferências e discursos proferidos em Portugal e em terras lusitanas e ex-lusitanas da Ásia, da África e do Atlântico.* São Paulo: É Realizações, 2010. First published 1953 by José Olympio (Rio de Janeiro).
Guicci, Guillermo, and Enrique Rodriguéz Larreta. *Gilberto Freyre, uma biografia cultural: A formação de um intelectual brasileiro, 1900–1936.* Rio de Janeiro: Civilização Editora, 2007.
Lessa, Almerindo. "A vocação ardente dos portugueses," *Mesas redondas internacionais,* 295–303. Lisbon: Edições Semana Médica, 1961.
———. "Expansão bio-social do homem português: Uma linha vertebral e dois exemplos de ocupação por 'extertia de homem'—Antropologia genética de Cabo Verde e de Macau." In *Convergência de raças e culturas: Biologia e sociologia da Mestiçagem,* 31–53. Évora: Universidade de Évora, 1983.
———. "O homem cabo-verdiano: Suas raízes, sua multiplicação, suas doenças (linha vertebral de um ensaio demográfico, com uma análise crítica dos métodos para o estudo do mestiço luso-tropical)." In *Seroantropologia das Ilhas de Cabo Verde: Mesa redonda sobre o homem cabo-verdiano,* 2nd ed., edited by Almerindo Lessa and Jacques Ruffié, 115–30. Lisbon: Junta de Investigações do Ultramar, 1960.
———. *Meridianos brasileiros: Metas políticas e sociais, fundamentos da administração, organização da ciência, presença de Portugal, posição do Brasil no espaço luso-tropical.* Lisbon: Junta de Investigações do Ultramar, 1960.
Lessa, Almerindo, and Jacques Ruffié, eds. *Seroantropologia das Ilhas de Cabo Verde: Mesa redonda sobre o homem cabo-verdiano.* Lisbon: Junta de Investigações do Ultramar, 1957.
Lima, Joaquim Alberto Pires de. "Influência dos mouros, judeus e negros na etnografia portuguesa." In *Congresso do Mundo Português,* vol. 18, book 2, 63–102. Lisbon: Comissão Executiva dos Centenários 1940.
Lopes, Baltasar. *Cabo Verde visto por Gilberto Freyre: Apontamentos lidos ao microfone de Rádio Barlavento.* Praia: Imprensa Nacional, 1956.
Lopes, João. "Apontamento." *Claridade* 1 (1936): 9.
Maio, Marcos Chor. "A crítica de Otto Klineberg aos teses de inteligência: O Brasil como laboratório racial." *Varia Historia* 33, no. 61 (2017): 135–61.
———. "Tempo controverso: Gilberto Freyre e o projecto UNESCO." *Tempo Social* 11, no. 1 (1999): 111–36.
Maio, Marcos Chor, and Thiago da Costa Lopes. "Entre Chicago e Salvador: Donald Pierson e o estudo das relações raciais." *Estudos Históricos* 30, no. 60 (2017): 115–40.
Moreira, Adriano. "O pensamento do Infante D. Henrique e a actual política ultramarina de África." *Boletim da Sociedade de Geografia de Lisboa* 78, nos. 4–6 (1960): 131–150.
———. *Política Ultramarina.* Lisbon: Junta de Investigação dop Ultramar, 1956.
Morgado, José. "Verdades científicas ou pataratas de um pseudo-científico." *Angola: Revista Mensal de Doutrina, Estudo e Propaganda Instrutiva* 11 (1934): 5.
Nash, Roy. *The Conquest of Brazil.* New York: Harcourt, Brace & Co., 1926.
Needell, Jeffrey D. "Identity, Race, Gender, and Modernity in the Origins of Gilberto Freyre's oeuvre." *American Historical Review* 100, no. 1 (1995): 51–77.
Nunes, Zita. *Cannibal Democracy: Race and Representation in the Literature of the Americas.* Minneapolis: University of Minnesota Press, 2008.
Oliveira, José Osório de. "A mestiçagem: Esboço duma opinião favorável." *O Mundo Português* 1, no. 11 (1934): 367–69.
———. "A suposta inferioridade do Mestiço." *O Mundo Português* 6, no. 62 (1939): 57–60.

Oliveira, Mário António de. "Influência da literatura brasileira sobre as literaturas portuguesas do Atlântico tropical." In *Reler África*, 233–274. Coimbra: Instituto de Antropologica, Universidade de Coimbra, 1990.

Pallares-Burke, Maria Lúcia Garcia. *Gilberto Freyre: Um vitoriano nos trópicos*. São Paulo: Editora Unesp, 2005.

———. *O trunfo do fracasso: Rüdiger Bilden, o amigo esquecido de Gilberto Freyre*. São Paulo: Unesp, 2012.

Raj, Kapil. "Beyond Postcolonialism ... and Postpositivism: Circulation and the Global History of Science." *Isis* 104, no. 2 (2013): 337–47.

Rodrigues, Eugénia. *A geração silenciada: A Liga Nacional Africana e a representação do branco em Angola na década de 30*. Porto: Afrontamento, 2003.

Roquette-Pinto, Edgard. *Ensaios de antrolopogia brasiliana*. Rio de Janeiro: Editora Nacional, 1934.

Schwarcz, Lilia Moritz. *The Spectacles of Races: Scientists, Institutions, and the Race Question in Brazil*. New York: Hill & Wang, 1999.

Seigel, Micol. "Beyond Compare: Comparative Method after the Transnational Turn." *Radical History Review* 91 (2005): 62–90.

Silva Correia, Alberto C. Germano da. *Os euro-africanos de Angola: Comunicação ao I Congresso Nacional de Antropologia Colonial*. Porto: Edições da 1. Exposição Colonial Portuguesa, 1934.

Sousa, Henrique Teixeira de. "Uma visita desejada," *Cabo Verde: Boletim de Propaganda e Informação* 27 (1951): 31.

Sousa, Vanderlei Sebastião de. "Ciência e miscigenação racial no início do século XX: Debates e controvérsias de Edgard Roquette-Pinto com a antropologia física norte-americana." *História, Ciências, Saúde—Manguinhos* 23, no. 3 (2016): 597–614.

Stepan, Nancy. *The Hour of Eugenics: Race, Gender, and Nation in Latin America*. Ithaca, NY: Cornell University Press, 1991.

Tamagnini, Eusébio. *Os problemas da mestiçagem: Conferência proferida na sessão plenária do I Congresso Nacional de Antropologia Colonial*. Porto: Edições da 1. Exposição Colonial Portuguesa, 1934.

Thomaz, Omar Ribeiro. "'The Good-Hearted Portuguese People': Anthropology of Nation, Anthropology of Empire." In *Empires, Nations, and Natives: Anthropology and State-Making*, edited by Benoît de L'Estoile, Federico Neiburg, and Lygia Maria Sigaud, 58–87. Durham, NC: Duke University Press, 2005.

CHAPTER 2

Gilberto Freyre
Racial Populism and Ethnic Nationalism

Jerry Dávila

There are many ways to interpret the significance of Gilberto Freyre and his work to the study of Brazilian race relations and of race relations in the Portuguese-speaking world. He is Brazil's seminal twentieth-century author, an accomplished and innovative writer of history, and the preeminent public intellectual defender of Portugal's last years as an imperial power. He occupies a seemingly permanent place in the literature on race relations and culture in Brazil, even—perhaps especially—for those who dismiss his conclusions or weigh his ideas as detrimental to the people about whom he wrote.

If Freyre is ubiquitous, how then do we weigh his influence? One way is to subtract him: to consider the ways in which race relations and their interpretation in Brazil in the 1930s and since then would be different in the absence of his work. When we do this, it becomes clear that many of the ideas that he is associated with survive without him. This is true for areas where he is regarded as having a positive contribution, such as the transition in intellectual thought from regarding race to regarding culture as the basis of human differences, and the idea that Brazil is a country shaped by social and cultural mixture. It is equally true of areas where criticism of him condenses: the association between Freyre and the concept that Brazil was a racial democracy, or the defense of Portuguese colonialism in Africa and South Asia.

These major elements of what is associated with Freyre would still exist without him, but other aspects of Freyre's influence would not have existed as he created them. It is in these areas that Freyre's significance can be most acutely felt. These aspects derive from the careful ways in which Freyre constructed an identity as a public intellectual: how he imbued that role with moral and scientific authority, and how he used that role to delegitimate the voices of Brazilians of African descent and subjects in Portuguese colonies who spoke out against and resisted the political, social, and cultural values systems to which they were subordinated. Freyre crafted a role for himself as a racial populist by curating an image of Brazil characterized by benign race relations, and he acted as an ethnic nationalist who promoted a belief in the cultural and moral superiority of the Portuguese and their descendants.

Drawing on Freyre's writing, and his life as a public intellectual, we can define racial populism as the act of a public figure to define the experience of a racial minority group in terms that reinforce a positive national image. This definition employs Michael Conniff's characterization of political populists, who "inspired a sense of nationalism and pride in their followers ... The individual could take pride in being a citizen of this nation. By the same token, populists held themselves up as defenders of the popular sovereignty against foreign pressures and exploitation."[1] A racial populist is someone who comes from outside the historical experience of the marginalized group but makes claims about that group's experience to assert that the nation's race relations are benign, particularly compared to those of other countries. This populist stance defends that positive national image against challenges, particularly those that come from the minority group itself or that come from abroad. The affirmations of a racial populist are directed toward the country's dominant social groups, who consume it as evidence that they are benign and moral and therefore do not need to make accommodations in the area of race relations.

Freyre's racial populism was connected to his assertion of ethnic nationalism. While many twentieth-century Brazilian intellectuals celebrated Brazil's racial mixture as a positive national characteristic, Freyre was distinctive in attributing this to a supposed moral and cultural endowment of the Portuguese. It is hard to say whether Freyre's views on race relations and miscegenation shaped his views on Portuguese ethnicity or vice versa: throughout his career as a writer and public figure, Freyre's thinking on race and ethnicity fed each other. While Freyre's ethnic nationalism gained its fullest expression in his defense of Portuguese colonialism in Africa in the 1960s, it was already evident in the years immediately following the publication of *Casa-grande & senzala*. In 1937, Freyre embarked on a lecture tour in Europe and while in Portugal declared:

> The Portuguese were everywhere, especially Brazil, splendidly creative in their efforts at colonization. The glory of their blood was not so much that of the imperial warrior who conquered and subjugated barbarians to dominate them and exploit them from above. It was mainly that of being the procreator of Europe in the tropics. He dominated native peoples mixing himself with them [elas] and loving with gusto the women of color.

The result was that, "in all places where this kind of colonization dominated, racial prejudice appears as insignificant."[2]

Freyre's Context

Gilberto Freyre was educated by Baptist missionaries, received a scholarship to attend Baylor University in Texas, and pursued a master's degree at Columbia University, making him one of the most educated Brazilians in a country with scarce educational opportunities and in which racial disparities in access to those opportunities were extraordinarily high. These disparities are reflected in the 1940 census, which conducted the earliest substantial examination of literacy and education rates correlated by race and by region. At that time, fewer than four in ten of Brazilians over age five would have had the literacy needed to read a book like *Casa-grande & senzala*. If Freyre and his readers were part of a national elite by virtue of their literacy, then racial disparities made access to that elite highly unequal. Brazilians identified by the 1940 census as black or brown had a literacy rate of 23 percent. In Freyre's home state of Pernambuco, which was also the region that epitomized for Freyre the themes of cultural mixture and miscegenation that defined Brazil, the disparities were even starker for members of his generation. Less than fifty thousand black or brown Pernambucans between the ages of thirty and forty-nine (Freyre turned forty in 1940) were literate.[3]

Freyre's educational opportunities, his platform as a writer, his readership, and the kinds of perspectives he could develop in his writing were constrained by the limits to educational opportunity in early twentieth-century Brazil, and these exacerbated the deep racial disparities that dominated all aspects of Brazilian life. A Brazilian of African descent was unlikely to have had the trajectory that Freyre did. As a result, the interpretation of Brazilian culture and national identity that Freyre synthesized was one that he formed out of the meanings he ascribed to people who lacked the comparable power to write (or for the most part, read) their history. As Fernando Henrique Cardoso writes in his preface to the forty-eighth edition of *Casa-grande & senzala*, "In the end, the history he tells was the history that Brazilians, or at least the elite who read and wrote about Brazil, wanted to hear."[4]

The extent to which disparities in access to literacy shaped the society in which Freyre produced his work, and within which his work was received, is reflected by the differences in literacy rates between Brazil and other countries such as the United States and Cuba. For instance, 77 percent of black Brazilians were not literate in 1940, in contrast to only 11.5 percent of people defined as "nonwhite" in the United States.[5] Consequently, the presence of African Americans in the US public sphere was much denser and more able to critically engage debates about race and nation than could have been the case in Brazil. The Columbia University anthropologist Franz Boas, whom Freyre called his mentor, had African American interlocutors including W. E. B. Du Bois, Booker T. Washington, the historian Carter Woodson, and Boas's advisee, the folklorist Zora Neale Hurston.[6] In Cuba, the proportion of literate Afro-Cubans in 1919 was 53 percent, a number that would not be reached among black and brown Brazilians until the late 1970s.[7] Since literacy was required for the right to vote until 1985 in Brazil, limited access to literacy compounded the marginalization of black Brazilians. The capacity to form political and advocacy organizations was hampered not only by literacy levels and the fact that most or many black Brazilians lacked political voice but also by political ruptures and the dictatorial regimes that suppressed speech and political organizations after 1937 and 1964.

As black intellectuals gained prominence in the 1950s and 1960s—a cohort that included the folklorist Edison Carneiro, the sociologist Alberto Guerreiro Ramos, and the theater director and journalist Abdias do Nascimento—Freyre had little dialogue with them. He invited Carneiro to participate in the First Afro-Brazilian Congress, which he organized in Recife in 1934 on the heels of the publication of *Casa-grande & senzala*. But when Carneiro invited Freyre to the Second Afro-Brazilian Congress, which Carneiro organized in Salvador in 1937, not only did Freyre not participate, but he also criticized the event for being "improvised" and political: "I believe that the problems of the black and mulatto in Brazil must be discussed frankly ... pointing out the social and even political oppression of people of color that are still observed today ... But I do not believe that the Afro-Brazilian congresses should slide into political advocacy or demagoguery of people of color."[8] Carneiro, for his part, declared that Freyre "exploited blacks," and criticized him as an "owner of the subject."[9]

Freyre was among the writers whom Guerreiro Ramos decried in 1953 for treating black Brazilians as "ethnographic material" and neglecting "their present sociopolitical problematics."[10] In a 1982 interview, Guerreiro Ramos went further: "I consider him a joke. Gilberto Freyre is the greatest Brazilian fallacy. He is nothing: not a sociologist; technically, he is a literary writer ... He is technically incorrect, a man who does not know what research is, does not know what science is: he is a literary figure."[11] From 1948 to 1950, Nascimento edited the newspaper *Quilombo*, which had a regular column called "Racial Democracy" that featured a commentary by Freyre in its first issue, but this was perhaps the only moment of collaboration between the two men. Nascimento would emerge as one of the most prominent critics of Freyre and his worldview within Brazil's black movement. For Nascimento, "a special talent of Freyre has been his coinage of euphemisms in the attempt to paint Brazilian racial harmony in the rosiest hues possible." He called Freyre a "fertile creator of mirages."[12] Carneiro, Guerreiro Ramos, and Nascimento were persecuted by the military regime that took power in 1964—a regime that Freyre cheered and that celebrated Freyre and his ideas.

Historian, Anthropologist, Sociologist

Freyre thrived on ambiguity about the nature of his graduate studies at Columbia. One of the most common fallacies is that he held a doctorate rather than the master's he completed in 1922. This misconception, or misrepresentation, is even part of Freyre's biography by the Fundação Joaquim Nabuco, the federal research institute whose creation Freyre sponsored as a member of Congress in 1949 (which is located next to the restored plantation house where Freyre lived and was directed by his son, Fernando de Mello Freyre, for several decades). Its website describes Freyre's "master's and doctorate in social science, politics, and law at Columbia University."[13] A more common perception, which Freyre cultivated, was that Franz Boas had been his mentor. Freyre used this perception to foster a public persona that moved fluidly and often strategically between identities as a historian, anthropologist, and sociologist.

Freyre attended Columbia during the peak years of Boas's training of a pathbreaking generation of anthropologists. Manuel Gamio, a Mexican anthropologist who worked on Indigenous institutions in Mexico, completed his PhD in 1920. In 1923, Ruth Benedict completed her dissertation on Native American religion, and Melville Herskovits completed his on cattle-herding cultures in East Africa. Margaret Mead completed her MA in 1924 and published her dissertation research on gender and adolescence in Samoa in 1928. Hurston, who completed her BA at Barnard College in 1928 and conducted research under Boas's supervision, studied African American folklore. Boas's students focused on ethnography and on linguistic anthropology, particularly among Native American communities but also on African American communities or in the Pacific. Freyre's work bore little resemblance to that of the anthropologists whose graduate training Boas supervised. In unpacking the origins of Freyre's thought, Maria Lúcia Pallares-Burke has carefully rolled back the inferences about the intellectual or academic relationship between Boas and Freyre that have grown out of his introduction to *Casa-grande*. She finds two courses taught by Boas on Freyre's academic record at Columbia: Anthropology 101 and 102. These courses do not appear to have been immediately influential to Freyre. More significant was Freyre's coursework in history, where he took six of his graduate courses, all in US and European history.[14]

Freyre's major interlocutors were historians: he sustained relationships with classmates Rüdiger Bilden and Francis Butler Simkins that he referenced in his preface to *Casa-grande & senzala*. Freyre's advisor was also a historian, William Shepherd, an early US scholar of Latin American history. Freyre's master's thesis was also a work of history. A version was published in the *Hispanic American Historical Review,* which Shepherd had helped establish four years earlier, as "Social Life in Brazil in the Middle of the Nineteenth Century." Freyre's thesis included a detailed discussion of how benign he interpreted Brazilian slavery to have been:

> The work people [slaves] of the plantations were well-fed, and attended to by their master and mistress as a "large family of children." They had three meals a day and a little rum (*caxaca*) in the morning ... On holidays it was customary on certain estates to have an ox killed for the slaves and a quantity of rum was given to make them merry. Then they would dance the sensuous measures of the *batuque* or other African dances or sing or play the *marimba*.
>
> As a rule, the slaves were not overworked in the households either in the plantations or the city. It is true that much was being said in the [1850s], of cruel treatment of slaves in Brazil, by the British anti-slavery propaganda. Later on, the British dark account of conditions was to be repeated in Brazil by Brazilian anti-slavery orators such as the young [Joaquim] Nabuco and Sr. Ruy Barbosa—men inflamed by the bourgeois idealism of Wilberforce as well as by a very human desire for personal glory—and they did it in so emphatic a language that the average Brazilian believes today that slavery was really cruel in his country. The powerful fancy won over reality. For, as a matter of fact, slavery in Brazil was anything but cruel. The Brazilian slave lived the life of a cherub if we contrast his lot with that of the English and other European factory-worker in the middle of the last century.[15]

To assert the moral and material superiority of Brazilian slavery to European free labor, Freyre dismissed evidence of the cruelty of slavery as the product of foreign propaganda or the self-aggrandizement of abolitionists. Freyre's suggestion that Brazilian slaves were better off than were British industrial workers emerged from his coursework with the only one of his faculty cited in the article, Carlton Hayes.[16] Hayes's focus on social history and the study of culture, reflected in his *Political and Social History of Modern Europe*, seem to have been particularly influential to Freyre's approach as a writer—far more so, thematically, empirically, and in narrative form, than Boas's work. His thesis reflects the extent to which a perception of Brazilian slavery as comparatively benign transcended Freyre's work from the beginning.

The notion that Boas was Freyre's mentor or advisor is one that Freyre first cultivated with the publication of *Casa-grande & senzala* in 1933, when he introduced his analytical framework by declaring that "the scholarly figure of Professor Boas is the one that to this day makes the deepest impression upon me ... It was my studies in anthropology under the direction of Professor Boas that first revealed to me the Negro and the mulatto for what they are—with the effects of environment or cultural experience separated from racial characteristics." In the preface to the second English-language edition, he added another reference to Boas: "It was at Columbia, years ago, that I did my graduate work with a scholar who was one of the first to think my experimental work not entirely worthless: Franz Boas."[17] Freyre's invocation of Boas formed part of his identity as a social scientist. He frequently described himself as a sociologist, a stance he employed when he used historical evidence to make arguments about contemporary society.

Anti-racism in Brazil, with and without Freyre

Gilberto Freyre frequently laid claim to ideas already in circulation as part of a practice of self-promotion. In the English-language editions of *The Masters and the Slaves,* he likened himself to Picasso and Freud and he cited praise of his work by scholars at prestigious universities in the United States and Europe. He described his own work as pioneering and adventurous. His self-references were a savvy step by a writer who eschewed faculty appointments and held one term as a federal deputy. Instead, Freyre was a public intellectual succeeded in no small part by promoting himself.

It is in this context that we should understand his identification with Boas and as part of a process of laying claim to the pivot from nature to nurture that overcame scientific racism in interpretations of Brazilians of African descent. As he presented himself as Boas's disciple, he described himself: "I do not believe that any Russian student among the romantics of the nineteenth century was more intensely preoccupied with the destiny of Russia than I was of Brazil at that time that I knew Boas. It was as if everything depended upon me and those of my generation, upon the manner in which we succeeded in solving age-old questions."[18] In other words, Freyre was critically engaged in a fundamental national problem that had to be solved. Through this construction, Freyre presented himself as the person who solved a problem—overcoming the doctrine of scientific racism, and the belief that blacks were inferior to whites more generally—even though the problem did not need him in order to be solved.

In Brazil, both racist and anti-racist theses abounded in the decades before Freyre published *Casa-grande.* The prominent nationalist Alberto Torres stands out as an anti-racist. In 1914, Torres criticized scientific racism, as well as projects promoting the whitening of Brazil through European immigration. He declared, "It would simply be vain pretension of ethnic nobility to affirm that black or Indigenous Brazilians are inferior to whites."[19] Torres invoked Boas and challenged the idea that mulattos or cafusos who resulted from race mixture were degenerate.[20] In *Ordem e progresso,* Freyre himself noted that Torres was "possibly the first Brazilian publicist [public figure?] to learn about the research on the relationship between races and physical and social environments that were being conducted by Franz Boas."[21]

The popular writer José Bento Monteiro Lobato made the transition from nature to nurture through the transformation of his character Jeca Tatú. In a 1914 story, Lobato condemned him as racially degenerate but four years later "redeemed" him as someone who "wasn't born that way, he became so," in the same kind of redemption allegory of both the subject and, by extension, its author that Freyre would execute in *Casa-grande & senzala*.[22] Within the field of anthropology in Brazil, the major critic of scientific racism and advocate for cultural readings of human populations was Edgard Roquette-Pinto, the director of the Museu Nacional's national school of anthropology. In a series of essays and lectures begun in 1912 and collected in 1927 in the volume *Seixos rolados (estudos brasileiros)*, Roquette-Pinto differentiated the field of genetics from the discussion of race. One of the early adherents to Mendelian genetics in Brazil, Roquette-Pinto believed that the practice of eugenics could improve the heredity of populations through selective reproduction, but he vehemently rejected the idea that this had anything to do with race or with race mixture, declaring, "Everything that we have discovered in the anthropology laboratory of the Museu Nacional confirms . . . our mixed population, when healthy, presents no characteristics of physical or psychic degeneracy."[23]

Roquette-Pinto went so far as to suggest that race mixture was even desirable from the standpoint of eugenics because "outcrossing" diluted "undesirable" recessive genetic traits. He framed the nature versus nurture question in his critique of Euclides da Cunha's account, *Os sertões*, of the late nineteenth-century rural rebellion in Canudos, Bahia: "Euclides' grand illusion was thus: he considered *inferior*, people who were simply backward; *incapable*, men who were just ignorant." Roquette-Pinto suggested: "Let us not forget, for love of cloaked or manifest prejudice, that the national problem is not to make Brazilian mestizos into white people. Our problem is educating those who find themselves there, light or dark."[24] Vanderlei de Souza explains that "all of Roquette-Pinto's discussion of racial miscegenation in Brazil was . . . guided by that effort to demonstrate, by means of modern scientific research in the field of biology, that the results of racial mixing should not be seen as negative for the development of the nation."[25]

Ricardo Ventura Santos argues that when Roquette-Pinto visited Franz Boas in 1926, "he was already converted to the idea that the causes of Brazil's backwardness were fundamentally sociopolitical rather than racial." In other words, Roquette-Pinto's anti-racist perspective emerged from his own research in physical anthropology genetics rather than from exposure to Boas and his work. This was significant because, as Santos argues, "it is not necessary to propose a diffusionist argument to explain the development of a certain antiracist current in physical anthropology, favorable to miscegenation, in early twentieth-century Brazil."[26] This was the opposite of the perspective expressed by Freyre, who stressed Boas's intellectual influence on his perception of race and miscegenation.

Arthur Ramos, an anthropologist who trained in medicine and psychiatry, engaged in work that was contemporary to Freyre's but kept its focus on

African cultures in Brazil. Ramos was influenced by American cultural anthropologists such as Melville Herskovits and Ruth Landes.[27] Beginning with *O negro brasileiro* (1934), Ramos characterized race relations in Brazil as softened by miscegenation and cultural contact, and, like Freyre, he rejected the idea that people of African ancestry bore "anthropological inferiority," citing Boas, among others.[28] But unlike Freyre, Ramos recognized both racial prejudice and formation of Afro-Brazilian organizations to "assert equal rights economically, politically, and culturally."[29] Ramos nonetheless held that Brazilians of African descent were the bearers of primitive cultures, and, drawing on his background in psychiatry, he argued that black Brazilians often bore problems of "mental hygiene." These beliefs placed him within what he called the "'nature-nurture' debate" on the side of those who believed that the purported backwardness of black Brazilians was a condition, and one that could be remedied through interventions like education. He declared, "Man is a product of his civilization and his society."[30]

In 1920s and 1930s Brazil, many influential social scientists, intellectuals, and politicians thought that Brazilians of African descent, or people of mixed ancestry, were racially inferior. Many others did not see African ancestry or race mixture through the lens of white racial supremacy, but they generally believed that Brazilians of African descent harbored cultural, educational, and health deficiencies that placed them in a condition of inferiority relative to whites. Freyre staked out this position as he laid claim to the intellectual transition from thinking of people in terms of cultures rather than races. And other social scientists such as Lobato, Roquette-Pinto, and Ramos held this position. This was a debate with high stakes: it shaped immigration policies and investments in public education and health. But the debate also occurred within a conceptual framework that elevated people who were of European origin over those of African origin or of mixed ancestry.

The Key Passage

Casa-grande & senzala stresses the significance of cultural mixture between Portuguese, African, and Indigenous peoples in shaping Brazil, particularly in Freyre's focus on family and popular culture in intimate areas such as food preparation and language. The book places cultures in dialogue. Freyre both focuses on the details of that dialogue and finds virtue within it. The voice that dominates in that dialogue is Portuguese. The history of Portuguese Christians, and their cultural, religious, and intimate encounters with Iberian Muslim and Jewish peoples, makes them into the historical protagonists that can catalyze and synthesize Indigenous and African influences. This is also Freyre's voice, as well as his perception of his readers. He writes:

> Every Brazilian, even the light-skinned blond ones, carries in their soul, when not in soul and body . . . the shadow, or at least the look, of the black . . . We all carry the unmistakable mark of black influence. Of the slave woman or "mammy" who lulled us to sleep. Who nursed us. Who fed us, mashing our food with her hands . . . To the mulatta . . . who initiated us in love . . . To the black boy who was our first playmate.[31]

The "us" in this passage, and throughout the book, is commonly male and predominantly—though, as Freyre emphasizes, not solely—white and of Portuguese descent. That was Freyre's public. And this is the context in which *Casa-grande & senzala* fit well: the major literary work is a milestone in Brazilian intellectual history and in the innovative cultural production of national identity. It is also an illustration of what the book was not: a study of race relations. The book would, however, become an object of race relations: though Freyre did not use the term "racial democracy" in it, the book's assertion that relations between slaves and masters was largely—but not solely—benign became foundation of the idea that Brazil was a "racial democracy," a term that would become more closely connected to Freyre than to any other Brazilian intellectual.

This relationship between author, reader, and subject provides the framework for the book's key passage. In the preface to *Casa-grande & senzala*, Freyre discusses his impression of a group of Brazilian sailors disembarking in New York:

> I once saw, after more than three full years absent from Brazil, a band of Brazilian sailors—mulattos and cafusos—disembarking, I don't recall if from the *São Paulo* or from the *Minas*, through the soft Brooklyn snow. They gave me the impression of being caricatures of men. It reminded me of a phrase from the book of an English or American traveler that I had just read about Brazil: "the fearfully mongrel aspect of the population." Miscegenation resulted in that. I lacked then someone who could tell me, as in 1929 Roquette-Pinto told the Aryanists of the Brazilian Congress of Eugenics, that the individuals whom I judged to represent Brazil were not simply mulattos or cafusos, but sickly cafusos and mulattos.[32]

Ricardo Benzaquén de Araújo reflects, "It would be difficult to overstate the importance of that passage, especially because the entire book conveys the sense of having been written to *refute it*."[33] Freyre agreed. In the preface to the second English-language edition, he called his passage on the Brazilian sailors and of Boas the interpretive key to the book: "It is upon this criterion of the basic differentiation between race and culture that the entire plan of this essay rests."[34] What does it mean that the sailors were sickly? How were they caricatures of men? The only indication that Freyre gives us is that they were racially mixed—"mulattos and cafusos" and "mongrel." The passage is intended to signal the significance of environment over heredity, which is one reason why Roquette-Pinto and Boas are immediately invoked. As the passage reads, the condition "sickly" supplants the state of being racially mixed. What is not in contention in this construction is that Freyre found them worthy of disdain.

In subsequent English-language editions, the sailors come from the states of São Paulo or Minas Gerais and are crossing the Brooklyn Bridge, a likely error in translation: in the original Portuguese, they are naval sailors disembarking from a Brazilian battleship, either the *Minas* or the *São Paulo,* in the Brooklyn Navy Yard. Freyre's choices in describing these sailors were significant. Had Freyre chosen to, he could have easily guided his Brazilian readers in 1933 to the other significance that racially mixed sailors on these battleships could have held. And he refers to the ships only by their name, without describing them, suggesting that Freyre recognized and presumed his reader would be familiar with these two naval vessels.

It was on these very battleships that in 1910 the predominantly black crews revolted, killing white officers and shelling the capital city of Rio de Janeiro. The vessels were the pride of the Brazilian Navy, dreadnought-class ships purchased from British shipyards shortly before World War I. Soon after the ships were delivered, the crews revolted in order to end punishment through whipping, a practice that persisted illegally in the Navy in the decades after the abolition of slavery. When Freyre saw these sailors, no more than a dozen years after the revolt, what role did "the slavery that is practiced in the Brazilian navy" that sailors had protested play in his perception?[35] They were not the same sailors: after the government agreed to their demands and approved an amnesty for the rebels, it reversed itself and imprisoned or killed the participants.

Freyre described the sailors through his perceptions about their color rather than through the recent history of racialized protest by their precursors. As José Luiz Passos and Valéria Costa e Silva explain, he employed the anecdote as a means of dramatizing a personal moral and intellectual conversion:

> A recurrent strategy in *The Masters and the Slaves* is Freyre's resorting to a self-referential mode in order to legitimate data, themes, and perspectives. In the passage, the move encompassed by Freyre's narrative is to present the author as possibly resembling the reader's own position with regard to the eugenic view of miscegenation; to suggest the limitation of the author's former stance as a misapprehension of the phenomena; and, finally, to offer a method through which both author and reader can properly overcome their mistakes.[36]

When we place Freyre's analytical and self-referential mechanisms alongside the alternative meanings that the racial identities that sailors from the battleships held in their time, the juxtaposition illustrates the power of racial populism. The 1910 revolt was one of the most significant racial revolts in post-emancipation Latin America, and one of the major upheavals that beset Brazil's republican regime. Yet, in Freyre's narrative, the sailors did not appear as people with a history. Instead, Freyre made them into symbols—who "represent Brazil"—that served his interpretation of race, culture, and national identity. In *Casa-grande & senzala*, the sailors appear only as the markers on which Freyre dramatizes a pivot from unreconstructed racism to enlightened paternalism. Freyre did not engage Brazilians of African descent, be they enslaved or free, as historical actors who of made claims and shaped their history.

Within its context, we can also interpret praise from anti-racist scholars and criticism from Afro-Brazilian intellectuals. Roquette-Pinto thought the book was "superb" in its differentiation of race and culture, and that it "will take a fitting place on the shelf alongside the books of Alberto Torres." Freyre applied the principles that Roquette-Pinto and Torres had espoused in a historical synthesis of Brazilian culture that was relevant to contemporary society. Souza explains that the contemporary significance that Roquette-Pinto saw were the debates in National Congress about racial and ethnic restrictions to immigration.[37] In 1934, the year following the publication of *Casa-grande & senzala*, Freyre was intellectually and politically the closest to the black communities whose role in Brazilian culture and society he had interpreted. In 1934, he organized the First Afro-Brazilian Congress in Recife. Most of the participants were white Brazilians, including Roquette-Pinto and Ramos. Many of the papers presented were steeped in eugenic thought, but Carneiro presented a paper on black marginalization, the theme also developed by one of the other few black participants included in the volume of published papers, a representative of the Frente Negra of Pelotas, Rio Grande do Sul.

Soon after, Carneiro made sharp criticisms of *Casa-grande & senzala*. In a 1935 newspaper column, he praised Freyre and other anti-racist scholars including Roquette-Pinto and Ramos for their "fraternal sympathy for the great oppressed race." But for Carneiro, this sympathy was not enough to overcome the "paternalistic ways" of these authors, whom he sees as treating blacks as an object of study and placing themselves above them:

> It is especially in Gilberto Freyre that the exploitation of blacks is present in greatest force. In his great book . . . there is always a bit of sadism (of the sadism of the masters that he describes so well), of pleasure for the anonymous suffering of the race, and of poorly disguised nostalgia for slavery . . . Naturally these are hereditary attitudes that do not reach the author's consciousness. But despite that, they tinge the entire work.

For Carneiro, Freyre and the others simply used blacks as "raw material." He laments: "The naked and cruel truth is that all of these writers lack the ability to put themselves in a black person's skin . . . They all feel like whites, as individuals who are distant from the race . . . All that remains is the hope that in the future the black race itself will produce the great intellectual that interprets their aspirations, their self-determination, their freedom."[38]

The Public Writer

Freyre's writing in the 1930s fit a context of "nationalistic optimism," as Souza describes Roquette-Pinto's work.[39] This nationalism coincided—and dialogued—with the political nationalism of Brazil's Vargas Era (1930–1945) and with the modernist art and literary movements that emerged in the 1920s. The nationalist context that Freyre wrote in was shaped by two forces he criticized: intensifying industrialization and political centralization under an increasingly authoritarian state. Paulina Alberto explains:

> Though Freyre's work was in many ways a reaction against the changes taking place under Vargas' regime, the ideas of a mixed national identity that he helped to popularize dovetailed with the regime's ongoing project of promoting a national culture capable of overarching the country's class, racial, and regional divisions. In his first decade of rule, Vargas made the ideas that Freyre popularized into the ideological core of his regime's cultural policy.[40]

Freyre's presentation of cultural and racial mixture as virtues fed Brazil's "nationalistic optimism" and was well matched to its political and cultural moment. Yet even at that early moment, this idea was better fitted to the perceptions and needs of white readers than of black communities in Brazil, and Portuguese culture already occupied a preeminence in Freyre's first books that anticipated his future work. In later decades, Freyre became a more rigid political figure who was often antagonistic to black assertions of political rights or expressions of black culture in Brazil but increasingly supportive of Portugal's dictatorship and its colonial project in Africa. As Brazil changed and as Freyre became less nuanced and more political. But the Portuguese ethnic nationalism and racial populism that increasingly isolated Freyre from the worlds of Brazilian social science and of black intellectuals were already present in his 1930s work.

Scholars began to distance themselves from Freyre in the 1950s: "The Freyre who advocated for 'Lusotropicology' seemed to us a shameless opportunist, whose privileges were guaranteed by Salazar's Portugal . . . His attitudes toward the 1964 coup, as well as the years of dictatorship that followed, only increased the hiatus."[41] In the 1960s and 1970s, critical readings of Freyre emerged, notably those of Carlos Guilherme Mota, who interpreted Freyre's "seigneurial view of the world" as a "search for a lost time. A return to the roots," in the context of Brazil's industrialization.[42] Subsequent readings of

Freyre continued to historicize his books published in the 1930s, separately from his later political persona. Araújo explains that his work on *Casa-grande & senzala* emerged from an interest in situating Freyre's work in the context of Brazil's modernist artistic and literary movements that emerged in the 1920s— movements that emphasized the originality of Brazilian cultures and explored regional traditions.[43]

Following the publication of *Casa-grande & senzala* and *Sobrados e Mucambos* (1936), Freyre transitioned into a lasting role as a public figure. He served as a cultural ambassador to Europe and South America during the Vargas regime that he often criticized, lectured frequently in the United States, and served a term as a federal deputy as a member of the conservative National Democratic Union. These roles kept him in the spotlight. A mutual admiration between Freyre and the historian Frank Tannenbaum helped cement Freyre's international reputation as a leading anti-racist intellectual, which in turn bolstered his image in Brazil. While he continued to publish books, including *Ordem e progresso* (1959), which completed the trilogy of social and cultural history that he began with *Casa-grande & senzala*, Freyre's major outlets were his columns in the popular illustrated magazine *Cruzeiro* and in the *Diário de Pernambuco* newspaper that were nationally syndicated by its parent company, Diários Asociados. Freyre also developed a close relationship with the dictatorship of António de Oliveira Salazar in Portugal, through which he amplified his interpretation of Brazil to suggest that Portuguese colonialism in Africa was producing "future Brazils."

The low point in Freyre's scholarship emerged from this embrace of Portuguese colonialism and his association with Salazar's dictatorship. Out of that association, Portuguese colonial officials commissioned two books from Freyre as part of the propaganda effort related to their colonial wars: *The Portuguese and the Tropics: Suggestions Inspired by the Portuguese Methods of Integrating Autochthonous Peoples and Cultures Differing from the European in a New, or Luso-tropical Complex of Civilization* (1961) and *Portuguese Integration in the Tropics: Notes Concerning a Possible Lusotropicology Which Would Specialize in the Systematic Study of the Ecological-Social Process of the Integration in Tropical Environments of the Portuguese, Descendants of Portuguese and Continuators of Portuguese* (1961). These oblique texts, despite the abundant copies distributed globally by the Portuguese colonial ministry, have fallen outside scholarly attention to Freyre's writing. In *Portuguese Integration in the Tropics*, Freyre proposes:

> When I refer to a Portuguese, it is a social Portuguese or a cultural Portuguese that I mean; and who can be either yellow, dark, red, black or white . . . if one day the Lusotropicological systematics here suggested is constituted into a science, one of its main objects of study will be this process of the surpassing of the ethnic condi-

tion by the cultural, by virtue of which the blackest of blacks of tropical Africa is considered Portuguese without having to renounce some of his dearest habits of an ecologically tropical man."[44]

Beginning in the early 1940s, Freyre increasingly turned to his columns to criticize protests by black Brazilians against discrimination, as well as assertions of an independent black identity. In 1941, he argued that "associations for the 'defense of the rights' of 'men of color' did not correspond to the needs of the Brazilian environment" and claimed that "there rigorously does not exist in Brazil an 'African minority' of any kind."[45] After he traveled as a guest of the Portuguese government to its colonies, Freyre extended this criticism to include African peoples seeking to end white colonial rule. For Freyre, these were the same cause: they merged his defense of Portuguese ethnicity to his attack on political or cultural independence asserted by African peoples under Portuguese rule or of people of African descent in Brazil. Salazar's dictatorship also provided a context for expressing his increasingly authoritarian thinking about Brazil: Freyre would advocate for the installation of a dictatorship, particularly by the armed forces, and when one was imposed, he cheered. "What we Brazilians need is not only a coup, but a good coup," Freyre told reporters from *Manchete* magazine ("as he called attention to the beautiful colonial furnishings he possesses in his home," the reporter added). The dictatorship "should resemble Oliveira Salazar's in Portugal . . . Portugal lives splendidly today, in an economic-financial, social, and political situation that is quite superior to ours."[46]

As Freyre came to advocate for political dictatorship, he also began to speak about "racial democracy." His first public use of the term came in a 1962 speech organized by the Portuguese political lobby in Rio de Janeiro to support Portugal's armed defense of its colonies. The term was frequently attributed to him, though he did not use it his earlier work. Antonio Sérgio Guimarães traces its origin to how "Arthur Ramos, Roger Bastide, and others translated the ideas expressed by Freyre in lectures" of the late 1930s and early 1940s.[47] Until the early 1960s, Freyre spoke and wrote of "ethnic democracy" or "social democracy," and often qualified his references by describing it as almost a reality or saying that Brazil was the country that came closest to achieving it. This ambiguity was characteristic of his earlier work. In turn, when he began to use "racial democracy," it was in a more explicitly political context and reflected the conceptual and ideological inflexibility that he increasingly brought to his defense of Portuguese colonialism or his opposition to black politics, movements, and studies.

As the independence wars waged by nationalist groups in Portuguese colonies intensified, Freyre published a newspaper commentary in 1962 that represented this assertion about racial democracy. In "Against Afro-Racism," he argues that African political leaders who sought to "de-Europeanize Africa reveal themselves to be racists as repugnant to socially and racially democratic Brazilians as are the racists of Europe and the United States." Criticizing the foreign policy of Brazil that at the time supported decolonization, he asked, "What affinity with these Afro-racists, cruelly hostile to the most precious democratic value being developed by the Brazilian people—racial democracy—could come from Brazil?"[48]

By the mid-1960s, Freyre commonly described any assertion about the existence of discrimination in Brazil, or any kind of black mobilization, as a form of Communist agitation (an accusation that was particularly menacing after the armed forces took power in 1964). Such "agents of Russian-Soviet Communism," he argued, sought to "create in Brazil a figure that sociologically does not exist: that of the Brazilian black. A black who is substantively black and only adjectively Brazilian." He accused journalists who reported on cases of discrimination of being anti-Brazilian agents of Communism for "seeking to exaggerate what racial or color prejudice to be found in Brazil."[49] Freyre's criticism of journalists in this 1969 commentary was directed at the emerging discrimination reports around the 13 May commemoration of the abolition of slavery, which had become a platform that black Brazilians used to generate public awareness of the existence of discrimination.

In 1974, the tensions between Freyre's ideologies of race and colonialism and the peoples they applied to appeared in perhaps their sharpest relief. It was the tenth year of the dictatorship that Freyre had repeatedly called for and celebrated. The military regime had purged scholars such as Florestan Fernandes and others at the University of São Paulo whose work challenged Freyre's worldview. The regime had even purged the category of race from the 1970 census and wrapped itself in the imagination that Brazil was a paradise of racial democracy, even though it had no political democracy. But this was also the year in which the Carnation Revolution overthrew Portugal's colonialist regime with which Freyre had identified so closely. On 25 April, war-weary military officers deposed the government and pursued swift decolonization. The leaders of the nationalist movements in Portugal's colonies were contemptuous of Freyre's vision. When the Brazilian activist José Maria Pereira traveled to Guinea-Bissau that year, a member of the African Party for the Independence of Guiné and Cabo Verde told him, "Freyre's idea of Lusotropicalism killed more people than the G3 [assault rifle used by the Portuguese Army]."[50] The critique of Freyre's ideas by people subjected to Portuguese colonialism in Africa was not new. Mário de Andrade, the founder of the Popular Movement for the Liberation of Angola, had written in 1955 that Freyre's theory of Lusotropicalism was simply "a method of colonization" and criticized Freyre's "religious belief in the exclusive Portuguese hereditary aptitude to live under the tropical sun and arrange for himself a woman of color . . . Influenced by this belief, we understand that the essential nature of the colonial situation escapes him."[51]

By 1974, the social, political, and cultural landscape in Brazil had also begun to shift away from Freyre's paradigms about racial mixture, as growing numbers of young Brazilians began embracing black identities with diverse national and global connections. These ranged from a reaffirmation of African cultural roots reflected in the musical and aesthetic choices of Ilê Aiyê, the fist Afro-centric carnival bloc in Salvador, founded in 1974. That same year, black activists in Rio de Janeiro founded the Society for Brazil-Africa Exchange, which drew inspiration from African liberation movements to explore challenges to racial discrimination in Brazil.[52] Amid these changes, Freyre took to his newspaper column to make caustic criticism of the Brazilian performance at the 1974 FIFA World Cup opening ceremony in West Germany:

> Brazilians who watched . . . [the ceremony] were shocked to see depicted as Brazilian folklore some *mungangas* in which they saw neither folklore nor Brazil . . .
>
> First, from the conch from which the supposed representatives of Brazilian folklore emerged, there appeared only super black Brazilians [*pretíssimos*], some perhaps painted black, as though this were the protest or advocacy of . . . the worst of negritude, that is, very dark politics. Africa only for black Africans, the politics of blacks against whites, the rejection of that magnificently Brazilian thing that is miscegenation, mixture, the crossing of bloods . . . beyond race, pure race overcome by brownness. The meta-race . . .
>
> Thus, the anti-Brazilianism of that group of good very dark blacks [*bons pretos retintos*]—a group that was exclusively Afro-black—with which it was intended to represent the folklore of our people at the inauguration of the '74 Cup. It just looks like it was the strategy of agents of "negritude" more exclusively or more fanatically negrophile . . .
>
> But this—which is grave—disfigures the ethnic-cultural situation of Brazil that is not that of a country in which a monolithic block of blacks who are Brazilian—instead of Brazilians who are black—appear in opposition to countrymen of other ethnic origins, and pretending to be the only authentic Brazil.[53]

Nascimento criticized Freyre's concept of a "meta-race" as a "café-au-lait universalism" used to condemn negritude and to pursue "the definitive disappearance of the African descendant, physically and spiritually" from Brazil.[54]

Thanks to YouTube, it is possible to see the Brazilian performance in the opening ceremony that so perturbed Freyre.[55] One by one, dancers representing different countries emerged from giant soccer balls on the field and performed folkloric dances. The various nations' performances were mostly popular expressions of cultural and ethnic stereotypes: dancing Aztec warriors representing Mexico, and milkmaids wearing bonnets and yokes representing the Netherlands. Several incorporated racialized and sexualized representations of women. The Brazilian dance was performed by a group called Brasil

Tropical, headed by a choreographer and a well-known capoeira mestre from Bahia (both of whom were white), which had been touring in recent years through Europe performing variety shows that introduced capoeira to many audiences.[56] The Brazilian performance was a carnivalesque mixture of samba and capoeira. None of the performers appeared to be painted black.

Freyre interpreted the performance as part of an "anti-Brazilian" agenda to express a distinct black identity, something that he repeatedly characterized as a threat in his newspaper columns. The language that Freyre employed in his criticism stands out. He refers to the performers as *mungangas,* a term he first used in *Casa-grande & senzala,* listing it as one of the words "we have adopted from the Negro dialects that have no history and no literature words that we have permitted to come up, along with the slave lads and Negro women, from the slave huts to the Big Houses."[57] In the Brazilian Northeast, the term came to be used to signify clownery, but its origin was the Central African Kimbundo language and was used in Afro-Brazilian religious rituals to refer to states of trance.[58] For Freyre, assertions of blackness or of Africanness in Brazil were only appropriate when they took place within the framework that he conceived, which subordinated them to a Portuguese colonial and cultural project. To do otherwise was to be illegitimate, "fanatically negrophile" representatives of Brazil who brought shame to the nation.

Conclusion

The idea of racial democracy in Brazil has meant many things, including its role as a concept that black activists of the 1940s and 1950s used as an opening to seek a more inclusive society. The "Racial Democracy" column in *Quilombo,* edited by Abdias do Nascimento, is one illustration of this. But the concept also lent itself to populism and demagoguery—roles that Gilberto Freyre readily embraced. These roles became a common thread between his early scholarship and his role in later years as an advocate of colonialism abroad, dictatorship at home, and the silencing of black protests or the expression of black identity.

From the very outset, Freyre's writing reflected his tendency to lay claim to concepts that were already in circulation in order to define himself as a public intellectual at the center of an effort to define Brazilian national identity. As the means of attaining that role, Freyre essentialized the experiences of Brazilians of African descent who mostly lacked the standing to build counter-narratives or to challenge his representations of race and nation. Freyre's increasingly strident defense of Portuguese colonialism and caustic attacks on black consciousness and political mobilization in Brazil were the culmination of his efforts at self-promotion, representing himself as the populist "defender of popular sovereignty against foreign pressures and exploitation," and the ethnic nationalist who defended above all the Portuguese way of being in the world.

JERRY DÁVILA is Jorge Paulo Lemann Chair in Brazilian History at the University of Illinois. He studies the influence of racial thought on public policy. He is the author of *Dictatorship in South America* (Wiley, 2013), *Hotel Trópico: Brazil and the Challenge of African Decolonization* (Duke University Press, 2010), and *Diploma of Whiteness: Race and Social Policy in Brazil* (Duke University Press, 2003). Most recently, he is a coeditor of *Brazil's Economy* (Routledge, 2018) and a coauthor of the eleventh edition of *A History of World Societies* (Bedford / St. Martins, 2018).

Notes

All translations in this chapter are my own unless otherwise indicated.
1. Michael Conniff, ed., *Populism in Latin America*, 2nd ed. (Tuscaloosa, AL, 2012), 5–6.
2. Gilberto Freyre, *Conferencias na Europa* (Rio de Janeiro, 1938), 7, 10, 14.
3. Instituto Brasileiro de Geografia e Estatística (IBGE), *Recenseamento Geral de 1940: Censo Demográfico, População e Habitação* (Rio de Janeiro, 1950), 28; IBGE, *Recenseamento Geral de 1940: Censo Demográfico, Série Regional, Parte IX—Pernanbuco* (Rio de Janeiro, 1950), 16.
4. Fernando Henrique Cardoso, "Prefácio: Um livro perene," in Gilberto Freyre, *Casa-grande & senzala: Formação da família brasileira sob o regímen de economia* (São Paulo, 2003), 22.
5. US Bureau of the Census, *Historical Statistics of the United States, Colonial Times to 1857* (Washington, DC, 1960), 214.
6. Vernon J. Williams, *Rethinking Race: Franz Boas and His Contemporaries* (Lexington, KY, 1996), 32.
7. Aline Helg, *Our Rightful Share: The Afro-Cuban Struggle for Equality, 1886–1912* (Chapel Hill, NC, 1995), 244; Kaizô Iwakami Beltrão and Maria Salet Novellino, *Alfabetização por raça e sexo no Brasil: Evolução no período 1940–2000* (Rio de Janeiro, 2002), 17.
8. "Em torno do II Congresso Afro-Brasileiro," *O Estado da Bahia,* 13 November 1936, in *Cartas de Édison Carneiro a Artur Ramos*, ed. Waldir Freitas de Oliveira and Vivaldo Costa Lima (São Paulo, 1987), 129; Gustavo Rossi, *O intelectual feiticeiro: Edison Carneiro e o campo de estudos das relações raciais no Brasil* (Campinas, 2015), 213.
9. Rossi, *O intelectual feiticeiro,* 213; Edison Carneiro and Adyano do Couto Ferraz, "Congresso Afro-Brasileiro da Bahia," in *O negro no Brasil: Trabalhos apresentados o 2° Congresso Afro-Brasileiro (Bahia)* (Rio de Janeiro, 1940), 8.
10. Marcos Chor Maio, "Cor, intelectuais e nação na sociologia de Guerreiro Ramos," *Cadernos EBAPE.BR* 13 (2015): 614; Paulina Alberto, *Terms of Inclusion: Black Intellectuals in Twentieth Century Brazil* (Chapel Hill, NC, 2011), 191.
11. Lucia Lippi Oliveira, *A sociolgia do guerreiro* (Rio de Janeiro, 1995), 158.
12. Abdias do Nascimento, *Brazil: Mixture or Massacre? Essays in the Genocide of a Black People* (Dover, MA, 1979), 71.

13. Lúcia Gaspar, "Gilberto Freyre," Fundação Joaquim Nabuco, last updated 28 August 2009, http://basilio.fundaj.gov.br/pesquisaescolar/index.php?option=com_content&id=272.
14. Maria Lúcia Garcia Pallares-Burke, *Gilberto Freyre: Um vitoriano nos trópicos* (São Paulo, 2012) 73n52; Columbia University Catalogue, 1919-1920, 82, 142-44. https://babel.hathitrust.org/cgi/pt?id=nnc2.ark:/13960/t6sx70f3t;view=1up;seq=1.
15. Gilberto Freyre, "Social Life in Brazil in the Middle of the Nineteenth Century," *Hispanic American Historical Review* 5, no. 4 (1922): 607-8.
16. Ibid., 609.
17. Gilberto Freyre, *The Masters and the Slaves: A Study in the Development of Brazilian Civilization*, 2nd ed., trans. Samuel Putnam (New York, 1956), xxv-xxvi, xix.
18. Ibid., xxvi.
19. Alberto Torres, *A organização nacional* (Rio de Janeiro, 1914), 84.
20. Alberto Torres, *O problema nacional brasileiro* (Rio de Janeiro, 1914), 48, 52-55.
21. Gilberto Freyre, *Ordem e progresso*, 6th ed. (São Paulo, 2004), 188.
22. Thomas Skidmore, *Black into White: Race and Nationality in Brazilian Thought* (Durham, NC, 1993), 185.
23. Edgard Roquette-Pinto, *Seixos rolados (estudos brasileiros)* (Rio de Janeiro, 1927), 201-2.
24. Ibid., 61-62, 294.
25. Vanderlei Sebastião de Souza, *Em busca do Brasil: Edgard Roquette-Pinto e o retrato antropológico brasileiro (1905-1935)* (Rio de Janeiro, 2017), 261.
26. Ricardo Ventura Santos, "Guardian Angel on a Nations Path: Contexts and Trajectories of Physical Anthropology in Brazil in the Late Nineteenth and Early Twentieth Centuries," *Current Anthropology* 53, no. S5 (2012): S30.
27. Arthur Ramos, *Introdução à antropologia brasileira, 1° volume: As culturas não européias* (Rio de Janeiro, 1943), 16.
28. Arthur Ramos, *O negro brasileiro* (Rio de Janeiro, 1934), 21.
29. Arthur Ramos, *A aculturação negra no Brasil* (São Paulo, 1942), 143.
30. Arthur Ramos, *A creança problema: A higiene mental na escola primária* (São Paulo, 1939), 3, 10.
31. Freyre, *Casa-grande & senzala*, 303.
32. Ibid., xii.
33. Ricardo Benzaquen de Araújo, *Guerra e paz*: Casa grande & senzala *e a obra de Gilberto Freyre nos anos 30.*, 2nd ed. (São Paulo, 2005), 25.
34. Freyre, *The Masters and the Slaves*, xxvii.
35. Zachary Morgan, *Legacy of the Lash: Race and Punishment in the Brazilian Navy and the Atlantic World* (Bloomington, IN, 2014), 3. See also Morel, Edmar, *A revolta da chibata* (Rio de Janeiro, 2016); Joseph L. Love, *The Revolt of the Whip* (Stanford, CA, 2012).
36. José Luiz Passos and Valéria Costa e Silva, "Gilberto Freyre's Concept of Culture in *The Masters and the Slaves*," in *Brazil in the Making: Facets of National Identity*, ed. Carmen Nava and Ludwig Lauerhass (Lanham, MD, 2006), 49.
37. Souza, *Em busca do Brasil*, 345.
38. Edison Carneiro, "Exploração do Negro," *Correio da Manhã*, 14 November 1935, 3.
39. Souza, *Em busca do Brasil*, 257.
40. Alberto, *Terms of Inclusion*, 114
41. Luiz Costa Lima, "Apresentação," in Araújo, *Guerra e paz*, 10.
42. Carlos Guilherme Mota, *Ideologia de cultura brasileira* (São Paulo, 1977), 54, 58.
43. Araújo, *Guerra e paz*, 17.
44. Gilberto Freyre, *Portuguese Integration in the Tropics* (Lisbon, 1961), 47.

45. Gilberto Freyre, "'Minorias Africanas' no Brasil?" *Correio da Manhã,* 22 April 1941, Artigos de Jornal de Gilberto Freyre, AJ-2 1941–1944, Fundação Gilberto Freyre (FGF).
46. "Gilberto Freire prega a ditadura," *Manchete,* 5 May 1955, WC 1952–1955, FGF.
47. Antonio Sérgio Guimarães, "Racial Democracy," in *Imagining Brazil,* ed. Jessé Souza and Valter Sinder (Lanham, MD, 2007), 133.
48. Gilberto Freyre, "Contra o afro-racismo," *O Cruzeiro,* 22 September 1962, Artigos de Jornal de Gilberto Freyre, AJ-11 1962 (O Cruzeiro), FGF.
49. Gilberto Freyre, "Africanistas'? Excesso de glorificação da negritude," *O Cruzeiro,* December 1963, Artigos de Jornal de Gilberto Freyre, AJ-11, FGF; Gilberto Freyre, "A propósito de preconceito de raça no Brasil," 18 May 1969, Artigos de Jornal de Gilberto Freyre, AJ-17 1969–1971 (O Cruzeiro), FGF.
50. Interview with José Maria Pereira, 23 June 2009.
51. Mário de Andrade, "O mito lusotropical," *Istoé,* 19 March 1980, 46–47.
52. Alberto, *Terms of Inclusion,* 260–71.
53. Gilberto Freyre, "Uma mistificação," Diários Associados, 23 June 1974, Artigos de Jornal de Gilberto Freyre, AJ-18, 1972–1974, FGF.
54. Nascimento, *Brazil: Mixture or Massacre?* 71–72.
55. "1974—Trecho da cerimônia de abertura da Copa do Mundo de 1974—TV Globo," video, 5:34, posted by MZL tresCY, 14 February 2013, originally broadcast on TV Globo, 13 June 1974, https://www.youtube.com/watch?v=8v4-t0XgtAQ.
56. Matthias Röhrig Assunção, *Capoeira: The History of an Afro-Brazilian Martial Art* (New York, 2005), 186.
57. Freyre, *The Masters and the Slaves,* 346.
58. Luís da Câmara Cascudo, *Dicionário do folclore brasileiro,* 3rd ed. (Brasília, 1972), 513.

Bibliography

Alberto, Paulina. *Terms of Inclusion: Black Intellectuals in Twentieth Century Brazil.* Chapel Hill: University of North Carolina Press, 2011.
Araújo, Ricardo Benzaquen de. *Guerra e paz:* Casa-grande & senzala *e a obra de Gilberto Freyre nos anos 30.* 2nd ed. São Paulo: Editora 34, 2005.
Assunção, Matthias Röhrig. *Capoeira: The History of an Afro-Brazilian Martial Art.* New York: Routledge, 2005.
Beltrão, Kaizô Iwakami, and Maria Salet Novellino. *Alfabetização por raça e sexo no Brasil: Evolução no período 1940–2000.* Rio de Janeiro: Escola Nacional de Ciências Estatísticas, 2002.
Câmara Cascudo, Luís da. *Dicionário do folclore brasileiro.* 3rd ed. Brasília: Instituto Nacional do Livro, 1972.
Cardoso, Fernando Henrique. "Prefácio: Um livro perene." In Freyre, *Casa-grande & senzala,* 19–28.
Carneiro, Edison, and Adyano do Couto Ferraz. "Congresso Afro-Brasileiro da Bahia." In *O negro no Brasil: Trabalhos apresentados o 2° Congresso Afro-Brasileiro (Bahia).* Rio de Janeiro: Civilização Brasileira, 1940, 5–11.
Conniff, Michael, ed. *Populism in Latin America.* 2nd ed. Tuscaloosa: University of Alabama Press, 2012.
Costa Lima, Luiz. "Apresentação." In Benzaquén de Araújo, *Guerra e paz,* 9–13.
Freyre, Gilberto. *Casa-grande & senzala: Formação da família brasileira sob o regímen de economia.* São Paulo: Global Editora, 2003. First published 1993 by Maia & Schmidt (Rio de Janeiro).

———. *Conferencias na Europa*. Rio de Janeiro: Serviço Gráfico do Ministério da Educação e Saúde, 1938.

———. *Ordem e progresso*. 6th ed. São Paulo: Global Editora, 2004. First published 1959 by José Olympio (Rio de Janeiro).

———. *Portuguese Integration in the Tropics: Notes Concerning a Possible Lusotropicology which would Specialize in the Systematic Study of the Ecological-Social Process of the Integration in Tropical Environments of the Portuguese, Descendants of Portuguese and Continuators of Portuguese*. Lisbon: Tipografia Silvas, 1961.

———. "Social Life in Brazil in the Middle of the Nineteenth Century." *Hispanic American Historical Review* 5, no. 4 (1922): 597–630.

———. *The Masters and the Slaves: A Study in the Development of Brazilian Civilization*. 2nd ed. Translated by Samuel Putnam. New York: Knopf, 1956.

———. *The Portuguese and the Tropics: Suggestions Inspired by the Portuguese Methods of Integrating Autochthonous Peoples and Cultures Differing from the European in a New, or Luso-Tropical, Complex of Civilization*. Translated by Helen M. D'O. Matthew and Fernando de Mello Moser. Lisbon: Executive Committee for the Commemoration of the 5th Centenary of the Death of Prince Henry the Navigator, 1961.

Guimarães, Antonio Sérgio. "Racial Democracy." In *Imagining Brazil*, edited by Jessé Souza and Valter Sinder. Lanham, MD: Lexington Books, 2007, 119–140.

Helg, Aline. *Our Rightful Share: The Afro-Cuban Struggle for Equality, 1886–1912*. Chapel Hill: University of North Carolina Press, 1995.

Instituto Brasileiro de Geografia e Estatística (IBGE). *Recenseamento Geral de 1940: Censo Demográfico, População e Habitação*. Rio de Janeiro: Serviço Gráfico do IBGE, 1950.

———. *Recenseamento Geral de 1940: Censo Demográfico, Série Regional, Parte IX—Pernanbuco*. Rio de Janeiro: Serviço Gráfico do IBGE, 1950.

Love, Joseph L. *The Revolt of the Whip*. Stanford, CA: Stanford University Press, 2012.

Maio, Marcos Chor. "Cor, intelectuais e nação na sociologia de Guerreiro Ramos." *Cadernos EBAPE.BR* 13 (2015): 605–30.

Morel, Edmar. *A revolta da chibata*. Rio de Janeiro: Paz e Terra, 2016.

Morgan, Zachary. *Legacy of the Lash: Race and Punishment in the Brazilian Navy and the Atlantic World*. Bloomington: Indiana University Press, 2014.

Mota, Carlos Guilherme. *Ideologia da cultura brasileira*. São Paulo: Attica, 1977.

Nascimento, Abdias do. *Brazil: Mixture or Massacre? Essays in the Genocide of a Black People*. Dover, MA: Majority Press, 1979.

Oliveira, Lucia Lippi. *A sociolgia do guerreiro*. Rio de Janeiro: Universidade Federal do Rio de Janeiro, 1995.

Passos, José Luiz, and Valéria Costa e Silva. "Gilberto Freyre's Concept of Culture in *The Masters and the Slaves*." In *Brazil in the Making: Facets of National Identity*, edited by Carmen Nava and Ludwig Lauerhass. Lanham, MD: Rowman & Littlefield, 2006, 45–70.

Ramos, Arthur. *A aculturação negra no Brasil*. São Paulo: Companhia Editora Nacional, 1942.

———. *A creança problema: A higiene mental na escola primária*. São Paulo: Companhia Editora Nacional, 1939.

———. *Introdução à antropologia brasileira, 1° volume: As culturas não européias*. Rio de Janeiro: Casa do Estudante do Brasil, 1943.

———. *O negro brasileiro: Ethnographia religiosa e psychanalyse*. Rio de Janeiro: Civilização Brasileira, 1934.

———. *Seixos rolados (estudos brasileiros)*. Rio de Janeiro: Machado & Machado, 1927.

Rossi, Gustavo. *O intelectual feiticeiro: Edison Carneiro e o campo de estudos das relações raciais no Brasil.* Campinas: Editora Unicamp, 2015.

Santos, Ricardo Ventura. "Guardian Angel on a Nations Path: Contexts and Trajectories of Physical Anthropology in Brazil in the Late Nineteenth and Early Twentieth Centuries." *Current Anthropology* 53, no. S5 (2012): S17–S32.

Skidmore, Thomas. *Black into White: Race and Nationality in Brazilian Thought.* Durham, NC: Duke University Press, 1993. First published 1974 by Oxford University Press (New York).

Souza, Vanderlei Sebastião de. *Em busca do Brasil: Edgard Roquette-Pinto e o retrato antropológico brasileiro (1905–1935).* Rio de Janeiro: Editora Friocruz, 2017.

Torres, Alberto. *A organização nacional.* Rio de Janeiro: Imprensa Nacional, 1914.

———. *O problema nacional brasileiro.* Rio de Janeiro: Imprensa Nacional, 1914.

US Bureau of the Census. *Historical Statistics of the United States, Colonial Times to 1957.* Washington, DC: US Department of Commerce, 1960.

Williams, Vernon J. *Rethinking Race: Franz Boas and His Contemporaries.* Lexington: University Press of Kentucky, 1996.

CHAPTER 3

Anthropology and Pan-Africanism at the Margins of the Portuguese Empire
Trajectories of Kamba Simango

Lorenzo Macagno

Kamba Simango[1] was born in 1890 in Machanga District, on the coast of present-day Mozambique. He was sent to the United States to study at the Hampton Institute in 1914 under the auspices of missionaries of the American Board of Commissioners for Foreign Missions[2] (hereafter, "American Board"). At the Hampton Institute, African Americans and young people from Africa came to learn science, literature, and manual skills. During his studies, he encountered the musicologist and folklorist Natalie Curtis. In 1919, the missionaries sent Simango to study at Teachers College, Columbia University, where he met Franz Boas and the pair immediately struck up a rapport. The "father" of modern North American anthropology encouraged Simango to become a native ethnographer (not merely an "informant"), armed with anthropological tools. Boas suggested that Simango write about his people, the Vandau or Mandau, independently of his commitments to the missionaries of the American Board. The two men began a correspondence that would continue for many years. Simango and Boas also had a friend in common: W. E. B. Du Bois, the Pan-Africanist leader and editor of *The Crisis* magazine.[3]

Portugal and its African colonies underwent intense changes in the early 1920s, with the *Estado Novo* (New State) emerging from 1926 to 1928. There followed a resurgence of economic and cultural nationalism promoted by the influence of Salazarism (1928–1968), which brought the colonial question to the fore. A new imperial grammar emerged in the Lusophone world, heralded by Gilberto Freyre's 1933 *Casa-grande & senzala*. In the mid-twentieth century, Portugal still envisaged a "Portuguese future" for its overseas provinces, including Mozambique. My aim here is to inquire, based on the life trajectory of Simango, into the paradoxes of Portuguese assimilationism. Although Simango was a subject of Portugal, his experience in the United States drew him further from the "Portuguese world" and closer to the English-speaking African diaspora.

Contemporary with these developments was the emergence in the 1920s of an ethnographic sensibility that would be decisive for the future of anthropology. At the same time, after the period of "effective occupation" in Africa, a new African elite took shape, influenced by a growing Pan-Africanist cosmopolitanism. Simango's exposure to both anthropologists and West African intellectuals—facilitated by the educational opportunities provided by a North American missionary organization with a tense relationship with colonial authorities—produced a particularist ethnic pride and Pan-Africanist sensibility. This chapter looks beyond the "biographical illusion" of Kamba Simango's life to the polysemy of experience at the juncture of these national, colonial, and intellectual arcs.

Kamba Simango and Franz Boas

Boas's work transitions through physical anthropology, linguistic anthropology, and into what would later be called cultural anthropology, punctuated by his ethnographic studies of the Eskimos, the Kwakiutl, and Tsimshian mythologies—future raw material for some of Claude Lévi-Strauss's works—and of the potlatch, the ritual that Marcel Mauss would later describe as a "total services of an agonistic type".[4]

Despite the vast literature on Boas, his ethnographic writings about Mozambique are little known, and his incipient Africanist sensibility remains obscure. Boas wrote five articles, one of which Simango coauthored, about the central region of present-day Mozambique, populated by the Ndau (pl. Mandau or Vandau) whose language is a variant of Shona (a language also spoken in present-day Zimbabwe). I argue that these publications reveal a "minimal history" of anthropology. Such histories must be understood simultaneously as political histories and diachronic ethnographies. Current ethnographical dilemmas shape our historical preoccupations, so Simango has rarely featured either in official colonial or postcolonial historiographies. Colonial historiography has struggled to categorize Simango. Because Simango was educated by North American Protestants, his place in the legal-colonial category of *assimilado* is precarious. Postcolonial historiography has also found Simango difficult to place. Was he a Ndau nationalist, a defender of the "tribalist" primordialisms of his people? Faced with this risk, the nationalists tried to posthumously erase these ethnicist traces to create a character after their independentist concerns: Kamba Simango as a "proto-nationalist," or precursor of Mozambican nationalism.

A pioneering article by the Angolan nationalist Mário Pinto de Andrade sees Simango's trajectory as "proto-nationalism" but does not look to his relationship with Boas to understand it.[5] John Keith Rennie also studies Simango in his 1973 dissertation, "Christianity, Colonialism, and the Origins of Nationalism among the Ndau of Southern Rhodesia, 1890–1935." At the time, it was no small detail that Rennie had analyzed the historical-political dynamics of a Ndau ethnic nationalism, a possibility that was certainly inconvenient to the nationalists tout court on both sides—Southern Rhodesia (Zimbabwe) and Mozambique. In fact, for the respective independentist leaders, the ethnicist attempt—"tribalist," they would say—should have been neutralized and domesticated in the name of national unity and the struggles against colonialism. These concerns may account for why Rennie's dissertation was never published. From 1975 on, especially in the former Portuguese colonies, it was not politically feasible to construct objects of analysis concerning "ethnic nationalism" or similar phenomena.[6]

This chapter studies Boas and Simango's relationship by analyzing an exchange of unpublished letters between them. I discovered these letters during my postdoctoral research in the Department of Anthropology at Columbia University, in which I conducted a documentary survey and visited the places where Simango lived during his time in New York.[7] The series includes twenty-eight letters written from 1917 to 1927.[8] Eleven were written directly between Boas and Simango, and the others—between Boas and Curtis, and Boas and the banker and philanthropist George Foster Peabody—also relate to the collaboration.

From Mozambique to New York

Simango's trajectory follows that of many other young Africans educated in the Protestant missions established on the African continent in the nineteenth and twentieth centuries. In 1905, Simango moved to Beira and began to attend the school of the American Board missionary Fred Bunker. The surrounding territories, Manica and Sofala, were then under the administration of the private Companhia de Moçambique (Mozambique Company) to which the Portuguese government had granted privileges for the exploitation of minerals, agriculture, and livestock. The missionary school was soon prohibited from continuing its activities due to conflicts with local authorities, and the students, including Simango, were relocated to another mission school in Mount Selinda, Southern Rhodesia, close to the Mozambique border.

In 1913, at the age of twenty-three, Simango was sent to study at the institutions that the American Board maintained in South Africa. He spent one year at Lovedale and a period at Adams College, in Natal. He received the missionaries' further support to study in Virginia. At the Hampton Institute, African Americans and African students learned "arts and trades" alongside theoretical subjects; Simango trained in carpentry. There, Simango met Natalie Curtis, who was familiar with Boas's work. Curtis sparked Simango's initial interest in ethnography, and he later helped her conceive of a project to record and transcribe Ndau music.[9] During this project, Curtis wrote to Boas to dispel doubts or clarify questions but did not mention Simango. On the eve of the publication of *Negro Folk-Songs*, she wrote to Boas of the challenges she had encountered while preparing it and referred to him as "an authority on African issues."[10] At this time, another character appears in the letters: George Foster Peabody. Born in Georgia, his life was paradigmatic for a banker-philanthropist of the era. He financially supported schools and universities from which many African Americans and Africans graduated, including the Hampton Institute.[11] He also served on the boards of numerous schools and philanthropic organizations.

Leaving the Hampton Institute in 1919, Simango began study at Teachers College, Columbia University under the supervision of Mabel Carney, an expert in rural education.[12] Curiously, during the four years when Simango remained under Carney's supervision, there was very little dialogue between her and Boas. Curtis finally presented Simango to Boas in a letter sent in November 1919. She mentioned Simango's deep interest in Boas's *The Mind of Primitive Man* (1911).[13] She spared no praise:

> My dear Dr. Boas,
> May I introduce to you Kamba Simango, from Portuguese East Africa, a full-blood [sic] native of the Vandau tribe, who speaks zulu as well as his own tongue and came to this country direct from Africa. He was sent by missionaries to take the industrial and Academic training at Hampton Institute, where he promoted last year. Simango is now studying at Columbia and is most anxious to met you because of his great interest in your book "The Mind of Primitive Man." If you have time to see Simango I should be most glad. He is extremely inteligent and has a fine, well-praised and capital mind. He was my principal informant in my study of the native African songs and songs-poems and is well versed in the love of his people as he comes original from a pagan kraal and is nephew of a diviner (or "witch doctor" as they are called by the whites).[14]

This would not be the first time that Curtis insisted on Simango's supposed cultural "purity." The musicologist had shown the same kind of primordialism when conducting musical surveys among North American Indians, and it would clash, in time, with Boas's anthropological arguments. Her concerns should be read in context: as specific derivations of broader concerns about the expansion of the frontier and increasing violence against Indian nations.

Simango and Boas met after Curtis's introduction and began collaborating in March and April 1920, concentrating primarily on the study of the grammar of the Ndau language. On 5 May 1920, Boas wrote to Peabody to secure funding for a project on Ndau culture. Simango had already canvased the details of this project with Peabody in person. Boas's plan consisted, literally, of "being able to capture and systematize everything that Simango knew [about Africa] and then to write it up and ultimately send it back in the form of a more refined anthropological analysis."[15] This would enable Simango to return to Africa with a core of anthropological material and a program—to illuminate whatever was left unclear. Boas praised Simango to Peabody, describing him as "very intelligent" and "deeply interested." He hoped to retain Simango for one academic year at Columbia in order to consolidate their ethnographic dialogue. The details of the project were addressed at Boas's house between Boas, Peabody, and Simango.

Peabody's response was immediate, and positive: all that was needed was a start date, and budgetary details for supporting Simango in New York.[16] Boas replied directly, presenting material details and displaying Boas's aptitude for negotiation—persuading Peabody of the need to supplement Simango's funds to meet the cost of living in New York.[17] Boas and Simango began their formal anthropological collaboration on 20 September 1920.[18] It would produce five academic articles but also profound consequences for the development of North American anthropology and African studies in the United States.

In early 1923, when Melville Herskovits arrived at Columbia, Boas put him in touch with Simango. The dialogue between the two would culminate in Herskovits's doctoral dissertation, "The Cattle Complex in East Africa," published in installments in the *American Anthropologist* in 1926, and an article about the Vandau, also published in the *American Anthropologist*, "Some Property Concepts and Marriage Customs of the Vandau."[19] In addition, after he returned to Mozambique, Simango gave valuable information to Henri-Philippe Junod, son of the eminent ethnographer and missionary Henri-Alexandre Junod. The details of their ethnographic dialogue are unknown, but from it Junod wrote two essays: "Les cas de possession et l'exorcisme chez les Vandau" (1934) and "Coutumes diverses des Vandau de l'Afrique Orientale Portugaise: Mariage. Divination. Coutumes et tabous de chasse" (1937).[20] Simango also collaborated with the missionary and ethnographer Dora Earthy, who in 1931 published the short essay "The Vandau of Sofala" in *Africa: Journal of the International African Institute*.[21] In these ways, Simango helped to produce the ethnographic sensibility that would be a signal part of the early development of African anthropology.

Pan-Africanism and Cosmopolitanism

On 1 June 1922, Kamba Simango and Kathleen Easmon (1891–1924) were married in the Wilton Connecticut Congregational Church. Born on the Gold

Coast (Ghana), Kathleen was the daughter of the physician John Farrell Easmon, born in Sierra Leone and descended from an important Creole (Krio) family. John Easmon had left Freetown in 1880 and moved to Accra, where he worked as chief medical officer for the Gold Coast government. At the time, there was an intense circulation in the Krio diaspora between London, Freetown, and Accra. Kathleen had been deeply influenced, both academically and politically, by her aunt Adelaide Casely-Hayford (married to the Gold Coast lawyer Joseph Ephraim Casely-Hayford). Her aunt was very active in Sierra Leone as president of the Freetown Young Women's Christian Association and, briefly, as the president of the local chapter of the Women's League, a branch of the Universal Negro Improvement Association founded by Marcus Garvey (1887–1940). Kathleen studied at the Royal College of Art, in South Kensington, London, and had met Simango at the Hampton Institute while traveling in the United States with her aunt to raise funds for educational activities in Africa.

Despite the research that Simango and Boas were conducting, the missionaries had other plans for the Simangos. The American Board was planning to launch a new missionary office in Mozambique. In 1907, it had clashed with local authorities, part of the recurring tensions between the colonial administration and the Protestant churches, which supposedly posed a "denationalizing" threat. The appointment of "nationals" like Simango could dissipate tension and make room for negotiations with the Portuguese administration. When Fred Bunker, who was in charge of the American Board, moved to Beira in 1905, the situation had seemed relatively straightforward. The Mozambique Company's director was granting Africans permission to attend night classes at the mission. The students responded with enthusiasm, but, a few months later, the new governor of Manica and Sofala, Alberto Celestino Ferreira Pinto Basto, came into office, and hostilities commenced. Rumors began to circulate that Bunker was inciting anti-Portuguese sentiment among the Africans. The permits and passes allowing Africans to attend the American Board school were revoked, although students continued to attend night classes clandestinely; there were persecutions and punishments. Finally, Bunker decided to close the school. He polled his students to find out who would be willing to move to Mount Selinda, where the American Board had another office. Simango was among the group of eighteen young Africans who decided to leave Beira.[22] Shortly afterward, in 1910, the Republic of Portugal was established, bringing with it a series of new changes in relation to the presence of missionaries in the colonies. According to Malyn Newitt, the idea was to establish "secular" missions.[23] It would prove to be a failure.

In 1923, having graduated, Simango was supposed to return to Mozambique to inaugurate and supervise the new missionary office in Gogoi, but the Portuguese administration required him to learn Portuguese. As a youth who had left Mozambique early, studying first in South Africa and then in the United States, Simango did not fluently speak Portuguese. The missionaries financed a brief trip to London, where both Kamba and Kathleen studied Portuguese grammar, followed by a period in Lisbon to perfect their language study. The trip was decisive for their Pan-Africanist and political experiences.

On 28 April 1924, Kathleen sent a detailed letter to the missionaries of the American Board, recounting their arrival in London and their first activities in Lisbon. The Simangos arrived in London on 3 June 1923 and took a summer course at King's College taught by the missionary council. Kamba also took classes in Portuguese phonetics at University College London. In London, they met many African students, participated in artistic events, and immersed themselves in the Pan-Africanist environment of the diaspora. In November, Kamba participated in the Third Pan-Africanist Conference, a planner of which was Du Bois, who was eager to raise awareness of the brutality of the forced labor Portugal imposed in Angola and São Tomé and Príncipe. The conference, which was held in London and Lisbon, was a pivotal moment in the history of Pan-Africanism and the criticism of Portuguese colonialism. Edward Alsworth Ross published a report on forced labor in the Portuguese colonies the following year, at the request of the League of Nations.[24]

The preparations for the meetings in Lisbon and London were difficult. There appeared to be some misunderstandings with the African representatives in Paris, who ended up not attending. Du Bois had originally hoped to hold a third session in Paris, but the French newspapers publicized the rumor that the event was associated with the polemic figure of Marcus Garvey. It was not—Du Bois's Pan-Africanist thinking was opposed to Garvey's exclusivist and radical ideas—but there were significant ramifications regardless. The London event took place 7–8 November 1923. As well as Du Bois, the delegates included the prominent British socialist Harold Laski (professor at the London School of Economics), Pan-Africanist and civil rights leader Ida Alexander Gibbs Hunt (teacher), Bishop Vernon (African Methodist Episcopal Church), Dr. John Alcindor (London), Chief Kofi Amoah III (Gold Coast Africa), and Sir Sidney Olivier (Governor of Jamaica), among others. Simango was also present and, though he was from Mozambique, delivered a discourse on the colonial situation in Angola. He would briefly sojourn briefly in Angola, where the missionaries of the American Board also had a mission, before returning to Mozambique.

The Lisbon session began on 1 December. José de Magalhães (1867–1937), who was born in Moçamedes, Angola, and studied medicine in Lisbon, had convinced Du Bois of the need for a session of the Congress in Portugal. He was appointed professor at the Instituto de Medicina Tropical in Lisbon after further studies at the Institute of Colonial Medicine in 1903 and 1904. Magalhães was close to important figures of the republican period, including António de

Brito Camacho. Following the republican revolution in 1910, Magalhães was called to head the committee for educational affairs.²⁵ Magalhães, a moderate socialist and reformist, played a central role in the Lisbon-based African League. The league was born out of the republican fervor, emerging from an internal split within the Junta de Defesa dos Direitos de África, a federation of the Portuguese Africans associations, founded in 1912. The faction that founded the African League adopted a more moderate, conciliatory tone toward Portuguese colonial interests. The league would include blacks, mestizos, and even whites among its leaders.

Arriving in Lisbon on 30 November 1923, Du Bois was received with all honors by the representatives of the African League. According to Du Bois's biographer, David Levering Lewis, the Lisbon session replicated the London session. Over two days, there were presentations on the history of the Pan-African movement, the condition of São Tomé (Portugal's most developed colony), African experiences in the United States, and the prospects for Pan-Africanism.²⁶ Kathleen and Kamba Simango were still in London and unable to take part in the Lisbon session. One week before her departure for Lisbon, Kathleen held a radio conference, becoming the first person of African descent to do so on English radio. "It was nice to feel that in spite of the fact that I had had to cancel all the speaking engagements that had been made for me," wrote Kathleen to the missionaries (she had had her appendix removed). "I was able to address a far larger audience than I would have done otherwise."²⁷

The Simangos arrived in Lisbon early in 1924, continuing their language study and living in a house provided by the missionaries together with other young American Board missionaries who were preparing to leave for Angola. They awaited the board's authorization to establish themselves in Mozambique, but also the permission of the Portuguese authorities. It was the eve of the *Estado Novo*, which was hostile to the Protestant churches. Kathleen returned to London in June 1924 to attend, where she developed an infection from peritonitis and died on 20 July. Boas was still hopeful that Simango would divert from his current course and take up anthropology more seriously. When he found out that Simango would be in Lisbon, Boas wrote a letter of recommendation for him to the most important Portuguese anthropologist at the time, José Leite de Vasconcelos (1958–1941). The letter, dated 28 May 1923, introduced Simango as a curious and competent student of the ethnology of "his people," the Vandau:

> My dear Sir:
> Permit me to introduce my friend Mr. Kamba Simango, a native of Portuguese Southeast Africa, who is going back there as a teacher after taking the steps demanded by the Portuguese administration in order to qualify for such a position.

> Mr. Simango is a capable and interested student of the ethnology of his people, the Vandau. He has worked here with me for several years, and I shall take the liberty of sending you some of the publications which he and I have prepared jointly. Mr Simango plans to use his time for advancing his study of the Vandau.
>
> Any help that you may be able to render him will be greatly appreciated.[28]

Simango likely never contacted Vasconcelos, however. His commitments to the missionaries, the death of Kathleen, and the ambiguous position of the Portuguese authorities on the mission in Mozambique did not allow him sufficient peace to return to anthropology. In October 1924, Simango sent a long letter to Boas from Lisbon, expressing concern over the future of their ethnographic collaboration; at times it reads almost as a farewell letter, slipping tonally in and out of academic formality. Simango thanked Boas for having taught him "to love and value the traditions of my people," and finally committed himself to completing their collaborating, mentioning some "pamphlets" Boas had sent him to correct—perhaps research forms relating to the ethnographic material he was compiling.[29] In this letter, we can see a close relationship and reciprocal recognition as the basic tissue for their ethnographic dialogue.

Simango married Christine Mary Coussey in March 1825, eight months after Kathleen's death. Coussey was also from the Gold Coast (Ghana), from Axim. She was Kathleen's cousin. She studied at Wesleyan Girls' High School in Cape Coast and then moved to England with her sister and her aunt, enrolling at Brighton College and then taking "home economics" in Kent. She was a secretary in London and then in Accra, in the recently formed Agricultural-Cultural Society of the Gold Coast. In 1923, she returned to London with her father and met up with her cousin Kathleen, then married to Simango. She and Simango began corresponding after Kathleen's death. Rennie argues that Coussey (who, like other members of the Krio elite of the West African Coast, had also visited Senegal and France) played an important role in strengthening Simango's Pan-Africanists convictions.[30]

The Last Dialogue

Before moving to Mozambique, Kamba and Christine Simango spent several months at the Chisamba Evangelical Mission in the central Angolan highlands. Finally, on 11 September 1926, they arrived in Beira, Mozambique, living first at the headquarters of the American Board in Mount Selinda. In 1927, with the approval of the Portuguese authorities, they moved to Gogoi (Gogoyo), the mission's only permanent base in the Manica and Sofala territories. In Gogoi, Kamba, in collaboration with Christine and Bede Simango, directed a school attended by one hundred students, dedicated chiefly to teaching Portuguese and the "industrial" arts.[31]

On 10 May 1927, Boas sent a letter to the Gogoi headquarters, asking if Simango wanted to continue the ethnographic work they had begun at Columbia. The second edition of Henri-Alexandre Junod's ethnography of the Thonga of southern Mozambique, *The Life of a South African Tribe*, had just appeared, and Boas wanted Simango to encourage Boas to return to writing about his country:

> My dear Mr. Simango,
> It is a very long time since I have heard from you. You wrote to me from Lisbon and I wrote you a long letter in reply . . . I am wondering whether you are still interested in the work that we were doing together here and whether you would not care to continue to do some work of the same kind, writing down the customs of your country as Dr. Junod has done so successfully for the Thonga. I think I should be able to get some money to repay you for your trouble if you would undertake to do such work.[32]

Simango was busy attending to the affairs of the new mission in Gogoi. The Portuguese administration had given authorization in April 1927. "Needless to say," however, he was "delighted" to hear from Boas "and very interested in what you ask about and suggest that I might do." Simango nevertheless wanted to continue the collaboration. The people living in the region around the mission remained "primitive," he wrote to Boas—untouched by "any kind of Western civilization." He hoped "to be able to gather some useful and interesting information about customs and folklore," and would send them for Boas "to make use of."[33]

Boas replied immediately. Not particularly interested in Simango's missionary activities, he emphasized the idea that the survey of the "customs" and "tales" of the group should be carried out in the local language, with "interleaved" translations. He asked whether Simango had received the volume of Junod's ethnography he had sent him. In that same year, Clement Martyn Doke's book about the Lamba of Northern Rhodesia had appeared, and Boas was willing to send Simango a copy of this too.[34]

Boas's mention of Doke was likely no accident. Doke was a former Baptist missionary who, in the 1930s, became one of the most important linguists and ethnographers of sub-Saharan Africa. Boas clearly wished for a similar path for Simango, but these anthropological hopes would not be fulfilled. Despite their mutual enthusiasm for the work, the various obstacles to its completion continued. The next few years would involve intense work for Simango and increasing conflict with his superiors at the American Board. During his training period in Portugal, Simango had received a full salary, equivalent to that of a European missionary. When he returned to Mozambique in 1926, however, his salary was cut in half in accordance with American Board policy. The board had no desire to elevate their African employees above their own compatriots, as the full salary would. It was the beginning of an irreversible conflict. Later, Simango would accuse his superiors of inconsistency with Christian principles. Behind this wage discrimination, he argued, lurked racial discrimination:

> From what we have received in the way of treatment from the Board, we can only deduce the following, that it is not that we do not have the qualifications to do the work here as most missionaries but simply because we are Africans and therefore considered a "problem" ... Could it be possible that the American Board in this year of our Lord 1931 can still be swayed by a spirit of dividing people into nationals to such an extent that they make us feel that we must be very different from the rest of workers?[35]

From 1934 to 1935, after a series of quarrels and mutual accusations, Simango broke from the missionaries completely. He turned his energies to the Negrophile Guild of Manica and Sofala ("Guild" was later replaced by "Nucleus"), founded in Beira in March 1935. The sources on Simango's role in the founding of the guild are ambiguous, but he clearly played a key role. The creation of the guild suggests that political considerations were an important element of the breakdown between Simango and the American Board, as well as the financial conflict and growing interpersonal distrust. Faced with this new challenge and no longer able to rely on the protection of the missionaries, Simango had to seek new ways to provide for his family. In March 1936, they migrated from Mozambique to Ghana, where his familiarity with the country through his wife, and his old "diaspora" colleagues, might have made the relocation less difficult. Little is known about Simango's activities in Ghana. He lived there until his death.[36]

The "Double Bind" of Portuguese Assimilationism

Was Kamba Simango merely representing the *assimilado*? Without doubt, his itineraries and experiences help us to understand the complexities of the problem of the *assimilado* in Mozambique. According to the legal-colonial discourse, an *assimilado* was an (ex)*indígena* (or African) who abandoned his "manners and customs" and adopted Portuguese cultural values. The law, which legally differentiated between *indígenas* and *assimilados*, reached its apogee with the Estatuto Político, Civil e Criminal dos Indígenas de Angola e Moçambique, which came into force in October 1926. The much-vaunted assimilation of the *indígenas* implied not only a legal categorical shift but also a long process of spiritual incorporation of the *indígenas* into the Portuguese world. Two models of colonization were therefore at stake: the British model of "separate development" through indirect rule, and the Portuguese model of tutelage by the *Indigenato* regime toward "assimilation," though this was a very far-off horizon.[37] The distinction between Indigenous and "assimilados" was not abolished until 1961, when, at least on paper, all inhabitants of Mozambique, Angola, and Guinea-Bissau became Portuguese citizens.

As the detailed work of Cláudia Castelo shows, only after the 1950s did Portuguese colonial policy begin to assume a more explicitly Luso-tropicalist grammar, inspired by the thinking of Gilberto Freyre.[38] Before this, Freyre's thinking was poorly received in Portugal, or "purely and simply ignored."[39] Given that our horizon of reflections is broad—the ambiguities of the supposed Portuguese racial exceptionalism, and its most recurrent grammar, Luso-tropicalism—it is significant that Simango and Freyre, the inventor of Luso-tropicalism, were both disciples of Boas and, indeed, were at Columbia University together for two years. Freyre was at Columbia from 1921 to 1922, Simango from 1919 to 1923. There was almost no personal relationship between Freyre and Boas, however, akin to that disclosed by the letters analyzed here. Maria Lúcia Pallares-Burke shows that the personal connection between Freyre and Boas was often more imagined than real. There is an anecdote—oddly ironic—that reveals the tenuous nature of this connection. In 1936, Boas asked Herskovits, who had discussed his thesis with Simango at Columbia, "could you tell me the title of the book and the name of the author, the Brazilian, whom you spoke about the other day?" "The name of Freyre's book is *Casa-grande & senzala*," replied Herskovits, "and his first name is Gilberto."[40] In the "Franz Boas Papers" at Columbia University, there is no evidence of any written exchanges between Boas and Freyre. Freyre, however, wrote emphatically of his intellectual relationship with Boas, both in the prefaces of his books and in various interviews.

Simango's career reveals the double bind of assimilationism; it offers a metaphor for the "colonial paradox" itself. "We want to teach the native to write, to read and to count," as Cardinal Cerejeira of Lisbon famously said, "but not make them doctors."[41] Salazar himself said that "a law recognizing citizenship takes minutes to draft . . . But a man fully and consciously integrated into civilized political society takes centuries to achieve."[42] Simango, perhaps realizing that neither the missionaries nor the Portuguese would allow him to become a "doctor," or a "citizen," opted to break away and exile himself. As the *Estado Novo* advanced and the *Indigenato* regime became consolidated, it came into more and more conflict with those who, like Simango, traversed colonial boundaries. If Simango's trajectory resembled that of the *assimilado*, it did so in a way that demonstrated the polysemic nature of that word, and the paradox of such a life.

Simango's displacement in New York and London was also decisive for fueling his political unease and expanding his worldview. His contact with anthropology in particular, together with his social ties to a series of eminent personalities, educators, and activists mostly from West Africa, produced a mixture of moderated ethnic pride and strong Pan-Africanist universalistic sensibility. However, it is necessary to set the coordinates of this "pride" within the context of a broader and more ambiguous narrative. The ideology of the missionaries consisted in making the Africans develop within their own sociocultural environment: in the segregationist language of the subsequent years, this amounted to "equal, but separate." African uniqueness was to be valued without sacrificing civilizatory imperatives, a dual requirement that condensed particularist-universalist tensions in the same place. Simango was not exempt from this apparent dilemma. It should be remembered, incidentally, that the years that Simango spent in New York coincided with the beginning of the Harlem Renaissance, a time when the burgeoning tropes of Pan-Africanism began to be heard among a host of black writers, poets, painters, sculptors, and musicians. In Simango's case, this milieu of Afrocentric "cultural" fervor was incorporated into the dialog with Boas.

The urban environment permeated by the Harlem Renaissance fed the aspirations of a wide gamut of Africans and African Americans in New York at the time. In April 1921, for example, Simango produced a musical and theatrical performance together with Kathleen Easmon and Madikane Cele at the Town Hall to benefit the Washington Conservatory of Music, a center where many African Americans studied. In April 1922, he participated as a dancer in the theater performance *Taboo,* presented at the Sam H. Harris Theatre in Harlem. The famous black actor Paul Robeson, who was a close friend of Simango, starred in the performance. Both Simango and his second wife, Christine, were also friends of the singer Roland Hayes, one of the first African American tenors to achieve international success.[43] These public rituals of "recognition," as well as Simango's ethnomusicological experiences with Natalie Curtis and the interest that Boas invested in him in their ethnographic discussions, contributed to his self-valorization of his African and Ndau background. Nonetheless—and this is the apparent paradox—this "return" to Africa was also the result of a markedly cosmopolitan and modern experience. In the person of Simango, both ethnic particularism and universalism coexisted, apparently without difficulty. Later, when the missionaries' paternalism became pronounced and untenable, Simango decided to break away from them—a rupture consistent with the emancipatory principles of that incipient modern cosmopolitanism.

Simango's life and career help us to understand the colonial experience *par le bas*, and to understand the construction of subjectivities and specific historicities from a less state-centered perspective.[44] Indeed, his trajectory challenges the commonplaces of national and colonial historiographies. On the other hand, it is not a matter of redeeming Simango's character through an apologetic or celebratory effort, something like a naïf denunciation of the monological power of ethnographic authority—the "authority" of Boas, in this case. In a range of ways, Simango's trajectory invites us to reflect on the collaborative dimensions of the construction of anthropological knowledge. Lyn Schumaker also adopts this approach in her work to address the importance of African assistants at the Rhodes-Livingstone Institute in Northern Rhodesia (Zambia).[45] It should also be remembered that Boas's intentions were simple. He desired to turn Simango, at best, into a good research assistant. Boas does, however, seem to have desired a bolder future for him, which is what we find when, in one of his letters, he expresses his wish for his young collaborator to become an ethnographer of the Ndau, in the same way in which the missionary Henri-Alexandre Junod became an ethnographer of the Thonga.

It should also be noted that when he met Simango, Boas's ethnographic experience was already immense. His model for the ethnographic "informant" was the Kwakiutl Indian George Hunt, with whom Boas maintained a professional relationship and a friendship over decades.[46] Without Hunt's collaboration (he was bilingual in English and Kwakiutl), Boas could never have conducted his research among the Kwakiutl, let alone develop his linguistic contributions about this group. The collaboration, however, was reciprocal in that Boas had provided Hunt with grammatical and phonetical methods to better transcribe the Kwakiutl language. The dialogue between Boas and Simango was, then, permeated by these previous ethnographic experiences.

Finally, Kamba Simango's biography is largely analogous to those described by Leo Spitzer in his book *Lives in Between*.[47] These "lives in between" seem to upset our fragile historiographical (Luso-tropical?) certainties. Or, after Michel de Certeau, these unique histories continue to challenge the "national political stabilities always postulated by [official] historiography."[48] In different ways, questioning these particular trajectories also allows us to achieve a temporary suspension of sociological and anthropological judgment, that is, a preliminary epistemological distrust of the operative and analytical scope of the well-established notions of our vocabulary—terms such as identity, ethnicity, nation, empire, colonialism, and Luso-tropicalism.

LORENZO MACAGNO is Associate Professor of Anthropology at the Federal University of Paraná. He has been conducting fieldwork in Mozambique since 1996. His main research interests focus on the Portuguese colonial imaginary and its consequences, transnational identities, multiculturalism, diasporas in the Lusophone world, and the history of anthropology in colonial contexts. His publications include *Outros muçulmanos: Islão e narrativas coloniais* (2006) and *O dilema multicultural* (2014), which was recently translated into Arabic by the Moroccan Institute for Hispanic-Lusophone Studies. He is also a researcher at the Brazilian National Council for Scientific and Technological

Development and a member of the Brazilian Association of Anthropology's Executive Board (2017–2018).

Notes

An earlier version of this chapter appeared in noncommercial, Portuguese-language form as Lorenzo Macagno, "Franz Boas e Kamba Simango: Epistorários de um diálogo etnográfico," in *Travessias antropológicas: Estudos em contextos africanos,* ed. Wilson Trajano Filho (Brasília: ABA Publicações, 2012). The first version of this chapter was presented on 6 April 2016 in Rio de Janeiro. On that occasion, I received valuable comments from the colleagues who were present. I would like to thank, in particular, Nélia Dias (Instituto Universitário de Lisboa), the principal discussant of my session. This chapter also owes a great deal to the conversations I had with Eric Morier-Genoud of Queen's University Belfast, a specialist in religious-political relations in Mozambique with whom I shared the same interest in the fascinating figure of Kamba Simango. My friend and mentor Peter Fry read an early version of this article. I am deeply indebted to him. Thanks also to James Dunk who worked hard to smooth out the rougher passages in English.

1. His full name was Columbus Kamba Simango. Apparently, he took that first name from Rev. Columbus Fuller, a missionary in Mount Selinda (Southern Rhodesia), where Simango studied. However, I will use "Kamba Simango," as he has been called in most sources. See also Eric Morier-Genoud, "Kamba Columbus Simango," in *Dictionary of African Biography,* ed. Henry Louis Gates Jr. and Emmanuel K. Akyeampong (Oxford, 2011).
2. A Presbyterian organization of the Congregationalist type, headquartered in Boston. Under the aegis of the London Missionary Society, already with a presence in South Africa, it received first the mandate to work among the Zulu and the Ndebele starting in the second half of the nineteenth century. Norman Etherington, "Kingdoms of This World and the Next: Christian Beginnings among Zulu and Swazi," in *Christianity in South Africa: A Political, Social and Cultural History,* ed. Richard Elphick and Rodney Davenport (Berkley, CA, 1997), 90.
3. Charles L. Briggs, "Genealogies of Race and Culture and the Failure of Vernacular Cosmopolitanisms: Rereading Franz Boas and W. E. B. Du Bois," *Public Culture* 17, no. 1 (2005): 75–100; Julia E. Liss, "Diasporic Identities: The Science and Politics of Race in the Work of Franz Boas and W. E. B. Du Bois, 1894–1919," *Cultural Anthropology* 13, no. 2 (1998): 127–66.
4. Macel Mauss (2002: 8) said: "We propose to reserve the term potlatch for this kind of institution that, with less risk and more accuracy, but also at greater length, we might call: total services of an agonistic type."
5. Mário Pinto de Andrade, "Proto-nacionalismo em Moçambique: Um estudo de caso— Kamba Simango (c. 1890–1967)," *Arquivo: Boletim do Arquivo Histórico de Moçambique* 6 (1989): 127–48.
6. See also Leon P. Spencer, *Toward an African Church in Mozambique: Kamba Simango and the Protestant Community in Manica and Sofala, 1892–1945* (Lilongwe, 2013).
7. My studies at Columbia University from November 2009 to July 2010 were possible thanks to a postdoctoral grant with the support of the Coordination for the Improvement of Higher Education Personnel (CAPES) foundation in the Brazilian Ministry of Education.
8. The original letters of Franz Boas are deposited in the archives of the American Philosophical Society (APS), in the collection "Franz Boas Papers" (FBP) in Philadelphia,

Pennsylvania. In preparing this chapter, I consulted a collection microfilmed by Scholarly Resources (SR) found in the Columbia University archives. The collection is organized chronologically, so, throughout the text, I will indicate the corresponding dates of the letters with APS-FBP-SR.
9. See Curtis, 2002. First published 1920 by G. Schirmer.
10. Natalie Curtis to Franz Boas, 20 March 1917 (APS-FBP-SR).
11. I am using the contemporary "African American," but the reader should be aware that the most common term employed at the time I am writing about was simply "negro."
12. Richard Glotzer, "Mabel Carney and the Hartford Theological Seminary: Rural Development, 'Negro Education,' and Missionary Training," *Historical Studies in Education* 17, no. 1 (2005): 58.
13. The second edition in English was published in 1938.
14. Natalie Curtis to Franz Boas, 24 November 1919 (APS-FBP-SR).
15. Franz Boas to George Foster Peabody, 5 May 1920 (APS-FBP-SR).
16. George Foster Peabody to Franz Boas, 7 May 1920 (APS-FBP-SR).
17. Franz Boas to George Foster Peabody, 14 May 1920 (APS-FBP-SR).
18. One was signed by both Boas and Simango: "Tales and Proverbs of the Vandau of Portuguese South Africa," *Journal of American Folklore* 35, no. 136 (1922): 151–204. The other four articles were signed by Boas, three of which were published in German and deal with religion, kinship, and everyday life: "Der Seelenglaube der Vandau," *Zeitschrift für Ethnologie* 52 (1920–1921): 1–5; "Das Verwandtschaftssystem der Vandau," *Zeitschrift für Ethnologie* 54 (1922): 41–51; "Ethnographische Bemerkungen über die Vandau," *Zeitschrift für Ethnologie* 55 (1923): 6–31; "The Avunculate among the Vandau," *American Anthropologist* 24, no. 1 (1922): 94–97. Of the three articles published in German, two were republished in English in Franz Boas, *Race, Language, and Culture* (New York, 1940).
19. Melville J. Herskovits, "The Cattle Complex in East Africa," *American Anthropologist* 28, no. 1 (1926): 330–72; Melville J. Herskovits, "Some Property Concepts and Marriage Customs of the Vandau," *American Anthropologist* 25, no. 3 (1923): 376–86.
20. Henri-Philippe Junod, "Les cas de Possession et l'Exorcisme Chez les Vandau," *Africa: Journal of the International African Institute* 7, no. 3 (1934): 270–99; Henri-Philippe Junod, "Coutumes diverses des Vandau de l'Afrique Orientale Portugaise: Mariage. Divination. Coutumes et Tabous de Chasse," *Africa: Journal of the International African Institute* 10, no. 2 (1937): 159–75.
21. Deborah Lyndall Gaitskell, "Religion Embracing Science? Female Missionary Ventures in Southern African Anthropology: Dora Earthy and Mozambique, 1917–1933," Basler Afrika Bibliographien working paper no. 5 (Basel, 1998).
22. Spencer, *Toward an African Church in Mozambique*.
23. Malyn Newitt, *A History of Mozambique* (Bloomington, IN, 1995), 435.
24 *Report on Employment of Native Labor in Portuguese Africa*. New York: The Abbott Press, 1925.
25. Robert A. Hill, ed., *The Marcus Garvey and Universal Negro Improvement Association Papers, Vol. IX: Africa for the Africans, June 1921–December 1922* (Berkeley, CA, 1995), 103.
26. David Levering Lewis, *W. E. B. Du Bois: The Fight for Equality and the American Century, 1919–1963* (New York, 2000), 116.
27. Letter from Kathleen Simango (but also signed by Kamba), sent from Lisbon and addressed to the missionaries of the American Board. It was published as "News from Mr. and Mrs. Simango," *Southern Workman* 53, no. 7 (1924): 334.
28. Franz Boas to José Leite de Vasconcelos, 28 May 1923 (APS-FBP-SR).

29. Kamba to Boas, 21 October 1924 (APS-FBP-SR).
30. John Keith Rennie, "Christianity, Colonialism and the Origins of Nationalism Among the Ndau of Southern Rhodesia, 1890–1935" (PhD diss., Northwestern University, 1973), 390–91.
31. Bede Simango was not a direct relative of Kamba (even though he appears in one of the official missionary sources in quotes as "his cousin"). He had received a solid missionary education, spending several years at the intermissionary school of the Swiss Mission in Lourenço Marques [Maputo], until he obtained authorization in 1927 to manage the Gogoi mission together with Kamba.
32. Franz Boas to Kamba Simango, 10 May 1927 (APS-FBP-SR).
33. Kamba Simango to Franz Boas, 8 October 1927 (APS-FBP-SR).
34. Franz Boas to Kamba Simango, 21 November 1927 (APS-FBP-SR).
35. Kamba Simango, quoted in Rennie, "Christianity, Colonialism and the Origins of Nationalism," 398.
36. Today, Eric Morier-Genoud, professor at Queen's University Belfast, conducts research on the Simango's period in Ghana.
37. Peter Fry, "Cultures of Difference: The Aftermath of Portuguese and British Colonial Policies in Southern Africa," *Social Anthropology* 8, no. 2 (2000): 117–43.
38. Cláudia Castelo, *"O modo português de estar no mundo": O luso-tropicalismo e a ideologia colonial portuguesa (1933–1961)* (Lisbon, 1998).
39. Marcos Cardão and Cláudia Castelo, *Gilberto Freyre: Novas leituras do outro lado do Atlântico* (São Paulo, 2015), 13.
40. Maria Lúcia Garcia Pallares-Burke, *O triunfo do fracasso: Rüdiger Bilden, o amigo esquecido de Gilberto Freyre* (São Paulo, 2012), 351.
41. Cardinal Cerejeira, quoted in Basil Davidson, "Portuguese Colonial Values," in *Portuguese Colonialism in Africa: The End of an Era*, ed. Eduardo de Sousa Ferreira (Paris, 1974), 26.
42. Quoted in Eduardo Mondlane, *Lutar por Moçambique* (Lisbon, 1976), 46.
43. Christopher A. Brooks and Robert Sims, *Roland Hayes: The Legacy of an American Tenor* (Bloomington, IN, 2015).
44. Jean-François Bayart, "Le politique par le bas en Afrique noire: Questions de méthode," *Politique Africaine* 1 (1981): 53–82.
45. Lyn Schumaker, *Africanizing Anthropology: Fieldwork, Networks, and the Making of Cultural Knowledge in Central Africa* (Durham, NC, 2001).
46. George Hunt was brought up in a Kwakiutl village but was the son of an English father and a Tlingit mother.
47. Leo Spitzer, *Lives in Between: Assimilation and Marginality in Austria, Brazil, West Africa, 1780–1945* (Cambridge, 1989).
48. Michel de Certeau, *A escrita da história* (Rio de Janeiro, 2008), 309.

Bibliography

Andrade, Mário Pinto de. "Proto-nacionalismo em Moçambique: Um estudo de caso—Kamba Simango (c. 1890–1967)." *Arquivo: Boletim do Arquivo Histórico de Moçambique* 6 (1989): 127–48.

Bayart, Jean-François. "Le politique par le bas en Afrique noire: Questions de méthode." *Politique Africaine* 1 (1981): 53–82.

Boas, Franz. "Das Verwandtschaftssystem der Vandau." *Zeitschrift für Ethnologie* 54 (1922): 41–51.

———. "Der Seelenglaube der Vandau." *Zeitschrift für Ethnologie* 52 (1920–1921): 1–5.
———. "Ethnographische Bemerkungen über die Vandau." *Zeitschrift für Ethnologie* 55 (1923) 6–31.
———. *Race, Language and Culture*. New York: Macmillan, 1940.
———. "The Avunculate among the Vandau." *American Anthropologist* 24, no. 1 (1922): 94–97.
Boas, Franz, and C. Kamba Simango. "Tales and Proverbs of the Vandau of Portuguese South Africa." *Journal of American Folklore* 35, no. 136 (1922): 151–204.
Briggs, Charles L. "Genealogies of Race and Culture and the Failure of Vernacular Cosmopolitanisms: Rereading Franz Boas and W. E. B. Du Bois." *Public Culture* 17, no. 1 (2005): 75–100.
Brooks, Christopher A., and Robert Sims. *Roland Hayes: The Legacy of an American Tenor*. Bloomington: Indiana University Press, 2015.
Cardão, Marcos, and Cláudia Castelo. *Gilberto Freyre: Novas leituras do outro lado do Atlântico*. São Paulo: Editora da Universidade de São Paulo, 2015.
Castelo, Cláudia. *"O modo português de estar no mundo": O luso-tropicalismo e a ideologia colonial portuguesa (1933–1961)*. Porto: Edições Afrontamento, 1998.
Certeau, Michel de. *A escrita da história*. Rio de Janeiro: Editora Forense Universitária, 2008.
Curtis, Natalie. *Songs and Tales from the Dark Continent*. Mineola, NY: Dover Publications, 2002. First published 1920 by G. Schirmer (New York).
Davidson, Basil. "Portuguese Colonial Values." In *Portuguese Colonialism in Africa: The End of an Era*, edited by Eduardo de Sousa Ferreira, 11–27. Paris: UNESCO, 1974.
Etherington, Norman. "Kingdoms of This World and the Next: Christian Beginnings among Zulu and Swazi." In *Christianity in South Africa: A Political, Social and Cultural History*, edited by Richard Elphick and Rodney Davenport, 89–106. Berkeley: University of California Press, 1997.
Fry, Peter. "Cultures of Difference: The Aftermath of Portuguese and British Colonial Policies in Southern Africa." *Social Anthropology* 8, no. 2 (2000): 117–43.
Gaitskell, Deborah Lyndall. "Religion Embracing Science? Female Missionary Ventures in Southern African Anthropology: Dora Earthy and Mozambique, 1917–1933." Basler Afrika Bibliographien working paper no. 5. Basel: Basler Afrika Bibliographien, 1998.
Glotzer, Richard. "Mabel Carney and the Hartford Theological Seminary: Rural Development, 'Negro Education,' and Missionary Training." *Historical Studies in Education* 17, no. 1 (2005): 55–80.
Herskovits, Melville J. "Some Property Concepts and Marriage Customs of the Vandau." *American Anthropologist* 25, no. 3 (1923): 376–86.
———. "The Cattle Complex in East Africa." *American Anthropologist* 28, no. 1 (1926): 330–72.
Hill, Robert A., ed. *The Marcus Garvey and Universal Negro Improvement Association Papers, Vol. IX: Africa for the Africans, June 1921–December 1922*. Berkeley: University of California Press, 1995.
Junod, Henri-Philippe. "Coutumes diverses des Vandau de l'Afrique Orientale Portugaise: Mariage. Divination. Coutumes et Tabous de Chasse." *Africa: Journal of the International African Institute* 10, no. 2 (1937): 159–75.
———. "Les cas de Possession et l'Exorcisme Chez les Vandau." *Africa: Journal of the International African Institute* 7, no. 3 (1934): 270–99.
Lewis, David Levering. *W. E. B. Du Bois. The Fight for Equality and the American Century, 1919–1963*. New York: Henry Holt & Co., 2000.

Liss, Julia E. "Diasporic Identities: The Science and Politics of Race in the Work of Franz Boas and W. E. B. Du Bois, 1894–1919." *Cultural Anthropology* 13, no. 2 (1998): 127–66.

Mauss, Marcel. *The Gift: The Form and Reason for Exchange in Archaic Societies.* London and New York: Routledge, 2000 [1950].

Mondlane, Eduardo. *Lutar por Moçambique.* Lisbon: Livraria Sá da Costa Editora, 1976.

Morier-Genoud, Eric. "Kamba Columbus Simango." In *Dictionary of African Biography*, edited by Henry Louis Gates Jr. and Emmanuel K. Akyeampong. Oxford: Oxford University Press, 2011.

Newitt, Malyn. *A History of Mozambique.* Bloomington: Indiana University Press, 1995.

Pallares-Burke, Maria Lúcia Garcia. *O triunfo do fracaso: Rüdiger Bilden, o amigo esquecido de Gilberto Freyre.* São Paulo: Editora Unesp, 2012.

Rennie, John Keith. "Christianity, Colonialism and the Origins of Nationalism among the Ndau of Southern Rhodesia, 1890–1935." PhD dissertation, Northwestern University, 1973.

Schumaker, Lyn. *Africanizing Anthropology: Fieldwork, Networks, and the Making of Cultural Knowledge in Central Africa.* Durham, NC: Duke University Press, 2001.

Spencer, Leon P. *Toward an African Church in Mozambique: Kamba Simango and the Protestant Community in Manica and Sofala, 1892–1945.* Lilongwe: Mzuni Press, 2013.

Spitzer, Leo. *Lives in Between: Assimilation and Marginality in Austria, Brazil, West Africa, 1780–1945.* Cambridge: Cambridge University Press, 1989.

PART II

Imaging a Mixed-Race Nation

CHAPTER 4

Eugenics, Genetics, and Anthropology in Brazil
The Masters and the Slaves, Racial Miscegenation, and Its Discontents

Robert Wegner and Vanderlei Sebastião de Souza

Caliban to Prospero:
This island's mine, by Sycorax my mother,
Which thou takest from me . . .
And show'd thee all the qualities o' the isle,
The fresh springs, brine-pits, barren place and fertile . . .
Which first was mine own king: and here you sty me
In this hard rock, whiles you do keep from me
The rest o' the island.

Prospero to Caliban:
Abhorred slave,
Which any print of goodness wilt not take,
Being capable of all ill! I pitied thee,
Took pains to make thee speak, taught thee each hour
One thing or other: when thou didst not, savage,
Know thine own meaning, but wouldst gabble like
A thing most brutish, I endow'd thy purposes
With words that made them known. But thy vile race,
Though thou didst learn, had that in't which
good natures
Could not abide to be with; therefore wast thou
Deservedly confined into this rock,
Who hadst deserved more than a prison.

— William Shakespeare, *The Tempest* (1611)

This chapter analyzes interpretations of Brazilian cultural and racial formation through a history of eugenics, and its interfaces with genetics and anthropology, in the late 1920s and early 1930s. We analyze the reflections of the anthropologist Edgard Roquette-Pinto and the physician Renato Kehl with respect to the controversies about the effects of miscegenation in the light of Mendelian genetics, as well as a similar clash of views between the geneticists Salvador de Toledo Piza Júnior and Octávio Domingues. This analysis is contrasted with Gilberto Freyre's influential book *Casa-grande & senzala* (*The Masters and the Slaves*), originally published in 1933, which, for its part, was steeped in the neo-Lamarckian tradition. In the formation of patriarchal society in the Northeast Region of Brazil, colonizers mixed with colonized peoples, inheriting certain features acquired in the process of adapting to their environment. To Freyre, the Portuguese were themselves the fruit of interracial and intercultural mixing. Between Europe and Africa, Christianity and Islam, the colonizers of Brazil were the expression of "opposites in equilibrium"; insofar as they were "plastic," they were Africanized in Africa and Americanized in the Americas.[1]

In the late nineteenth century, Hispanic America witnessed the beginnings of an influential tradition of essayists whose reflections on the formation of the continent's nations and the Spanish colonial experience were based on Shakespeare's *The Tempest*. One seminal work in this tradition was *Ariel*, published in 1900, by the Uruguayan writer José Enrique Rodó.[2] The character of the Spanish colonizer takes the form of Prospero, who, in the play, settles on an unnamed island with his daughter, Miranda, and becomes its ruler. The nations formed in the Americas as a result of its colonization are identified with Ariel, the spirit dweller of the island and Prospero's faithful servant, who hopes to eventually be granted his freedom. Finally, Prospero's rebellious slave, Caliban, a misshapen creature, neither man nor beast, is taken to represent the great power of the North, which, in its urge to grow economically, has lost all touch with any spiritual values and given itself up to pure utilitarianism. This interpretation of Rodó's was, as mentioned, a fruit of his involvement with a network of intellectuals from the Americas and Spain who were keen to highlight the value of *hispanidad*, especially after the United States' traumatic 1898 intervention in the Caribbean and the defeat of Spain.

This is not the only way the play has been interpreted. Cuban writer Roberto Fernández Retamar's essay "Caliban," from 1971, clearly expresses a quite different approach, arguably for the first time, even though such a change in tone could actually be traced back even to before Rodó, in the writings of José Martí (1853–1895). In this version, the Spanish colonizer is still Prospero, but now he is the usurper of the island, while Caliban—the rebellious slave—represents the colonized peoples, the natives of the Americas and legitimate occupiers of the land, who were only deformed in the eyes of the colonizers.[3]

In Brazil, Shakespearean metaphors have not been so widespread in reflections about Portuguese colonization and the formation of the nation, but that does not mean they cannot serve any purpose in analyzing these processes. As such, we propose here to reflect on the history of eugenics and the debate about miscegenation through the characters of *The Tempest*. The science of eugenics can be thought of as the occult powers that Prospero developed even when he was Duke of Milan and which, once stranded on the island, he put into practice to tame and control Caliban. Native and mixed-race populations—like Caliban—were seen as more monstrous in the eyes of some eugenicists than others, and while some believed this deformity to be intrinsic to their nature, others saw it as the result of disease. Prospero stands for not just physicians, geneticists, anthropologists, and eugenicists, but also—as many of the Hispanic American essays indicate—the actual colonizers of the Americas as a whole. Yet, the Portuguese colonizer portrayed in *Casa-grande & senzala* is so malleable that he takes power almost without imposing himself; he colonizes by allowing himself to be colonized, like a kind of pliable, enervated Prospero. It is arguably this image of the Portuguese that is so much up for debate—being contended and confirmed—among the Luso-tropicalists and their discontents.

Eugenics in Brazil: History and Historiography

In the early twentieth century, at the height of nationalist and imperialist policies, eugenics emerged in different parts of the world as an enticing means of intervening in the formation of national populations. Generally speaking, the ideas of eugenics were seen as a way of speeding up human evolution by drawing on the techniques and rationale of science, selecting and educating more racially "suitable" individuals and eliminating or preventing the reproduction of those who were "unsuitable." Based on evolutionary biology and theories about race, eugenics was quickly ushered into discussions about racial mixing, immigration, marriage control, and human reproduction. In many countries, intellectuals, scientists, and public figures appropriated eugenics in a variety of ways, adapting their plans for human biological improvement according to the racial and ideological realities prevailing in their respective national settings.[4] While the eugenics movement took on more radical proportions in the United States and parts of Europe, nurtured by ideas of racial purification,[5] it was manifested in Latin America in a "milder" form, incorporating social medicine and neo-Lamarckian inheritance, according to which social and environmental reforms could bring about improvements for future generations.[6]

As the historian Nancy Stepan points out, the history of eugenics in Brazil was marked by a special kind of scientific and social knowledge produced and shaped by local political, historical, and cultural variables. Rather than a "negative" eugenics, which prompted radical measures such as sterilization and strict racial segregation policies, Brazil's eugenicists mostly favored the development of "preventive" measures, focusing on sanitation and social reform projects to improve the characteristics of the population.[7]

To understand the emergence of eugenics in Brazil, we must not overlook the most pressing concerns of the intellectuals, the state, and parts of the ruling classes in the early 1900s when it came to the racial makeup of the country, the sanitation and public health conditions in its rural and urban parts, and the abject poverty and levels of illiteracy of a high proportion of its people. At this time, Brazil was often represented as a nation in the throes of degeneration, especially in view of the great many black people who had recently been released from slavery, the high proportion of *mestiços* and Indigenous people, and the country's tropical, disease-ridden climate. In the eyes of many foreign travelers, intellectuals, and officials, and even the country's elites and some of its foremost thinkers, Brazil was tainted by racial inferiority, economic and political backwardness, and its people's lack of civilization.[8]

At the same time, notwithstanding the different opinions about the country's racial future, Brazil seems to have gone through a period of deep political and social change. Industrialization, immigration, and urban development in the main cities held out the promise of a new scenario, but the devastation wrought by World War I shook its political and intellectual elites to the core and forced them to look inward in their efforts to shape the fate of their own country. In these circumstances, scientists, intellectuals, and social thinkers were keen to avoid any deterministic theories in their diagnoses of the problems that Brazil was facing in order to forge a less pessimistic discourse about its future.[9] The will to drag Brazil out of its civilizatory backwaters sparked intense debate about the nature of the country, leading to the formulation of some of the most original and long-lasting ideas about Brazil and the Brazilian identity. According to Sérgio Carrara, "Brazil's scientists were trying to make it possible, or at least conceivable, to reposition their country and themselves in what was then called the *concert of nations*."[10]

The subject of national identity and race went through major changes as of 1930, when Getúlio Vargas came to power and ushered in a new regime, which Stepan describes as being "marked by the desire to create a homogeneous consciousness of nationhood as the basis of social and political life." Under a more politically and administrative centralizing government, "new state apparatuses were developed to create such consciousness, to mobilize patriotism, to generate a sense of national unity and to level 'ethnic disparities.'"[11] At a time when eugenics was being taken to extremes in other parts of the world—including the growing affirmation of racial hygiene, which flowed into Nazi policies—a form of eugenics that was identified more closely with public hygiene and as being compatible with racial mixing gained ground in Brazil and the conception of racial democracy emerged.[12] The mixing of races ceased to be a problem and started to be viewed as a boon for Brazilian civilization. As such, as Stepan goes on, "intellectually, the representative figure of the 1930s was the Brazilian sociologist Gilberto Freyre." Freyre was both a child of his time and an entrencher of its tendencies: what he wrote "provided the key ideas that dominated domestic interpretations of Brazilian history and nationality for the next thirty years."[13]

While *Casa-grande & senzala* shaped the debate on social identity and race relations in the next thirty years in Brazil and even Portugal—as other chapters demonstrate—its influence could also have restructured how the period before its publication has been seen historically. It is possible that it influenced the view that the eugenics put into practice in the 1910s and 1920s was "milder," notwithstanding the radical and racist voices at that time, as Stepan is careful to note. Finally, it is important to problematize the supposedly absolute predominance of neo-Lamarckian thinking in Brazilian eugenics in that twenty-year period. In the foreword to the first edition of *Casa-grande & senzala*, Freyre aligns himself with neo-Lamarckism, mentioning several writers and a set of arguments supporting not only the inheritance of acquired traits but also the physical transformation of a race in a single generation. The most notable reference Freyre makes is to the German-American anthropologist Franz Boas, whose work he first read in the early 1920s.

By this time, Boas, who had been living in the United States since the late 1800s, was already an authority in the field of anthropology, especially for his criticisms of evolutionism and scientific racism.[14] Starting with his studies in physical anthropology in the early 1900s, Boas gained international repute for questioning some of the guiding principles of evolutionary anthropology. In "Instability of Human Types," presented in 1911 at the First Universal Races Congress in London, and in "Changes in the Bodily Form of Descendants of Immigrants," published the following year, Boas had already regarded the environment as a crucial factor in shaping anthropological features. At a time when studies on Mendelian genetics were gaining ground and consolidating the assumption about the absolute stability and immutability of physical types, Boas's research on European immigrants living in America proved that there was a varying degree of plasticity in bodily forms, including in the shape and size of the skull, taken as paradigmatic in physical anthropology. The result of his studies demonstrated that when individuals moved from one geographical environment to another, they underwent physical and even mental changes that were then inherited by future generations.[15] Clearly, then, Boas incorporated the assumptions of neo-Lamarckian evolutionary theory about the heredity of acquired characteristics. Although he was not a "committed Lamarckian," as the historian George Stocking puts it:

there is much in Boas' work to tie him to the tradition of neo-Lamarckian direct environmentalism which was so widespread in the late nineteenth century. Several of his intellectual antecedents, including Rudolf Virchow, clearly entertained the possibility that acquired characteristics were inherited. Boas himself constantly emphasized the functional and environmental modification of physical type.[16]

The immediate success of *Casa-grande & senzala,* with its scientific underpinnings, may have had the effect, in hindsight, of making the intellectual circles immediately before its publication appear predominantly neo-Lamarckian, a view that recent studies have tended to moderate. With its extraordinary power, *Casa-grande & senzala* was surely an influence for at least the three decades after its publication, but it equally shaped how historians have interpreted the twenty years that preceded it.

Neo-Lamarckism and Its Discontents

Despite the widespread influence of the neo-Lamarckian theory of evolution among Brazilians, Gregor Mendel's theories also attracted the support of some key figures in the eugenics movement, including Kehl, Roquette-Pinto, Domingues, and Toledo Piza Júnior. While they held opposing positions on eugenics and how to deal with racial theories, these authors shared the understanding that the uses of eugenics should be restricted to the study and application of the laws of Mendelian inheritance. In their view, education, hygiene, or any other policy to promote social welfare and living conditions could indeed contribute to the development of individuals and the nation as a whole, but they bore no relation to the practice of eugenics or interventions in human inheritance.[17]

While neo-Lamarckian thinking in Brazil was, as Stepan[18] points out, a result of contact with French scientific traditions, constructing a model of "Latin eugenics," the Brazilian eugenicists' acceptance of Mendelian genetics derived from their interaction with other scientific paradigms. As leaders in the fields of physical anthropology, genetics, and eugenics, Brazilian scientists of a Mendelian bent were more geared toward the scientific traditions of Germany, Britain, and the United States, taking in other theories that guided the study of evolutionary biology. Incidentally, these countries were the global leaders in modern genetic research in the early twentieth century, which gave credence to the idea held by one group of Brazilian eugenicists that Mendelian explanations were indispensable in any investigation of inheritance and eugenics. As had been the case in the United States and Northern Europe, the Brazilians' adoption of Mendel's theories was accompanied by a total rejection of neo-Lamarckian thinking, such that they completely disregarded environmental and social issues in their analyses of the workings of human inheritance.[19]

Nonetheless, Mendelian genetics was put into play in a variety of ways that did not share a common theoretical or ideological foundation, especially when it came to how racial mixing and more radical eugenics measures were addressed. Clear examples of such divergences can be seen in the clash between Roquette-Pinto and Kehl. Following quite distinct intellectual trajectories and projects, they were both trained in medicine in the early 1900s and devoted their scientific careers to the study of Brazil's racial formation.[20] Like the whole generation of scholars who came of age in the late imperial period and early republican years, they saw themselves as public figures with a responsibility to guide the nation into the future, putting their faith in science and technical rationality as instruments for transforming society and for setting the country on track toward progress and modernity. To this generation of intellectuals, Kehl and Roquette-Pinto included, science held out the promise of solving the country's supposedly delayed development, the possibly deleterious effects of racial mixing, and all the suffering related to the "social question," like poverty, diseases, malnutrition, and illiteracy.[21]

The Anthropologist and the Physician

Edgard Roquette-Pinto had acquired experience as an anthropologist and ethnographer at the National Museum (Museu Nacional) in Rio de Janeiro, highly regarded in Brazil for its research in evolutionary biology. His interests ranged across subjects as diverse as the languages, habits, and social conditions of Indigenous and *sertão*-dwelling population groups, and "racial types" and the meaning of miscegenation in the formation of Brazil.[22] As a researcher at the National Museum, his main efforts were geared toward a wide-ranging study of "racial types," building up an extensive archive of anthropometric data on populations from different parts of the country from 1910 to 1920. His aim was to distinguish the anatomic, physiological, and psychological nature of the different "racial types" of Brazil and the factors that determined their anthropological makeup. In line with the Mendelian genetics research of his day, Roquette-Pinto had classified the anthropological types by analyzing the physical and constitutional traits of the Brazilian types, making detailed anthropometric studies that recorded everything from eye color and hair type to height, thorax circumference, muscle strength, cephalic and nasal indices, the effects of miscegenation, and the formation of psychological character.

Roquette-Pinto was keen to refute the theories that reaffirmed the existence of inferior and superior races and looked down on racial mixing. Not surprisingly, his anthropological work was marked by a strong defense of the *mestiço* population and severe criticism of theses expounding the degeneration of the Brazilian population—ideas that were repeatedly propagated by foreign travelers and scientists, who saw miscegenation as Brazil's Achilles' heel. In the second and third decades of the twentieth century, well before the publication of *Casa-grande & senzala*, Roquette-Pinto was already consistently rebutting theories of Aryan supremacy and scientific racism, stressing that the country's problems had nothing to do with racial mixing or any other factor of a racial or biological nature.

Unlike Freyre, who drew on the work of Boas to develop his anti-racism arguments, Roquette-Pinto's position against racism emerged from his idiosyncratic study of physical anthropology, sustained by his particular interpretation of Mendelian genetics and his strongly nationalistic position. While he was familiar with Boas's work and ideas, and even his ideological leanings, particularly with regard to miscegenation, Roquette-Pinto was not in any way influenced by cultural anthropology. Indeed, his understanding of the role of the anthropologist set him quite apart from Boas.[23] While Boasian anthropology started out from physical anthropology and moved toward cultural anthropology, Roquette-Pinto was ever a staunch supporter of evolutionary anthropology, both in its positive version and in its expression that linked it to studies of eugenics and human genetics. While he recognized Boas as a "master" of anthropology, as he put it in a letter to the German historian Rüdiger Bilden,[24] he did not use his work as a reference. Mentioning the "two currents" that vied with one another to explain the hereditary constitution of the human species in "Notas sobre os tipos antropológicos do Brasil" (Notes on the anthropological types of Brazil), published in the late 1920s, he went to the point of saying that his own research had led him to prefer the Mendelian observations of Charles Davenport over Boasian ones that insisted on environmental influences.[25]

An advocate of Mendelian genetics, Roquette-Pinto took on board the evolutionary theses about the immutability of inherited characteristics, aligning his work closely with American and German anthropologists and geneticists. In the talk he gave at the First Brazilian Congress on Eugenics (Primeiro Congresso Brasileiro de Eugenia), in 1929, he staked out his position alongside the main defenders of Mendelian eugenics, including Davenport and Eugen Fischer. However, unlike them, he drew on Mendel's theories to demonstrate that nothing in the genetic makeup of the Brazilian *mestiço* population indicated any sign of degeneration. Rather than blaming racial mixing for the production of genetic anomalies, as Davenport did, Roquette-Pinto held that racial mixing should be seen as a "combination of hereditary factors," since "they followed biological laws [that are] already known"[26] and documented by science, making reference to the researches he had undertaken at the National Museum. This assumption of miscegenation as "combination" implied a synthetic understanding of what happened in racial mixing. Around 1930, some Mendelians had come to believe there was not a preponderance of the characteristics of one race over another but instead a combination of factors, which justified their rejection of the existence of superior or inferior races. Thus, they were convinced that it was possible to form a country that was simultaneously mixed race and eugenic.

Renato Kehl, a physician who made his name as a staunch advocate of the Brazilian eugenics movement, defended an opposing position. Not only did Kehl publish more than twenty books on eugenics, he also devoted his whole career to its institutionalization in Brazil. He was one of the people behind the creation of the Eugenics Society of São Paulo (Sociedade Eugênica de São Paulo) (1918) and the *Boletim de Eugenia,* a key journal in the communication of ideas on eugenics from 1929 to 1933. In the early 1930s, Kehl was also responsible for forming the Central Brazilian Commission on Eugenics (Comissão Central Brasileira de Eugenia), a think tank that advised the Brazilian government on eugenics policy-related issues. Two of his key publications were *Lições de eugenia* (Lessons of eugenics) (1929) and *Sexo e civilização: aparas eugênicas* (Sex and civilization: Fragments of eugenics) (1933), in which he summed up his ideas on eugenics and its interface with scientific racism.

Although Kehl began his career as a member of the sanitary reform movement, which defended a model of "preventive" eugenics much like social medicine and neo-Lamarckism, he veered theoretically and ideologically toward "negative" eugenics and Mendelian genetics in the late 1920s. His conversion to a more radical interpretation of eugenics came about as a result of closer contact with the ideas being put into practice in Germany and the United States. From 1920 to 1930, when eugenics was flourishing in countries like Germany, Sweden, Denmark, and Norway, he made several visits to Northern Europe.[27] His contact with these foreign eugenicists and eugenics institutions both reinforced his negative views on racial mixing and justified the adoption of stricter eugenic interventions like selective immigration and racial segregation, marriage control, and the sterilization of people who were mentally ill, criminals, or regarded as "dangerous" for the formation of future generations.[28]

Putting forward racist and biologically deterministic theories derived from German Mendelian genetics, Kehl held that Brazil's problems could not be solved without developing a radical "biological policy" inspired by racial hygiene—in reference to the eugenics program being developed in Germany. As he saw it, Brazil's greatest hurdle was its "racial ill" (*mal de raça*), so the government should prevent the proliferation of racially "undesirable" (*indesejáveis*) individuals, even if this implied using such extreme measures as those being proposed in Germany and the United States, like racial segregation, eugenic sterilization, and euthanasia.[29] He published such beliefs in his book *Sexo e civilização: Aparas eugênicas* (1933) a year after his second visit to Germany. Around this time, he even voiced praise for the newly created Nazi eugenics court, which had passed laws on sterilization to be enforced throughout the

Reich. As he wrote in the second edition of *Lições de eugenia*, Germany was the country where eugenics was practiced "more broadly and courageously," as borne out by the passing of compulsory sterilization laws. As he saw it, "the German eugenic system of racial protection has impressed the scientists and leaders of many countries, especially in the north of Europe, which are gradually adopting the same regulatory measures."[30]

The Geneticists

Almost ten years younger than Kehl and Roquette-Pinto, Octávio Domingues and Salvador de Toledo Piza Júnior graduated in experimental genetics of animals and plants at the agricultural college Escola Superior de Agricultura Luiz de Queiroz (ESALQ). It had been founded in 1901 as a "practical school" in the state of São Paulo, which boasted the most advanced agricultural practices in the country, based primarily on coffee cultivation. Established by the state government in the town of Piracicaba, the school focused on agricultural research in a bid to diversify and modernize the state's farming methods.[31]

Domingues graduated there in 1917, returning to work as a teacher and researcher from 1924 to 1935, when he transferred to a school of agronomy, Escola Nacional de Agronomia, in Rio de Janeiro, then the capital city. While at ESALQ, he worked with zootechnics and played an important role in adapting and genetically improving the zebu breed of cattle in Brazil. He was one of the pioneers in Brazil in the genetic improvement of cattle, publishing an important book on the subject, *Introdução ao estudo do melhoramento dos animais domésticos* (Introduction to the study of improvement of domestic animals), in 1928. Domingues's research and zebu campaigns took him to far-flung reaches of Brazil, as well as the United States and some countries in Europe.[32]

Toledo Piza Júnior graduated from ESALQ in 1921, and one year later he traveled to Europe, where he studied biology, genetics, and especially protozoa and invertebrates at the schools of agriculture and veterinary science in Berlin. He then joined the faculty at ESALQ, where he taught zoology, anatomy, and the comparative physiology of domestic animals. He remained at the same institution throughout his working life. Domingues and Toledo Piza, together with Nicolau Athanassof from Bulgaria, joined forces in 1926 to establish the *Revista de Agricultura* (Journal of Agriculture), that it might serve as a forum for new techniques for improving the farming practices in the state of São Paulo. Soon afterward, in 1930, the two professors joined the eugenics movement. Like geneticists from other countries, they were keen to link their science to eugenics.

In 1929, the year of the First Brazilian Congress on Eugenics, Domingues published *A hereditariedade em face da educação* (Inheritance in the face of education), in which he proposed eugenic policies through descriptions of the Mendelian mechanisms of inheritance. Within the context of such policies, the very act of divulging the mechanisms could lead, he believed, to a greater public awareness of eugenics. Domingues believed, quoting staunch British eugenicist Reginald Ruggles Gates (1882–1962), that "probably an intelligent and enlightened public opinion is more efficacious than any law that could be devised. And a large element of that enlightenment will consist in an understanding of the nature, the laws and the ubiquity of heredity."[33]

In 1930, Toledo Piza Júnior published a review of Kehl's book *Lições de eugenia* in which he made several "small repairs" (*pequeninos reparos*).[34] Kehl replied to the article in a letter, admitting that many of the errors had been caused by the speed with which he had written the book, but generally welcoming the geneticist's criticisms. Indeed, he not merely accepted the corrections with good grace but actually incorporated them into the second edition, published in 1935.[35] This was quite likely the juncture at which Kehl—a physician educated at the Faculty of Medicine of Rio de Janeiro and the activist most closely identified as a eugenicist per se—started to see Domingues and Toledo Piza Júnior as potential allies in the field of genetics. He invited them into the Central Brazilian Commission on Eugenics, created in March 1931, as well as the editorial team of the *Boletim de Eugenia*, which he had launched in 1929.

Arguably, from Kehl's perspective, everything seemed to slot into place, and through the *Boletim*, the eugenics movement in Brazil became more cohesive and drew closer to the classic form seen in the United States, where eugenics was primarily a case of modern Mendelian genetics applied to humans. In September 1931, still under Kehl's exclusive editorship, the *Boletim* published an interview with Domingues on his acceptance as an associate member of the American Genetic Association. In it, Domingues stated his belief that "genetics is a science of this century. It was born precisely in the first year of the twentieth century." He argued that "the improvement of plants, with the teachings of genetics, is a current practice in modern agriculture," while "improving cattle, in turn, is one of the best proofs in existence that the principles of genetics are true." He concluded: "Indeed, applying this knowledge, from the animal world to Man, is a measure that cries out to be taken. It is no longer permissible for us to deny that Man is an animal. Thus, why not take advantage of these laws of genetics applicable to animals, to apply them to humans?"[36]

All this is consistent with William Provine's observation that "in many countries geneticists lent their prestige and support to the early eugenics movement."[37] It is as if the eugenics movement, led by Kehl, was effecting an *aggiornamento* (updating) on a national scale using Mendelism and scientific knowledge legitimized by genetics. It could stand up to physical anthropology, at least in the form that it was conceived of by National Museum Director Roquette-Pinto, who was already vocal in his criticism of Kehl's arguments against racial mixing. However, things were not that simple, because dissension over so crucial a theme as miscegenation ultimately would destabilize the whole edifice.

Miscegenation and Its Discontents: Salvador de Toledo Piza Júnior, Ally of Kehl

In a series of articles published in the *Boletim de Eugenia,* Toledo Piza Júnior considered the consequences of the "marriage of whites with blacks in the light of biology." The first article, published in the April/June 1932 issue, explained Mendelism, the mechanism of inheritance, and the segregation of genetic factors. Toledo Piza Júnior presented the combination of dominant and recessive genes in the results of crossbreeding rabbits in successive generations and the genetic combinations of red and white flowers. In the next issue, Piza Toledo Júnior explained that human skin color depended not solely on one Mendelian factor but rather on the interaction of several, as yet unknown by geneticists. The matter was a "factorial complex in which diverse Mendelian units are involved."[38] In the third and final article, Toledo Piza Júnior expounded his views on the consequences of racial mixing. He explained that the study of human genetics at that time was restricted merely to observing and transposing experiments on plants and animals to the human reality. Echoing the first two articles, he claimed, "There can no longer be the slightest doubt that man is an animal, as his behavior shows, reacting to the environment in a fundamentally identical way to other animals," but "man cannot be experimented on."[39]

He went on to observe that despite the scientific clarity of Mendel's laws of inheritance and their validity for humans, "the endocrine apparatus also has an influence on pigmentation." The introduction of the action of the "endocrine apparatus" to Toledo Piza Júnior's analysis, considering that "the products generated by the different internal secretion glands have a powerful influence on the ... general metabolism," allowed him to restate the complexity of the human being, concluding that "the white man and the black man are so different in such a variety of aspects that they could well be regarded as belonging to different species." This led him to deduce that "from an anthropological viewpoint ... unions between whites and blacks are not natural."[40] Toledo Piza Júnior was categorical about the incompatibility of unions between black and white people since, he sustained, they belonged to different species.[41]

Similar racist conceptions can be seen in the writings of Charles B. Davenport in the United States and Jon Alfred Mjöen (1860–1939) in Norway, among others. Mjöen's speech at a 1930 meeting of the International Federation of Eugenics Organizations contains cognate ideas and was vehemently against racial mixing. Given that this speech was published in translation in the *Boletim de Eugenia* the following year, it is fair to infer that his research on population groups became an important reference for both Toledo Piza Júnior and Kehl, who, in the introduction to the text, recommended its reading to all eugenicists, sociologists, and anthropologists, stressing that the negative effects of miscegenation among the "Nordics" and "Lapps" whom Mjöen studied were of "great scientific value, especially for the study and appraisal of the consequences arising from the mixing observed among us."[42]

In his anthropological studies in northern Norway and Sweden, a region Mjöen saw as an open-air laboratory for the study of racial mixing because "very different races" came into contact there, the Norwegian eugenicist focused his attentions on the development and mixing of two races in particular: the "Mongoloid Lapps" and the "Nordics."[43] Over twenty years, he made several visits to the tundra, studying around six hundred Nordics, six hundred Lapps, and "over three hundred hybrids," both men and women, measuring their muscle strength and the volume of their lungs. His graphs containing the results of these tests show that around 30 percent of the hybrid men and women had indices that were superior to those of the pure Lapps but inferior to the Nordics. However, the hybrids' muscle strength and lung volume were overall inferior to the Lapps', whose measurements were in turn inferior to those of the Nordics.

Mjöen correlated these data with height to analyze the "harmony" of the individuals from each group, concluding that hybrids possessed more physical or mental disharmonies than did the individuals from one or other of the races. While showing no data on the subject, he added that "the most surprising discovery was the lower mental capacity combined with the relatively good overall appearance." Aligning himself with Fischer and Davenport, Mjöen put this down to the thesis of a "mosaic heritance . . . which gives rise to the series of disharmonies in hybrids." Like all the Mendelian geneticists, he was sure that the genetic factors of the progenitors did not "blend" in the descendants but were instead "combined." Yet, these combinations could be mutually disharmonious. These disharmonies were, he argued, more evident in the "functioning of the various endocrine glands," for "the growth of the body stands in close relation to the function of the glands," such that the descendant of parents of different races was very likely to manifest some glandular disturbance, which would have a negative impact on their development. But this glandular disturbance could have impacts beyond their physical makeup, also resulting in "mental and moral" instability and "a want of balance." Hybrids were therefore more at the mercy of their drives and less capable of exerting self-control.[44]

When he spoke at the meeting of the International Federation of Eugenics Organizations, Mjöen was already under a good deal of pressure in Norway. As Nils Roll-Hansen has noted, the young physician Otto Lous Mohr

(1886–1967) since the 1910s had dismissed him as a "dilettante in medicine and biology." Attacks on Mjöen's scientific legitimacy gained force as genetics was institutionalized in the country. Kristine Bonnevie, a specialist in cytology and genetics, and Kristian Schreiner, a professor of anatomy and eminent physical anthropologist, warned that Mjöen's eugenic views bore false hopes and he "did not understand that the young science of eugenics was not yet ripe for application in practical politics,"[45] nor did he fully master the underlying scientific principles. As Mjöen was gradually ostracized from serious medical, biological, and genetic circles in his country, he turned his writings more directly to the lay public and threw his energies into sustaining his legitimacy by taking part in international eugenics institutions. His reception in Brazil indicates a degree of success in this strategy.

If the new discoveries in endocrinology were opening up new fields for eugenics and raising "a question that is of practical importance in, for example, my native land, owing to the Nordic-Lapp alliances,"[46] then, for Kehl, the Norwegian eugenicist's study served as a warning against miscegenation between whites and blacks in Brazil. Meanwhile, Toledo Piza Júnior's series of articles on mixing between white and black people suffered from a paucity of research of the human populations in question and merely presented the functioning of Mendel's laws of heredity in plants and animals. His affirmation that racial mixing between whites and blacks was harmful and would bring about disharmony was derivative, drawing on the conclusions of Mjöen's study of Lapps and Nordics in Northern Europe and applying them to the mixing of white and black people in Brazil. In all cases, hybrids were, it seemed, disharmonious, insofar as their glands were apparently so. As such, Kehl and Toledo Piza Júnior held that what Freyre subsequently conceived as the great virtue of the Portuguese—their plasticity and openness to miscegenation—was actually their biggest flaw, leaving a harmful legacy that eugenics must now address, including warning Brazilians, in a great crusade, that miscegenation had been a mistake that must be reverted. Prospero must acknowledge his superiority and govern the island without ever having mixed with Caliban.

Roquette-Pinto and Domingues in the Defense of Miscegenation

As we have seen, Mendelian genetics was central to the formulation of Roquette-Pinto's interpretations of Brazilian racial composition. Racial mixing was not a problem but rather an advantage for the formation of the nation, since it conciliated the different genetic characteristics existing in the country. Like Roquette-Pinto, Domingues used Mendelian genetics to refute theses about the existence of "pure races" or racial hierarchies. Science, he argued, had already demonstrated convincingly that miscegenation was commonplace the world over and that "purity of races is of no importance to the improvement of the species."[47] As for Brazilian racial mixing, Domingues saw it as "a special and precious example of the encounter of the three races. . . . It is the most complete miscegenation history has ever recorded."[48] According to Stepan, interpretations like Domingues's can be seen as forerunners of Freyre's thesis on racial democracy in Brazil and the formation of civilization in the tropics.[49]

Another interpretation common to Roquette-Pinto and Domingues can be seen in the role they attributed to racial mixing as an element of eugenization. While Roquette-Pinto believed miscegenation resulted from simple eugenic combination—the outcome of a biological amalgam—Domingues emphasized that successful miscegenation in the Brazilian past would become ever more important for its population in the future due to the need to absorb migratory flow taking place in the modern world.[50] In this sense, the crux of the matter for both Roquette-Pinto and Domingues was not just refuting scientific racism and extreme ideas about the negative impacts of racial mixing but rather the chance to think about the formation of a more biologically homogeneous and integrated nation. It is no surprise that their interpretations about the future of the Brazilian nation did not get away from either racial democracy or the theory of whitening, ideologies widely held by Brazilian intellectuals as they took miscegenation on board as a positive element of the formation of Brazil.

Roquette-Pinto and Domingues believed in the constant improvement of human races, envisaging eugenics as an effective tool for the transformation of society. However, they were against more radical measures, like state-sanctioned eugenic sterilization, racial segregation, and birth control. Rather, they believed in a positive eugenics capable of encouraging spontaneous measures on the part of individuals in terms of their matrimonial choices and reproductive care. Both saw education as pivotal for promoting eugenic awareness and the overall development of individuals. Although they championed Mendel's theses and believed that the environment did not affect heredity in future generations, they understood that education, hygiene and health care, and social reform policies were nonetheless decisive for individual improvement, enhancing the population's intellectual, aesthetic, and physical vigor, irrespective of racial origins.

Concluding Remarks

As we have seen, eugenics and Mendelian genetics manifested in various forms during this period in Brazil and produced a series of clashes and controversies, especially when it came to the issue of miscegenation. Such disagreements can be seen, for instance, at the First Brazilian Congress on Eugenics, attended by more than a hundred eugenicists, physicians, educators, and intellectuals with links to the eugenics movement. One major point of contention concerned the radical positions defended by Renato Kehl in *Lições de eugenia*, which he launched at the congress. Essentially, the book argued strongly against miscegenation and for strict eugenic policies of selected immigration, sterilization, and birth control. Kehl's proposals were contested not just by Edgard Roquette-Pinto but also by Alvaro Fróes da Fonseca, an anthropologist who also worked at the National Museum. In his talk, Fróes da Fonseca positioned himself against Kehl's anti-racial mixing and anti-*mestiço* views, pointing out that it was well established that "miscegenation does not create in us any conditions of inferiority and does not offer us any insoluble problem." In strictly scientific circles, he said, credence was no longer given to the putative inferiority of black people, Indigenous people, and *mestiços*—as was preached by "the advocates of Aryan blood," referring to Kehl and his followers.[51]

In Roquette-Pinto's speech opening the conference, he followed a similar line to Fróes da Fonseca. He argued that it was necessary to deconstruct the prejudiced eugenic conceptions that condemned Brazilian *mestiços* as inferior or degenerate. Citing his own research findings about the anthropological formation of Brazil, he said, "None of the Brazilian population types has any stigma of anthropological degeneration." Quite the contrary: "The characteristics of all of them are the best one could hope for." Brazilian *mestiços*, whom the defenders of a "false biology" (*falsa biologia*) regarded as degenerate or dysgenic (referring to authors like Kehl), were actually uneducated, sick, and debilitated by the pathological circumstances in which they lived.[52]

Roquette-Pinto's words reverberated strongly not only inside the eugenics movement but also in the field of sociology. Recent historiographical research has shown how strong an impact this anthropologist's studies had on the thinking of Gilberto Freyre.[53] It is fair to say that even before *Casa-grande & senzala*, a seminal work in the constitution of a new interpretative paradigm for the social reality in Brazil, Roquette-Pinto and, to a lesser extent, Octávio Domingues had already sketched out the general thrust of the ideas that subsequently took shape in Freyre's groundbreaking work, especially when it came to the thesis that miscegenation was ethnically beautiful, healthy, and culturally enriching. Indeed, Freyre himself indicated Roquette-Pinto's influence on his perception of the significance of racial mixing in Brazil—a subject of such importance to him and his generation of intellectuals—in the foreword to the first edition of this work. In the same passage in which he stressed the importance of having interacted with Franz Boas in conceiving the difference between race and culture, Freyre highlighted that his negative view of Brazil's *mestiços* changed following his contact with Boas in New York. Freyre also noted that there were anthropologists in Brazil, including Roquette-Pinto, who opposed the view that racial mixing was intrinsically negative, as the outcome would depend on concomitant environmental conditions, especially exposure to disease.[54]

Other chapters in this book demonstrate that the story does not end here but instead ramifies out in time and space. Freyre's ideas and work went on to take new shape in Luso-tropicalism and the argument that, as Claudia Castelo puts so succinctly, "the Portuguese possessed a special capacity to adapt to life in the tropics" and that "in the areas of Portuguese influence, 'hybrid forms of men and culture,' a 'third man or a third culture' was in the making." Luso-tropicalism, a formulation developed by Freyre in the 1950s, as other chapters explain, was certainly an offshoot of *Casa-grande & senzala,* its reception in Portugal and its colonies, and Freyre's new interpretations and new voyages to parts of Africa. Essentially, Luso-tropicalism had meanings that involved different translations, betrayals, deceptions, reviews, and negotiations. For some Portuguese scholars like António Augusto Mendes Correia (discussed by Ricardo Roque) and Alberto Germano da Silva Correia (discussed by Cristiana Bastos) the Portuguese man's unbridled urge toward miscegenation was not as desirable as Freyre would have it or even constant, varying according to the specific circumstances of each colonization process and the characteristics of the native peoples. Meanwhile, as Castelo discusses, Baltasar Lopes da Silva (a scholar from Cape Verde) and Osório de Oliveira (a Portuguese publicist) start out with an enthusiastic reading of *Casa-grande & senzala,* only to face disappointment with Freyre, who on a visit to Cape Verde regarded its population as being "so negroid" (*tão negróide*) and did not find the beneficial racial mixing he had expected.

In *Ecos do Atlântico Sul* (Echoes from the South Atlantic), the Brazilian anthropologist Omar Ribeiro Thomaz suggests that Freyre defined a two-way "cannibalism" in Brazil, while his theory of Luso-tropicalism in the broader context of the Portuguese empire represented a one-way cannibalism, "and the cannibal was [just] the Portuguese colonizer. It was therefore necessary for 'African cannibalism' to be eliminated and for the Indigenous 'difference' to be established and to assure, for many centuries, they were swallowed by the Portuguese empire."[55] Interpretations and appropriations of Freyre in the South Atlantic range from a vision of the Portuguese colonizer as a malleable Prospero, adaptable to all tropical environments and peoples, to one in which Prospero takes his original form, dictating to Caliban both his "purposes" and the "words that made them known."[56] Finally, this latter interpretation seems to have predominated in the third era of the Portuguese Empire. The former shaped Freyre's interpretation of the colonization of Brazil and, as has been restated throughout this chapter, prevailed for many years. However, as is argued by Marcos Chor Maio in this volume, the questions about the actual existence of this paradoxical Prospero—who colonizes without dominating, who fraternizes with those he enslaves—already started to be voiced in Brazil as early as World War II.

Robert Wegner is a historian affiliated with the Oswaldo Cruz Foundation. He is also Professor in the Department of Social Sciences at the Pontifical Catholic University of Rio de Janeiro. He received his PhD in sociology from University Research Institute in Rio de Janeiro in 1999. He is the author of *A conquista do Oeste: A fronteira na obra de Sérgio Buarque de Holanda* (1999) and several articles published in scientific journals. His research interests are in the history of modernism and eugenics.

Vanderlei Sebastião de Souza is Adjunct Professor of History at the Universidade Estadual do Centro-Oeste do Paraná and holds a PhD in the history of science from Casa de Oswaldo Cruz. He is the author of *Em busca do Brasil: Edgard Roquette-Pinto e o retrato antropológico brasileiro—1905-1935* (2017). His research interests include the history of science and intellectual history, with a focus on history of eugenics; history of physical anthropology, race, nation, and social thought in Brazil; and intellectual trajectories and biographies.

Notes

All translations in this article are our own unless otherwise indicated.
1. Gilberto Freyre, *Casa-grande & senzala: Formação da família brasileira sob o regime de economia patriarcal* (Rio de Janeiro, 1983), 8.
2. José Enrique Rodó, *Ariel y Proteo selecto* (Caracas, 1993).
3. Roberto Fernández Retamar, *Todo Caliban* (Buenos Aires, 2004), 37–43.
4. Mark Adams, *The Wellborn Science: Eugenics in Germany, France, Brazil, and Russia* (New York, 1990); Nancy Stepan, *The Hour of Eugenics: Race, Gender, and Nation in Latin America* (Ithaca, NY, 1991).
5. Daniel Kevles, *In the Name of Eugenics: Genetics and the Uses of Human Heredity* (Berkeley, CA, 1985); Robert Proctor, "The Origins of Racial Hygiene," in *Racial Hygiene: Medicine Under the Nazis*, Robert Proctor (Cambridge, MA, 1988), 10–46; Alexandra Minna Stern, *Eugenic Nation: Faults and Frontiers of Better Breeding in Modern America* (Berkeley, CA, 2005).
6. Stepan, *The Hour of Eugenics*.
7. Ibid.
8. Thomas Skidmore, *Preto no branco: Raça e nacionalidade no pensamento brasileiro*, trans. Raul de Sá Barbosa (Rio de Janeiro, 1976); Lilia M. Schwarcz, *O espetáculo das raças: Cientistas, instituições e questão racial no Brasil, 1870–1930* (São Paulo, 1993); Marcos Maio and Ricardo Ventura Santos, eds., *Raça, ciência e sociedade* (Rio de Janeiro, 1996).
9. Gilberto Hochman, Nísia Lima, and Marcos Maio, "The Path of Eugenics in Brazil: Dilemmas of Miscegenation," in *The Handbook of the History of Eugenics*, ed. Alison Bashford and Philippa Levine (Oxford, 2010).
10. "Os cientistas brasileiros tentavam tornar possível, ou pelo menos concebível, o reposicionamento de seu país e deles próprios no então chamado concerto das nações." Sérgio Carrara, "Estratégias anticoloniais: sífilis, raça e identidade nacional no Brasil do entreguerras" in *Cuidar, controlar, curar: Ensaios históricos sobre saúde e doença na*

América Latina e Caribe, ed. Gilberto Hochman and Diego Armus (Rio de Janeiro, 2004), 430.
11. Nancy Stepan, *The Hour of Eugenics: Race, Gender, and Nation in Latin America* (Ithaca, NY, 1991), 174.
12. Ibid., 177.
13. Ibid., 176.
14. George Stocking, *Race, Culture, and Evolution: Essays in the History of Anthropology* (Chicago, 1968).
15. Franz Boas, "Instability of Human Types," in *Papers on Inter-racial Problems Communicated to the First Universal Races Congress, Held at the University of London, July 26–29,* ed. Gustav Spiller (London, 1911), 101–2.
16. Stocking, *Race, Culture, and Evolution,* 184.
17. Vanderlei Sebastião de Souza, "Brazilian Eugenics and Its International Connections: An Analysis Based on the Controversies Between Renato Kehl and Edgard Roquette-Pinto, 1920–1930," *História, Ciências, Saúde—Manguinhos* 23 (2016): 93–110; Robert Wegner, "Dois geneticistas e a miscigenação: Octavio Domingues e Salvador de Toledo Piza no movimento eugenista brasileiro (1929–1933)," *Varia Historia* 61, no. 33 (2017): 79–107.
18. Stepan, *The Hour of Eugenics.*
19. Souza, "Brazilian Eugenics."
20. Ibid.
21. Hochman et al., "The Path of Eugenics in Brazil."
22. Ricardo Santos, "Guardian Angel on a Nation's Path: Contexts and Trajectories of Physical Anthropology in Brazil in the Late Nineteenth and Early Twentieth Centuries," *Current Anthropology* 53, no. S5 (2012): S17–S32; Nísia Trindade Lima and Dominichi Miranda de Sá, eds., *Antropologia brasiliana: ciência e educação na obra de Edgard Roquette-Pinto* (Rio de Janeiro, 2008); Vanderlei Sebastião de Souza, *Em busca do Brasil: Edgard Roquette-Pinto e o retrato antropológico brasileiro, 1905–1935* (Rio de Janeiro, 2017).
23. Nísia Trindade Lima, "Antropologia, raça e questão nacional: Notas sobre as contribuições de Edgard Roquette-Pinto e um possível diálogo com Franz Boas," in *Ciência, civilização e república nos trópicos,* ed. Alda Heizer and Antonio Videira (Rio de Janeiro, 2010), 268.
24. Correspondência de Edgard Roquette-Pinto a Rüdiger Bilden [Correspondence from Edgard Roquette-Pinto to Rüdiger Bilden], Rio de Janeiro, 15 October 1929, Roquette-Pinto personal archive, Centro de Memória da Academia Brasileira de Letras, Rio de Janeiro.
25. Edgard Roquette-Pinto, "Notas sobre os tipos antropológicos do Brasil," in *Actas e trabalhos do Primeiro Congresso Brasileiro de Eugenia* (Rio de Janeiro, 1929), 139.
26. "combinação de fatores hereditários . . . . seguiam leis biológicas já conhecidas." Ibid., 146.
27. Souza, "Brazilian Eugenics"; Proctor, "The Origins of Racial Hygiene"; Sheila Weiss, "The Race Hygiene Movement in Germany 1904–1945," in Adams, *The Wellborn Science,* 8–68.
28. Renato Kehl, *Lições de eugenia* (Rio de Janeiro, 1929); Renato Kehl, *Sexo e civilização: Aparas eugênicas* (Rio de Janeiro, 1933).
29. Kehl, *Sexo e civilização.*
30. "com mais amplitude e coragem . . . . O sistema eugênico alemão de proteção racial impressionou os cientistas e governantes de vários países, especialmente do norte eu-

ropeu que, aos poucos, estão adotando os mesmos dispositivos regulamentares." Renato Kehl, *Lições de eugenia*, 2nd ed. (Rio de Janeiro, 1935), 25–26.
31. Paula Habib, "Agricultura e biologia na Escola Superior de Agricultura Luiz de Queiroz (Esalq): Os estudos de genética nas trajetórias de Carlos Teixeira Mendes, Octavio Domingues e Salvador Toledo Piza Jr. (1917–1937)" (PhD diss., Casa de Oswaldo Cruz, 2010), 30–32.
32. Ibid., 120–22.
33. Octávio Domingues, *A hereditariedade em face da educação* (São Paulo, 1929), 154.
34. Salvador de Toledo Piza Jr. "Anotações à margem das Lições de Eugenia do Dr. Renato Kehl," *Revista de Agricultura* 5, nos. 1–2 (1930): 46.
35. Carta de Renato Kehl a Salvador de Toledo de Piza Júnior, Rio de Janeiro, 24 March 1930 and 19 August 1930, Fundo Pessoal Renato Kehl, Departamento de Arquivo e Documentação, Casa de Oswaldo Cruz.
36. "Genética é uma ciência deste século. Nasceu precisamente no 1º ano do século XX"; "o melhoramento das plantas, com os ensinamentos da Genética é uma prática corrente na agricultura moderna. . . . O aperfeiçoamento dos gados, por sua vez, é uma das melhores provas que se tem de que os princípios da Genética são verdadeiros. . . . Ora, passar a aplicação desses conhecimentos, do mundo animal para o Homem, é medida que se impõe por si mesma. Negar que o Homem é um animal, já não é mais permitido hoje. Logo, porque não aproveitar essas leis da Genética aplicáveis aos animais, para aplicá-las aos humanos?" Domingues, "Em torno dos problemas eugênicos," *Boletim de Eugenia* 3, no. 33 (1931): 3.
37. William Provine, "Geneticists and Race," *American Zoologist* 26, no. 3 (1986): 865–66.
38. "casamento do branco com o preto à luz da biologia . . . . complexo fatorial em que diversas unidades mendelianas se encontram envolvidas." Salvador de Toledo Piza Jr., "A hereditariedade da cor da pele no casamento branco-preto," *Boletim de Eugenia* 4, no. 39 (1932): 31.
39. Salvador de Toledo Piza Jr., "A hereditariedade da cor da pele no casamento branco-preto (conclusão)," *Boletim de Eugenia* 5, no. 41 (1933): 6.
40. "Não resta a menor dúvida que, sendo o homem um animal, como tal ele se comporte, reagindo ao meio de maneira fundamentalmente idêntica aos outros animais." "Não se pode experimentar com o homem." "Também sobre a pigmentação influi o aparelho endócrino." "Os produtos elaborados pelas diferentes glândulas de secreção interna influem poderosamente sobre o . . . metabolismo geral." "O branco e o preto são tão diferentes sob tão variados aspectos, que bem poderiam ser considerados como pertencentes a espécies distintas." "Ponto de vista antropológico . . . as uniões de branco com preto não são naturais." Ibid., 10–12.
41. The following observation by Kevles on the stance of the American eugenicist Charles Davenport could equally apply to Toledo Piza: "He combined Mendelian theory with incautious speculation. He knew that certain traits expressed combinations of elements—that is, were polygenic in origin—and had advanced the notion in his own research on skin color, yet his analysis of mental and behavioral traits usually neglected polygenic complexities." Kevles, *In the Name of Eugenics*, 48.
42. "grande valor científico, especialmente para o estudo e avaliação das consequências resultantes dos cruzamentos verificados entre nós." Kehl in the presentation of Jon Alfred Möjen, "Cruzamento de raças," *Boletim de Eugenia* 32 (1931): 1.
43. Ibid., 3.
44. Ibid., 4–5.

45. Nils Roll-Hansen, "Norwegian Eugenics: Sterilization as Social Reform," in *Eugenics and the Welfare State: Norway, Sweden, Denmark, and Finland,* ed. Gunnar Broberg and Nils Roll-Hansen (East Lansing, MI, 2005), 159.
46. Möjen, "Cruzamento de raças," 6.
47. "Pureza de raças não tem importância para o melhoramento da espécie." Domingues, *A hereditariedade em face da educação,* 145.
48. "um exemplo especial e precioso do encontro das três raças . . . . É o mestiçamento mais completo que a história registra." Ibid., 146.
49. Stepan, *The Hour of Eugenics,* 160.
50. "face desse fenômeno sociológico que se chama imigração." Domingues, *A hereditariedade em face da educação,* 146.
51. "que a mestiçagem não nos cria nenhuma condição de inferioridade e não nos oferece nenhum problema insolúvel"; "os pregoeiros do sangue ariano." Alvaro Fróes da Fonseca, "Os grandes problemas da anthropologia," in *Actas e trabalhos do Primeiro Congresso Brasileiro de Eugenia* (Rio de Janeiro, 1929), 78.
52. "Nenhum dos tipos da população brasiliana apresenta qualquer estigma de degeneração antropológica . . . As características de todos eles são as melhores que se poderiam desejar." Roquette-Pinto, "Notas sobre os tipos antropológicos," 145, 146.
53. Maria Lucía Garcia Pallares-Burke, *Gilberto Freyre: Um vitoriano nos trópicos* (São Paulo, 2005); Vanderlei Sebastião de Souza, "As 'leis da eugenia' na antropologia de Edgard Roquette-Pinto," in Lima and Sá, *Antropologia brasiliana,* 213–46; Santos, "Guardian Angel on a Nation's Path."
54. "Faltou-me quem me dissesse então, como em 1929 Roquette-Pinto aos arianistas do Congresso de Eugenia, que não eram simplesmente mulatos ou cafusos os indivíduos que eu julgava representarem o Brasil, mas cafusos e mulatos doentes." Freyre, *Casa-grande & senzala,* lvii.
55. "e o antropófago seria [apenas] o colonizador português. Havia, portanto, que eliminar a 'antropofagia africana', fixar a 'diferença' indígena e garantir, por muitos séculos, a deglutição imperial portuguesa." Omar Ribeiro Thomaz, *Ecos do Atlântico Sul: Representações sobre o terceiro império português* (Rio de Janeiro, 2002), 279–80.
56. William Shakespeare, *A tempestade* (Rio de Janeiro, 1999), 36.

Bibliography

Adams, Mark B., ed. *The Wellborn Science: Eugenics in Germany, France, Brazil, and Russia.* New York: Oxford University Press, 1990.

Boas, Franz. "Changes in the Bodily Form of Descendants of Immigrants." *American Anthropologist,* New Series, 14, no. 3 (July–September 1912): 530–62. Accessed 12 March 2018. https://www.jstor.org/stable/659886.

———. "Instability of Human Types." In *Papers on Inter-racial Problems Communicated to the First Universal Races Congress, Held at the University of London, July 26–29,* edited by Gustav Spiller, 99–103. London: P.S. King & Son, 1911.

Carrara, Sérgio. "Estratégias anticoloniais: Sífilis, raça e identidade nacional no Brasil do entreguerras." In *Cuidar, controlar, curar: Ensaios históricos sobre saúde e doença na América Latina e Caribe,* edited by Gilberto Hochman and Diego Armus, 427–53. Rio de Janeiro: Editora Fiocruz, 2004.

Domingues, Octávio. *A hereditariedade em face da educação.* São Paulo: Editora Melhoramentos, 1929.

Fonseca, Alvaro Fróes da. "Os grandes problemas da anthropologia." In *Actas e trabalhos do Primeiro Congresso Brasileiro de Eugenia,* 63–83. Rio de Janeiro: s/editora, 1929.

Freyre, Gilberto. *Casa-grande & senzala: Formação da família brasileira sob o regime de economia patriarcal.* Rio de Janeiro: José Olympio Editora, 1983.

Habib, Paula. "Agricultura e biologia na Escola Superior de Agricultura Luiz de Queiroz (Esalq): Os estudos de genética nas trajetórias de Carlos Teixeira Mendes, Octavio Domingues e Salvador de Toledo Piza Jr. (1917–1937)." PhD dissertation, Casa de Oswaldo Cruz, 2010.

Hochman, Gilberto. *A era do saneamento: As bases da política de saúde pública no Brasil.* São Paulo: Editora Hucitec/ANPOCS, 1998.

Hochman, Gilberto, Nísia Trindade Lima, and Marcos Chor Maio. "The Path of Eugenics in Brazil: Dilemmas of Miscegenation." In *The Handbook of the History of Eugenics,* edited by Alison Bashford and Philippa Levine, 493–510. Oxford: Oxford University Press, 2010.

Kehl, Renato. *Lições de Eugenia.* Rio de Janeiro: Editora Livraria Francisco Alves, 1929.

———. *Lições de Eugenia.* 2nd ed. Rio de Janeiro: Editora Livraria Francisco Alves, 1935.

———. *Sexo e civilização: Aparas eugênicas.* Rio de Janeiro: Editora Francisco Alves, 1933.

Kevles, Daniel. *In the Name of Eugenics: Genetics and the Uses of Human Heredity.* Berkeley, CA: University of California Press, 1985.

Lima, Nísia Trindade. "Antropologia, raça e questão nacional: Notas sobre as contribuições de Edgard Roquette-Pinto e um possível diálogo com Franz Boas." In *Ciência, civilização e república nos trópicos,* edited by Alda Heizer and Antonio Videira, 255–76. Rio de Janeiro: Mauad X, 2010.

Lima, Nísia Trindade, and Dominichi Miranda de Sá, eds. *Antropologia brasiliana: Ciência e educação na obra de Edgard Roquette-Pinto.* Belo Horizonte / Rio de Janeiro: UFMG / Fiocruz, 2008.

Maio, Marcos Chor, and Ricardo Ventura Santos, eds. *Raça, ciência e sociedade.* Rio de Janeiro: Editora Fiocruz, 1996.

Möjen, Jon Alfred. "Cruzamento de raças." *Boletim de Eugenia* 32 (1931): 1–6.

Pallares-Burke, Maria Lucía G. *Gilberto Freyre: Um vitoriano nos trópicos.* São Paulo: Editora Unesp, 2005.

Proctor, Robert. "The Origins of Racial Hygiene." In *Racial Hygiene: Medicine under the Nazis,* Robert Proctor, 10–46. Cambridge, MA: Harvard University Press, 1988.

Provine, William. "Geneticists and Race." *American Zoologist* 26, no. 3 (1986): 857–87.

Retamar, Roberto Fernández. *Todo Caliban.* Buenos Aires: Consejo Latinoamericano de Ciencias Sociales, 2004.

Rodó, José Enrique. *Ariel y Proteo selecto.* Caracas: Biblioteca Ayacucho, 1993.

Roll-Hansen, Nils. "Norwegian Eugenics: Sterilization as Social Reform." In *Eugenics and the Welfare State: Norway, Sweden, Denmark, and Finland,* 2nd ed., edited by Gunnar Broberg and Nils Roll-Hansen. East Lansing: Michigan State University Press, 2005.

Roquette-Pinto, Edgard. "Notas sobre os tipos antropológicos do Brasil." In *Actas e trabalhos do Primeiro Congresso Brasileiro de Eugenia,* 119–47. Rio de Janeiro, 1929.

Santos, Ricardo Ventura. "Guardian Angel on a Nation's Path: Contexts and Trajectories of Physical Anthropology in Brazil in the Late Nineteenth and Early Twentieth Centuries." *Current Anthropology* 53, no. 5 (2012): S17–S32.

Schwarcz, Lilia M. *O espetáculo das raças: cientistas, instituições e questão racial no Brasil, 1870–1930.* São Paulo: Companhia das Letras, 1993.

Shakespeare, William. *The Tempest.* Indiana: Indiana Publishing House, 1864. Translated by Barbara Heliodora as *A tempestade* (Rio de Janeiro: Lacerda, 1999).

Skidmore, Thomas. *Preto no branco: raça e nacionalidade no pensamento brasileiro.* Translated by Raul de Sá Barbosa. Rio de Janeiro: Paz e Terra, 1976.
Souza, Vanderlei Sebastião de. "As 'leis da eugenia' na antropologia de Edgard Roquette-Pinto." In Lima and Sá, *Antropologia brasiliana: Ciência e educação na obra de Edgard Roquette-Pinto,* 213–46.
———. "Brazilian Eugenics and its International Connections: An Analysis Based on the Controversies Between Renato Kehl and Edgard Roquette-Pinto, 1920–1930." *História, Ciências, Saúde—Manguinhos* 23 (2016): 93–110.
———. *Em busca do Brasil: Edgard Roquette-Pinto e o retrato antropológico brasileiro, 1905–1935.* Rio de Janeiro: Editora Fiocruz, 2017.
Stepan, Nancy. "Eugenia no Brasil, 1917–1940." In *Cuidar, controlar, curar: ensaios históricos sobre saúde e doença na América Latina e Caribe,* edited by Gilberto Hochman and Diego Armus, 330–91. Rio de Janeiro: Editora Fiocruz, 2004.
———. *The Hour of Eugenics: Race, Gender, and Nation in Latin America.* Ithaca, NY: Cornell University Press, 1991.
Stern, Alexandra Minna. *Eugenic Nation: Faults and Frontiers of Better Breeding in Modern America.* Berkeley: University of California Press, 2005.
Stocking, George W., Jr. *Race, Culture and Evolution: Essays in the History of Anthropology.* Chicago: University of Chicago Press, 1968.
Thomaz, Omar Ribeiro. *Ecos do Atlântico Sul: Representações sobre o terceiro império português.* Rio de Janeiro: Editora Universidade Federal do Rio de Janeiro / Fapesp, 2002.
Toledo Piza, Salvador de, Jr. "A hereditariedade da cor da pele no casamento branco-preto." *Boletim de Eugenia* 4, no. 39 (1932): 62–67.
———. "A hereditariedade da cor da pele no casamento branco-preto. (Conclusão)." *Boletim de Eugenia* 5, no. 41 (1933): 5–12.
———. "Anotações à margem das Lições de Eugenia do Dr. Renato Kehl." *Revista de Agricultura* 5, nos. 1–2 (1930): 46–49.
Wegner, Robert. "Dois geneticistas e a miscigenação: Octavio Domingues e Salvador de Toledo Piza no movimento eugenista brasileiro (1929–1933)." *Varia Historia* 33, no. 61 (2017): 79–107.
Weiss, Sheila Faith. "The Race Hygiene Movement in Germany 1904–1945." In Adams, *The Wellborn Science,* 8–68.

CHAPTER 5

Gilberto Freyre and the UNESCO Research Project on Race Relations in Brazil

Marcos Chor Maio

In the early 1950s, UNESCO sponsored a set of studies on race relations in Brazil. The initiative was part of the anti-racist agenda adopted by the agency in the context of the post-Holocaust era, at a moment when blatant racism persisted in countries like the United States and South Africa, decolonization was sweeping Asia and Africa, and the Cold War was dawning. Brazil was selected as the site of the UNESCO race relations research project in part because the notion had taken hold, under the influence of Gilberto Freyre's scholarship, that race relations were benign in Brazil, and it was hoped its lessons could be applied elsewhere. Although this idea found some footing among the social scientists who participated in the project both inside and outside UNESCO, it neither clouded their vision of racism and inequalities in Brazil nor deterred them from their goal of investigating the problems stemming from a process of modernization in a traditional society where racism was becoming visible. The initial project was expanded and refined by a transatlantic network of social scientists from the United States, France, and Brazil, including Charles Wagley, Roger Bastide, Virginia Leone Bicudo, Luiz de Aguiar Costa Pinto, Oracy Nogueira, Aniela Ginsberg, Florestan Fernandes, René Ribeiro, Edson Carneiro, and Marvin Harris. The researchers eventually concluded that Brazil's racial dynamics were more complex than first thought, while modernization was also making its impact felt. The project, which was conducted in both traditional and modern regions, including Rio de Janeiro, São Paulo, Pernambuco, and Bahia, produced a broad, new, diversified interpretative framework of race relations in Brazil.[1]

As early as the 1930s, Freyre had been a critic of racism, an ideology embraced by much of Brazil's educated elite. While most Brazilian scholars then shared the pessimistic outlook that the country's sizeable black population and intense miscegenation were roadblocks to modernity, Freyre emphasized the importance of ethnoracial "cooperation" among the Portuguese, blacks, and Indians, whom he saw as equal participants in shaping the national identity. While Freyre more than once highlighted the extreme violence of the relations between black and white that were engendered by the slave-owning plantation monoculture, the overriding idea in his classic *Casa-grande & senzala* (1933) (*The Masters and the Slaves*, 1946), based on his dialectic perspective of "antagonisms in balance," is one of relative fellowship among the races, deemed a hallmark of Brazilian society.[2] As a refined interpretation of the myth of Brazilian racial democracy, the Freyrean view of racial coexistence formed one of the main ideological pillars in the construction of a collective identity. If Brazilian society had previously been condemned by race, then, from Freyre's perspective, it would be saved by miscegenation, an Iberian legacy.

Freyre's prestige grew internationally from the 1930s through the 1950s. He presented lectures and seminars in the United States and Europe; published books and articles in countries such as the United States, France, England, Portugal, and Argentina; and participated in forums sponsored by multilateral agencies like the UN and UNESCO. The mid-1940s brought the first critiques of his sociological scholarship, labeled "essayistic" by many.[3] Paradoxically, while Freyre's portrait of Brazil as a country with civilizing lessons to offer inspired UNESCO's anti-racist policy, this interpretation also became construed in the 1950s as an intellectual discourse that lent legitimacy to Portugal's colonial empire, in the form of Luso-tropicalism.[4]

This chapter explores relations between Freyre and UNESCO in the context of the agency's research project on race relations in Brazil. After a brief overview of Freyre's analysis of race relations in Brazil, it describes the beginnings of UNESCO's race relations project and the role played by Brazilian scholars including Freyre and Arthur Ramos. The chapter next addresses Freyre's role in expanding the UNESCO project, above all by reinforcing the presence of the Northeast Region of Brazil through the inclusion of Recife, where Freyre had a substantial voice in the race relations study led by the anthropologist René Ribeiro. The focus then moves to Ribeiro and his work in leading the UNESCO studies in Recife. This is followed by a brief evaluation of Freyre's legacy that highlights his rebuttals to criticisms of his work, many of which were sparked by the release of the UNESCO research findings. The chapter concludes with remarks about Freyre's role in the UNESCO project.

Gilberto Freyre and the Topic of Race Relations in Brazil

In August 1950, during the design of the research project on race relations in Brazil, the anthropologists Alfred Métraux and Ruy Coelho—then with the Division of the Study of Racial Questions within UNESCO's Department of Social Sciences—drafted an evaluative overview of ethnoracial relations, in which Freyre was mentioned as "the most well-known Brazilian sociologist."[5] Métraux and Coelho saw *Casa-grande & senzala* as a landmark publication that had heightened intellectuals' awareness of Brazilian problems. In the preface to the first edition, Freyre said that his early 1920s encounter with Franz Boas, a professor of anthropology at Columbia University, had influenced his own identity as a member of the intelligentsia concerned with Brazil's fate. One of his main concerns dealt with miscegenation:

> I do not believe that any Russian student of the nineteenth-century Romantics showed graver concern for the fate of Russia than I for Brazil at the time I met Boas. It was as if everything depended on me and those of my generation, on our way of resolving long-standing questions. And of Brazil's issues, none bothered me as much as miscegenation.[6]

In the same preface, Freyre said Boas had taught him to draw the needed distinctions between race and culture, "between the effects of purely genetic relations and those of social influences, cultural heritage, and environment."[7] He also revealingly said Boas had taught him to valorize blacks and those of mixed race. When he omits references to non-European races like Indigenous peoples, Freyre is implicitly recognizing that the quintessential symbol of the racial mixing that lent Brazilian society its unique makeup is the black. Therefore, his evaluation of this process focused on relations between whites and blacks, which find expression in the contrasting terms appearing not only in the title of *Casa-grande & senzala* (literally, plantation house and slave quarters) but also in his second book, *The Mansions and the Shanties*, released in Portuguese in 1936.

The in-depth analysis of race relations presented in *Casa-grande & senzala* reveals a complex picture, where the master's cruelty and his intimate relations with slaves coexisted in balanced tension. More sophisticated than a mere idyllic depiction of Brazil's colonial past, Freyre's argument was that the complex relations between master and slave in colonial Brazil were interwoven with contrasts, reflecting tensions between an economic system that divided society into two extreme poles and an intimate coexistence within this society, evinced by miscegenation. The controversial belief in a Brazilian racial democracy thus became one of the most important ideological cornerstones of racial integration. This belief was substantial enough to attract international attention, including UNESCO's.

UNESCO's Anti-racist Agenda

UNESCO was established in the wake of the global upheaval of World War II. One of the agency's major goals was to arrive at an understanding of the international conflict and its most perverse consequence, the Holocaust. The statement of principles found in the preamble to its charter reflected the institution's liberal leanings and its psychological vision of World War II: "Since wars begin in the minds of men, it is in the minds of men that the defenses of peace must be constructed."[8] Within UNESCO, issues dealing with racial prejudice and discrimination had at first been linked to the project "Tensions Affecting International Understanding," an initiative of its Department of Social Sciences, approved during the Second Session of the General Conference, held in Mexico City in 1947. The aim of the study, over which Freyre wielded some influence, was to explore the causes of war, national rivalries, and racial stereotypes and prejudice against minorities and immigrants.[9]

Project Coordinator Otto Klineberg published findings on the causes of international conflict in *Tensions Affecting International Understanding: A Survey of Research*. In the chapter "Influences Making for Aggression," Brazil is cited as an example of a country with limited racial tensions. Klineberg, who was influenced by *Casa-grande & senzala*, wrote:

> It would be untrue to say that there is absolutely no race prejudice in Brazil, but there is only a fraction of what is usually found among White Americans in the United States. No restrictions of any kind are legally sanctioned anywhere in the country, and although individuals often exercise their preference for White as contrasted with Negro associates, the general picture of race relations in Brazil can be described as friendly.[10]

It was against this backdrop that Freyre was invited to take part in the "Tensions That Cause Wars" seminar, sponsored by the tensions project. Participants included Max Horkheimer, George Gurvitch, and Gordon Allport.[11] Freyre, the sole Latin American in attendance, called for a research agenda whose parameter would be a different West: one of the periphery and not ruled by the virulent racism exemplified by the United States. At a time when the Cold War was advancing, Freyre also identified Latin America as a region that could offer a recipe for alternative social relations.[12]

After the seminar, Freyre was invited to head UNESCO's Department of Social Science, at the suggestion of Hadley Cantril, a professor of social psychology at Princeton University and a symposium coordinator:

> I have talked in the past few days with those most responsible for the running of UNESCO. They have been kind enough to ask my advice about a candidate to serve as Head of the Social Science Department here. [The Sociologist Arvid] Brodersen

is Acting Head. As our program expands and takes on life, it becomes more and more essential to have a head who has standing in the field [of social sciences], some mellow wisdom, and all the other qualifications you would know better than I. I mentioned your name and was asked if I would write quite informally to inquire if you would be interested in the position. It would need to be for at least one year, the hope of course, that you would be interested for even a long time.[13]

While an invitation from an eminent international institution like UNESCO was frank recognition of Freyre's worldwide prestige, he nevertheless turned it down, probably because he was then a federal deputy for Pernambuco, representing the conservative National Democratic Union (União Democrática Nacional, UDN), and was deeply committed to establishing the Joaquim Nabuco Institute, a regional center for sociological research in Recife. Furthermore, in keeping with his positive view of miscegenation and his valorization of Afro-Brazilian culture, Freyre was involved in the fight against racial prejudice in the late 1940s and early 1950s and took part in several initiatives sponsored by black movements, particularly Abdias do Nascimento's Black Experimental Theater (TEN), Brazil's foremost expression of black activism. Moreover, he was heavily engaged in the debate that led to the 1951 enactment of the Afonso Arinos Law, Brazil's first anti-racist legislation.[14]

The Afonso Arinos Law, submitted by Deputy Afonso Arinos de Melo Franco (UDN-DF), came in response to a racist incident in São Paulo, where Katherine Durham, a black ballerina and anthropologist from the United States, was refused lodging at a well-known hotel.[15] Addressing the Chamber of Deputies during discussions of the draft bill, Freyre insisted that such racism was paradoxical in a country noted for its racial tolerance. He also mentioned the December 1949 debate on the heuristic value of the concept of race that had occurred under the auspices of UNESCO, as well as the agency's June 1950 decision to sponsor research on race relations in Brazil.[16] Freyre stated:

> At a time when men of science from nearly all corners of the world, certain that there are no superior or inferior races and stirred by Brazilian research, turn to Brazil and the Brazilian culture . . . as an example of a peaceful solution to the struggles between human groups that are prompted by racial prejudice, it is quite sad and even shameful for all of us Brazilians that no one less than an artist, an anthropologist, a woman with the intelligence and sensitivity of Katherine Dunham, whose dances . . . have brought the world the blending of blood and of different forms of body and culture, was brutishly barred from lodging at a São Paulo hotel.

Brazilian miscegenation and sociability was not compatible with this act of racism. Freyre saw the incident of discrimination as an exception, an attitude divergent from racial mixing, practiced by "someone who only appeared to have become part of the São Paulo community, to whose grandeur men of various bloods have contributed."[17]

Like Freyre, Arthur Ramos was a social scientist directly engaged with Afro-Brazilian culture. He became known for his research into the social conditions, culture, and religiosity of black Brazilians in the 1930s and 1940s, under the influence of acculturation theory. He also conducted research that displayed a growing concern with sociological aspects of Afro-Brazilian culture. After World War II, Ramos became a sympathizer of the Brazilian Communist Party and worked in collaboration with the black movement, especially with the TEN. He was invited to head UNESCO's Department of Social Sciences after Freyre turned the post down.[18] The decision to invite first Freyre and then Ramos was also a reflection of Latin America's marked presence during the early years of UNESCO, especially in key agency posts. Paulo Estevão de Berredo Carneiro (1901–1982), a chemical engineer and positivist, was the Brazilian representative on the Executive Council. Ramos also enjoyed the backing of Klineberg and Mexican UNESCO Director-General Jaime Torres Bodet (1902–1974), an educator, writer, and diplomat.

Ramos felt that part of the UNESCO social sciences program should be focused on the study of non-European human groups, especially black and Indigenous populations. In tune with the Brazilian intellectual elite, his perspective was driven by concern over the country's belated capitalist development and, its social and racial inequalities, and by the hope that Brazil would enter modernity. In other words, the program that Ramos outlined for the Department of Social Sciences prioritized the problems of nations of the periphery and the colonial world.[19] Freyre and Ramos shared the belief that UNESCO's social science research agenda should include experiences from the periphery.

The UNESCO Project under Construction

UNESCO's Department of Social Sciences began by choosing Bahia as the focus of its research.[20] The state had a sizeable mixed-race population, as well as research on African religions in Salvador, undertaken by scholars like Nina Rodrigues, Manoel Quirino, and, later, Ramos, dated to the late nineteenth century. Developed by Brazilian and foreign intellectuals alike, especially in the 1930s and 1940s, the image of a traditional cordial society averse to racial conflict dovetailed well with initial expectations within UNESCO.[21] The "great Brazilian 'black metropolis,'" characterized by intense miscegenation and harmony, had drawn the attention of social scientists, primarily in the United States.[22] Interest in Bahian society was also fueled by the disputes between the competing anthropological and sociological viewpoints held by scholars like Franklin Frazier and Melville Herskovits, who disagreed over black integration into US and Brazilian societies and how to fight racism in the United States.[23]

UNESCO wanted to analyze not only the race situation in Bahia but also the processes of social change and development that were occurring in the periphery during the postwar era. This is evident in the resolutions passed by the Fifth Session of the General Conference in Florence, which set as a goal the reduction of tensions that were caused as modern technology was introduced in nonindustrialized and industrializing nations.[24] Such an opportunity arose during project planning, when the anthropologist Charles Wagley contacted UNESCO. He had been working in Brazil since the late 1930s and was coordinating a joint project between Columbia University and the state of Bahia that was the brainchild of the educator Anísio Teixeira. The project, which was also assisted by the anthropologist Thales de Azevedo (Faculdade de Filosofia, Ciências e Letras da Bahia) and the sociologist Luiz de Aguiar Costa Pinto (Universidade do Brasil), entailed a set of studies to gather information in rural Bahian communities, ultimately to inform analyses aimed at fostering modernization in education and health in the countryside.

According to Wagley, Azevedo, and Costa Pinto, the project would "investigate the cultural changes associated with the introduction of Western technology and ideology, alongside complex administrative procedures in a backwards area where the process is now proceeding apace."[25] Wagley offered to work with the UNESCO project, a proposal that was well received by Métraux and Coelho, who also suggested investigating black social mobility in the city of Salvador, signaling UNESCO staff interest in social ascent and the role of race within a traditional urban center in transformation.[26] Azevedo was assigned this task.

Believing that processes of industrialization, social change, and racial tension were likewise relevant, Klineberg, Wagley, Costa Pinto, and Bastide proposed that the UNESCO project be broadened to include Rio de Janeiro and São Paulo.[27] Concomitantly, Brazil's black movement pressed for the research to move beyond the walls of academe. At the First Congress of Brazilian Blacks, held in Rio de Janeiro in August 1950 under the sponsorship of the TEN, Alberto Guerreiro Ramos, then a young sociologist and an active participant in the black movement, recognized UNESCO's salient role in "integrating racial minorities in countries where they are discriminated to greater or lesser extents." He also argued that the agency should ground its struggle against racism in "practical suggestions, avoiding studies of an academic or merely descriptive nature, which led to a false consciousness of racism."[28] Further, he had no interest in the race relations project, arguing instead that UNESCO, as a multilateral institution, should sponsor an International Congress on Race Relations to define a politically guided agenda for social intervention.

The final version of the UNESCO race relations project was defined in the second half of 1951 and was to include the study of race relations in Recife. As mentioned earlier, Freyre, in his capacity as a federal deputy, had been working since the 1940s to open the Joaquim Nabuco Institute, whose task would be sociological research on the living standards of rural workers in the Brazilian Northeast; it would also serve as a center for training students in sociological research methods at higher education and technical schools in the Northeast.[29] Freyre's initiative tied in with several early 1950s projects, such as the project to study the social and economic impact of dam construction on the São Francisco River and initiatives sponsored by the Institute of Social Anthropology (linked to the Smithsonian Institute) and the Special Public Health Service, the latter a partnership between the United States and Brazil.[30]

In August 1951, at a meeting with Métraux at the UNESCO headquarters in Paris, Freyre proposed that the project include the newly created Joaquim Nabuco Institute.[31] Métraux subsequently invited the anthropologist and physician René Ribeiro (1914–1990) to join the project and study the influence of Catholicism, Protestantism, and Afro-Brazilian religions on race relations in Recife.[32] In his push to include Recife, Freyre wanted not only to reinforce the institutionalization of research activities at the struggling new institute, and possibly internationalize it, but also to preserve his intellectual legacy within a climate of criticisms and controversy.

UNESCO Project in Recife

At the time of the First Afro-Brazilian Congress, held in 1934 and centered on the valorization of Afro-Brazilian culture, Ribeiro developed ties with Freyre.[33] But Ribeiro's definitive conversion to anthropology came through his contact with Melville Herskovits, a professor of anthropology at Northwestern University, who held that every culture should be understood in its own terms and according to its specific contributions to civilization. As Herskovits saw it, black cultural experiences in the Americas were characterized by the persistence of African elements alongside modernity, something apparent in his research into African culture in the United States, Africa, and Latin America.[34]

In September 1941, Herskovits arrived in Bahia to conduct a study that would explore the preservation of "cultural aspects originating in Africa [and] also the unique adaptation of African standards to the demands of a modern city, like Salvador, with a relative absence of challenges in reconciling these two styles of life."[35] In a lecture on possession in Afro-Brazilian religions, given in Recife and attended by Ribeiro, Herskovits presented the phenomenon as something not pathological but cultural. This contact would have a major impact on Ribeiro, ultimately shifting the direction of his research and drawing him into the controversy between Herskovits and Franklin Frazier over the influence of the African cultural legacy on Brazilian society.[36]

In the early 1940s, Frazier, a black professor of sociology at Howard University, extended his research to Haiti, Jamaica, and Brazil to observe family universes distinct from those found in the United States and to analyze the role these universes played in the assimilation of Western cultural values.[37] Frazier concluded that long-enduring African traditions in Bahia were nearly vanishing in response to ongoing social change.[38] He believed that intense miscegenation, the crisis of the patriarchal family, and black social mobility, especially in the face of Brazil's new urban-industrial impetus, would transform the Candomblé tradition into a kind of popular, folk culture. In his view, Salvador's black population was assimilating to Luso-Brazilian culture. In his critique of Frazier, Herskovits emphasized the persistence of African traits within Brazilian culture, manifested in clothing, food, religion, music, language, family structure, and gender roles.[39] When Herskovits interrogated Frazier's view of Bahian families, especially the poorest, whom the former saw as living largely outside of institutional bounds, he cited the cultural practice of *amasiamento* (cohabitation between a white man and black woman outside marriage), whose roots he traced to African polygamy.[40]

Ribeiro joined the debate, addressing the nature of *amasiamento* and aligning with Herskovits. Based on two studies conducted in 1939 and 1943, Ribeiro concluded that Pernambuco society construed the relationship as a legitimate conjugal union subject to moral sanctions. He believed that because a large contingent of enslaved Africans had come from a region dominated by the Yoruba and Daomé cultures, where polygamy was commonplace, *amasiamento* could be explained as a process of acculturation. Under this process, an African tradition had been adapted to the Western cultural standard of monogamous marriage through certain social and cultural practices characteristic of slavery, patriarchalism, and miscegenation, favoring unions of people from different socioeconomic levels.[41] Ribeiro's article seconded Herskovits's stance on the influence of African culture in Brazil and his position that *amasiamento* represented a variant of legal, religiously sanctioned monogamy rooted in African polygamy.[42] In 1945, Ribeiro's study was translated by Herskovits and released in the *American Sociological Review,* the same journal that published the controversy between Herskovits and Frazier. From 1948 to 1949, at Herskovits's invitation, Ribeiro did his master's at Northwestern. His thesis, "The Afro-Brazilian Cult Groups of Recife: A Study in Social Adjustment" (1949), was an ethnographic study of the structure, belief system, and rituals of the Xangô in Recife. In it, he explored the intersections between psychiatry and anthropology from the perspective of the school of culture and personality, led primarily by Ruth Benedict and Margaret Mead.[43]

After he returned from the United States, Ribeiro accepted Freyre's invitation to serve as head of the Department of Anthropology at the fledgling Joaquim Nabuco Institute. Shortly thereafter, Métraux invited Ribeiro to research the influence of religion in the shaping of race relations in Recife, a study that blended cultural anthropology, sociology, history, and social psychology. The Brazilian anthropologist began by analyzing the social formation in the Northeast and race relations in what was a miscegenated society. He grounded his work in arguments derived from *Casa-grande & senzala,* that is, that Portuguese settlers had a limited consciousness of race; that the framework was an agrarian, patriarchal, slave-owning colonial society; that the region had few white women; and that Catholicism there was of Luso bent: flexible, tolerant, and open to incorporating traditional Indigenous and African religious traditions in Brazil.

Drawing inspiration from Freyre, Ribeiro held that miscegenation wielded power as an instrument for democratizing social life but that this did not offset the weight of the exploitative system of slavery, which had swept across the New World and allowed for only selective integration of blacks. Colonial Brazil was no stranger to prejudice, as attested by the exclusion of black and mixed-race people from certain religious orders and by the formation of brotherhoods such as the Irmandade de Nossa Senhora do Rosário whose philanthropic work was directed specifically at the black population.[44] Like several social scientists in the UNESCO project, Ribeiro believed that the late-nineteenth-century abolition of slavery had not been accompanied by any substantive changes to capitalism or, consequently, by any shift from a rigidly hierarchical social structure reminiscent of a caste society to a class society. The monoculture system based on large estates limited social mobility, hampered formation of both a middle class and an internal market, and held back the incipient process of industrialization. Despite the absence of any formal barriers to black or mixed-race social mobility, economic and social conditions impeded ascent.

Concentrating his UNESCO research on relations between blacks and whites in Recife in the 1940s and 1950s, Ribeiro concluded that racial tensions intersected with gender relations and the preservation of social status, in that the white middle and upper classes, as well as the less privileged, reacted negatively when a family's social status was threatened by marriage between whites and blacks. At the same time, conflict was mitigated by a kind of interracial etiquette that required Brazilians to proceed with a certain caution when relating to those of another color; lighter-skinned Brazilians tried "not to offend blacks," while the darker skinned endeavored to avoid friction in their relations with whites. Because of slavery, skin color became associated with class, with darker-skinned people assigned to the bottom rungs of the social ladder. Still, Ribeiro credited the Northeast with a pattern of race relations more permeable to the social mobility of men of color, albeit still selective. In his words:

The longtime persistence of slavery and its abolition less than one century ago; extreme social stratification, deriving from the economic system and consequent constraints on social mobility still detected today; the pattern of male dominance in our culture; and the social importance of the family have led to relative immobility among the various ethnic groups in certain socioeconomic categories, hence resulting in hierarchization according to color and social position.[45]

Although Ribeiro's study bears the imprint of historical and sociological arguments, his rich ethnographic findings portrayed situations of racial bias and discrimination that were often at odds with his general hypotheses and conclusions, of a Freyrean nature, and they are open to alternative readings. The above passage clearly distinguishes the arguments that Ribeiro borrowed from Freyre from his own empirical research, grounded in ethnographic data that substantiated social and racial inequality and that approached from a perspective similar to that adopted by various other studies conducted as part of the UNESCO investigations by Fernandes, Costa Pinto, Bicudo, and Azevedo.[46]

Times of Controversy: The Legacy of Gilberto Freyre

Freyre became the target of political and academic criticism starting in the mid-1940s. His valuing of miscegenation in Brazilian society was challenged in the recurrent debate on the formation of the Brazilian national identity. In a controversial article, "Negros do Brasil" (Blacks of Brazil), that pointed to racial prejudice in the city of São Paulo, published in April 1947 in the prominent newspaper *O Estado de S. Paulo,* Paulo Duarte—a journalist, politician, ethnologist, and professor at the Universidade de São Paulo (USP)—attacked Freyre.

Duarte blamed the *Estado Novo* dictatorship for racial tensions in São Paulo. He held that Vargas populism encouraged the formation of black social movements, engendering an "inverted racism." He drew ties between the Vargas government and the work of Freyre and his followers. He fired criticism at the "minor sociology of the Northeast ... [comprised of] some romanticists who have revolved around the sociology of Mr. Gilberto Freyre, whose lightness is pleasant, often accurate, but on many points tinged with fantasy, meant to impose a Brazilian black or mixed-race type as the only legitimate Brazilian type." Duarte accused Freyre of confusing a Northeastern kind of miscegenation with a Brazilian kind and argued that the makeup of the population could hardly be considered cemented, given the country's ability to absorb new waves of migration. He also stated categorically that "Brazil wants to be a white country, not a black one."[47] This aligned him with the thinking of various Brazilian intellectuals of the era, like Oliveira Viana, one of Brazil's leading intellectuals, a proponent of the ideology of "whitening," and a main target of Freyre's criticism in *Casa-grande & senzala*. Duarte's positions were supported by such intellectuals as Vivaldo Coaracy and Sergio Milliet, while some representatives of the black movement and some Northeast writers—like Rachel de Queiroz and José Lins do Rego—defended Freyre.

Freyre came under further attack in the social sciences. Seeking to professionalize their field and enforce scientific rigor, social scientists in São Paulo had begun framing earlier scholarship, including Freyre's work, as backward and prescientific, bound to essayistic traditions and characterized by historical narrative. They wanted to discard the descriptive approach that had marked the 1920s and 1930s in favor of an objective language with precise empirical descriptions.[48] Attention was called to shortcomings in Freyre's work, including his alleged lack of scientific rigor, culturalist perspective, and literary style. For example, in the view of the sociologist Antonio Candido, from USP, Freyre had slipped into the "most regrettable social and historical sentimentalism, into conservatism and traditionalism. Enamored by his Brazilian cultural cycle, he is impelled to design a certain world, where progress is combined with the conservation of earlier characteristics."[49] At the same time, the sociologist Florestan Fernandes found fault with Freyre's book *Sociologia*, claiming it was devoid of original research, essayistic in style, imprecise in the scientific definition of sociological concepts, "verbose," and inspired by an "amphibian science" in detriment of "sociological exclusivism."[50] For his part, Costa Pinto criticized Freyre's modernist style.[51] Donald Pierson once stated that although Freyre had pioneered research into social and cultural relations in the Northeast, his analyses were normative and somewhat more literary than scientific.

In 1946, the first English translation of *Casa-grande & senzala* (*The Masters and the Slaves*) also drew disapproval. While Pierson, who played a decisive role in the development and institutionalization of social science research in Brazil in the 1940s and 1950s as a professor and researcher at the Free School of Sociology and Politics (Escola Livre de Sociologia e Política, ELSP), shared the view that race relations caused little strife in Brazil compared with the United States, he raised doubts about certain generalizing statements in the book. In his review of *The Masters and The Slaves*, he rebuked Freyre for maintaining concepts reminiscent of biological determinism, such as "economic instinct." In step with Pierson, Wagley deemed parts of the book outdated, like those addressing intelligence tests, "without mentioning the work of Otto Klineberg (*Racial Differences*, 1935)," the social psychologist who challenged the scientific character of intelligence measures as indicators of racial asymmetries.

Freyre's classic was also blasted for painting the Northeast as a general representation of Brazil when in fact, critics like Pierson argued, there were "several Brazils."[52] Wagley was one of those who felt Freyre generalized his historical and sociological findings on the Northeast.[53] In step with Pierson and Wagley, Sergio Buarque de Holanda charged that no matter how much the historical and sociological analysis of the sugar economy featured in *Casa-grande & senzala* was meant to decipher the formation of Brazilian society, it fell short even of explaining the Northeast as a whole:

> In the Northeast itself, [these criteria and perspectives] would barely apply, for example, to the regions where cropping and even slave labor did not play a stronger role. Or on the São Paulo plateau, where, during most of the colonial period, a certain form of polyculture dominated on a large scale. Or, further, in the far north, [where] extractive industries and forest gathering were broadly practiced. Or in the lands of Minas Gerais and especially in the fields of southern Brazil, where many of the features that the author from Pernambuco seems to attach inexorably to his portrait of our civilization, rooted in patriarchy and the slave system, are quite frankly missing.[54]

Freyre replied to his critics, especially to those from the stream of sociology prevalent at ELSP and USP in the 1940s and 1950s, in his lengthy preface to Ribeiro's *Religião e relações raciais*.[55] Central to the discord was the matter of more essayistic sociological language versus language concerned with empirical objectivity. Pierson and Fernandes were the voices of greatest weight during these discussions.

Addressing these objections, Freyre argued that his was the stance of a sociologist, citing as support recent publications in the United States that underscored the importance of the interface between literature and the social sciences, especially in the case of studies on racial prejudice. In that sense, Freyre contended, those who felt his work was "impressionistic," "picturesque," and "anecdotal"—critiques often found in the works of Costa Pinto and Guerreiro Ramos, the latter working at the Getúlio Vargas Foundation in Rio de Janeiro—failed to realize that his insights, perspicacious discernment, impressionism, and even "sensitivity for the picturesque" could open fertile new paths for academic sociology.[56] Freyre also highlighted the presence of modern social sciences at the Joaquim Nabuco Institute, whose staff included social scientists trained at Columbia and Northwestern. Without naming names, Freyre took aim at the social scientists involved in the UNESCO race relations project, especially those from southeastern Brazil:

> In 1950, when I detected that anthropologists and sociologists (some perhaps biased) who had been charged by UNESCO with conducting an investigation on race relations in Brazil intended to exclude from active participation in this investigation Recife, which had a flourishing social research institute specialized in regional studies—the Joaquim Nabuco Institute—I, in Paris, vehemently voiced my protest over this absurdity to the wise Professor Alfred Métraux: it was incomprehensible that an investigation of this nature could be undertaken in Brazil without relying on the collaboration of the new researchers from the [Institute].[57]

Freyre did not confine his complaints about UNESCO's initial exclusion of Recife and his institute from the race relations project to methodological concerns. Responding to those who criticized his view that Brazil was a country of benign race relations and his belief in a racial democracy, Freyre defended himself from accusations that he was one of those "merely lyrical sociologists or anthropologists who felt there had never been any form of racial prejudice among either the Portuguese or Brazilians." He also denied that *Casa-grande & senzala* offered an idealization of harmonious ethnoracial coexistence in Brazil:

> [Racial] prejudice among the Portuguese—right from their contact with blacks and the assimilation policy of the Infante [D. Henrique]—and Brazilians has always been, and still is, minimal as compared with its harsh expressions found among Europeans and other groups. Which would give Brazil the right to deem itself an advanced ethnic democracy, just as Switzerland considers itself—and is considered—an advanced political democracy, despite the fact, underscored by more than one observer, that there are among the Swiss not a few followers of [Charles] Maurras and his antidemocratic political ideas.[58]

For Freyre, the notion of a Brazilian racial democracy was a kind of Weberian ideal type. From his perspective, the presence of empirical elements incompatible with the elements used to construct this type did not negate the analytical value of the concept of racial democracy, nor did signs of racism alter the Luso cultural tradition that informed social interactions in Brazil. In the wake of the UNESCO project, which rejected the myth of a Brazilian brand of racial harmony, Freyre's interpretations, and particularly the historical and sociological arguments that underpinned his optimistic interpretation of Brazilian society in matters of race, had become the target of numerous criticisms.[59] Moreover, contradicting Freyre's outlook, the Recife branch of the UNESCO project, grounded in Ribeiro's ethnographic studies, ultimately uncovered a broad gamut of situations of prejudice and racial discrimination.

Closing Remarks

When Freyre was in Paris in August 1951 to wrap up the agreement bringing Pernambuco into the UNESCO research project, Métraux invited him to write a brief introductory book for the project, one that would summarize *The Masters and the Slaves* and *The Mansions and the Shanties* and offer a broad panorama of the history of blacks in Brazil. Freyre accepted the invitation but some months later made this task contingent on his prior access to the papers produced under the UNESCO project. Métraux saw no point to Freyre's precondition, since the Swiss ethnologist's idea was for the book to be historical in nature and thus not overlap with any contemporary sociological or anthropological studies on race relations in Brazil.[60] In asking Freyre to write along historical, essayistic lines, Métraux was in effect reinforcing the voices of various social scientists who accused Freyre of not engaging in scientific sociology. It may well be that Freyre felt his proviso would offer him an opportunity to respond to his critics.

Freyre eventually ended up writing a brief introductory article to a dossier compiling some of the research findings.[61] Edited by Métraux, the dossier was published in *Courier,* UNESCO's science communication journal, as "An Inquiry on Race Relations in Brazil" (1952). The text was written around the time of Freyre's trip to the Portuguese Empire and displayed signs of his Luso-tropicalism. In his introduction, "The Negro's Role in Brazilian History," Freyre reiterated the notion of Iberian exceptionalism and his contention that blacks played a valuable role in the formation of Brazilian society. He offered an ambivalent view of Brazilian slavery, where social life in mansion houses and slave quarters was permeated by "antagonisms in balance." He thus maintained his argument that slavery had been characterized by both violence and a certain closeness between masters and slaves, feeding an intense process of miscegenation that in turn favored the emergence of a broad, diversified cultural and religious universe where the presence of blacks figured large.[62]

In principle, within the context of the UNESCO research project, Freyre's perspective on race relations in Brazil did not change. His preface to Ribeiro's *Religião e relações raciais* reaffirmed the theses about the democratizing, integrating force of Brazilian miscegenation as laid out in *The Masters and the Slaves.* Yet, Freyre appeared to relativize the significance he had previously attributed to the category "ethnic democracy," now identifying it as an operational concept, or "ideal type," and no longer as the expression of a substantive reality. This seems to be how Freyre reacted to the critiques of his work and analyses of his "legacy" within the context of the UNESCO project and managed to restate, albeit somewhat subtly, his own interpretations.

In 1956, Ribeiro published *Religião e relações raciais,* a major product of the UNESCO research project. Although Freyre's historical and sociological arguments wielded great influence over Ribeiro, the book cast the Northeast as a region in transition, where an agrarian, patriarchal, monoculture system, wrapped in a sugarcoated Catholicism, had failed to become a more dynamic, open economy, typical of industrialized societies. At the same time, this process of change sharpened ethnic-racial divisions. Further, Ribeiro held that Brazil's slave-owning past had produced a selective, filtered brand of miscegenation, where the division into classes corresponded to a pattern of racial divides, with blacks and darker-skinned individuals making up the bulk of the lower tiers, while the light skinned and whites comprised the upper. Further according to Ribeiro's study, prejudice against blacks and those of mixed race—manifested, for example, in resistance to miscegenation—was more acutely visible in the white middle and upper strata. Ribeiro had also uncovered the race etiquette that tends to camouflage situations of ethnoracial conflict. As identified by his research, the intensification of bias and racial discrimination in Recife was not consistent with the picture of harmonious race relations so dear to Freyre or with UNESCO's initial idea that Brazil represented an example of racial democracy.

MARCOS CHOR MAIO is Researcher and Professor of History of Science and Health at the Casa de Oswaldo Cruz. He received his PhD in political science from the Instituto Universitário de Pesquisas do Rio de Janeiro and has been a visiting scholar in the Department of History at New York University (2011–2012). He is the author of *Nem Rotschild nem Trotsky: O pensamento anti-semita de Gustavo Barroso* (1992) and the coeditor of *Raça, ciência e sociedade* (1996) and *Raça como questão: História, ciência e identidades no Brasil* (2010). Currently, he is studying the relationship between social psychology, sociology, and anthropology on the studies of race and racism (1940–1960).

Notes

This chapter was translated by Diane Grosklaus Whitty.
1. On the series of studies made as part of the UNESCO race relations project, see Charles Wagley, Thales de Azevedo, and Luiz Costa Pinto, "Uma pesquisa sobre a vida social no estado da Bahia, Salvador," *Publicações do Museu do Estado / Secretaria de Educação e Saúde* 11 (1950); Thales de Azevedo, *Les élites de couleur dans une ville brésilienne* (Paris, 1953); Luiz de Aguiar Costa Pinto, *O negro no Rio de Janeiro: Relações de raças numa sociedade em mudança* (São Paulo, 1953); Roger Bastide and Florestan Fernandes, eds., *Relações raciais entre negros e brancos em São Paulo* (São Paulo, 1955); Oracy Nogueira, "Relações raciais no município de Itapetininga," in Bastide and Fernandes, *Relações raciais,* 362–554; Virginia L. Bicudo, *Atitudes raciais de pretos e mulatos em São Paulo* (São Paulo, 2010); Aniela Ginsberg, "Pesquisas sobre as atitudes de um grupo de escolares de São Paulo em relação às crianças de cor," in Bastide and Fernandes, *Relações raciais,* 311–61; René Ribeiro, *Religião e relações raciais* (Rio de Janeiro, 1956). On the history of the UNESCO race relations project, see Marcos Chor Maio, "UNESCO and the Study of Race Relations in Brazil: Regional or National Issue?" *Latin American Research Review* 36, no. 2 (2001): 118–36.
2. Ricardo Benzaquen de Araújo, *Guerra e paz: Casa-grande & senzala e a obra de Gilberto Freyre nos anos 30* (Rio de Janeiro, 1994); Élide Rugai Bastos, *As criaturas de Prometeu: Gilberto Freyre e a formação da sociedade brasileira* (São Paulo, 2006).
3. Luiz Antonio Castro Santos, "O espírito da aldeia: Orgulho ferido e vaidade na trajetória intelectual de Gilberto Freyre," *Novos Estudos Cebrap* 27 (1990): 45–66; Simone Meucci, "Gilberto Freyre e a sociologia no Brasil: Da sistematização à constituição do campo científico," PhD diss., Instituto e Filosofia e Ciências Humanas, 2006.
4. Cláudia Castelo, *"O modo de estar no mundo": O luso-tropicalismo e a ideologia colonial portuguesa (1933–1961)* (Porto, 1999); Omar Ribeiro Thomaz, "Do saber colonial ao Luso-Tropicalismo: 'Raça' e 'nação' nas primeiras décadas do salazarismo," in *Raça,*

ciência e sociedade, ed. Marcos Chor Maio and Ricardo Ventura Santos (Rio de Janeiro: Editora Fiocruz, 1996), 85–106.

5. Alfred Métraux and Ruy Coelho, "Suggestions for Research on Race Relations in Brazil," Race Questions & Protection of Minorities (RQ&PM), REG 323.1, Part II up to 31/VII/50 (BOX REG 145), UNESCO Archives, 1.
6. Gilberto Freyre, *Casa-grande & senzala: Formação da família brasileira sob o regímen de economia patriarchal* (Rio de Janeiro, 1933), xii, trans. Samuel Putnam as *The Masters and the Slaves: A Study in the Development of Brazilian Civilization* (Knopf: New York, 1946).
7. Today we tend to relativize the influence that Boas's criticism of racial determinism had on Freyre's work. Freyre did not actually replace the concept of race with that of culture but in fact tried to integrate the two viewpoints from a neo-Lamarkian perspective. Nancy L. Stepan, *"The Hour of Eugenics": Race, Gender, and Nation in Latin America* (Ithaca, NY, 1991); Araújo, *Guerra e paz*; Marcos Chor Maio, "Estoque semita: A presença dos judeus em Casa-grande & senzala," *Luso-Brazilian Review* 36, no. 1 (1999): 95–110.
8. UNESCO, *Conference for the Establishment of the United Nations Educational, Scientific and Cultural Organisation: Held at the Institute of Civil Engineers, London, from the 1st to the 16th November, 1945*, ECO/CONF./29 (Paris, 1945), 2.
9. Otto Klineberg, "A Challenge to the Sciences of Man," *International Social Science Bulletin* 1, nos. 1–2 (1949): 11–21.
10. Otto Klineberg, *Tensions Affecting International Understanding* (New York, 1950), 192.
11. Letter from Hadley Cantril to Gilberto Freyre, 13 August 1948, Arquivo do Instituto Gilberto Freyre.
12. Gilberto Freyre, "Internationalizing Social Science," in *Tensions That Cause Wars*, ed. Hadley Cantril (Urbana, 1948), 149.
13. Letter from Cantril to Freyre, 13 August 1948.
14. Monica Grin and Marcos Chor Maio, "O antirracismo da ordem no pensamento de Afonso Arinos de Melo Franco," *Topoi* 14, no. 26 (2013): 33–45.
15. George Reid Andrews, *Blacks and Whites in São Paulo, Brazil, 1888–1988* (Madison, WI, 1991).
16. Marcos Chor Maio and Ricardo Ventura Santos, "Antiracism and the Uses of Science in the Post–World War II: An Analysis of UNESCO's First Statements on Race (1950 and 1951)," *Virtual Brazilian Anthropology* 12, no. 2 (2015): 1–26.
17. Gilberto Freyre, "Discurso de Gilberto Freyre na Câmara dos Deputados no dia 17 de julho de 1950," *Quilombo* 10 (1950): 9 (this and the previous extract).
18. Arthur Ramos, "Os grandes problemas da Antropologia brasileira," *Sociologia* 10, no. 4 (1948): 213–26; Mariza Corrêa, *As ilusões da liberdade: A Escola Nina Rodrigues e a antropologia no Brasil* (Rio de Janeiro, 2013); Jerry Dávila, *Diploma of Whiteness: Race and Social Policy in Brazil, 1917–1945* (Durham, NC, 2003); Marcos Chor Maio, "Caminhos de Arthur Ramos: A busca do Brasil como projeto civilizatório," in *Médicos intérpretes do Brasil*, ed. Gilberto Hochman and Nísia Trindade Lima (São Paulo, 2015), 362–89.
19. Maio, "UNESCO and the Study of Race Relations in Brazil."
20. Alfred Métraux, "UNESCO and the Racial Problem," *International Social Science Bulletin* 2, no. 3 (1950): 384–90.
21. Beatriz G. Dantas, *Vovó nagô e papai branco: Usos e abusos da África no Brasil* (Rio de Janeiro, 1988).
22. Alfred Métraux, "Brazil: Land of Harmony for All Races?" *UNESCO Courier* 4, no. 4 (1951): 3; Robert Park, "Introduction: The Career of the Africans in Brazil," in *Negroes*

in Brazil: A Study of Race Contact at Bahia, by Donald Pierson (Chicago, 1942); Lorenzo Dow Turner, "Some Contacts of Brazilian Ex-slaves with Nigeria, West Africa," *Journal of Negro History* 27 (1943): 55–67; Ruth Landes, *The City of Women* (1947; repr., Albuquerque, 1994); Franklin Frazier, "The Negro Family in Bahia, Brazil," *American Sociological Review* 7, no. 4 (1942): 465–78; Donald Pierson, *Brancos e pretos na Bahia: Estudo de contato racial* (São Paulo, 1945); Melville Herskovits, "The Negro in Bahia, Brazil: A Problem in Method," *American Sociological Review* 8, no. 4 (1943): 394–404.

23. Livio Sansone, "USA and Brazil in Gantois: Power and the Transnational Origin of Afro-Brazilian Studies, *Vibrant Brazilian Journal* 8, no. 1 (2011): 536–67.
24. UNESCO, *Records of the General Conference of the United Nations Education, Scientific and Cultural Organization: Fifth Session, Florence, 1950—Resolutions* (Paris, 1950), 40.
25. Wagley et al., "Uma pesquisa sobre a vida social," 14.
26. Letter from Charles Wagley to Alfred Métraux, 18 June 1950, RQ&PM, REG 323.1, Part I up to 30/VI/50 (BOX REG 145), UNESCO Archives, 1; letter from Ruy Coelho to Charles Wagley, 27 July 1950, RQ&PM, REG 323.1, Part II up to 31/VII/50 (BOX REG 145), UNESCO Archives; letter from Otto Klineberg to R. C. Angell (Head, Department of Social Sciences), comments on memorandum regarding Research on Race Relations in Brazil, 1 August 1950, RQ&PM, REG 323.1, Part II up to 31/VII/50 (BOX REG 145), UNESCO Archives, 4.
27. Letter from Klineberg to Angell, 1 August 1950; letter from Charles Wagley to Ruy Coelho, 6 September 1950, RQ&PM, REG 323.1, Part II up to 31/VII/50 (BOX REG 145), UNESCO Archives, 2; letter from Luiz de Aguiar Costa Pinto to Alfred Métraux, 31 July 1950, statement on race, REG file 323.12 A 102, Part I (BOX REG 146), UNESCO Archives, 1; letter from Alfred Métraux to Roger Bastide, 18 August 1950, RQ&PM, REG 323.1, Part II up to 31/VII/50 (BOX REG 145), UNESCO Archives.
28. Alberto Guerreiro Ramos, "A UNESCO e as relações de raça," in *O negro revoltado*, ed. Abdias do Nascimento (Rio de Janeiro, 1982), 237.
29. "O Instituto Joaquim Nabuco de Pesquisa Social," *Boletim do Instituto Joaquim Nabuco* 1, no. 1 (1952): 113.
30. Marcos Chor Maio, Nemuel da Silva Oliveira, and Thiago da Costa Lopes, "Donald Pierson e o Projeto do Vale do Rio São Francisco: Cientistas sociais em ação na era do desenvolvimento," *DADOS—Revista de Ciências Sociais* 56, no. 2 (2013): 245–84; André Luiz V. de. Campos, *Políticas internacionais de saúde na era Vargas: O Serviço Especial de Saúde Pública, 1942–1960* (Rio de Janeiro, 2006).
31. Alfred Métraux, "Rapport au Directeur Géneral sur mission au Brésil," 29 October–12 December 1951, RQ&PM, REG 323.1, Part II up to 31/VII/50 (BOX REG 145), UNESCO Archives, 1.
32. Gilberto Freyre, "Mestre Métraux em Salvador da Bahia," *O Cruzeiro*, 8 September 1951, 2; Paul Freston, "Um império na província: O Instituto Joaquim Nabuco em Recife," in *História das ciências sociais no Brasil*, vol. 1, ed. Sérgio Miceli (São Paulo, 1989), 316–58.
33. René Ribeiro, "Tempo de experiência," *Revista de Ciências Sociais* 14–15, nos. 1–2 (1984): 83–100.
34. Walter Jackson, "Melville Herskovits and the Search for Afro-American Culture," in *Malinowski, Rivers, Benedict and Others: Essays on Culture and Personality*, ed. George W. Stocking Jr. (Madison, WI, 1986), 96–98.
35. Herskovits, "The Negro in Bahia, Brazil," 264.
36. René Ribeiro, "Melville J. Herskovits: O estudo da cultura e o fator humano," *Revista do Museu Paulista* 14 (1963): 287; Kevin Yelvington, "Melville J. Herskovits e a insti-

tucionalização dos estudos Afro-Americanos," in *Projeto UNESCO no Brasil: Textos críticos,* ed. Cláudio Luiz Pereira and Livio Sansone (Salvador, 2007), 149–72; Jerry Gershenhorn, *Melville J. Herskovits and the Racial Politics of Knowledge* (Lincoln, NE, 2004).
37. David E. Hellwig, "E. Franklin Frazier's Brazil," *Western Journal of Black Studies* 15, no. 2 (1991): 87.
38. Frazier, "The Negro Family," 478.
39. Herskovits, "The Negro in Bahia, Brazil"; Melville Herskovits, "Pesquisas etnológicas na Bahia," *Afro-Ásia* 4–5 (1967): 89–106.
40. Frazier, "The Negro Family," 477.
41. René Ribeiro, "On the *Amaziado* Relationship and Other Aspects of Family in Recife," *American Sociological Review* 10, no. 1 (1945): 51.
42. Ibid., 50.
43. René Ribeiro, *Cultos afro-brasileiros do Recife: Um estudo de ajustamento social* (1962; repr., Recife, 1978), 141–44.
44. Ribeiro, *Religião e relações raciais,* 66–67.
45. Ibid., 106.
46. Roberto Motta, "Gilberto Freyre, René Ribeiro e o Projeto UNESCO," in Pereira and Sansone *Projeto UNESCO no Brasil,* 38–60; Marcos Chor Maio, "Florestan Fernandes, Oracy Nogueira, and the UNESCO Project on Race Relations in São Paulo," *Latin American Perspectives* 38, no. 3 (2011): 136–14; Marcos Chor Maio, "Educação sanitária, estudos de atitudes raciais e psicanálise na trajetória de Virgínia Leone Bicudo," *Cadernos Pagu* 35 (2010): 309–55; Antonio Sergio Guimarães, "Cor, classe e status nos estudos de Pierson, Azevedo e Harris na Bahia: 1940-1960," in *Raça, ciência e sociedade,* ed. Marcos Chor Maio and Ricardo Ventura Santos (Rio de Janeiro, 1996).
47. Paulo Duarte, "Negros do Brasil," *O Estado de S. Paulo* 16 April 1947, 5–6.
48. Meucci, "Gilberto Freyre e a sociologia no Brasil."
49. Antonio Candido, "Depoimento," in *Plataforma da nova geração,* ed. Mário Neme (Porto Alegro, 1945), 39.
50. Florestan Fernandes, "*Sociologia*," *Jornal de São Paulo,* 3 and 8 January 1946, Fundo Florestan Fernandes, Universidade Federal de São Carlos.
51. Luiz de Aguiar Costa Pinto, "O negro no futebol brasileiro," *Sociologia* 9, no. 2 (1947): 182.
52. Donald Pierson, Review of *The Masters and the Slaves: A Study in the Development of Brazilian Civilization, American Sociological Review* 12, no. 5 (1947): 609.
53. Charles Wagley, Review of *The Masters and the Slaves: A Study in the Development of Brazilian Civilization, Political Science Quarterly* 61, no. 4 (1946): 626–27.
54. Sérgio Buarque Holanda, "Sociedade patriarcal (partes 1–2)," *Folha da Manhã,* 10 and 13 November 1951.
55. Gilberto Freyre, "Prefácio," in Ribeiro, *Religião e relações raciais,* 5–31.
56. Ibid., 8–9. For typical critiques of Freyre, see Costa Pinto, *O negro no Rio de Janeiro*; Alberto Guerreiro Ramos, "O problema do negro na Sociologia Brasileira," *Cadernos do Nosso Tempo* 2, no. 2 (1954): 189–230.
57. Freyre, "Prefácio," 18.
58. Ibid., 21–22.
59. Nogueira, "Relações raciais no município de Itapetininga"; Costa Pinto, *O negro no Rio de Janeiro*; Bastide and Fernandes, *Relações raciais.*
60. Letter from Alfred Métraux to René Ribeiro, 31 March 1952, and letter from Alfred Métraux to René Ribeiro, 21 April 1952, Arquivo da Família de René Ribeiro.

61. Texts by the following social scientists were also included in the dossier published in the journal *Courier*: Roger Bastide, Charles Wagley, Harry William Huntchinson, Luiz de Aguiar Costa Pinto, and Thales de Azevedo.
62. Gilberto Freyre, "The Negro's Role in Brazilian History," *UNESCO Courier* 5, nos. 8–9 (1952): 7–8.

Bibliography

"O Instituto Joaquim Nabuco de Pesquisa Social." *Boletim do Instituto Joaquim Nabuco* 1, no. 1 (1952): 113.
Araújo, Ricardo Benzaquen de. *Guerra e paz: Casa-grande & senzala e a obra de Gilberto Freyre nos anos 30*. Rio de Janeiro: Editora 34, 1994.
Azevedo, Thales de. *Les élites de couleur dans une ville brésilienne*. Paris: UNESCO, 1953.
Bastide, Roger, and Florestan Fernandes, eds. *Relações raciais entre negros e brancos em São Paulo*. São Paulo: Editora Anhembi, 1955.
Bastos, Élide Rugai. *As criaturas de Prometeu: Gilberto Freyre e a formação da sociedade brasileira*. São Paulo: Global, 2006.
Bicudo, Virginia L. *Atitudes dos Alunos dos Grupos Escolares em relação com a Cor dos seus Colegas*. São Paulo: Sociologia e Política.
Campos, André Luiz V. de. *Políticas internacionais de saúde na era Vargas: O Serviço Especial de Saúde Pública, 1942–1960*. Rio de Janeiro: Editora Fiocruz, 2006.
Candido, Antonio. "Depoimento." In *Plataforma da nova geração*, edited by Mário Neme, 29–40. Porto Alegre: Editora Globo, 1945.
Castelo, Cláudia. *"O modo de estar no mundo": O luso-tropicalismo e a ideologia colonial portuguesa (1933–1961)*. Porto: Edições Afrontamento, 1999.
Castro Santos, Luiz Antonio. "O espírito da aldeia: Orgulho ferido e vaidade na trajetória intelectual de Gilberto Freyre." *Novos Estudos Cebrap* 27 (1990): 45–66.
Corrêa, Mariza. *As ilusões da liberdade: A Escola Nina Rodrigues e a antropologia no Brasil*. Rio de Janeiro: Editora Fiocruz, 2013.
Costa Pinto, Luiz de Aguiar. "O negro no futebol brasileiro." *Sociologia* 9, no. 2 (1947): 181–84.
———. *O negro no Rio de Janeiro: Relações de raças numa sociedade em mudança*. São Paulo: Companhia Editora Nacional, 1953.
Dantas, Beatriz G. *Vovó nagô e papai branco: Usos e abusos da África no Brasil*. Rio de Janeiro: Graal, 1988.
Dávila, Jerry. 2003. *Diploma of Whiteness: Race and Social Policy in Brazil*. Durham, NC: Duke University Press, 2003.
Frazier, Franklin. "The Negro Family in Bahia, Brazil." *American Sociological Review* 7, no. 4 (1942): 465–78.
Freston, Paul. "Um império na província: O Instituto Joaquim Nabuco em Recife." In *História das ciências sociais no Brasil*, vol. 1, edited by Sérgio Miceli, 316–58. São Paulo: IDESP/Vértice/Finep, 1989.
Freyre, Gilberto. *Casa-grande & senzala: Formação da família brasileira sob o regímen de economia patriarchal*. Rio de Janeiro: Editora Maia & Schmidt, 1933. Translated by Samuel Putnam as *The Masters and the Slaves: A Study in the Development of Brazilian Civilization* (Knopf: New York, 1946).
———. "Discurso de Gilberto Freyre na Câmara dos Deputados no dia 17 de julho de 1950." *Quilombo* 10 (1950): 9.

———. "Internationalizing Social Science." In *Tensions That Cause Wars*, edited by Hadley Cantril, 139–65. Urbana: University of Illinois Press, 1949.
———. "Prefácio." In Ribeiro, *Religião e relações raciais*, 5–31.
———. "The Negro's Role in Brazilian History." *UNESCO Courier* 5, nos. 8–9 (1952): 7–8.
Gershenhorn, Jerry. *Melville J. Herskovits and the Racial Politics of Knowledge*. Lincoln: University of Nebraska Press, 2004.
Ginsberg, Aniela. "Pesquisas sobre as atitudes de um grupo de escolares de São Paulo em relação às crianças de cor." In Bastide and Fernandes, *Relações raciais*, 311–61.
Grin, Monica, and Marcos Chor Maio. "O antirracismo da ordem no pensamento de Afonso Arinos de Melo Franco." *Topoi* 14, no. 26 (2013): 33–45.
Guerreiro Ramos, Alberto. "A UNESCO e as relações de raça." In *O negro revoltado*, edited by Abdias do Nascimento, 233–42. Rio de Janeiro: Nova Fronteira, 1982.
———. "O problema do negro na Sociologia Brasileira." *Cadernos do Nosso Tempo* 2, no. 2 (1954): 189–230.
Guimarães, Antonio Sergio. "Cor, classe e *status* nos estudos de Pierson, Azevedo e Harris na Bahia: 1940–1960." In *Raça, ciência e sociedade*, edited by Marcos Chor Maio and Ricardo Ventura Santos, 143–157. Rio de Janeiro: Editora Friocruz, 1996.
Hellwig, David. "E. Franklin Frazier's Brazil." *Western Journal of Black Studies* 15, no. 2 (1991): 87–94.
Herskovits, Melville. "Pesquisas etnológicas na Bahia." *Afro-Ásia* 4–5 (1967): 89–106. First published 1943 by Governo do Estado (Salvador).
———. "The Negro in Bahia, Brazil: A Problem in Method." *American Sociological Review* 8, no. 4 (1943): 394–404.
Jackson, Walter. "Melville Herskovits and the Search for Afro-American Culture." In *Malinowski, Rivers, Benedict and Others: Essays on Culture and Personality*, edited by George W. Stocking Jr., 95–186. Madison: University of Wisconsin Press, 1986.
Klineberg, Otto. "A Challenge to the Sciences of Man." *International Social Science Bulletin* 1, nos. 1–2 (1949): 11–21.
———. *Tensions Affecting International Understanding*. New York: Social Science Research Council, 1950.
Landes, Ruth. *The City of Women*. 1947. Reprint, Albuquerque: University of New Mexico Press, 1994.
Maio, Marcos Chor. "Caminhos de Arthur Ramos: A busca do Brasil como projeto civilizatório." In *Médicos intérpretes do Brasil*, edited by Gilberto Hochman and Nísia Trindade Lima, 362–89. São Paulo: Editora Hucitec, 2015.
———. "Educação sanitária, estudos de atitudes raciais e psicanálise na trajetória de Virgínia Leone Bicudo." *Cadernos Pagu* 35 (2010): 309–55.
———. "Estoque semita: A presença dos judeus em *Casa-grande & senzala*." *Luso-Brazilian Review* 36, no. 1 (1999): 95–110.
———. "Florestan Fernandes, Oracy Nogueira, and the UNESCO Project on Race Relations in São Paulo." *Latin American Perspectives* 38, no. 3 (2011): 136–49.
———. "UNESCO and the Study of Race Relations in Brazil: Regional or National Issue?" *Latin American Research Review* 36, no. 2 (2001): 118–36.
Maio, Marcos Chor, and Ricardo Ventura Santos. "Antiracism and the Uses of Science in the Post–World War II: An Analysis of UNESCO's First Statements on Race (1950 and 1951)." *Virtual Brazilian Anthropology* 12, no. 2 (2015): 1–26.
Maio, Marcos Chor, Nemuel da Silva Oliveira, and Thiago da Costa Lopes. "Donald Pierson e o Projeto do Vale do Rio São Francisco: Cientistas sociais em ação na era do desenvolvimento." *DADOS—Revista de Ciências Sociais* 56, no. 2 (2013): 245–84.

Métraux, Alfred. "Brazil: Land of Harmony for All Races?" *UNESCO Courier* 4, no. 4 (1951): 3.
———. "UNESCO and the Racial Problem." *International Social Science Bulletin* 2, no. 3 (1950): 384–90.
Meucci, Simone. "Gilberto Freyre e a sociologia no Brasil: Da sistematização à constituição do campo científico." PhD dissertation, Instituto e Filosofia e Ciências Humanas, 2006.
Motta, Roberto. "Gilberto Freyre, René Ribeiro e o Projeto UNESCO." In Pereira and Sansone, *Projeto UNESCO no Brasil*, 38–60.
Nogueira, Oracy. "Relações raciais no município de Itapetininga." In Bastide and Fernandes, *Relações raciais*, 362–554.
Park, Robert. "Introduction: The Career of the Africans in Brazil." In *Negroes in Brazil: A Study of Race Contact at Bahia*, by Donald Pierson, 39–49. Chicago: University of Chicago Press, 1942.
Pereira, Cláudio Luiz, and Livio Sansone, eds. *Projeto UNESCO no Brasil: Textos críticos.* Salvador: Editora da Universidade Federal da Bahia, 2007.
Pierson, Donald. *Brancos e pretos na Bahia: Estudo de contato racial.* São Paulo: Companhia Editora Nacional, 1945.
———. Review of *The Masters and the Slaves: A Study in the Development of Brazilian Civilization. American Sociological Review* 12, no. 5 (1947): 607–9.
Ramos, Arthur. *A aculturação negra no Brasil.* São Paulo: Companhia Editora Nacional, 1942.
———. "Os grandes problemas da Antropologia brasileira." *Sociologia* 10, no. 4 (1948): 213–26.
Ribeiro, René. *Cultos afro-brasileiros do Recife: Um estudo de ajustamento social.* 1952. Reprint, Recife: Edições Institution Joaquim Nabuco de Pesquisas Sociais, 1978.
———. "Melville J. Herskovits: O estudo da cultura e o fator humano." *Revista do Museu Paulista* 14 (1963): 377–422.
———. "On the *Amaziado* Relationship and Other Aspects of Family in Recife." *American Sociological Review* 10, no. 1 (1945): 44–51.
———. *Religião e relações raciais.* Rio de Janeiro: Ministério da Educação e Cultura, 1956.
———. "Tempo de experiência." *Revista de Ciências Sociais* 14–15, nos. 1–2 (1984): 83–100.
Sansone, Livio. "USA and Brazil in Gantois: Power and the Transnational Origin of Afro-Brazilian Studies. *Vibrant Brazilian Journal* 8, no. 1 (2011): 536–567.
Stepan, Nancy L. *"The Hour of Eugenics": Race, Gender, and Nation in Latin America.* Ithaca, NY: Cornell University Press, 1991.
Thomaz, Omar Ribeiro. "Do saber colonial ao Luso-Tropicalismo: 'Raça' e 'nação' nas primeiras décadas do salazarismo." In *Raça, ciência e sociedade*, edited by Marcos Chor Maio and Ricardo Ventura Santos, 85–106. Rio de Janeiro: Editora Fiocruz, 1996.
Turner, Lorenzo Dow. "Some Contacts of Brazilian Ex-slaves with Nigeria, West Africa." *Journal of Negro History* 27 (1943): 55–67.
UNESCO. *Conference for the Establishment of the United Nations Educational, Scientific and Cultural Organisation: Held at the Institute of Civil Engineers, London, from the 1st to the 16th November, 1945.* ECO/CONF./29. Paris: UNESCO Archives, 1945.
———. *Records of the General Conference of the United Nations Education, Scientific and Cultural Organization: Fifth Session, Florence, 1950—Resolutions.* Paris: UNESCO Archives, 1950.
Wagley, Charles, ed. 1952. *Race and Class in Rural Brazil.* Paris: UNESCO, 1952.
———. Review of *The Masters and the Slaves: A Study in the Development of Brazilian Civilization. Political Science Quarterly* 61, no. 4 (1946): 625–27.

Wagley, Charles, Thales de Azevedo, and Luiz Costa Pinto. "Uma Pesquisa sobre a vida social no estado da Bahia: Salvador." *Publicações do Museu do Estado / Secretaria de Educação e Saúde* 11 (1950): 7–38.

Yelvington, Kevin. "Melville J. Herskovits e a institucionalização dos estudos Afro-Americanos." In Pereira and Sansone, *Projeto Unesco no Brasil*, 149–72.

CHAPTER 6

"An Immense Mosaic"
Race Mixing and the Creation of the Genetic Nation in 1960s Brazil

Rosanna Dent and Ricardo Ventura Santos

In the mid-1960s, the Brazilian geneticists Francisco M. Salzano and Newton Freire-Maia collaborated to synthesize the existing genetic knowledge of the Brazilian nation into a slender volume with the unassuming title, *Populações brasileiras: Aspectos demográficos, genéticos e antropológicos* (Brazilian populations: Demographic, genetic, and anthropological aspects). At a moment when Salzano and Freire-Maia were emerging as key architects of the field of human genetics in Brazil, their 1967 publication consolidated their expertise; it sought to "summarize the main results obtained in the field of the genetics of human populations in Brazil and to integrate them into a wider context."[1] Shortly after its release, they published the 1970 English-language version, *Problems in Human Biology: A Study of Brazilian Populations,* aiming for an international audience.

As they drew on data points from across countless publications in biomedicine and physical anthropology, the geneticists participated in the long tradition of commenting on the exceptional nature of the Brazilian nation. Indeed, the geneticists' "wider context" was profoundly informed by preexisting imaginaries of *mestiçagem*. Echoing earlier sociological tracts, including notions made famous by Gilberto Freyre's *Casa-grande & senzala* (1933), the geneticists highlighted the particularities of Portuguese colonialism, the ostensibly inevitable mixing of colonists with Indigenous peoples, and the dynamics of Brazilian slavery as they rendered a genetic portrait of Brazil.

At the time, producing a book-length synthesis of genetic data on a single country was an unusual practice for the nascent field of human genetics. Apart from some prewar volumes, and conference proceedings with specific national topics, few monographs were published on national populations defined by state borders.² Rather, genetic profiles were regionally and ethnically specific. While papers often specified the country of study, longer treatments usually tackled geographic areas or populations defined by linguistic determinates or perceived ethnic group: "populations of the Pacific," "Australian Aborigines," or "Arctic populations." Genetic profiles of individual countries would become more common from the mid-1970s on, almost ten years after the Portuguese-language publication of Salzano and Freire-Maia's project. This raises the question of how and why these two geneticists conceived of and developed their account. What prompted them to embark on such a synthesis? Why was Brazil one of the first countries to be described *genetically*?

In this chapter, we show that Salzano and Freire-Maia's leap to consider Brazil as a nation in genetic terms was facilitated by the foundation of social-scientific work that conceived of Brazil's exceptionalism in racial terms. We argue that *Populações brasileiras* and *Problems in Human Biology* constructed a new kind of national population, one legible in genetic terms. Moreover, by drawing on discourses that defined a tri-hybrid origin and valorized race mixing as a central aspect of Brazilian identity, Salzano and Freire-Maia's monographs contributed to the consolidation of the authority of genetics as a site to discuss and comment on the biological nation.³

As diverse works in the history and anthropology of science show, the twenty-first-century constitution of the field of human genetics is the direct inheritance of the human genetics research of the mid-twentieth century.⁴ Furthermore, recent anthropological studies have emphasized the salience of discourses of nation in late-twentieth- and early-twenty-first-century Latin American genomics. This chapter traces the origin of these practices to 1960s Brazil, linking them to longer histories of race thinking and nation building. While race "appears and disappears" in contemporary genomics, comprising what Peter Wade and colleagues refer to as an "absent presence,"⁵ race and associated constructs were not only explicitly present but perhaps even hegemonic in the geneticists' narratives of the 1960s. This chapter thus offers a starting point to trace the eliding of explicit racial thinking as it developed over the second half of the twentieth century.

Race thinking and predominant ideas about *mestiçagem* were central to the geneticists' promotion of Brazil as a site of research. At a moment of political and social uncertainty, three years into a military dictatorship and in the midst of the global Cold War, their synthetic vision of the Brazilian nation was an argument for the importance of the "immense mosaic" of the Brazilian population to answer pressing questions for the field of human genetics.⁶ Echoing both Freyre's early work and his subsequent *Luso-tropicalismo*, the geneticists set Brazilian bodies and genes apart from other populations due to historical, environmental, and cultural factors, particularly *mestiçagem* (race mixing), promoting Brazil as a site of cognition.⁷

Salzano and Freire-Maia's portrayal of Brazilian genetics shared the conflicted legacy of Freyre's oeuvre, which ambiguously critiqued racism while celebrating harmonious racial mixing. However, dedicated to progressive causes and anti-racist (if still profoundly racial) science, the geneticists aligned themselves with Freyre's critics rather than with the Pernambucan sociologist himself. In the early years of the Brazilian military-civilian dictatorship, *Luso-tropicalismo* held little appeal even as Freyre's earlier thinking pervaded the new genetic imaginary of the nation.

Geneticizing the Sociological Nation

We begin from the idea that populations are not, in fact, natural kinds. Populations are made, with priorities and values inherent in the process of their making.[8] When humans are grouped, whether through state-led bureaucratic processes, scientific counting and categorization, or some combination thereof, the results are politically salient. As Jenny Bangham and Soraya de Chadarevian have argued for post–World War II studies of human heredity, "much practical and conceptual work went into making populations into appropriate social and biological entities," and the processes of deciding who constituted part of a population was "fraught scientifically and politically."[9]

Although the nation may seem to be a logical unit of analysis, its relevance was not a foregone conclusion. Modern projects to quantify and characterize human variation have often parted from the notion that the populations under analysis were coherent biological entities even while preexisting social categories defined these groupings. Why, from a biological perspective, did it make sense to combine data from a community of *índios* from Central Brazil, *negros* from the Northeast, and a sample of *brancos* from the southern state of Rio Grande do Sul in a single table of blood group frequencies? Separated by hundreds of miles and vastly different environments, these groups could scarcely be considered part of the same reproductive pool.[10] It was Brazilian borders—a political category—and a particular imaginary regarding the past, present, and future of Brazil that determined the geneticists' analysis. *Populações brasileiras* must therefore be understood as a nationalist project. The key connection between political and biological classification, the link that justified the project in scientific terms, was the idea that *mestiçagem* had forged a unique national body.

The geneticists' vision grew out of a deep history of nationalist accounts that centered pacific race mixing as the origin of the nation.[11] As soon as the authors introduced "neo-Brazilians"—referring to colonial settlers—they emphasized race mixing: "Since there were no white women, miscegenation occurred almost at once."[12] Salzano and Freire-Maia went on to describe the three founding "stocks" of the Brazilian population, emphasizing that the Portuguese were "one of the genetically most heterogeneous people of the continent" of Europe, and that enslaved Africans also came from heterogeneous backgrounds.[13] The geneticists located the notion of a "tri-hybrid" racial origin at the heart of their account. Rather than focusing on genetic distribution according to region, state, socioeconomic class, or rural versus urban dwelling, the primary axis of analysis fell along *branco, mulatto, negro* and *índio*.

Prior scholarship has shown that early research topics in human genetics consistently paralleled contemporary social scientific ideas about national identity in Brazil and across Latin America more broadly.[14] *Populações brasileiras* and *Problems in Human Biology* are strong examples of this phenomenon, echoing social science analyses of *brasilidade*. However, despite clear conceptual continuities with earlier works and their stated commitment to incorporating social scientific thinking into their analyses, the geneticists were selective regarding the sociological works they cited.

Of particular interest is the absence of reference to Gilberto Freyre. Even as the scientists rendered an account that geneticized the vision of Brazil made famous by Freyre, they drew no explicit connections to his work. Reflecting on this absence in 2015, Salzano reflected, "There are no references to Gilberto Freyre in [*Problems in Human Biology*], really, even though we were familiar with *Casa-grande & senzala*, probably because the text did not offer any quantitative data regarding interethnic mixing."[15] However, it may also have been relevant that during the 1960s the work of the *pernambucano* sociologist was under intense criticism.

The social scientists Florestan Fernandes, Octavio Ianni, and Fernando Henrique Cardoso, from the Universidade de São Paulo (USP), were particularly vocal critics of Freyre, and, incidentally, their analyses were the sociological works most cited by Salzano and Freire-Maia.[16] Beyond the academic question of the treatment of race and racial inequity, Freyre's public image had also fluctuated greatly, and by the 1950s he was seen as a conservative.[17] As diverse scholars have indicated, Freyre's support of the military regime and the uptake of Freyrean *Luso-tropicalismo* both in Brazil and under Salazar in Portugal led Freyre to be closely associated with the right in the eyes of academic and lay publics.[18] In a 1990 interview, Darcy Ribeiro, a great admirer of *Casa-grande & senzala* and *Sobrados e Mucambos*, said Freyre was "uma peça reacionaríssima" (an extremely reactionary figure).[19] Yet, among university students of the mid-to late 1960s, "[Freyre] did not attract much interest, since his support for the military dictatorship (1964–1985) alienated many students."[20] Freyre, perhaps, alienated the geneticists as much as the students. Even as Salzano and Friere-Maia endeavored to cross disciplinary boundaries and integrate knowledge, they cited their social scientists selectively.

Their "attempt to show how social, historical, demographic, and environmental variables influence the results of calculations . . . of the modern population geneticist" was met with varying appraisals.²¹ The anthropologist and influential Brazilianist Charles Wagley of Columbia University lauded this approach in his preface to the volume: to the benefit of holistic understandings of human biology, "in Brazil, scientific disciplines are not isolated cubicles into which each specialist is catalogued and isolated."²² For the geneticist Newton Morton, situating genetic data within a larger anthropological frame was part of what made the "general account" an important and exciting addition to the field.²³ The physical anthropologist Hermann Bleibtreu was least charitable in his assessment, appreciating the goal of interdisciplinarity but considering the volume unsuccessful as an anthropological treatise.²⁴

The passages of texts that most resonate with Freyrean *Luso-tropicalismo* attracted reviewers' attention, particularly the geneticists' celebrations of the arrival and establishment of the Portuguese on the South American continent; evaluations were mixed. Morton praised their efforts to synthesize: "The authors write with obvious pride and affection about the extraordinary conquest of Brazil by a handful of Portuguese and mulattoes and the immigration of successive racial groups." He went on to suggest that those unacquainted with the history of Brazil and Brazilian race relations would "be fascinated by their brief but well-balanced account."²⁵

However, others differed on the success of the geneticists' treatment of the colonial past. One anthropologist found the celebratory focus on colonial origins misplaced: "The ultimate interpretation of the genetic and demographic substance of the book might have profited from less attention to, say, Portuguese dynastic succession and more to modern Brazilian social anthropology."²⁶ Hermann Bleibtreu was even more put off by the opening chapter: "Thirteen of twenty-five pages are devoted to the history of the Portuguese in Brazil, leaving short shrift to the 'Negro' and the 'Indian.' There is one page devoted to the prehistory of Brazil but three devoted to a rather romantic history of Portugal."²⁷

The framing of the volume with an account of the "extraordinary conquest" of Brazil contextualized the essence of the project: an analysis of racial mixing and the tri-hybrid constitution of Brazil as measured in Brazilian genes. Here we turn to the practical work of geneticizing preexisting social scientific account. In order to do this, the scientists had to construct populations, a theoretical and technical challenge that occupied their attention as well as that of their reviewers.

"The Population Pie": Raça, Cor, and Human Hybridity

Aiming for a comprehensive profile of the national population, the two geneticists compiled results from dozens of studies, including both their own swiftly growing bodies of publications and those of Brazilian and foreign colleagues. Combining research that had been conducted with different methodologies, research questions, and objectives raised several challenges. The first, and perhaps most difficult, was that of blending data by using distinct systems of classification. Salzano and Freire-Maia tackled the technical difficulty of aligning data by employing the most salient and consistent value reported by their colleagues: race.

The scientists were careful to define their terms. Only a few years earlier, Salzano had participated in the 1964 UNESCO meetings in Moscow, which resulted in the third UNESCO statement on "Proposals on the Biological Aspects of Race."[28] As such he was well acquainted with the challenges of reaching consensus on the meaning of "race." In the glossary of their books, the geneticists defined race as a "group of individuals that occupy a certain geographic area, who cross among themselves and are genetically distinct from other groups of the same species... By this definition a race explicitly is: (1) a population; (2) predominantly endogamic; and (3) characterized by a gene pool different from those characterizing other populations." They finalized their definition noting that contact between different races had increased since "the time of the great navigations" (or "descobrimentos" in Portuguese), "thus creating new races by differential crossing."[29] Salzano and Freire-Maia understood races as "biological open systems," with the possibility for change and the emergence of new races.[30]

However, while Salzano and Freire-Maia had a specific definition of race, the terms their colleagues used to characterize Brazilian populations were almost as varied as the populations themselves. They included geographical ancestry, national ancestry, geographical location, racial categories, racial types, ethnic groups, and varying designations of human hybridity. To give a sense of how this manifested in the text the discussion of one polymorphic system, the MNSs antigen blood group system, occupied a mere paragraph in the chapter on genetic polymorphisms. This short section included the following classifications: "Caiuá Indians," "trihybrid (white/Indian/Negro)," "white," "Negro," "mulatto," "dark mulatto," "light mulatto," "Indian Carajá," "Xavante," and "Caingang Indians and mestizos."[31] Each classification was linked to a numerical percentage identifying the range of variation for this gene. A great deal of work was needed to extract and then simplify these data into legible categories.

Although the particular system of racial classification varied from section to section, most data sets were broken down into *Brancos, Negros,* and *Mulatos* (Whites, Negroes, and Mulattoes in the translation) with *Índios* and *Mestiços* (Indians and Metizos) occasionally included.[32] When source studies failed to classify by race, it augmented the authors' difficulty to include the study in the synthetic overview. For example, one paper that examined associations between blood group B and tuberculosis infection was all but dismissed due to small sample size and the fact that "neither the samples nor the controls were classified according to race."[33]

Moreover, the uneven use and reporting of categories was the most critiqued aspect of the work in reviews published in international journals. One anthropologist reviewed *Problems in Human Biology*, saying, "Often, it seems, the population 'pie' will be cut one way for one investigation, say along racial lines, and quite a different way, say along a rural-urban continuum, for another, leaving the reader wondering about the unassessed interaction of these variables." The reviewer acknowledged, however, that this may have been the result of "bringing together heterogeneous reportage."[34] The most critical review also harped on this issue, saying that the "delimitation of the unit of study" is the beginning of any population research:

> The Brazilian populations discussed in this book dance from 'populations' in the most loose sense of the term (Negro populations of Brazil) to primitive isolates (Xavante). One wishes the authors would have discussed the theoretical and methodological problems in identifying populations. A note on the difficulties involved in generalizing from one population to another would also have seemed appropriate."[35]

While a national lens was salient enough to motivate the analysis and to structure the approach to the data, it alone was insufficient to convince reviewers of national borders as biological boundaries. Brazilian race mixing had not yet proceeded to such an extent that colleagues, or even the geneticists themselves, considered the nation homogenous. The heterogeneity was part of what made Brazil an interesting place to study. Yet, implicit in some portions of the geneticists' text was the idea that Brazil was a "nation of progress" and that racial relations and the trend toward increased homogeneity were inherently linked to the biological future of the nation.

Social Commentary and the Future (of the) Brazilian Race

As the geneticists situated coefficients of consanguinity and patterns of polymorphism distribution in the wider context of demographics, geography, and history, they also claimed authority to comment on Brazil's present and future. The nation's genes were accompanied by discussion of national issues, imbued with the concerns of the Cold War. Their commentary ranged from attention to development and underdevelopment to racial prejudice and birth control, articulating the relevance of such topics for the vitality of the body politic and its genetic composition. A fundamental concern, as with prior treatises on the racialized nation, was Brazil's future and its potential as a world power.

The geneticists used the forum of *Populações brasileiras* and *Problems in Human Biology* to offer a nationalist interpretation of a few key topics, some aimed at national readers and others specifically prepared for the English-language version. They asserted opinions elaborated in contrast to predominant visions emanating from the United States. For example, on the question of "population control" and the risks of the population explosion, Salzano and Freire-Maia took a different approach from prominent US geneticists.[36] Warning against overzealous implementation, they wrote that birth control policies "should be just an aid to strong measures of social and economic nature, aiming at real progress based on economic development." By rendering "unexplored areas and resources" productive, a growing population could drive economic growth, they posited, largely in keeping with the developmentalist discourses that successive Brazilian governments had promoted in the 1950s and 1960s. Furthermore, rather than framing population growth among poorer sectors of society as a risk for the advance of communism, they suggested demographic pressure would "focus" the need for development measures that would benefit the population broadly.[37]

Some discussions were prepared specifically with an international audience in mind; in *Problems in Human Biology*, Salzano and Freire-Maia added a section on how forms of social, economic, and technological progress would also "drastically change" selective pressures on human populations. Focusing on rates of malnutrition compared to those of chronic and degenerative disease, they contrasted "underdeveloped, developing, and developed countries." The radically uneven distribution of hunger and malnutrition in Brazil, they noted, "seriously disturb our ethical feelings as well as the democratic principle of opportunity for all." They went on to critique the coexistence of technological advancement and social inequity: "At a time when men are reaching the moon, people from different nations should be able to live side by side without these enormous and unfair differences in living conditions." The geneticists proposed investment in "more integrated studies of human beings" in order to better understand and govern these changing health and lifestyle dynamics.[38]

But beyond these progressive points, by far the most prominent social commentary of the monographs addressed the fraught topic of racism. Like "race," "racism" received an entry in the glossary, which succinctly defined it as "racial prejudice, which has no scientific basis."[39] Interestingly, most of their discussion came in a chapter on immigration and admixture, emerging out of research on interracial marriage. While Salzano and Freire-Maia held that intragroup marriages within racial groups were "justified" as preference for marriage between people of similar socioeconomic level, national origin, or height, if motivated by "hatred of another race, they can be considered a racist attitude." From here they launched into a three-page discussion of racism, prejudice, and proposed solutions to the problem in Brazil.

The geneticists acknowledged discrimination across social institutions and criticized whites who erroneously believed in the biological superiority of white over black and brown. Furthermore, "racism has deep roots since it almost always masks purposes of social, economic, or political domination."[40] Characterizing racism as primarily aimed at "the Negro" and particularly predominant in "the higher classes of the society," Salzano and Freire-Maia commented on how explanations without "racial overtones" often masked racial discrimination in the Brazilian case. The authors went on to proclaim the role of education in fighting racist attitudes:

> A good weapon is education for whites. This education for understanding would show that racism has no scientific basis and that it is rather the consequence of socioeconomic tensions, hatred, umbrage, and fear. Further, there is evidence that the racist himself is a socially inferior personality since he creates conflicts in a place where mutual help and collaboration should exist.

But even as Salzano and Freire-Maia proclaimed the presence and evil of racism in Brazil, they drew sharp distinctions with racism in other regions of the world. "We in Brazil," they wrote, "are very far from the tragic situation which exists in South Africa, Rhodesia, or even the United States; and we hope never to arrive there."[41] Following the model of social-scientific treatises in drawing comparisons between Brazil and other nation-states, the geneticists participated in constructing the nation through comparison, a practice with a long history.[42] While maintaining that racism was a problem in Brazil, the text also portrayed a kinder, gentler racism. In fact, some passages presented a seemingly irreconcilable contrast between historical violence, current political possibilities, and future harmony: "Brazil's history shows more understanding, despite the slavery of the Negro and the extermination of the Indian . . . Brazilians think that the Negro and the white have equal political rights . . . [and] the unfair prejudice against the Negro that is present is not poisoned by hate."[43] This ambivalent position with prejudice but no hate allowed the geneticists to imagine a future that aligned key social visions for Brazil—particularly that present in *Casa-grande & senzala* and in other works by Freyre—with their genetic vision.

This social vision for Brazil was one that even with acknowledgment of inequity emphasized racial harmony and the later iteration, racial democracy. In circulation for many decades, under the reformist governments of Jânio Quadros and João Goulart in the early 1960s, discourses of racial democracy "reached new heights of institutionalization and international visibility."[44] As a myth in the broadest sense, racial democracy served as both a descriptor and an aspiration; diverse actors mobilized the concept in conservative attempts to defend the status quo and in progressive calls for the nation to enact its promised equality.[45]

Although never invoking the term directly, the geneticists drew on these predominant notions of racial harmony. They did not suggest the absence of racism and prejudice but, in a positivist vision of racial progress, envisioned the future disappearance of biological races in the *povo brasileiro*. "Reduced racial discrimination" in some parts of the country led to "a tendency toward higher genetic homogeneity." Over time, these decreased preferences for intraracial marriage combined with internal migration and the "breakdown of isolates" meant that the myth of racial harmony would become a genetic reality: genetic variability, they wrote, "is not going to be expressed predominantly in the form of distinct racial blocks, but spread more uniformly over the total population. Thus, the genes of Caucasian, Negro and Indian origin which constitute the people are going to be found together in the same individuals with a higher frequency than today."[46] Over time, Brazilians would become increasingly genetically homogenous, resulting in the emergence of "new races," or perhaps a new national race. For Salzano and Freire-Maia, science had a role to play as a means of educating against racist ideas. After all, "as was stressed by the anthropologist Alfred Métraux . . . 'modern science confirmed and ratified the ethics of human fraternity.'"[47]

Personal and Professional Contexts

Understanding Salzano and Freire-Maia's career trajectories is essential to make sense of how and why they came together to work on this project. Their backgrounds, training, and the rising position of human genetics as a field structured their collaboration. In many respects, the relationship between the two authors encapsulates the early period of institutionalized genetics research in Brazil. Their personal and professional relationship can be understood as a microcosm of key forces in the development of human genetics as a field of academic inquiry in Brazil, much as their coauthored overview of Brazilian populations is a clear product of the conditions of their training.

The two geneticists first met at USP. In the 1940s and 1950s, USP was emerging as a key site for genetics in Brazil, with the Rockefeller Foundation funding the visit of famous geneticist Theodosius Dobzhansky and other prominent figures.[48] In 1951, Salzano and Freire-Maia overlapped only long enough for Freire-Maia to offer the younger biologist an "autographed set of reprints" and some encouragement.[49] As Salzano began his doctoral studies, Freire-Maia completed a two-year course in biology and returned to his home state to found a genetics laboratory at the Universidade Federal do Paraná in Curitiba.[50] Similarly, Salzano joined the nascent Department of Genetics at the Universidade do Rio Grande do Sul in 1954 while still completing his doctoral studies.

Following early fruit fly work, both southern Brazilian scientists turned their attention to what Salzano would describe as "an area of studies that, at that time, was not considered very promising: human genetics."[51] This shared interest would lead to a much more extensive period of interaction, this time in the United States. Again with funding and support from the Rockefeller Foundation, the geneticists found themselves together as visiting fellows at the University of Michigan in the laboratory of the human geneticist and physician James V. Neel. They overlapped for a large portion of the 1956–1957 academic year, living in adjacent apartments, navigating the fraught Ann Arbor winter and frozen pipes with their wives and children.[52] There, their professional relationship grew into a friendship based on intellectual exchange and shared experience. While in Ann Arbor, Salzano reminisced in a 2003 obituary for his colleague, their conversations "were so lively that our American colleagues would come to see if we were not fighting!"[53]

The months in Ann Arbor were influential for both scientists' careers. During the fellowship period, Salzano, Freire-Maia, and Neel held "informal discussions about research possibilities in Brazil," to help them develop their research agendas.[54] When Freire-Maia and Salzano returned to Brazil, these experiences would help them build two of the most important centers for the study of human genetics in South America. In Salzano's case, he also returned well prepared for large-scale international collaborations that would be fundamental to these efforts.[55] Much like other Brazilian scholars who studied in the United States in the first half of the twentieth century, they returned with both critiques and admiration of certain aspects of what they witnessed. Much as witnessing the Jim Crow era in the United States had crystalized Freyre's notions of lusophone excpetionalism, segregation and the civil rights movement made a strong impression.[56] Ten years later, Salzano and Freire-Maia would collaborate to take stock of and consolidate scholarship on the human genetics of Brazil.

Selling Brazil as a Research Site

Salzano and Freire-Maia were both instrumental in building Brazilian human genetics through their active research programs, mentorship, and promotion of the field. They authored *Populações brasileiras* only a decade and a half after the founding of their academic departments. Stopping to assess the state of their field in the late 1960s was part of a vigorous promotion of their research agenda at a time of academic and political uncertainty. Their work to construct a coherent national population—in genetic terms—helped make a case for the legitimacy of their intellectual projects and declare their immediate relevance to high-profile political debates. *Populações brasileiras* and *Problems in Human Biology* can be read not only as a project to create a coherent genetic category out of the classification "Brazilian" but also as an attempt to promote human genetics on the national and international stage. At a moment of political change and instability, and in the context of prior positive experiences of international collaboration, the geneticists' text invited investment in Brazilian human genetics research.

The late 1950s to the early 1960s was a period of institutionalization but also turmoil in the Brazilian academy, reflecting Brazilian politics more broadly. Under President Goulart, the União Nacional dos Estudantes (National Union of Students) had reached new levels of organization and militancy, demanding educational reform and increases in the number of students accepted into the federal university system.[57] Before his deposition by the military-civilian coup of 1964, Goulart had proposed higher education reform as part of his broad sweeping *reformas de base,* which promised to expand access to university education and provide additional protections for academic freedom.[58] The instability continued under the military government; while those in power implemented reforms and expansions in the university system beginning in 1966, they also initiated investigations and purging of academics with ties to communist or socialist political organizations.[59] The unstable economic situation added to researchers' worries about investment in higher education and funding for laboratory and fieldwork.

The early years of military rule, when the geneticists were drafting *Populações brasileiras,* was an "era of apprehension."[60] Salzano and Freire-Maia felt the impact of military rule both directly and indirectly, where "the simple fact of not wearing a tie was enough to arouse suspicion."[61] Even before the most stringent crackdowns and academic purges, seventeen colleagues were fired or forced to retire at Salzano's home institution of the Universidade Federal do Rio Grande do Sul in 1964.[62] The closing of the Universidade de Brasília caused particular consternation, where colleagues' newly established biology program was disbanded.[63] Freire-Maia was investigated because of his socialism but, unlike some of his friends and colleagues, was never imprisoned.[64] It was a period of challenges for the geneticists.

It was in this context that Salzano and Freire-Maia used their monograph to argue for the relevance of Brazil for human genetics and, although to a lesser extent, for the relevance of human genetics for Brazil. Previous researchers often positioned Brazil and its people as a resource for understanding race, race relations, and racism. Salzano and Freire-Maia were far from the first to take this tactic but were the first to do so for the "new science of genetics." Their monograph opened with this argument: "Because of the extreme variety of their original ethnic groups, the widespread miscegenation, and their distribution in all kinds of environmental conditions, the eighty-five million people who live in Brazil present the geneticist and anthropologist an excellent opportunity for the study of complex and fascinating problems."[65] In their conclusions, the geneticists reiterated the characteristics they had highlighted throughout the text that made their country so well suited to studies of human variation. First, "Indian populations . . . can furnish important data about the factors which may have influenced the evolution of our species in remote times." Next, "interracial relations which are different from those prevailing in many other countries" set Brazil apart, while high incidence of infectious disease and heterogeneity would allow for certain kinds of questions to be answered, despite the methodological challenges heterogeneity presented. In the space of one page, the Brazilian population was described as "excellent material," "ideal material," and "an excellent field for research."[66]

The simple act of translating the book into English shows how highly the authors valued international readership. Making their work accessible in these circles was an important strategy: their work was an invitation to foreign colleagues to explore Brazil's genetic variation. By the time Salzano and Freire-Maia decided to coauthor their survey of Brazil, they had each benefitted from collaboration and support with international funders and colleagues. The Rockefeller Foundation had been essential in providing training and equipment. The World Health Organization, the Pan American Health Organization, the US Atomic Energy Commission, the German National Research Council, and the US Public Health Service had all supported collaborations with scholars from Europe and the United States.[67]

Through the relationships that they had formed while abroad and in their close work with the Rockefeller Foundation, Freire-Maia and Salzano gained visibility in the field and accompanying opportunities to participate in conferences and workshops in Europe and the United States. In fact, many of the studies cited in the text were conducted in conjunction with scholars from abroad, including a large portion of the research emerging from Salzano's lab. Against this backdrop and in the context of uncertainty regarding the national economic and political situation, attracting international collaboration through *Problems in Human Biology* could lend stability and opportunity. The reviewers understood this message. As one anthropologist noted, over the course of the small volume, "there emerges moreover a clear indication of the opportunities that exist in Brazil for genetic studies of human evolution in progress."[68] Another enthusiastic review concluded, "The problem of hybridization of three different racial groups and the evolutionary subsequences is indeed a fascinating and important genetic problem, one which helps in the understanding of several theoretical problems."[69]

In the new English version of the text, Salzano and Freire-Maia took the opportunity to include some updated data and additional reflections on the state of the field. They also added several comparisons between Brazil and the United States. On the question of racial violence, they included a clause in an existing question regarding the future of racism in Brazil: "And how may Brazilians not fear that the present racism may explode, *as presently is happening in the United States*, or develop into a form of genocide similar to the great Nazi crime?"[70] The "explosion of racism" in the United States was the backlash of whites against demands of black citizens for equality.

As Micol Seigel has argued, comparisons, particularly those on race relations between Brazil and the United States, have often served not only to describe but also to construct truths about the natural order of existing hierarchies or the potential for change. "Comparers of racial systems," she writes, "plant their social positions deeply in the work they produce."[71] Salzano and Freire-Maia's comparisons aligned smoothly with many contemporary Brazilian social scientists. In the process, they rendered what they proposed as relatively pacifistic relations between racial groups into a resource for continued comparative study. Their approach to human genetics located Brazilian racial harmony in the genes of the nation, and invited scientists and funders at home and abroad to invest in their exploration.

Conclusion

Salzano and Freire-Maia's volume followed a long tradition of ambiguous critique and celebration of Brazilian race relations. Drawing on the exceptionalism articulated by Freyre, but eschewing his conservatism, the two geneticists constructed a new geneticized vision of the nation. In this biological account of populations, ancestry was a central concern, assumed to be stabilized and located in the trihybrid past. However, equally important were the notions of heterogeneity and malleability. The variety of environments and levels of development easily accessed within Brazil constituted a resource for study of human variation, as did the potential to track race mixture as it occurred. As they synthesized and packaged knowledge of genes within state borders, *Populações brasileiras* and *Problems in Human Biology* portrayed Brazil as an open question for national and international researchers.

The geneticists positioned their work as contributing more broadly to what Sebastián Gil-Riaño has described as an anti-racist "moral economy" of mid-century human sciences, committed to "overcoming notions of 'race' that are overly concerned with fixity and hierarchy and that serve to oppress rather than enable."[72] As discussed earlier, their commentary on social and political realities focused on a critique of global inequality and argued explicitly for the education of white people to dispel racism. They even included an appendix in both versions of their book that featured the text of the 1951 "Lei Afonso Arinos," or the "Brazilian Antiracist Law," as they translated the title. They referenced the existence of the law against racial prejudice as evidence that discrimination on the basis of race or color did in fact exist in Brazil.[73] The appendix served as a reminder that even as they classified and calculated based on race, racial discrimination was officially illegal in Brazil. Moreover, the remedy that the two geneticists proposed was the "dissemination of scientific evidence that demonstrates the fallacious nature of racist theories."[74] They called for a scientific worldview, appeals to fellow citizens' rationality, and greater support of research as much needed remedies.

However, Salzano and Freire-Maia's reliance on categories that were inextricable from longer histories of enslavement, colonialism, and oppression complicated the ability of their scholarship to work against hierarchical ideas about race, much as Veronika Lipphardt has argued for the case of contemporary human genomics.[75] When the geneticists framed race mixing as inevitable and amicable, they reiterated earlier sociological tracts that had obscured histories of dispossession, genocide, and sexual violence; they simplified these human histories into "a reduced idiom of biological processes, and hence contribute[d] to an unparalleled reification of human history."[76] In the process of synthesizing information on many Brazilian populations into a single monograph on Brazil, they also extended the authority of the young field of human genetics to address the social issues of the nation.

Rosanna Dent is Assistant Professor in the Federated Department of History at the New Jersey Institute of Technology and Rutgers-Newark. She holds a PhD in history and sociology of science from the University of Pennsylvania and completed a Mellon Postdoctoral Fellowship in the Department of History and Classical Studies at McGill University. She is currently working on a book manuscript on the history of twentieth-century human sciences research in Indigenous territories in Brazil.

Ricardo Ventura Santos is an anthropologist affiliated with the Fundação Oswaldo Cruz (Oswaldo Cruz Foundation) in Rio de Janeiro and Professor in the Department of Anthropology at the National Museum of Brazil. He received his PhD in anthropology from Indiana University Bloomington in 1991. He has been a visiting scholar in MIT's Program on Science, Technology, and Society (1998–1999) and at the Max Planck Institute for the History of Science (2012–2013). He recently received a Wellcome Trust Senior Investigator Award in Humanities and Social Science (2017–2021).

Notes

The work for this chapter was supported by the Wellcome Trust, the Fundação Carlos Chagas Filho de Amparo à Pesquisa do Estado do Rio de Janeiro (FAPERJ), the Mellon Foundation, and a Social Science Research Council International Dissertation Research Fellowship. Susan Lindee, Elaine LaFay, Melissa S. Creary and anonymous reviewers provided valuable feedback. All translations are by Rosanna Dent unless otherwise noted. While this chapter was in final revisions, Professor Francisco Salzano passed away. In addition to being one of the most important scholars of human population genetics in Brazil, he was intellectually generous and always interested in cultivating interdisciplinary dialogue. Over the past ten years, he kindly agreed to numerous interviews with us about his career. We dedicate this work to his memory.

1. Francisco M. Salzano and Newton Freire-Maia, *Problems in Human Biology: A Study of Brazilian Populations* (Detroit, MI, 1970), xvi, originally published as *Populações brasileiras: Aspectos demográficos, genéticos e antropológicos* (São Paulo, 1967).
2. Two exceptions include a monograph on Turkey (1946) and another on Sweden (1959). See Nermin Aygen, *Türklerin kan grupları ve kan gruplarının antropolojik karakterlerle ilgisi üzerine bir araştırma* (Ankara, 1946); Lars Beckman, *A Contribution to the Physical Anthropology and Population Genetics of Sweden: Variations of the ABO, Rh, MN and P Blood Groups* (Lund, 1959).
3. Before the rise of genetics, discussions of race and the biological realities of the Brazilian nation took place in the fields of physical anthropology and medicine. See Ricardo Ventura Santos, "Guardian Angel on a Nation's Path: Contexts and Trajectories of Physical Anthropology in Brazil in the Late Nineteenth and Early Twentieth Centuries," *Current Anthropology* 53, no. S5 (2012): S17–S32; Vanderlei de Souza and Ricardo Ventura Santos, "The Emergence of Human Population Genetics and Narratives about the Formation of the Brazilian Nation (1950–1960)," *Studies in History and Philosophy of Biological and Biomedical Sciences* 47 (2014): 97–107; Nancy Leys Stepan, *The Hour of Eugenics: Race, Gender, and Nation in Latin America* (Ithaca, NY, 1991).
4. See M. Susan Lindee, *Moments of Truth in Genetic Medicine* (Baltimore, MD, 2005); Nathaniel Comfort, *The Science of Human Perfection: How Genes Became the Heart of American Medicine* (New Haven, CT, 2012); Jenny Reardon, *Race to the Finish: Identity and Governance in an Age of Genomics* (Princeton, NJ, 2004); Ricardo Ventura Santos, Michael Kent, and Verlan Gaspar Neto, "From Degeneration to Meeting Point: Historical Views on Race, Mixture, and the Biological Diversity of the Brazilian Population," in *Mestizo Genomics: Race Mixture, Nation, and Science in Latin America*, ed. Peter Wade, Carlos López López Beltrán, Eduardo Restrepo, and Ricardo Ventura Santos (Durham, NC, 2014).
5. Peter Wade, Vivette García Deister, Michael Kent, María Fernanda Olarte Sierra, and Adriana Díaz del Castillo Hernández, "Nation and the Absent Presence of Race in Latin American Genomics," *Current Anthropology* 55, no. 5 (2014): 498, https://doi.org/10.1086/677945.
6. Salzano and Freire-Maia, *Problems*, 176–77.
7. On "sites of cognition," see Warwick Anderson, "Hybridity, Race, and Science: The Voyage of the *Zaca*, 1934–1935," *Isis* 103, no. 2 (2012): 229–53.
8. Lisa Gannett, "Making Populations: Bounding Genes in Space and in Time," *Philosophy of Science* 70, no. 5 (2003): 989–1001, https://doi.org/10.1086/377383.
9. Jenny Bangham and Soraya de Chadarevian, "Human Heredity after 1945: Moving

Populations Centre Stage," *Studies in History and Philosophy of Biological and Biomedical Sciences* 47, Part A (2014): 46, https://doi.org/10.1016/j.shpsc.2014.05.005.
10. On definitions of "population" circulating at this time, see Gannett "Making Populations," 990–95.
11. Doris Sommer, *Foundational Fictions: The National Romances of Latin America* (Berkeley, CA, 1993), 138–71; Tracy Devine Guzmán, *Native and National in Brazil: Indigeneity after Independence* (Chapel Hill, NC, 2013).
12. Salzano and Freire-Maia, *Problems*, 25.
13. Ibid., 41.
14. Souza and Santos, "The Emergence of Human Population Genetics"; Wade et al., "Nation and the Absent Presence of Race"; Peter Wade, Vivette García Deister, Michael Kent, and María Fernanda Olarte Sierra, "Social Categories and Laboratory Practices," in Wade et al., *Mestizo Genomics*, 183–209, esp. 188–92.
15. Personal correspondence, Francisco M. Salzano to Ricardo Ventura Santos, 14 December 2015.
16. On criticisms of Freyre during the 1950s and 1960s, see Antônio Sérgio Alfredo Guimarães, *Racismo e anti-racismo no Brasil* (Rio de Janeiro, 1999), 51–58; Luís Rodolfo Vilhena, *Ensaios de antropologia* (Rio de Janeiro, 1997), 132–34; Peter Burke and Maria Lúcia Garcia Pallares-Burke, *Gilberto Freyre: Social Theory in the Tropics* (Oxford, 2008). For Salzano and Freire-Maia's use of Ianni, Fernandes, and Cardoso, see Salzano and Freire-Maia, *Problems*, 54, 58. All three sociologists would be forced to retire in the dictatorship's purges of 1969 when open criticisms of racism were considered a threat to the nation. On these forced retirements, see Paulina L. Alberto, *Terms of Inclusion: Black Intellectuals in Twentieth-Century Brazil* (Chapel Hill, NC, 2011), 250; Edward E. Telles, *Race in Another America: The Significance of Skin Color in Brazil* (Princeton, NJ, 2004), 40–42.
17. Burke and Pallares-Burke, *Gilberto Freyre,* 119.
18. Jerry Dávila, *Hotel Trópico: Brazil and the Challenge of African Decolonization, 1950–1980* (Durham, NC, 2010), 14–23.
19. Darcy Ribeiro, *Darcy Ribeiro: Encontros* (Rio de Janeiro, 2007), 205.
20. Burke and Pallares-Burke, *Gilberto Freyre,* 13. Furthermore, the dictatorship's aggressive promotion of Brazil as a racial democracy undermined the usefulness of the concept for anti-racist activists and intellectuals of color who had used the concept as an aspirational vision for Brazil in the 1940s and 1950s. See Alberto, *Terms of Inclusion,* 245–96.
21. Hermann Bleibtreu, "Review of *Problems in Human Biology: A Study of Brazilian Populations,*" *American Anthropologist* 73, no. 4 (1971): 942, https://doi.org/10.1525/aa.1971.73.4.02a00930.
22. Charles Wagley, "Preface," in Salzano and Freire-Maia, *Problems,* xx.
23. Newton E. Morton, "Review of *Problems in Human Biology: A Study of Brazilian Populations,*" *American Journal of Human Genetics* 23, no. 3 (1971): 327.
24. Bleibtreu, "Review," 942.
25. Morton, "Review," 327–28.
26. Eugene Giles, "Review of *Problems in Human Biology: A Study of Brazilian Populations* and *The Ongoing Evolution of Latin American Populations,*" *American Journal of Physical Anthropology* 37, no. 1 (1972): 155, https://doi.org/10.1002/ajpa.1330370121.
27. Bleibtreau, "Review," 942.
28. For a discussion of the UNESCO meetings, see Perrin Selcer, "Beyond the Cephalic Index: Negotiating Politics to Produce UNESCO's Scientific Statements on Race," *Cur-*

rent Anthropology 53, no. S5 (2012): S173–S84; Sebastián Gil-Riaño, "Historicizing Anti-racism: UNESCO's Campaigns against Race Prejudice in the 1950s" (PhD diss., University of Toronto, 2014).
29. Salzano and Freire-Maia, Problems, 190; Salzano and Freire-Maia, Populações brasileiras, 168.
30. Over the long course of his career, Salzano has maintained that there are social and biological definitions of race and that racial biological differences exist. Francisco M. Salzano, "Raça, racismo e direitos humanos," Horizontes Antropológicos 11, no. 23 (2005): 225–27. For a useful discussion of Dobzhansky's definitions of race from 1962, which Salzano and Freire-Maia seem to have shared, see Reardon, Race to the Finish, 34–35.
31. Salzano and Freire-Maia, Problems, 154–55.
32. See, e.g., ibid., 149; Salzano and Freire-Maia, Populações brasileiras, 131.
33. Salzano and Freire-Maia, Problems, 162.
34. Giles, "Review," 155.
35. Bleibtreu, "Review," 943.
36. James Neel, for example, echoed US-led programs' discourse of urgency to reduce population growth in countries "at risk" of communist infiltration due to high poverty rates. See James V. Neel, Physician to the Gene Pool: Genetic Lessons and Other Stories (New York, 1994), 281–301. An extensive literature discusses how Latin American intellectuals alternately embraced and resisted US programs to promote birth control. See, e.g., Raúl Necochea López, A History of Family Planning in Twentieth-Century Peru (Chapel Hill, NC, 2014).
37. Salzano and Freire-Maia, Problems, 66.
38. Ibid., 176.
39. Ibid., 190.
40. Ibid., 59 (this and the previous quotation).
41. Ibid., 60 (this and the previous extract).
42. For a compelling discussion of the discursive power of comparative studies, see Micol Seigel, "Beyond Compare: Comparative Method after the Transnational Turn," Radical History Review 91 (2005): 62–90.
43. Salzano and Freire-Maia, Problems, 60.
44. Alberto, Terms of Inclusion, 201.
45. Here we follow Alberto and others who have understood "myth" in the anthropological sense as "a discourse that guided discussion of what it meant to be a Brazilian and shaped individual and collective choices" and which explains the power and persistence of ideas about racial harmony across diverse actors to the present day. See ibid., 16.
46. Salzano and Freire-Maia, Problems, 179.
47. Ibid., 61.
48. Thomas F. Glick, "The Rockefeller Foundation and the Emergence of Genetics in Brazil, 1943–1960," in Missionaries of Science: The Rockefeller Foundation and Latin America, ed. Marcos Cueto (Bloomington, IN, 1994), 149–64; Souza and Santos, "The Emergence of Human Population Genetics," 99; Francisco M. Salzano, ed., Recordar é viver: A história da sociedade brasileira de genética (Riberão Preto, 2011), 12.
49. Francisco M. Salzano, "Newton Freire-Maia (1918–2003): From Boa Esperança to the World," Genetics and Molecular Biology 26, no. 3 (2003): 1–2.
50. Newton Freire-Maia, O que passou e permanece (Curitiba, 1995), 142.

51. Francisco M. Salzano, "Apresentação de Newton Freire-Maia," 1968, Personal Papers of Francisco M. Salzano, Porto Alegre.
52. Francisco M. Salzano, interview with Rosanna Dent, 11 July 2012, Porto Alegre; Salzano, "Newton Friere-Maia," 1.
53. Salzano, "Newton Friere-Maia," 2.
54. Francisco M. Salzano to Rockefeller Foundation, "Report of Francisco M. Salzano," 20 August 1957, RG 10.1, Folder 305E, Rockefeller Archive Center.
55. Initially, Salzano would collaborate closely with Neel promoting the study of so-called primitive groups. His Rockefeller Foundation experience led him to much future international collaboration.
56. Salzano, interview, 11 July 2012; Freire-Maia, *O que passou e permanece*.
57. Leslie Bethall, "Politics in Brazil under the Liberal Republic, 1945–1964," in *The Cambridge History of Latin America: Brazil since 1930*, ed. Leslie Bethall (Cambridge, 2008), 149.
58. Luciana Quillet Heymann, "Desafios e rumos da política educacional," Fundação Getulio Vargas CPDOC, accessed 9 October 2018, https://cpdoc.fgv.br/producao/dossies/Jango/artigos/NaPresidenciaRepublica/Desafios_e_rumos_da_politica_educacional.
59. On higher education under military rule, see Rodrigo Patto Sá Motta, *As universidades e o regime militar: Cultura política brasileira e modernização autoritária* (Rio de Janeiro, 2014).
60. Salzano, *Recordar é viver*, 41.
61. Freire-Maia, *O que passou e permanece*, 217.
62. Salzano, *Recordar é viver*, 40.
63. Nine members of the genetics department at Salzano's home institution moved to the Universidade de Brasília in 1963 to help found their program. See ibid., 37–52; Salzano, interview, 11 July 2012.
64. Freire-Maia referred to himself as a "terrified hero" as he confronted the major in charge of the university's investigation, saying, "If being a socialist is a crime, then I am a criminal!" Freire-Maia, *O que passou e permanece*, 217–20.
65. Salzano and Freire-Maia, *Problems*, xv.
66. Ibid., 178.
67. See, e.g., James V. Neel, Francisco M. Salzano, Friedrich Keiter, David Maybury-Lewis, and P. C. Junqueira, "Studies on the Xavante Indians of the Brazilian Mato Grosso," *American Journal of Human Genetics* 16, no. 1 (1964): 52; Freire-Maia, *O que passou e permanece*, 177–88, 226–27.
68. D. F. Roberts, "Review of *Problems in Human Biology: A Study of Brazilian Populations*," *Quarterly Review of Biology* 46, no. 3 (1971): 325.
69. Michael H. Crawford, "Review of *Problems in Human Biology: A Study of Brazilian Populations*," *Human Biology* 46, no. 3 (1974): 599.
70. Salzano and Freire-Maia, *Problems*, 61.
71. Seigel, "Beyond Compare," 66.
72. Gil-Riaño, "Historicizing Anti-racism," 34.
73. Salzano and Freire-Maia, *Populações brasileiras*, 46.
74. Salzano and Freire-Maia, *Problems*, 61.
75. Veronika Lipphardt, comment on Wade et al., "Nation and the Absent Presence of Race," 512.
76. Veronika Lipphardt, "The Body as a Substrate of Differentiation: Shifting the Focus from Race Science to Life Scientists' Research on Human Variation," *Varia Historia* 33, no. 61 (2017): 123.

Bibliography

Alberto, Paulina L. *Terms of Inclusion: Black Intellectuals in Twentieth-Century Brazil*. Chapel Hill: University of North Carolina Press, 2011.
Anderson, Warwick. "Hybridity, Race, and Science: The Voyage of the *Zaca*, 1934–1935." *Isis* 103, no. 2 (2012): 229–53.
Aygen, Nermin. *Türklerin kan grupları ve kan gruplarının antropolojik karakterlerle ilgisi üzerine bir araştırma*. Ankara: Ankara Üniversitesi, 1946.
Bangham, Jenny, and Soraya de Chadarevian. "Human Heredity after 1945: Moving Populations Centre Stage." *Studies in History and Philosophy of Biological and Biomedical Sciences* 47, Part A (2014): 45–49. https://doi.org/10.1016/j.shpsc.2014.05.005.
Beckman, Lars. *A Contribution to the Physical Anthropology and Population Genetics of Sweden: Variations of the ABO, Rh, MN and P Blood Groups*. Lund: Berlingska Boktryck, 1959.
Bethall, Leslie. "Politics in Brazil under the Liberal Republic, 1945–1964." In *The Cambridge History of Latin America: Brazil since 1930*, edited by Leslie Bethall, 87–164. Cambridge: Cambridge University Press, 2008.
Bleibtreu, Hermann. "Review of *Problems in Human Biology: A Study of Brazilian Populations*." *American Anthropologist* 73, no. 4 (1971): 942–943. https://doi.org/10.1525/aa.1971.73.4.02a00930.
Burke, Peter, and Maria Lúcia Garcia Pallares-Burke. *Gilberto Freyre: Social Theory in the Tropics*. Oxford: Peter Lang, 2008.
Comfort, Nathanial. *The Science of Human Perfection: How Genes Became the Heart of American Medicine*. New Haven, CT: Yale University Press, 2012.
Crawford, Michael H. 1974. "Review of *Problems in Human Biology: A Study of Brazilian Populations*." *Human Biology* 46, no. 3 (1974): 598–600.
Dávila, Jerry. *Hotel Trópico: Brazil and the Challenge of African Decolonization, 1950–1980*. Durham, NC: Duke University Press, 2010.
Freire-Maia, Newton. *O que passou e permanece*. Curitiba: Editora Universidade Federal do Paraná, 1995.
Gannett, Lisa. "Making Populations: Bounding Genes in Space and in Time." *Philosophy of Science* 70, no. 5 (2003): 989–1001. https://doi.org/10.1086/377383.
Gil-Riaño, Sebastián. "Historicizing Anti-racism: UNESCO's Campaigns against Race Prejudice in the 1950s." PhD dissertation, University of Toronto, 2014.
Giles, Eugene. "Review of Problems in *Human Biology: A Study of Brazilian Populations* and *The Ongoing Evolution of Latin American Populations*." *American Journal of Physical Anthropology* 37, no. 1 (1972): 155–56. https://doi.org/10.1002/ajpa.1330370121.
Glick, Thomas F. "The Rockefeller Foundation and the Emergence of Genetics in Brazil, 1943–1960." In *Missionaries of Science: The Rockefeller Foundation and Latin America*, edited by Marcos Cueto, 149–64. Bloomington: Indiana University Press, 1994.
Guimarães, Antônio Sérgio Alfredo. *Racismo e anti-racismo no Brasil*. Rio de Janeiro: Editora 34, 1999.
Guzmán, Tracy Devine. *Native and National in Brazil: Indigeneity after Independence*. Chapel Hill: University of North Carolina Press, 2013.
Heymann, Luciana Quillet. "Desafios e rumos da política educacional." Fundação Getulio Vargas CPDOC. Accessed 9 October 2018. https://cpdoc.fgv.br/producao/dossies/Jango/artigos/NaPresidenciaRepublica/Desafios_e_rumos_da_politica_educacional.
Lindee, M. Susan. *Moments of Truth in Genetic Medicine*. Baltimore: Johns Hopkins University Press, 2005.

Lipphardt, Veronika. "The Body as a Substrate of Differentiation: Shifting the Focus from Race Science to Life Scientists' Research on Human Variation." *Varia Historia* 33, no. 61 (2017): 109–33.

Morton, Newton E. "Review of *Problems in Human Biology: A Study of Brazilian Populations*." *American Journal of Human Genetics* 23, no. 3 (1971): 327–28.

Motta, Rodrigo Patto Sá. *As universidades e o regime militar: Cultura política brasileira e modernização autoritária*. Rio de Janeiro: Zahar, 2014.

Necochea López, Raúl. *A History of Family Planning in Twentieth-Century Peru*. Chapel Hill: University of North Carolina Press, 2014.

Neel, James V. *Physician to the Gene Pool: Genetic Lessons and Other Stories*. New York: J. Wiley, 1994.

Neel, James V., Francisco M. Salzano, Friedrich Keiter, David Maybury-Lewis. "Studies on the Xavante Indians of the Brazilian Mato Grosso." *American Journal of Human Genetics* 16, no. 1 (1964): 52–140.

Reardon, Jenny. *Race to the Finish: Identity and Governance in an Age of Genomics*. Princeton, NJ: Princeton University Press, 2004.

Ribeiro, Darcy. *Darcy Ribeiro: Encontros*. Rio de Janeiro: Beco do Azougue, 2007.

Roberts, D. F. "Review of *Problems in Human Biology: A Study of Brazilian Populations*." *Quarterly Review of Biology* 46, no. 3 (1971): 324–25. https://doi.org/10.1086/406987.

Salzano, Francisco M. "Newton Freire-Maia (1918–2003): From Boa Esperança to the World." *Genetics and Molecular Biology* 26, no. 3 (2003): 1–2.

———. 2005. "Raça, racismo e direitos humanos." *Horizontes Antropológicos* 11, no. 23 (2005): 225–27.

———, ed. *Recordar é viver: A história da sociedade brasileira de genética*. Riberão Preto: Sociedade Brasileira de Genética, 2011.

Salzano, Francisco M., and Newton Freire-Maia. *Populações brasileiras: Aspectos demográficos, genéticos e antropológicos*. São Paulo: Companhia Editora Nacional, 1967.

———. *Problems in Human Biology: A Study of Brazilian Populations*. Detroit: Wayne State University Press, 1970. Originally published as *Populações brasileiras: Aspectos demográficos, genéticos e antropológicos* (São Paulo: Universidade de São Paulo, 1967).

Santos, Ricardo Ventura. "Guardian Angel on a Nation's Path: Contexts and Trajectories of Physical Anthropology in Brazil in the Late Nineteenth and Early Twentieth Centuries." *Current Anthropology* 53, no. S5 (2017): S17–S32.

Santos, Ricardo Ventura, Michael Kent, and Verlan Gaspar Neto. "From Degeneration to Meeting Point: Historical Views on Race, Mixture, and the Biological Diversity of the Brazilian Population." In Wade et al., *Mestizo Genomics*, 33–54.

Seigel, Micol. "Beyond Compare: Comparative Method after the Transnational Turn." *Radical History Review* 91 (2005): 62–90.

Selcer, Perrin. "Beyond the Cephalic Index: Negotiating Politics to Produce UNESCO's Scientific Statements on Race." *Current Anthropology* 53, no. S5 (2012): S173–S84.

Sommer, Doris. *Foundational Fictions: The National Romances of Latin America*. Berkeley: University of California Press, 1993.

Souza, Vanderlei de, and Ricardo Ventura Santos. "The Emergence of Human Population Genetics and Narratives about the Formation of the Brazilian Nation (1950–1960)." *Studies in History and Philosophy of Biological and Biomedical Sciences* 47, Part A (2014): 97–107.

Stepan, Nancy Leys. *The Hour of Eugenics: Race, Gender, and Nation in Latin America*. Ithaca, NY: Cornell University Press, 1991.

Telles, Edward E. *Race in Another America: The Significance of Skin Color in Brazil*. Princeton, NJ: Princeton University Press, 2004.

Vilhena, Luís Rodolfo. *Ensaios de antropologia*. Rio de Janeiro: Editora Universidade do Estado do Rio de Janeiro, 1997.
Wade, Peter, Vivette García Deister, Michael Kent, and María Fernanda Olarte Sierra. "Social Categories and Laboratory Practices." In Wade et al., *Mestizo Genomics*, 183–209.
Wade, Peter, Vivette García Deister, Michael Kent, María Fernanda Olarte Sierra, and Adriana Díaz del Castillo Hernández. "Nation and the Absent Presence of Race in Latin American Genomics." *Current Anthropology* 55, no. 5 (2014): 497–522. https://doi.org/10.1086/677945.
Wade, Peter, Carlos López López Beltrán, Eduardo Restrepo, and Ricardo Ventura Santos, eds. *Mestizo Genomics: Race Mixture, Nation, and Science in Latin America*. Durham, NC: Duke University Press, 2014.

PART III
The Colonial Sciences of Race

CHAPTER 7

The Racial Science of Patriotic Primitives
António Mendes Correia in Portuguese Timor

Ricardo Roque

This chapter investigates how race and affect, racialized notions of biological primitivism and nationalistic imageries of affect, could come together into one consequential form of Luso-colonial racial science in the postwar years. I explore Portuguese racial conceptions beyond Luso-tropicalist emphasis on miscegenation, to call attention to the pervading significance of (physical) anthropological research on the "native tribes" of the Portuguese colonial empire. After World War II, colonialist imageries and racial theories that circumvented miscegenation and emphasized biological difference, I argue, were articulated in conjunction with ideas of spiritual unity and "cross-racial" affect between Portuguese and Indigenous. Interest in the colonized populations as racially different and primitive was not a preserve of the prewar years. It was a cherished theme of field research in the 1950s and 1960s, the Luso-tropicalist era, mobilizing a wealth of scientific experts, colonial administrators, Indigenous subjects, and state funding, until the demise of the Portuguese Empire and the fall of the *Estado Novo* dictatorship, in 1974. Colonial anthropology then came to appear as an affective mode of racial conceptions—a project of both racialization of the "primitive" other, and patriotic affinity with that same "primitive" simultaneously. Ideas of racial alterity and spiritual similitude could thus be productively articulated together, sustaining a singular vision of Portuguese colonial and racial exceptionalism, both alternative and parallel to the Brazilian anthropologist Gilberto Freyre's Luso-tropical concepts. This affective racial science, here paradigmatically revealed by the physical anthropologist António Mendes Correia's approach to Timor, added force rather than weakness to pervasive colonial and scientific idioms of racialization of Indigenous peoples. Hence, original modalities of scientific racism could find fertile ground in an affective idiom, in which emphasis on biological difference and the primitivism of Indigenous flesh joined hands with a stress on spiritual affinity and the patriotism of Indigenous spirit.

To investigate this hypothesis, I consider the history of the "colonial anthropological missions," a set of metropolitan and state-sponsored field expeditions sent to Mozambique (1936–1956), Angola (1948–1955), Guinea Bissau (1945–1947), and East Timor (1953–1963) by official initiative of the Junta das Missões Geográficas e de Investigações Coloniais (JMGIC—Board of Geographical Missions and Colonial Research)—renamed in 1951 the Junta de Investigações do Ultramar (JIU—Overseas Research Board)—within the Portuguese Ministry of the Colonies (renamed Overseas Ministry). The anthropological missions—funded by the imperial state, conducted and supervised by university experts, locally supported by colonial administrations (the latter expected to be the ultimate beneficiaries of the missions' scientific results)— were arguably the largest and most ambitious fieldwork project of Portuguese human sciences until 1960. The definition of "anthropological" encompassed physical anthropology, archaeology, linguistics, and ethnography—but the core program was in fact a kind of racial and physical anthropological science, an "anthropobiology." The object of the missions was the "ethnic tribes" inhabiting the Asian and African colonies under Portuguese rule—including, and especially, those considered most primitive. Important to my argument, then, European *mestizo* populations were not a primary focus of research; they did not enter the concerns of the missions.

The anthropological missions were both heirs to and agents of a nationalist and racialist tradition concerned with purity, primitivism, and aboriginality, in an anti-racist and Luso-tropical era. In the 1950s, rather than presenting a corruption, "variant," or "appropriation" of Freyrean visions, they configured an autonomous and productive form of Portuguese colonial anthropology. I will not address here the many and complex aspects of these missions. I intend to put forward a working hypothesis concerning the underlying mind-set of the expeditions by drawing on the theories of their architect, also a passionate and prolific Timor ethnology scholar, the physical anthropologist António Mendes Correia. I will focus on his meaningful attachment to the study of the races of Portuguese Timor and how it accompanied the Missão Antropológica de Timor (MAT—Timor Anthropological Mission), the latest to appear (but not for that reason least significant) of the anthropological missions. Headed by Mendes Correia's acolyte, the medical doctor and anthropologist António de Almeida, MAT surveyed the Portuguese colony of eastern Timor in a first and major collective campaign in 1953 and 1954, followed by smaller-scale field visits in 1957 and 1963.[1] Although he did not executively lead the MAT (Almeida did), Mendes Correia set up the research program and guiding scientific theories. He himself went on a visit to Timor, as part of the first field campaign of MAT, in 1953—a "visit" that will become the story line for this chapter.

I begin with considerations on Mendes Correia's outline of the anthropological missions and the apparent omission of race mixing and "mixed-race peoples" as objects of research. I then focus on his visit to the colony of Portuguese Timor in the context of the first MAT campaign. I read his visit as a field experience framed by a double theory: a theory of racial or anthropogenetic mutationism, through which the Timorese were presented as an utterly different and archaic racial form of mutants, beyond race mixing; and a theory of affect, through which the Portuguese and the Timorese were understood as spiritually affine. This, I argue, points toward an original scientific project of affective racial science, a distinctive form of racial exceptionalism beyond Luso-tropicalism, in the twentieth-century Portuguese-speaking world.

Racial Science beyond Luso-tropicalism

Mixed race communities were clearly peripheral rather than central to the original program for "Portuguese colonial anthropology" launched in the 1930s by Mendes Correia at the University of Porto, in the context of which the anthropological missions became prominent.[2] Even before 1945, mixed-race peoples in the colonies had hardly been the focus of systematic physical anthropological work. In the 1920s and 1930s, the Goan anthropologist Alberto C. Germano da Silva Correia investigated the racial vitality and (im)purity of the *luso-descendentes* in Goa and Angola, while Mendes Correia, through a questionnaire sent to colonial officials, tentatively inquired about the social usefulness and biological vigor of the Cape Verdean and Macanese mixed-race groups.[3] These attempts had little echo in concrete researches in subsequent years. Meaningful in this regard is that Mendes Correia did not premeditate anthropological missions in Goa, Macau, and Cape Verde, where mixed-race groups were presumably more visible and socially significant in the colonial populations. Miscegenation was practically excluded as a primary research object and as a research problem of colonial anthropology—and excluded, as we will see, at least in the case of Mendes Correia's ethnogenic theories for Timor, from raciological explanations.

The anthropological missions did not pursue race mixing as a research problem. Instead, they were anchored in the imagination of colonial Portugal's primitive ethnic others—"pure-race" Indigenous inhabitants of the colonial territories, beyond metropolitan soil. Importantly to my considerations, the "bio-ethnic" focus on "native tribes" did not die out with the declared end of scientific racism or the advent of Luso-tropicalism. It persisted after World War II, even when the Portuguese regime began to gradually adopt and adapt Freyre's theories as an official ideology. Such emphasis on racial primitivism, purity, and aboriginality apparently bears contrast with one of the marks of

Freyre's Luso-tropical views of Portuguese colonial and racial exceptionalism: miscegenation. The Portuguese settlers' special inclination to produce harmonious worlds based on the proliferation of socially and biologically benign *mestiços* was a main tenet of *luso-tropicalismo*. The impact of Freyre's work on Portuguese human sciences and political ideology has been considerable. In the late 1950s, the label *luso-tropicalismo* became political *doxa* and explicitly inspired a new wave of social sciences research in the colonies, including in human biology, notably Almerindo Lessa's investigations on the *mestiço luso-tropical* in Macau and Cape Verde.[4]

Nevertheless, Portuguese intellectuals interacted with Freyre's miscegenation argument in a nuanced and, not uncommonly, skeptical manner.[5] More than any other Luso-tropicalist argument, Freyre's celebratory views of race mixing divided his Portuguese readers before and *after* 1950. Suspicion concerning miscegenation was more openly declared in the interwar years. But even later, at the height of the regime's political use and abuse of Freyre's theory, the theme of miscegenation remained controversial. Anti-miscegenation critics did not simply disappear. While Luso-tropicalism gained ground, ambivalent and even negative views on racial hybridity could still hold sway in some Portuguese circles.[6] Mendes Correia stands out as an original representative of this latter tendency. Throughout his life, he remained a firm advocate of the social, cultural, and ethnic superiority of the Portuguese race as white colonizers; he naturalized the evolutionary inferiority of natives as "backward peoples" (*povos atrasados*) in the colonies. He also did not retract his earlier skepticism about the degrading potential of mixing for the white Portuguese overseas. In addition, he excluded miscegenation as a *leitmotif* of his fieldwork projects for expeditions in colonial anthropology.

Mendes Correia has been portrayed as a prominent opponent of Freyre's pro-race-mixing vision until late in life; he was arguably *never* a "Luso-tropicalist." Freyre was aware of this tension. He first met Mendes Correia in 1937 and apparently held him in high esteem as an academic.[7] Yet, in his *Aventura e rotina*, the travelogue resulting from his 1951–1952 tour to the Portuguese colonies, he distances himself from Mendes Correia's criticism of miscegenation and his contrasting exaltation of whiteness and purity. With verve, Freyre refers to Mendes Correia's "certain inclination to a Caucasian ethnocentrism."[8] Mendes Correia's racialism, however, was far more than a solitary crusade of an aged and old-fashioned physical anthropologist, beset, as it were, by a new generation of Luso-tropicalists. The historical persistence of the colonial anthropological missions as a collective and institutional project—as an institutional assemblage of experts, technicians, and officials; a policy vision; a fieldwork endeavor; and a producer of vast collections, archives, and scientific publications—bears evidence to this latter possibility. In the 1950s, scientific research on "primitive" others prospered in the colonies. In the missions, Mendes Correia's idealization of the patriotic primitive superseded Freyre's "Luso-tropical *mestiço*" as both an object of racial research and ideological celebration. In the postwar years, indeed, there was more to Portuguese theories of race than met the Luso-tropical eye.

Luso-colonial anthropology implied nationalist ideas of a benign Portuguese colonial empire broken into many different (and ultimately hierarchically related) biological races held together by one same spiritual force—patriotism and faith—that had been introduced by a gentle type of Portuguese colonization. With regard to its sentimental and Christian-centric dimensions, this orientation could perhaps coexist pacifically with Freyre's Luso-tropicalism; both apparently overlapped in the celebration of the Christian and humane Portuguese exceptionality in empire building.[9] A concern with (Portuguese) whiteness, too, may not be simply absent from Freyre's approach to race mixing in the colonies.[10] Nevertheless, Mendes Correia's Luso-colonial anthropology did stand for a distinctive mode of racial thought and practice that offered competing answers to postwar anxieties about the specificity and the future of the Portuguese Empire, in an internationally hostile anticolonial and anti-racist environment. My hypothesis is that this originality resided in a combination of ideas of alterity and similarity, primitive otherness and patriotic selfhood, articulated through a double emphasis on *affect* and *difference*.

This twofold emphasis constituted a single, interlaced, modality of race science, whereby a colonial and nationalistic theory of affect joined hands with racial theories of essentialized biological difference and primitivism. This combined approach, moreover, was presented as specific to Portugal as a colonial nation and, concomitantly, to its colonial sciences. Depending on the specific territories and scientific actors involved, this conjunction of race and affect, difference and community, could be made manifest in different degrees and forms in the anthropological missions. In the case of the "Angola Bushmen," for instance, as Samuël Coghe shows in this volume, racialized primitivism was paramount to anthropological considerations. Yet, I believe affect and patriotic-spiritual affinity remained an underlying idiom of scientific racialization in late Portuguese colonial anthropology. It was engrained in the missions' program since their inception in the 1930s; after World War II, with scientific racism discredited or at least unpopular, perhaps the affective dimension achieved greater relevance.

The event of Mendes Correia's field visit to Portuguese Timor in 1953 is an illuminating and exemplary instance of these visions. Both coeval and alternative to the rise of Freyre's *Luso-tropicalismo*, the visit acquires additional interest for yet another reason: Timor was (along with Macau) the only Portuguese territory that Freyre did not visit during his well-known travels by invitation of the regime; there he did not put Luso-tropicalism to the test of his bodily and visual experience. In 1951 and 1952, in order to bear proof to his theories, Freyre went on a tour to the Portuguese Asian and African colonies sponsored by the regime of António de Oliveira Salazar. The tour inspired him to further elaborate on the framework of Luso-tropicalism and this tour also became a landmark of its ideological embroilments with Portuguese late imperialism. In an early draft of Freyre's itinerary, all colonies were on the list, including Timor, where Freyre should have been exposed to the Timorese *"liurais'* loyalty" to Portugal, including a visit to relatives of the martyr Timorese *régulo* Dom Aleixo Corte-Real—a key figure, as we will see, in Mendes Correia's imagery of patriotic primitives and to whom he paid tribute in publications and in his visit. Freyre's exposure to evidence of Indigenous patriotic spirituality was thus planned.

However, for reasons unmentioned, Salazar instructed Overseas Minister Manuel Maria Sarmento Rodrigues to persuade Freyre to eliminate Timor from his itinerary (a change that Freyre accepted willingly).[11] Political reasons to do with the devastation caused by recent war may have been behind the dictator's decision ("Above all I did not want to show him Timor," Sarmento Rodrigues states without further ado in a letter to Salazar).[12] Perhaps intent was to avoid showing the eminent foreigner a country destroyed, or perhaps the Portuguese authorities thought Timor simply was not worth a visit, because the Brazilian anthropologist would not find any suitable evidence for his theory of Portuguese exceptionalism. In any case, Timor's absence in Freyre's *Luso-tropicalist* tour of 1951–1952, makes the Portuguese anthropologist's upcoming visit to the country all the more significant. Hence, Mendes Correia's trip can eventually be explored as a revealing alternative counterpart of the "Portuguese world" envisioned by Freyre.

Beyond Luso-tropicalism, Mendes Correia's engagement with Timor epitomizes—perhaps almost as an ideal type—the sort of postwar conjunction of affect and race in Luso-colonial anthropology. Although never a field leader or executive chief of the expeditions (he always saw himself as a data coordinator and armchair anthropologist, not a fieldworker), Mendes Correia masterminded the research program of the anthropological missions. With regard to Timor in particular, he offered the scientific theories for which the field research ought to provide the evidence. His understanding of a national empire made of bonds of intangible patriotic affect, rather than flesh, was expressed in his belief in a communal relationship with the East Timorese, as spiritually affine to the metropolitan Portuguese. However, over the years he simultaneously elaborated on a sophisticated racial theory of the ultimate biological and evolutionary primitivism of the East Timorese. The following is an analysis of this apparent "double bind" in Mendes Correia's racial thought, before and after his participation in the 1953 MAT campaign.

Proto-Malayans: An Archaic Race of Mutants

"I have read, studied, and published so much on Timorese subjects," Mendes Correia recalled in a lecture widely broadcast on Portuguese national radio after his return to Lisbon, in 1955, "that, on setting foot on Timor's soil, I felt an intimate, profound, joy, almost as if I was before a sacred vision, a mystery unveiled, a dream come true!"[13] On the morning of 23 August 1953, after a long journey from Lisbon, Professor António Mendes Correia landed in the modest airport of Dili, the capital of the smallest, most remote, and most isolated colony of the vast Portuguese Empire, Portuguese Timor. He came out "joyous," a witness wrote, holding the jacket by his arm, and came straight to greet the local authorities who awaited him at landing, to pay his respects: the governor, all principal members of colonial administration, and the recently arrived staff of the Timor Anthropological Mission headed by his fellow anthropologist, Dr. António de Almeida.[14] "Big chief" (*grande chefe*)—as Almeida subserviently and reverently treated Mendes Correia in his private diary—had arrived (fig. 7.1).[15]

Mendes Correia's appearance was a stately occasion. His arrival and his subsequent itinerary, on a government car, traveling across the country during the following month were meticulously planned and pompously staged by the colonial government authorities. His one-month visit to the country was accompanied by constant ceremonials prepared especially for him by local colonial authorities, on occasion of his every visit to a village. This included flag-raising ceremonies, welcome receptions by Timorese crowds, folklore displays, and martial parades. The government attentions toward Mendes Correia are indicators of his high status as a figure of authority in the Portuguese colonial world. The pompous arrangements suggest his arrival was prepared in the image of the recent official visit paid to Timor, just one year before, in 1952, by Minister Sarmento Rodrigues himself. Indeed, Mendes Correia was no ordinary visitor. He had come as president of the Overseas Research Board, by appointment of the same influential minister; then aged sixty-five, he was at the height of his political and scientific powers.

Mendes Correia, arguably the most influential Portuguese racial and physical anthropologist of the first half of the twentieth century, was also a major figure of the *Estado Novo* elite. In the early 1910s, he headed the institutionalization of anthropology at the University of Porto and launched a new academic field, "colonial anthropology," a discipline ruled by metropolitan academics, supported by the state, and closely allied with the imperial project. He went on to a highly successful political and scientific career. An avowed nationalist and imperialist, he became prominent as a scientific expert on race with the establishment of Salazar's dictatorship in 1933. He was a prolific writer on criminology, eugenics, archaeology, and prehistory. Initially, he

Figure 7.1. António Mendes Correia upon his arrival at Dili in 1953. *From left to right:* António de Almeida (Head of the Timor Anthropological Mission), César Serpa Rosa (Governor of Timor), Mendes Correia, and the plane pilots. Photographer unknown. IICT Photography Collection, INV. ULISBOA-IICT-MAT27773. Courtesy of Museu Nacional de História Natural e da Ciência, Lisbon.

was primarily concerned with the origins and racial constitution of the Portuguese metropolitan population. Over time, Mendes Correia became growingly interested in studying the Indigenous populations in the Portuguese colonies. In the 1930s, his scientific career prospered, as did his political career within the fascist dictatorship. He presided over the Porto City Council from 1936 to 1942 and became a deputy to the National Assembly from 1945 to 1956. Above all, he gained uncontested prominence as the head and ideologue of scientific policy for the colonies. In 1941, the government requested him, as a member of the National Education Board, to design a plan for colonial scientific research (specifically for anthropology). In 1946, he was appointed to the presidency of the JMGIC/JIU, which he held until his retirement in 1958. From 1951, moreover, his figure became omnipresent. He dominated all scientific institutions with a bearing on colonial matters in metropolitan Portugal, accumulating the JMGIC/JIU presidency with the directorship of the Colonial School and the presidency of the Lisbon Geographic Society.

The official purpose of his trip was to formally inaugurate the Centre of Timorese Studies in Dili, which the minister had promised in his former visit in 1952. However, the anthropologist also brought to Timor a personal agenda. He wanted to pursue his own researches, to collect and confirm certain hypotheses about Timorese "ethnic groups." Given his decades-long dedication to the problem of East Timorese ethnogeny, it is no wonder his one-month field visit to Timor in 1953 would become, in his own words, a "dream come true."

Rejecting Indigenous Miscegenation: An Anthropogenetic Theory

A self-declared armchair scholar, Mendes Correia never visited Timor until 1953. Yet, he had written and theorized extensively about its races since his early years as an anthropologist at Porto. He was prolific author on many topics, but, in what concerned the colonies, Timor was his favorite subject. Decades earlier, in his youth, in 1916, he published a set of articles on the racial classification of Portuguese Timor, based on anthropometric records from a late colonial officer, Fonseca Cardoso. Mendes Correia's anthropological reflections on Timor were framed by a lasting international debate, originated in nineteenth-century ethnology, on the distribution of human variety in Oceania and particularly in the Malay Archipelago. In this international context, Timor was especially interesting because it seemed to confusingly combine characteristics of the main regional race types. Timor was understood as a land of mixed-race types about which there was no classificatory agreement. In the 1910s, Mendes Correia (like many scholars of his time) was eager to achieve recognition by interfering with Alfred Russel Wallace's ethnological divide of the archipelago into two zones, two race types, the Malayan and the Papuan. Against Wallace, he particularly aimed at reclassifying (East) Timor as Malayan, rather than Papuan, therefore forcing a change in the ethnological map of the archipelago.[16]

Where to place the Portuguese colony of Timor in relation to Wallace's ethnological line was a driving force of Mendes Correia's research. It was also expected to be a driving force of MAT. In 1941, answering a request by the ministry to establish a plan for anthropological studies in the colonies, Mendes Correia expanded this personal interests into a collective research endeavor. He turned his anti-Wallace hypothesis into the commanding problematic for the planned Timor Anthropological Mission. "In what concerns Timor," he wrote, "the contribution of anthropological studies on the Timorese tribes would be of the highest importance for clarifying the intricate problem of the origins and relationships of the native peoples of Melanesia and Insulindia and *to criticize* Wallace's famous dividing line."[17] Thus, he planned a major fieldwork expedition to give credence to his long-standing argument, providing him hard data to disprove Wallace and validate his own Malayan hypothesis. For Wallace, *all* Timorese belonged to the Papuan race. But for Mendes Correia, the Portuguese part of Timor belonged to the Malayan race type, and particularly to a most primitive and archaic modality, the Proto-Malayan or Proto-Indonesian. This classificatory argument was originally presented in the mid-1910s and later on developed extensively in Mendes Correia's magnum opus on the ethnology of Portuguese Timor, the 1944 monograph *Timor português*. In this work, Mendes Correia elaborated on his arguments for classifying the East Timorese as representatives of the Proto-Malayan race. However, in the same monograph (and in subsequent articles), he added to his long-standing classificatory argument a novel anthropogenic theory.

In countercurrent with prevailing opinions, he challenged the accepted wisdom about the mixed-race nature of the Timorese. Whereas most scholars understood the Timorese imbroglio as the outcome of race mixing—a "mix," "juxtaposition," "mingle" of different races—Mendes Correia proposed a contrasting ethnogenic perspective, interpreting such racial uncertainty as an archaic moment in biological evolution, an instance of bio-ethnic mutation. Thus, he rejected "miscegenation" and "migrations" as explanatory forces in the formation of the races of Timor, instead putting forward a singular polygenetic theory of anthropogenetic mutationism. According to him, the island was an exemplary illustration of a broader mutationism, common to the whole Malay Archipelago: it was an origin center of *Homo sapiens,* a birthplace of racial mutations: "In Timor, one may feel at the same time the racial archaism of such a human evolution, and the germinal sprouting of its evolutionary possibilities."[18] In a 1945 essay, he summarized: "The ethnic influences of New Guinea and, in general, of Melanesia [in Timor] have been, in our view, exaggerated, but also even the genesis through mixing or miscegenation of numerous elements from the most varied provenances[;] instead our understanding is that the heterogeneity recorded therein results from a biological process of mutability, which has been underway in Indonesia, for reasons unknown."[19]

Mendes Correia designated this theory as "mutationism." Endless racial crossing between Indigenous types did not cause the Timorese ethnic mosaic. Miscegenation did not explain racial heterogeneity. Neither did a long history of maritime inter-island movements and influx of foreign migrants. Timorese "mixture" in reality stood for an archaic moment of biological differentiation of human types. Thus, Timor instead constituted an independent origin-center of racial creation and differentiation—a site of an ongoing evolutionary process that one could witness, at its most primitive stage, in the modern heart of the twentieth century.

Human variety had been created *ab nuovo* in the island itself. The Timorese in the present were archaic mutant forms of a human type born in the island, still undefined. This polygenetic vision of the mutant primitivism of the "Portuguese Timor" aborigines, so to speak, provided a model for explaining racial diversity across the Malay Archipelago as a whole. Mendes Correia thus rejected the miscegenation of the primitives in order to interfere with the ethnological line and the international discussion on the origins of races in the Malay Archipelago. However, his resilience to inter-Indigenous miscegenation as explanation perhaps also articulated a critique of race mixing as an essential feature of the Portuguese nation and its empire. His approach to Timor is one more piece of his views of the intrinsic value of aboriginal racial purity, part of a broader imagination of the potentially nefarious consequences of *mestiçagem* upon Portugal as colonial nation, and finally a broader expression perhaps too of his inner attempt to undermine Freyre's imagination of a Luso-tropical sexualized and mixed-race world.

Mendes Correia's rejection of "inter-native" miscegenation among the Timorese ethnic *other*, in a far corner of the Portuguese colonial empire, also reads as an expression of his celebrations of ethnic purity and correlate critiques of the degenerative impact of interracial mixing, among the Portuguese "self" at home in particular. Since the 1930s, he had theorized about the ethnic national character of the (metropolitan) Portuguese. He posited the white racial purity of the Portuguese nation both in the metropole and in the colonies, arguing against the degrading presence of African and Muslim blood in the ethnic character of the Portuguese, which he saw as genetically, inherently, "white European."[20] In the colonies, although he could be ambivalent about the practical value of mestizos as a resource in colonization policies, he nonetheless defended that race mixing as such could *not* form the basis for a scientific colonial policy.[21] A mestizo population could be pragmatically useful for administrative purposes. However, cross-racial mixing should not be encouraged, uncontrollably, because it would lead ultimately to the degeneration and even dissolution of the Portuguese racial stock. As such, cross-racial sexual intercourse and consequent biological mixing could put the purity and integrity of the "Portuguese race" at risk overseas.

Mendes Correia's eugenic arguments in detriment of race mixing express moral rejection of the bonds of flesh and sexual intercourse. Thus, his apparent abhorrence of race mixing (including, as we will see, in its affective and spiritual dimension) arguably stems from a conservative Catholicism, evoking an implicit moral opposition between flesh and spirit, body and soul, central to Western Judeo-Christian traditions.[22] In these traditions, the vile nature of the human flesh and the sinful nature of sexuality were depreciated, in contrast with the sublime condition of the human soul. Mendes Correia's rejection of racial crossing as a way to create a biologically strong and pure national-imperial community suggests the presence of these imageries. In the 1950s, this presence gained new strength, with added emphasis on the psychological character of the Portuguese to affectively—*not* sexually or biologically—connect to other peoples overseas. Furthermore, Timor apparently could be a perfect case study for Mendes Correia's idealization of a colonial empire free of race mixing. This was not a white settlers' colony; the Portuguese community in Timor had over the centuries been confined to Dili, limited to a handful of Europeans; only few Portuguese-Timorese descendants were visible. He thus could utterly dismiss miscegenation in the making of a Portuguese world that transcended the bodily boundaries of race.

In landing in Timor in 1953, therefore, Mendes Correia was anxious to find evidence for his ethnogenic theory of mutationism. He expected not only to disprove Wallace again but also to counter the theories about the formative powers of race mixing in island Southeast Asia. Back in the 1940s, in order to articulate his hypotheses about Timorese ethnology, he had drawn on anthropometric observations on living people and a number of photographic portraits while also conjecturing inventively on demographic data from recent census in Portuguese Timor. In 1953, he saw his visit to Timor as an opportunity to collect evidence that would confirm *in loco* his former anthropological theories—and such a confirmation he claimed to have found in Timorese legends and in his observations on a Timorese red-haired community.[23] His encounter with the latter community convinced him that such white race biological traits could not definitively be the outcome of European-Indigenous mixing; they were instead local anthropogenetic mutants, evidence after all of ongoing human evolution in the island, at its most primitive stage.

Despite the Portuguese administration's efforts for upbringing "civilization," the anthropologist drew a strict racial boundary between Portuguese and Timorese peoples and elaborated on the archaic evolutionary condition of the native populations. Yet, this was simultaneous to his nationalistic understanding of the Timorese as profoundly patriotic and spiritually Portuguese. His racial theory of bio-ethnic and genetic differentiation went along with a colonial theory of affective communion and interracial spiritual "fusion": "affectivity," he conceptualized in 1954, "is what regulates in degree and meaning the majority of the intellectual, volitional, and social activities of the Portuguese," including in the work of colonization.[24] Often on the same pages, in the same publications, Mendes Correia brought his hard approach to the racialization of the "primitive" together with a vision of spiritual and affective cross-racial union.

Affect and the Patriotic Primitive

The idea that Portuguese and Timorese were connected by mutual affect toward the Portuguese nation was a central motivation of Mendes Correia's anthropological research. An avowed nationalist, he saw the empire as one same spiritual body, a brotherhood of nationalistic love, where distinct races (distinct also in the hierarchical scale of evolution) came together by force of shared affect toward the motherland. Divided by flesh but united by spirit. Differentiated by race as a force of nature but brought together as one community of shared patriotic feelings. Thus, in 1944, in the introduction to *Timor português*, Mendes Correia framed his research approach to the anthropological study of the Timorese:

> It is a Portuguese tradition the desire to understand scientifically the varied peoples that live under our flag; the desire to seek their well-being and prosperity, to attract them affectionately to being together with the population of metropolitan origin. Timor . . . has had the gift to arise, to special degree . . . hard working and valuable research and affective interest. [25]

Mendes Correia's racial science was affective by motivation; his interest in Timor a gauge of his love and feelings of patriotism. Morever, he felt the Timorese were affectively *alike* the Portuguese. They were patriotic kindred spirits. From the perspective of this unifying spiritual patriotism, Deputy Mendes Correia, during the constitutional revision of 1951, criticized (though partially) the infamous *Indigenato* regime that since 1926 denied "natives" in the colonies equal citizenship rights and gave forced labor a free hand. He also praised the Acto Colonial of 1930, which reinforced a differential status for Indigenous people before Portuguese law, for giving legal acknowledgment to separate "ethnic realities."

But Mendes Correia now argued for further "national unification" between metropole and overseas provinces by eliminating the term *indígena* (native) from the Portuguese Constitution, in the same spirit then guiding the regime's idiomatic cosmetics of the postwar empire, replacing "colonies" with "overseas provinces." In his view, *indígenas* were in effect "overseas brothers" (*irmãos de além-mar*), so the term itself incorrectly conveyed two "blocs or casts of Portuguese, that is, citizens and natives." Such divide was "contrary to the precepts of Christian fraternity" and the utterly unique "spiritual traditions" of the centuries-old Portuguese colonization, which bore contrast with Anglophone forms of colonialism. He argued that *indígena* itself (just like *colónia*) was a foreign word imported from the English "native"; it was not a purely autochthonous Portuguese word; it wrongly conveyed the unique nature of Portuguese colonialism and as such should be eradicated from the Constitution: "Let us leave the juridical designations *native, African*, etc. for the other [colonizing] peoples. For us, in the Constitution there are and shall be only Portuguese, our brothers, souls, human beings like us, collaborators in a Christian mission, humane and universalist that was imposed upon us by History, our convictions and our highest aspirations."[26] An invisible and indivisible patriotic bond, a kind of spiritual kinship, united metropolitan and overseas peoples as a single Portuguese national soul. Hence, Mendes Correia's "special" scientific interest in Timor was grounded on his belief in the intrinsic destiny of Portugal as a Christian universalist nation in expansion, and in a quasi-religious understanding of the empire-nation as spiritual organism, which should extend, according to nationalist credo, from "Minho [a province in metropolitan Portugal] to Timor."

Mendes Correia's ideas of cross-racial patriotic affectivity arguably followed in the wake of a tradition of messianic and mystical interpretations of the universalistic and spiritual vocation of the Portuguese Empire.[27] They similarly evoked a more recent wave of ethnological scholarship that, since the outset of ethnology in Portugal in the 1870s, concerned the "ethnic psychology" of the Portuguese nation.[28] Finally, Mendes Correia's notions were also in harmony with a then contemporary nationalist emphasis on the central role of Christian religion and evangelization in empire building (a feat of the cross rather than the sword)—themes also present in Freyre's "Christo-centric" Luso-tropical arguments. "Who can deny," Lieutenant Colonel Leite de Magalhães, Mendes Correia's close acquaintance and loyal collaborator in his Timor studies, asked rhetorically in 1934, "the strong spirituality orienting and feeding all the wonders that the hands of ancient Portugal have risen up upon Earth?"[29] In the particular historical context of the 1940s, moreover, Mendes Correia's self-declared affective racial science especially resonated a pervading nationalist interpretation of Timor that developed during the war years in Portugal. For many decades, East Timor and its inhabitants had been perceived negatively as useless and problematic backwater colony. But after the war, Timor came to acquire a rather generalized positive connotation. By the 1940s, built on a nationalist-imperialist language, Timor moved from the margins to the center in the imagination of the Portuguese Empire as a national community of affect.

Timor's Patriotic Martyrdom in World War II

During World War II, Portugal followed a policy of neutrality. Yet, the isolated island of Timor held a strategic significance that with difficulty would avoid its involvement in the war. Despite Portugal's vehement attempts, first the Allies and then the Japanese army took positions in Timor. In 1942, the Japanese decided for an effective military occupation, forcing the Portuguese to flee.

Terrible violence followed; many East Timorese remained attached to the Portuguese and took the side of the Allies. Only after the Allied victory was Portuguese administration reestablished in East Timor in 1945. These events were followed attentively in Portugal. They had a strong impact on strengthening a nationalist-imperialist reading of the unique spiritual essence of Portuguese colonization, which, as noted earlier, held sway in Portuguese intellectual and political circles since at least the nineteenth century. In this wake, moreover, a common explanation for the apparent weakness of Portuguese rule in Timor was founded on patriotic-spiritualist arguments. The idea of Portuguese colonial domination sustained only by intangible energies, rather than by material and military strength, was deeply embedded in colonial discourse on Timor, at least since the mid-nineteenth century—and resumes in passages of Mendes Correia's writings.[30]

Japanese occupation reactivated a nationalist language of affective colonial ties. In the war events in Timor, Portuguese nationalists found ultimate evidence of Portugal as a single and integral national and imperial entity held together by feelings of Christian faith and patriotic devotion, a "sacred heritage" from the Age of Discovery that could not be desecrated. "Timor was a continuous and painful preoccupation in the hearts of the Portuguese," Salazar declared in a public statement after Timor was "liberated" from its Japanese occupants and Portuguese sovereignty reestablished in October 1945. "Never, not in a single moment has Timor left our spirit and occupied our attention . . . We vividly congratulate ourselves and congratulate the population of the Colony for their dedication and loyalty to the Motherland, duly appreciating its long sacrifice."[31] The East Timorese supposedly patriotic resistance to Japanese occupation, accordingly, came to be seen as demonstration of Portugal's colonizing capacity to transform even the most remote natives into true "Portuguese" by heart. In a public reaction to Salazar's message, the newly appointed governor of Timor, Óscar Ruas, reinstated the point: "Portugal's rights in this country are not established upon the right of force, but they reside essentially in the heart and conscious will of all his European and native inhabitants."[32]

These ideas were exacerbated after 1942 and 1943, as news on the war front arrived from Timor. In Portugal, the news of Japanese occupation was soon followed by accounts of some East Timorese having heroically defended Portuguese administration, dying in martyrdom in the name of Portugal and the national flag. For Mendes Correia, these events brought the metropolitan Portuguese and the Timorese closer than ever in spirit: "I do not think the metropolitan mind has forgotten Portugal's distant overseas province," he wrote on his return from Timor. "Quite on the contrary, I consider it always present in our spirit and close to our heart. Recent events [World War II, 1942–1945] have intensified those feelings of proximity and affect."[33] Indeed, the events of the occupation of Timor left a very vivid impression on Mendes Correia's spirit. With nationalist verve, then, he dedicated his anthropological monograph of 1944 to this very ideal:

> Thus, at a time in which the national sentiment, cruelly wounded, vibrates with indignation with the unfair attack to the Portuguese sovereignty in Timor, a publication that deals with the Timorese people represents evidently the animation of an indestructible solidarity between the metropole and all those who, regardless of their blood and their color, in those faraway places, do not repudiate the old and strong ties with Portugal. At the same time, this [publication] is a new manifestation of the firm and affective Portuguese interest in that pulsating parcel of the empire's living body.[34]

Portuguese "in their hearts," the Timorese stood as ultimate evidence of the benign "specificity" of Portuguese colonial history as a work of spiritual expansion of Christian and patriotic ideals and ties. From this perspective, the great feat of Portuguese colonization over the centuries was an achievement of spiritual assimilation, of which the main agent had been the diffusion of Catholicism over the centuries. "Throughout our colonization, spiritualism," wrote Lieutenant Colonel Luna de Oliveira after a visit to Mozambique, a few years before he signed his two-volume history of Timor, *Timor na História de Portugal* of 1949, "has been the most secure bond that has tied the colonizing body to the colonized body ... Other colonial nations, even if they treat well the Negro [*preto*], are not interested in making him similar to themselves in the psychological aspect."[35] Mendes Correia not only shared this vision of an empire made exceptionally of spiritual-patriotic similitude, as he also elaborated further on its significance in the framework of his bioanthropological understanding of racial alterity. In fact, he merged the two aspects, as mutually reinforcing images, in one same racialist anthropological conceptualizing.

Above all, one real historical figure stood out in this imagination of race and affective community: Aleixo Corte-Real, better known as Dom Aleixo, a Timorese *liurai* who fought against the Japanese occupants in the name of his loyalty to Portugal and the Portuguese flag. His tragic murder by Japanese forces in 1943 bore deeply on Mendes Correia's thoughts. Indeed, his luxuriously edited and illustrated *Timor português* opened with a fine watercolor portrait of Dom Aleixo, dressed up in his Indigenous traditional costumes of *liurai*: "This is a fair consecration," he explained, "of *régulo* D. Aleixo who died recently for Portugal!"[36] The pride of place given to the Timorese leader in the volume was Mendes Correia's homage to the sacrificial and heroic Portugueseness of the Indigenous Timorese—biologically different, spiritually Portuguese. It may not have been indifferent to this homage the fact that Mendes Correia had met Dom Aleixo in person, years before. In 1934 (and again in the great Portuguese World Exhibition of 1940), Dom Aleixo and his relatives came especially to the exhibition at Porto to be exhibited as representatives of the "native races" of Timor—as well as loyal primitive subjects of Portugal. Mendes Correia and his team at Porto also took this opportunity to observe and measure the Timorese as anthropological specimens. Back then, the *liurai* had already been treated doubly as racialized object and converted Portuguese patriot.[37] The body and soul of Aleixo Corte-Real epitomized Mendes Correia's imagination of the patriotic primitive. The news of his sacrificial death in defense of Portuguese administration in 1943 was, for Mendes Correia, a supreme revelation of that double truth.

Field Evidence of Affective Community

Mendes Correia's colonial theory of a national empire cemented by spiritual ties, rather than by the vile bonds of sex and flesh, expressed his own sense of a science inspired by feelings of patriotism that presumed an imagined communal spirituality among all subjects of Portugal, including the Timorese. Accordingly, his field visit of 1953 came to represent more than a means to gather data for his theories on Timorese racial taxonomy and ethnogeny. In his own account, field encounters stood as validation of his views about the spiritual fusion of patriotic hearts that had been achieved, over the centuries, by the Portuguese Empire in the country. The receptions that awaited Mendes Correia in the Timorese villages constituted transcendent moments of validation of the exceptionalism of Portuguese spiritual colonization. Flag-raising ceremonies and Timorese flag cults above all produced on Mendes Correia's self an inner validation of the bonds of patriotic affect and feeling that united him to the Timorese natives around. "I was moved in assisting to the homage paid by the *moradores* [Timorese auxiliary forces] and population in general to our flag . . . It is undeniable that [the Portuguese], throughout their history, with their processes of native policy, mainly with the absence of feelings and restrictions of racial discrimination, the Portuguese conquered the good dispositions, even the sympathies of the native peoples" (fig. 2). He continued, further illustrating his point with a reference to his emotional encounter with relatives of his admired hero: "D. António Corte-Real, *régulo* D. Aleixo's brother, gloriously killed on occasion of the Japanese occupation, let himself be photographed in his warrior or native chief outfit, but he requested a photo of himself holding a small Portuguese flag that he brought with himself from his house."[38]

He was touched to the verge of tears: Mendes Correia's field trip to Timor was not simply to corroborate an anthropogenetic theory of races; it was also to collect evidence of his notions on Portuguese Timorese affective *communitas*. It was a sentimental journey, as scientific as religiously colonial and nationalistic. In the field, Mendes Correia felt himself like the Timorese; he felt

Figure 7.2. António Mendes Correia and his reception at Ossu, Timor Anthropological Mission, 1953. Photographer unknown. IICT Photography Collection, INV. ULISBOA-IICT-MAT26663. Courtesy of Museu Nacional de História Natural e da Ciência, Lisbon.

the Timorese affectively *affine* to the Portuguese. The visit to Timor validated both his hypothesis on primitive mutationism and his ideas on the spiritual ties between Portugal and the *indígenas*. Mendes Correia's part in the anthropological mission, in sum, manifested the affective race science of patriotic primitives that, in his vision, only within the Portuguese colonial world could come into existence. The almost mystical language used to remember and retell the events of his visit are signs that his was not simply a fieldwork in search of racial origins and differences but also a metaphysical quest of ethereal, almost mystical, affective affinities.

Conclusion

In this chapter, I have called attention to a form of affective racial conceptions in the Portuguese-speaking world in the second half of the twentieth century. I reassessed the Luso-tropicalist emphasis on miscegenation by shifting attention to the programs, theories, ideas, agents, institutions, and field experiences that—from the 1930s to the 1960s—lay the focus on racial difference and primitivism of the Indigenous populations in the Portuguese colonies. Yet, this focus on difference went together with a nationalist colonial ideology that celebrated interracial affective and spiritual fusion, beyond the carnal bonds of miscegenation. I have argued that the research collectives of the anthropological missions represent this dualistic approach to race at an institutional and collective level, and at a cross-colonial scale. Here, I have explored particularly the theories of the missions' mentor, Mendes Correia, and his visit to Timor in 1953, to paradigmatically bring out the intimate conjunction between affect and race in the imagination of what I have tentatively called the "patriotic primitive."

The theme of "miscegenation" has dominated historical considerations on the character of Lusophone racial conceptions in the postwar years. Critical reassessments of the impact and "reception" of the Luso-tropical ideology of race on Portuguese conceptions have accordingly emphasized the miscegenation theme. Although this critique is required, the emphasis on miscegenation has resulted in detrimental considerations about other modalities of Portuguese racial science, where hybridity and racial mixing played a minor role—such as the one represented, I argued here, by the colonial anthropological missions and, importantly, by the influential vision of the missions' ultimate mentor and theorist, António Mendes Correia. Mendes Correia's studies and reflections on Timor epitomize this approach. His affective racial science for Timor expressed a singular merge of political/colonial theory of nationalism, on the one hand and scientific racial theories of "native race types" that downplayed the significance of miscegenation on the other. Only contradictory in appearance, this merge of affect and racialization, of communion and difference, was in fact one common theory. The benevolent nature of Portuguese colonialism as an imagined national community of affect went parallel to the imagined racial alterity and primitivism of the East Timorese; as such, these conceptions carried with them also a colonial ideology of domination and a racist assertion of the purity and superiority of the "white European race" of Portuguese colonizers.

This case study points to a racialized science of the primitive in the company of a language of cross-racial affect; it shows how alterity and similitude could be brought together in late twentieth-century racial conceptions. Mendes Correia saw a strict biological boundary between Portuguese and Timorese peoples and, despite the Portuguese administration's efforts, fully acknowledged the backward condition of the latter. Yet, this was simultaneous to his nationalistic understanding of the Timorese as profoundly patriotic and spiritually Portuguese. Racial miscegenation was a corporeal exercise that tainted the imagination of a mystical empire; in no way could it be seen as the cement for one same Portuguese world. Hybridity or mixture would not characterize the making of a benign and non-racist Portuguese world. Instead, it was an invisible flow of common sentiments and reciprocal affection for the Portuguese nation, more akin perhaps to a Durkheimian vision of a "conscience collective," a psychological force made of emotions, affect, and sentiments. Thus, grounded on Portuguese nationalist traditions, Christian universalism, and eugenic skepticism toward race mixing, Mendes Correia engaged with the challenges posed to postwar racial sciences in Portugal by anticolonialism, anti-racism, and Freyrean Luso-tropicalism.

His form of affective racialization of the primitive was also made manifest, I argue, in the anthropological missions that surveyed the colonies in the postwar years. In line with Mendes Correia's plans, a programmatic singularity of the late anthropological missions resided in fostering the racialization of primitives while also acknowledging cross-racial affective bonds as distinctive of the Portuguese colonial world and colonial sciences. Racial theories emphasizing primitivism and devaluing miscegenation thus prospered in connection with a nationalistic vision of transracial affective communion, presented as distinctively and uniquely "Portuguese." Certainly, this general hypothesis may require qualification and nuances beyond the case of Timor, in relation to the anthropological missions in Angola, Mozambique, or Guinea, for example. Beyond self-perceptions of Portuguese exceptionalism, moreover, international connections and comparisons are worth investigating in more detail. In that same historical period, the study of Indigenous "isolates" and "primitives" was in vogue in international human biology.[39] In this light, imperial rhetoric and colonial politics notwithstanding, the sustained focus of the anthropological missions on Indigenous pure and primitive ethnic groups perhaps was not so eccentric.

The concern with mass collecting anthropometry and blood grouping also had companions elsewhere. A case especially worth considering was Léon Palès's Mission Anthropologique de l'Afrique Occidentale Française of 1945–1951,[40] which, Mendes Correia, in effect, emulated in 1945 as a model in his defense of the significance of the Portuguese expeditions.[41] These transnational and comparative dimensions of the race sciences of the Portuguese anthropological missions require further research. But they clearly cannot be reduced to mere dying "vestiges" or "survivals" from past colonial racial sciences. They were a vigorous project worth exploring for the contemporary significance and the issues they addressed in their own times, in a postwar imperial and colonial context. We thus must understand better the longevity of this kind of racial formations in the twentieth-century Portuguese-speaking world, why and how they came into being, and perhaps how and why their impact may have lasted even beyond the end of the Portuguese colonial empire.

RICARDO ROQUE is Research Fellow at the Institute of Social Sciences (ICS) in the University of Lisbon (Instituto de Ciências Sociais da Universidade de Lisboa), and Honorary Associate in the Department of History at the University of Sydney. He works in the history and anthropology of colonialism, human sciences, and cross-cultural contact in the Portuguese-speaking world, from 1800 to the twentieth century. He has published widely on the history of racial science and the anthropology of colonialism, and on the theory and ethnography of colonial archives and museum collections. He is the author of *Headhunting and Colonialism* (Palgrave, 2010) and the coeditor of *Engaging Colonial Knowledge* (Palgrave, 2012). At the ICS, he coordinates the research group Empires, Colonialism and Postcolonial Societies.

Notes

An earlier version of this chapter was presented in Rio de Janeiro in April 2016. I thank the other attendees for a productive discussion and especially Warwick Anderson, Frederico Ágoas, James Dunk, Cláudia Castelo, Ilana Lowy, and Ricardo Ventura Santos for comments on earlier versions. I am grateful to Cláudia Castelo for generously sharing research materials. All translations from Portuguese are mine.

1. Exact dates of the late official campaigns remain uncertain, as most visits to Timor after 1953 were individual trips of the original expedition leader, António de Almeida.
2. See Ricardo Roque, "A antropologia colonial portuguesa (c. 1911–1950)," in *Estudos de sociologia da leitura em portugal no século XX*, ed. Diogo Ramada Curto (Lisbon, 2006), 789–822; Rui M. Pereira, "Raça, sangue e robustez: Os paradigmas da antropologia física colonial portuguesa," *Cadernos de Estudos Africanos* 7–8 (2005): 209–41.
3. See António A. Mendes Correia, "Os mestiços nas colónias portuguesas," in *Trabalhos do I Congresso Nacional de Antropologia Colonial*, vol. 1 (Porto, 1934), 331–49. On Alberto Correia, cf. Ricardo Roque, "'Portugueses da Índia': Germano Correia e a antropologia dos luso-descendentes de Goa," in *Actas do VI Congresso Luso-Afro-Brasileiro de Ciências Sociais*, ed. Rui Centeno and António Custódio Gonçalves (Porto, 2002), 339–46; Cristiana Bastos, "Um luso-tropicalismo às avessas: Colonialismo científico, aclimação e pureza racial em Germano Correia," in *Fantasmas e fantasias imperiais no imaginário português contemporâneo*, ed. Margarida Calafate Ribeiro and Ana Paula Ferreira (Porto, 2003), 227–53.
4. On the reception of Freyre's view of miscegenation in Portugal and beyond, see Cláudia Castelo, this volume.
5. Cf. Valentim Alexandre, "Portugal em África (1825–1974): Uma perspectiva global," *Penélope* 11 (1993): 53–66; Cláudia Castelo, *"O modo português de estar no mundo": O luso-tropicalismo e a ideologia colonial portuguesa* (Porto, 1998), chap. 3; Richard Cleminson, *Catholicism, Race and Empire: Eugenics in Portugal* (Budapest, 2014), 30.
6. The possibility of anti-miscegenation ideas continuing in Portugal after 1945 is perceptively suggested, but in reality not explored further, by Castelo, *O modo português*, 115; Cleminson, *Catholicism*, 207, 242–43.
7. Freyre first met Mendes Correia in person in his 1937 visit to Rio de Janeiro and was impressed by his reputation and lecturing skills. He wrote in a letter to Melville Herskovits: "At present we have in Rio, a prominent Portuguese anthropologist and sociol-

ogist: Professor Mendes Corrêa. He is a very good lecturer." In 1951, Freyre met him again in Portugal, but he was never part of Freyre's network of Portuguese correspondents. Letter from Gilberto Freyre to Melville J. Herskovits, 15 May 1937, box 7, folder 40, Melville Herskovits Papers, Northwestern University Archives. I thank Cláudia Castelo for this reference.
8. Gilberto Freyre, *Aventura e rotina: Sugestões de uma viagem à procura das constantes portuguesas de carácter e acção* (Lisbon, 1953), 74.
9. Valentim Alexandre has argued for the importance of preexisting nationalist intellectual traditions in the Portuguese reception and adaptation of Freyre's work. Freyre's Christo-centric notions and views of Portuguese character perhaps indicate his theory of *luso-tropicalismo* could also borrow from intellectual traditions of Portuguese nationalism, rather than simply the other way around. Cf. Valentim Alexandre, "O império e a ideia de raça (séculos XIX e XX)," in *Novos racismos: Perspectivas comparativas*, ed. Jorge Vala (Oeiras, 1999), 133–44; Valentim Alexandre, "Prefácio," in Castelo, *O modo português*, 5–6.
10. According to some readers of Freyre, he praises miscegenation in the Portuguese colonies, especially when it reveals traces of Portugueseness, a sort of benign persistence of racial whiteness within mixed-race groups. His disappointment with the dominant black African character of Cape Verdean *mestiços* is an example. See Rémy Lucas, "Aventura e rotina: Gilberto Freyre et l'Afrique," *Lusotopie* 4 (1997): 245; Michel Cahen, "A mestiçagem colonialista: Ou a colonialidade de Gilberto Freyre na colonialidade do Brasil," paper presented at the Lusophone Studies Association Congress, Aracajú (Sergipe), 28 June–2 July 2017.
11. Freyre also did not visit Macau, apparently by his own choice. [José Osório de Oliveira], Proposta de Itinerário de Gilberto Freyre, September 1951, Processo n.º 29 A: Visita de Gilberto Freyre ao ultramar português (1951–1953), Sala 2, n.º 87, Arquivo Histórico Ultramarino. I thank Cláudia Castelo for drawing my attention to this and the following reference.
12. [Manuel Maria] Sarmento Rodrigues to [António] Oliveira Salazar, 4 September 1951, nº 560, in Arquivo Salazar/AOS/CP-242, Pt. 7.242.16.
13. António A. Mendes Correia, "Um mês em Timor: Palestras na emissora nacional, na série 'A Ciência ao Serviço da Humanidade' em 26 de Fevereiro, 5, 12 e 26 de Março, 2 e 9 de Abril de 1955," *Boletim da Sociedade de Geografia de Lisboa* 73, no. 4–6 (1955): 187.
14. António Almeida Marques Jr., Diário da Missão Antropológica de Timor, 23 August 1953, Arquivo Histórico do Instituto de Investigação Científica Tropical (IICT), Universidade de Lisboa, Espólio das Missões Antropológicas.
15. António Almeida, "Caderno de campo 1: Missão Antropológica de Timor 1953," unpublished manuscript, Arquivo Histórico do IICT, Universidade de Lisboa, Espólio das Missões Antropológicas.
16. I here build on arguments explored at greater length in Ricardo Roque, "The Colonial Ethnological Line: Timor and the Racial Geography of the Malay Archipelago," *Journal of Southeast Asian Studies* 49, no. 3 (2018): 387–409.
17. António A. Mendes Correia, Plano de Estudos Antropológicos Coloniais, criado por indicação da Junta de Missões Geográficas e de Investigações Coloniais, 12 March 1941, Arquivo Histórico do IICT, Universidade de Lisboa, Espólio das Missões Antropológicas, Processo 150 (emphasis added).
18. António A. Mendes Correia, *Timor português: Contribuições para o seu estudo antropológico* (Lisbon, 1944), 213–15 (English in the original).
19. António A. Mendes Correia, "Gente de Timor," *Boletim Geral das Colónias* 21, no. 245 (1945): 126.

20. See João Luís Cardoso, "O Professor Mendes Corrêa (1888–1960) e as investigações sobre o *Homo Afer Taganus* dos concheiros mesolíticos de Muge," *Estudos Arqueológicos de Oeiras* 18 (2010–2011), 631–55; Patrícia Ferraz de Matos, "Mendes Correia e a Escola de Antropologia do Porto: Contribuição para o estudo das relações entre antropologia, nacionalismo e colonialismo (de finais do século XIX aos finais da década de 50 do século XX)" (PhD. diss., University of Lisbon, 2012), 172–95; see also José M. Sobral, "Identidade nacional portuguesa no século XX: Representações oriundas de Portugal e do Brasil," in *Identidade nacional: Entre discurso e a prática,* ed. Maria de Fátima Amante (Porto, 2011), 165–86.
21. Mendes Correia's negative views on miscegenation have been presented and analyzed elsewhere, as opposed to Freyrian approaches. E.g., Castelo, *O modo português,* 110–20; Patrícia Ferraz de Matos, *As côres do império: Representações raciais no império português* (Lisbon, 2006), 148–59; Matos, "Mendes Correia," 232–54; Miguel Vale de Almeida, "Longing for Oneself: Hybridism and Miscegenation in Colonial and Postcolonial Portugal," *Etnográfica* 6, no. 1 (2002): 181–200.
22. See Roy Porter, *Flesh in the Age of Reason: The Modern Foundations of Body and Soul* (New York, 2003).
23. See Mendes Correia, "Um mês em Timor."
24. António A. Mendes Correia, *Antropologia e história* (Porto, 1954), 227–63.
25. Correia, *Timor português,* 5.
26. António A. Mendes Correia, ["Intervenção parlamentar,"] in *Diário das Sessões: V Legislatura, Assembleia Nacional, Sessão nº 103* (Lisbon, 1951), 946–47. Mendes Correia's proposal, however, was not accepted. The *Indigenato* regime was basically maintained until its abolition in 1961. See also Matos, "Mendes Correia," 313–15.
27. Ideas of Portuguese Christian universalism (recognizable in Mendes Correia's discourse) can be traced back to the early modern period and possibly connect to the lasting presence of so-called messianic nationalist myths of Portugal's Fifth Empire (*Quinto Império*) since the seventeenth century.
28. See João Leal, *Etnografias portuguesas (1870–1970): Cultura popular e identidade nacional* (Lisbon, 2000), 83–104.
29. António Leite de Magalhães, *A cruz e a espada ao serviço do império* (Porto, 1934), 11.
30. Ricardo Roque, *Headhunting and Colonialism: Anthropology and the Circulation of Human Skulls in the Portuguese Empire, 1870–1930* (London, 2010), 49–54. See, e.g., Mendes Correia, "Um mês em Timor," 175.
31. António de Oliveira Salazar, "A libertação de Timor: Uma mensagem telegráfica de S. Exa. o Presidente do Conselho ao Governador da Colónia," *Boletim Geral das Colónias* 21, no. 44 (1945): 15–16.
32. Óscar Ruas, "A libertação de Timor: A resposta do Sr. Governador de Timor," *Boletim Geral das Colónias* 21, no. 244 (1945): 16.
33. Mendes Correia, "Um mês em Timor," 173.
34. Mendes Correia, *Timor português,* 7.
35. Luna de Oliveira, "O espiritualismo da nossa colonização," *Boletim Geral das Colónias* 21, no. 245 (1945): 197.
36. Correspondence from António A. Mendes Correia to President of JMGIC, 10 March 1944, Arquivo Histórico do IICT, Universidade de Lisboa, Processo individual de Mendes Correia.
37. Gonçalo Antunes, "Timorenses em Portugal: Antropologia e representação na Exposição Colonial do Porto de 1934," in *Atas do colóquio Timor: Missões científicas e antropologia colonial,* ed. Vitor R. Marques, Ana Cristina Roque, and Ricardo Roque (Lisbon, 2011).

38. Mendes Correia, "Um mês em Timor," 174, 178. Mendes Correia also paid an emotional visit to the widow of Dom Aleixo (173, 190).
39. See Susan Lindee and Ricardo Ventura Santos, eds., "The Biological Anthropology of Living Human Populations: World Histories, National Styles, and International Networks," special issue, *Current Anthropology* 53, no. S5 (2012).
40. However, unlike Mendes Correia's anthropological missions, the French mission was apparently a failed institutional project that ended in 1951. See Emmanuelle Sibeud, "A Useless Colonial Science? Practicing Anthropology in the French Colonial Empire, circa 1880–1960," *Current Anthropology* 53, no. S5 (2012): S90–S93.
41. António A. Mendes Correia, "O estudo das populações e o futuro do ultramar," *Boletim da Sociedade de Geografia de Lisboa* 69, nos. 7–8 (1951): 20.

Bibliography

Alexandre, Valentim. "O império e a ideia de raça (séculos XIX e XX)." In *Novos racismos: Perspectivas comparativas*, edited by Jorge Vala, 133–44. Oeiras: Celta, 1999.
———. "Portugal em África (1825–1974): Uma perspectiva global." *Penélope* 11 (1993): 53–66.
———. "Prefácio." In Castelo, *O modo português*, 5–6.
Almeida, Miguel Vale de. "Longing for Oneself: Hybridism and Miscegenation in Colonial and Postcolonial Portugal." *Etnográfica* 6, no. 1 (2002): 181–200.
Antunes, Gonçalo. "Timorenses em Portugal: Antropologia e representação na Exposição Colonial do Porto de 1934." In *Atas do Colóquio Timor: Missões científicas e antropologia colonial*, edited by Vitor R. Marques, Ana Cristina Roque, and Ricardo Roque. Lisbon: Instituto de Investigação Científica Tropical / Instituto de Ciências Sociais, 2011. http://www.historyanthropologytimor.org/?page_id=65.
Bastos, Cristiana. "Um luso-tropicalismo às avessas: Colonialismo científico, aclimação e pureza racial em Germano Correia." In *Fantasmas e fantasias imperiais no imaginário português contemporâneo*, edited by Margarida Calafate Ribeiro and Ana Paula Ferreira, 227–53. Porto: Campo das Letras, 2003.
Cahen, Michel. "A mestiçagem colonialista: Ou a colonialidade de Gilberto Freyre na colonialidade do Brasil." Paper presented at the Lusophone Studies Association Congress, Aracajú (Sergipe), 28 June–2 July 2017.
Cardoso, João Luís. "O Professor Mendes Corrêa (1888–1960) e as investigações sobre o *Homo Afer Taganus* dos concheiros mesolíticos de Muge." *Estudos Arqueológicos de Oeiras* 18 (2010–2011): 631–55.
Castelo, Cláudia. "*O modo português de estar no mundo*": *O luso-tropicalismo e a ideologia colonial portuguesa*. Porto: Afrontamento, 1998.
Clemminson, Richard. *Catholicism, Race and Empire: Eugenics in Portugal*. Budapest: Central European University Press, 2014.
Freyre, Gilberto. *Aventura e rotina: Sugestões de uma viagem à procura das constantes portuguesas de carácter e acção*. Lisbon: Livros do Brasil, 1953.
Leal, João. *Etnografias portuguesas (1870–1970): Cultura popular e identidade nacional*. Lisbon: D. Quixote, 2000.
Lindee, Susan, and Ricardo Ventura Santos, eds. "The Biological Anthropology of Living Human Populations: World Histories, National Styles, and International Networks." Special issue, *Current Anthropology* 53, no. S5 (2012).
Lucas, Rémy. "Aventura e rotina: Gilberto Freyre et l'Afrique." *Lusotopie* 4 (1997): 237–45.

Magalhães, António Leite de. *A cruz e a espada ao serviço do império*. Porto: Editora A Primeira Exposição Colonial Portuguesa, 1934.

Matos, Patrícia Ferraz de. *As côres do império: Representações raciais no império português*. Lisbon: Instituto de Ciências Sociais, 2006.

———. "Mendes Correia e a Escola de Antropologia do Porto: Contribuição para o estudo das relações entre antropologia, nacionalismo e colonialismo (de finais do século XIX aos finais da década de 50 do século XX)." PhD diss., University of Lisbon, 2012.

Mendes Correia, António A. *Antropologia e história*. Porto: Imprensa Portuguesa, 1954.

———. "Gente de Timor." *Boletim Geral das Colonias* 21, no. 245 (1945): 126–27.

———. ["Intervenção parlamentar."] In *Diário das Sessões: V Legislatura, Assembleia Nacional, Sessão nº 103*, 947. Lisbon: Secretaria da Assembleia Nacional, 1951.

———. "O estudo das populações e o futuro do ultramar." *Boletim da Sociedade de Geografia de Lisboa* 69, nos. 7–8 (1951): 1–28.

———. "Os mestiços nas colónias portuguesas." In *Trabalhos do I Congresso Nacional de Antropologia Colonial*, vol. 1, 331–49. Porto: Editora da Primeira Exposição Colonial Portuguesa, 1934.

———. *Timor português: Contribuições para o seu estudo antropológico*. Lisbon: Imprensa Nacional, 1944.

———. "Um mês em Timor: Palestras na emissora nacional, na série 'A Ciência ao Serviço da Humanidade' em 26 de Fevereiro, 5, 12 e 26 de Março, 2 e 9 de Abril de 1955." *Boletim da Sociedade de Geografia de Lisboa* 73, nos. 4–6 (1955): 173–91.

Oliveira, Luna de. "O espiritualismo da nossa colonização." *Boletim Geral das Colónias* 21, no. 245 (1945): 197.

Pereira, Rui M. "Raça, sangue e robustez: Os paradigmas da antropologia física colonial portuguesa." *Cadernos de Estudos Africanos* 7–8 (2005): 209–41.

Porter, Roy. *Flesh in the Age of Reason: The Modern Foundations of Body and Soul*. New York: W. W. Norton & Co., 2003.

Roque, Ricardo. "A antropologia colonial portuguesa, c. 1911–1950." In *Estudos de sociologia da leitura em Portugal no século XX*, edited by Diogo Ramada Curto, 789–822. Lisbon: Fundação Calouste Gulbenkian, 2006.

———. *Headhunting and Colonialism: Anthropology and the Circulation of Human Skulls in the Portuguese Empire, 1870–1930*. London: Palgrave Macmillan, 2010.

———. "'Portugueses da Índia': Germano Correia e a antropologia dos luso-descendentes de Goa." In *Actas do VI Congresso Luso-Afro-Brasileiro de Ciências Sociais*, vol. 1, edited by Rui Centeno and António Custódio Gonçalves, 339–46. Porto: Universidade do Porto / Tipografia Nunes, 2002.

———. "The Colonial Ethnological Line: Timor and the Racial Geography of the Malay Archipelago." *Journal of Southeast Asian Studies* 49, no. 3 (2018): 387–409.

Ruas, Óscar. "A libertação de Timor: A resposta do Sr. Governador de Timor." *Boletim Geral das Colónias* 21, no. 244 (1945): 16.

Salazar, António de Oliveira. "A libertação de Timor: Uma mensagem telegráfica de S. Exa. o Presidente do Conselho ao Governador da Colónia." *Boletim Geral das Colónias* 21, no. 44 (1945): 15–16.

Sibeud, Emmanuelle. "A Useless Colonial Science? Practicing Anthropology in the French Colonial Empire, circa 1880–1960." *Current Anthropology* 53, no. S5 (2012): S83–S94.

Sobral, José Manuel. "Identidade nacional portuguesa no século XX: Representações oriundas de Portugal e do Brasil." In *Identidade nacional: Entre discurso e a prática*, edited by Maria de Fátima Amante, 165–86. Porto: Fronteira do Caos / Centro de Estudos da População Economia e Sociedade, 2011.

CHAPTER

8

Reassessing Portuguese Exceptionalism
Racial Concepts and Colonial Policies toward the "Bushmen" in Southern Angola, 1880s–1970s

Samuël Coghe

From the nineteenth century onward, the so-called "Bushmen"[1] living scattered over the western half of southern Africa (nowadays South Africa, Namibia, Botswana, and Angola) were turned into objects of vivid anthropological research and imaginations and increasingly subjected to the policies of expanding colonial states. This chapter focuses on the case of Angola: it examines how racial concepts and colonial policies regarding the "Bushmen" in southern Angola evolved under Portuguese colonial rule from the late nineteenth century until decolonization in 1975. By doing so, it makes an important contribution to the field of "Bushman" studies: while the history of the "Bushmen" and the role of "Bushman anthropology" in the construction of scientific racism, popular imaginary, and governmental policies has received broad scholarly attention for most of southern Africa, the Angolan side of this story has largely remained untold.[2]

Yet, this chapter does more than to fill a research gap. Taking a comparative and transnational perspective, it evaluates what was (and what was not) distinctive about Portuguese concepts and policies. And, most importantly, it explores the implications of this case study for the debate on racial thought and policies in the Portuguese-speaking world. Since Gilberto Freyre and his theory of Luso-tropicalism, which became integral to the official ideology of the Portuguese Empire in the 1950s, this debate has turned around the question of whether the Portuguese and their Lusophone descendants in Brazil and elsewhere conceptualized and dealt with racial alterity in a different, more tolerant way and hence were more benign colonizers than their European competitors.[3]

This chapter makes three intertwined arguments. First, it argues that Portuguese views of the Angolan "Bushmen" as part of a distinct, dying, and useless aboriginal race, which dominated anthropological debate during the late nineteenth and early twentieth century, were increasingly challenged after World War II. While Portuguese scientists began to reinterpret physical particularities as the outcome of biological adaptation processes and genetic malleability instead of as racial markers, most administrators now emphasized the capacity of "Bushmen" for cultural and socioeconomic adaptation. I argue that these reconceptualizations were mutually constitutive and entangled with new colonial policies but that, overall, they were slow to gain ascendancy. Practices often remained ambiguous and the idea of racial difference did not entirely disappear.

Second, it claims that many aspects of "Bushman" anthropologies and policies in Angola were not inherently Portuguese. Shifting anthropological views, scientific practices, and administrative policies with regard to the "Bushmen" in Angola were most often paralleled by and/or intimately connected with developments in "Bushman" studies and policies in the rest of southern Africa and with global shifts in racial science. Finally, this chapter maintains that these transnational and global connections were more important in shaping "Bushman" views and policies in Angola than were discussions about race in Portugal and the wider Lusophone world. By doing so, it questions the often-asserted exceptionality of Portuguese racial thought and practices in the twentieth century and, consequently, the pervasiveness of Luso-tropicalist ideology in the Portuguese Empire.

Racializing the "Bushmen"

First references in Portuguese writings can be traced to the mid-nineteenth century,[4] but only in the 1880s did the presence of "Bushmen" on Angolan territory begin to receive increasing attention from Portuguese colonial officials and explorers.[5] They portrayed the Mucassequeres and Mucuancalas, as they were called, as clearly different from the surrounding populations, not only because of their "strange" click language but also in physical and cultural terms. In contrast to the tall and dark-skinned pastoralists and agriculturalists in the region, the "Bushmen" were represented as small, thin, and yellowish creatures leading a miserable and backward existence as nomadic hunter-gatherers; few in number and on the brink of extinction, they strode in small groups through the woods of southern Angola on the search for food. The "Bushmen," the explorer Serpa Pinto concluded, were "the real savages of southern tropical Africa."[6]

Beyond these utterly negative views, which reiterated long-standing commonplaces from ethnographic accounts on the "Bushmen" living farther south in South and South West Africa,[7] Portuguese observers also adopted the idea that the "Bushmen" in Angola were part of a larger "Hottentot race" that "extended from the area north of the Cape into the region between the Cubango and Cuando rivers" [i.e., into southern Angola] and was distinct from the "Negro" race.[8] Indeed, by the 1880s, most anthropologists had, based on somatic criteria, come to believe that the Bushmen, together with the pastoralist but physically similar "Hottentots," constituted a race or subrace in their own right.[9]

In the following decades, the idea that Angola was inhabited by at least two distinct "native" races—"Bushmen" (or "Boximanes") and "Negroes"—became a standard feature in Portuguese colonial literature.[10] It was cemented in the 1910s, when Manuel Alves da Cunha, the vicar capitular of the diocese of Congo and Angola, wrote the first more systematic ethnographic account on the "Bushmen" in Angola and when this text, originally published in 1913, was included in José de Oliveira Ferreira Diniz's *Populações indígenas de Angola* (1918), the first (and for a long time only) comprehensive ethnographic overview of Angola's "native" populations.[11] Significantly, Alves da Cunha's argument was no longer based solely on physical and cultural distinctions; it also encompassed new theories about race migration and language groups. He characterized the "Bushmen" as the vanishing remnants of an old "aboriginal" race that had been repelled toward the south by invading representatives of the "Negro race." This "aboriginal" race had once occupied the whole of tropical Africa, from the Sahara to the Kalahari, he stated, and the "Bushmen" were hence linked to other survivors such as the so-called "Pygmies" or Batwa in the Central African rain forest.[12]

Alves da Cunha's racial taxonomies and explanations reflected several decades of international debates. The notion of the "Bushmen" as an "aboriginal race" had gained prominence in the 1870s and 1880s through the work of the German anatomist and anthropologist Gustav Fritsch, who posited that, as the "most primordial, most ancient inhabitants of the continent," they had probably once inhabited the whole of southern Africa but had been pushed back by migrating races into the Kalahari Desert.[13] Unlike the latter, he stated, the "Bushmen" had not made any significant progress: they were an *Ur-Rasse* that "had remained almost unchanged in their development for thousands of years."[14] In the 1880s and 1890s, other scientists like the ethnographer George Stow and the historian George Theal, both based in South Africa, further disseminated this view, thereby clearly differentiating between the "Bushmen" and the "Hottentots," whom they defined as the result of racial admixture between "Bushmen" and invading "Negroes."[15]

That the idea of the "Bushmen" as an ancient and dying race quickly became a widely accepted theory was hardly a coincidence. It throve on—and simultaneously contributed to—widely circulating diffusionist ideas about the migration of races and social Darwinist theories about the resulting clashes between them and the survival of the fittest ones. For many observers, the primordiality of the "Bushmen" provided a plausible explanation for their physical inferiority and their primitive way of life. Being hunter-gatherers, they represented an early stage in the evolution of humankind and as such were naturally inferior to (and hence dominated by) more modern races that had more advanced modes of subsistence as pastoralists ("Hottentots"), agro-pastoralists (Bantu), or industrialists (Europeans).[16] In such views, which saw economic life, physical appearance, cultural practices, and collective power as mutually constitutive, racial hierarchies were naturalized as hierarchies in time: they reflected different stages in human evolution.[17] Moreover, the idea of the "Bushmen" as a dying race tapped into an older imperial discourse according to which "primitive" or "savage races" all over the world, from Tasmania to North America, were prone to extinction when they came into contact with more advanced and "civilized races" such as white Europeans. This discourse, as Patrick Brantlinger has shown, had already emerged around 1800; social Darwinism and scientific racism only further consolidated it.[18]

Significantly, the German explorer and botanist Georges Schweinfurth applied the same social Darwinist explanatory scheme to the small-statured Aka people in the equatorial forests of Central Africa whom he had "discovered" in the early 1870s. In his opinion, invading "Negro" people had equally repelled these "Pygmies," as they came to be called after the mystic, diminutive people in Greek and medieval writings, who were also hunter-gatherers. He defended that, before these invasions, "Pygmies" and "Bushmen" had formed a single race that had inhabited the whole of tropical and southern Africa.[19] For decades, this theory would find large support, also in Portuguese colonial writings, until genetic research increasingly cast doubt on it.[20]

The conceptualization of the "Bushmen" as an ancient race connected to other small-statured nomadic hunter-gatherers across Africa was further buttressed by linguistic evidence. Their click language was considered fundamentally different from most languages spoken in Central and Southern Africa, which Wilhelm Bleek had categorized as "Bantu" languages ("Bantu" being the word for "people" in most of them).[21] In order to explain the similarities between these Bantu languages, the British explorer, colonial servant, and natural scientist Harry Johnston (1858–1927) had, in a series of books and articles from the mid-1880s to the 1910s, influentially proposed and gradually refined the hypothesis that all Bantu speakers shared common origins. Laying the foundations of what continues to be discussed—though in somewhat different terms and without the racial overtones—as the Bantu expansion,[22] Johnston claimed that, in various waves of migration starting some two thousand to twenty-five hundred years ago, large numbers of Bantu speakers had moved from their homeland in Central Africa into Southern Africa, thereby also diffusing their language. In the course of these migratory movements, Johnston argued, the original inhabitants ("Bushmen" and "Pygmies") had been exterminated, assimilated, or repelled into inhospitable regions: the "Bushmen" into the Kalahari Desert, the "Pygmies" into the Central African rain forest.[23] Linguistic evidence, hence, bolstered existing theories about migration, social Darwinist selection and racial difference. Even if most anthropologists (and later Johnston) rejected the idea of a physically and culturally identifiable "Bantu race," language, culture and race were often conflated.[24] In Angola, "Bantu race" was often used synonymously with "Negro race" (*raça negra*) and in a binary opposition to the "Bushman race" until at least the 1950s.[25]

For decades, these internationally circulating theories, as well as further ethnographic, linguistic, and physical anthropological field research on the "Bushmen" in South Africa and Namibia, would prove essential in the racialization of the "Bushmen" in Angola.[26] This is also because of the almost complete absence of proper Portuguese anthropological research on the matter. This striking neglect corresponds with the slow institutionalization of colonial anthropology in Portugal. In the first decades of the twentieth century, physical anthropologists were gaining predominance in Portuguese academia but still hardly doing any fieldwork in the colonies, whereas cultural anthropology would only become firmly established in the late 1950s with the work of Jorge Dias and the study missions on ethnic minorities to Mozambique and Angola.[27] It is hence no coincidence that, throughout the interwar years, the study of the Angolan "Bushmen" remained the prerogative of a few "lay" anthropologists like the medical doctor Francisco Venâncio Silva or the veterinary doctor António Lebre, both stationed in southern Angola in the 1930s (but whose short ethnographic accounts were of little interest to the international scientific community), and of foreign scholars like Dorothea Frances Bleek and the Alsatian Catholic missionary Charles Estermann.[28]

Anthropological neglect was doubled by administrative neglect. Indeed, until after World War II, most "Bushmen" on Angolan territory were practically exempt from registration, taxation, and labor requirements—key elements of the colonial *Indigenato* regime.[29] This was not a legal privilege, as the successive labor laws that reigned the system did not differentiate between the "Bushmen" and other "natives." Practical exemption in part rested on the cultural concept of a completely different, inferior, and dying race—one that was viewed as unfit for labor and hence was not a target of biopolitical efforts aimed at increasing their quantity and quality.[30] As an administrator worded it in 1940: "It is a race that soon will disappear and that even today does not have any value, neither from a demographic, political or economic perspective."[31] But exemption from the *Indigenato* regime was also the consequence of the "Bushmen's" nomadic life and the concomitant difficulties for the colonial administration to locate and control them. This was especially true since most lived close to the southern border or in the southeastern Cuando Cubango province, areas where Portuguese colonial presence and influence remained very weak.

This administrative neglect stood in contrast with policies on the Namibian side of the border. Certainly, in the areas closest to the border, German and later South African interference with "Bushman" lives was also fairly limited before 1945, as these areas were situated outside the police zone, which officially delineated settler territory and was governed through indirect rule. This was, for instance, the case for the Khwe "Bushmen" in western Caprivi.[32] But this laissez-faire policy did not apply to the "Bushmen" living within or just beyond the police zone, like the Hai||om. In the last years of German colonial rule before World War I, "Bushmen" in the Outje and Grootfontein districts were increasingly accused of stealing stock and of robbing migrant laborers from Ovamboland and Okavango who crossed their territories. Many of them were killed by settlers or police patrols. Others were, often forcibly, integrated into the colonial economy as settler farm and diamond mine workers.[33] After the South African takeover in 1915, violence diminished but, also because of continuing settler encroachment on their ancestral territory, the "Bushmen" were further incorporated in the colonial economy, mainly as cheap and often temporary farm workers.[34] Arguably, the fundamental difference underlying these diverging policies between Angola and Namibia was the presence of a powerful and expanding white settler society in Namibia in or close to areas where "Bushmen" lived.

The Anthropobiological Mission to Angola (1950–1955) and the Persistence of Physical Anthropology

After 1945, anthropological neglect turned into its counterpart: the Angolan "Bushmen" became the target of various anthropological, medical, and demographic studies conducted by Portuguese scientists. Compared with their marginal demographic weight of a few thousand individuals, they became one of the best studied population groups in Angola. This shift was mainly due to the various research expeditions to the "Bushmen" undertaken by the Anthropobiological Mission to Angola in 1950, 1952, and 1955.[35] Led by António de Almeida, a medical doctor and professor of colonial ethnography at the Escola Superior Colonial in Lisbon, this research mission aimed to conduct an anthropological survey of all Angolan population groups.[36] Yet, it had a strong focus on the "Bushmen" and other so-called pre-Bantu population groups in southern Angola, whom Almeida had already studied on previous expeditions in 1948 and 1949.[37]

During their prolonged stays in southern Angola, Almeida and his collaborators—most notably, the biologist Maria Emília de Castro e Almeida (his daughter) and the physical anthropologist António Marques de Almeida Jr.—observed more than two thousand "Bushmen" in many different locations. Aided by local administrators and interpreters, they gathered a very broad set of data, ranging from ethnographic observations on material, religious, and social life to linguistic recordings, demographic statistics, archaeological data, and, most prominently, comprehensive physiological data.[38] Indeed, beyond a vast series of (about sixty) anthropometric measurements on more than one thousand "Bushmen," the team determined the blood groups of many hundreds of them and performed physiological tests such as measuring body temperature, blood pressure, and visual and auditory acuity.[39] This approach was typical of anthropobiology, a new strand of physical anthropology that looked beyond the static, morphological features analyzed in classical anthropometry to include more dynamic, biological data.[40]

This orientation of the Angola Anthropobiological Mission reflected the existing power relations within academic anthropology in Portugal, where anthropobiology had been introduced in the 1930s by António Mendes Correia, a professor of anthropology at the University of Porto and an outspoken proponent of the discipline's physical and biological aspects.[41] In the 1930s, Mendes Correia had managed to put colonial anthropology on the scientific and political agenda in Portugal and become its most powerful representative, not to mention one of the country's most powerful colonial scientists tout court. By the late 1940s, he was not only Almeida's direct superior as director of the Escola Superior Colonial but also the president of the Junta das Missões Geográficas e de Investigações Coloniais (JMGIC), the institution—created by the Colonial Ministry in 1936 to coordinate scientific research in the colonies—that funded the Angola Anthropobiological Mission.[42] Moreover, as director of the JMGIC's anthropological program since 1936, he had already left his anthropobiological mark on earlier state-funded anthropological missions to Mozambique (1936–1956) and Guiné (1945–1947), and later to Timor (1953–1970s), a mission that was led by Almeida as well.[43] Mendes Correia had also incited Almeida to devote particular attention to the "Bushmen" during his Angolan missions, given their "great scientific importance" and their imminent extinction.[44]

Although the dominance of physical anthropology in the colonial realm was perhaps particularly striking in the Portuguese case, as it was not counterbalanced by an academic tradition of cultural anthropology until the late 1950s, its persistence after World War II as such was not per se exceptional. Thus, the French government organized a vast anthropological survey in French West Africa in the late 1940s with a similar orientation.[45] And, more specifically, the international field of "Bushman" studies experienced a real revival of studies in physical and biological anthropology in the 1950s and 1960s. A pivotal figure in this revival was Phillip Tobias, a South African physical anthropologist who would later turn famous for his paleoanthropological work. After studying the

Auen and Naron "Bushmen" in 1951,[46] Tobias became a founder of the Kalahari Research Committee (KRC) in 1956. Based at the University of Witwatersrand, the KRC organized more than twenty research expeditions in the late 1950s and 1960s to investigate the biology of the "Bushmen" in Namibia, Botswana, and South Africa. The voluminous scientific output of these expeditions ranged from classical anthropometry to more biology-oriented studies on blood groups, physiological parameters, psychology, growth indices, and pathology.[47] Certainly in the 1950s, many of these studies, including Tobias's own writings, were still underwritten by the idea of identifiable biological races.[48] From the late 1950s onward, these studies increasingly became a point of reference for Almeida. Conversely, Tobias seems to have been unfamiliar with the work of the anthropobiological mission in Angola until the late 1950s, when he invited Almeida to give a series of lectures at the newly founded Institute for the Study of Man in Africa in Johannesburg.[49]

Between Racial Typologies and Human Adaptability

According to Ricardo Roque in this volume, the anthropobiological missions in the Portuguese Empire (1930s–1970s) were driven by the firm belief in racial difference and by the aim of categorizing the races of empire. They constituted a modality of Portuguese racial science that eschewed ideas of race mixing and fluidity and persisted even when the Portuguese colonial state began to adopt Luso-tropicalism as an ideological framework. While this might generally be the case, a closer examination of António and Maria Emília de Castro e Almeida's writings on the "Bushmen" in the 1950s and 1960s suggests that the Angolan mission had a messier and increasingly more hesitant understanding of racial difference. Besides a strong methodological tendency toward categorization, their work also reveals an eroding or at least vacillating belief in the racial alterity of the "Bushmen" vis-à-vis the surrounding "Bantus."

Before further exploring this issue, it must be noted that analyzing the Almeidas' stance toward racial difference is not an easy task for at least two reasons. In the 1950s, the Angola Anthropobiological Mission collected the largest series of anthropobiological data on the "Bushmen" in the whole of southern Africa thus far,[50] but only a small portion of these data was subsequently analyzed in academic publications—and often only many years or even decades later, after António de Almeida's death (1980), by his daughter.[51] One explanation certainly is that Almeida and some of his team members were also caught up in other anthropological missions, especially in Timor, and hence lacked time to process the "Bushman" data quickly. However, it also raises the question to what extent collecting became an autonomous and self-perpetuating operation, meaningful in itself and not primarily geared toward producing new knowledge. Beyond the possibility of their later use, extracting and storing a massive amount of data on Indigenous populations like the "Bushmen" or Timorese already showed to the world that Portugal was finally measuring up with other colonial powers and scientifically occupying its colonies, as Portuguese scientists and officials had demanded for many years.[52] The second, even bigger problem for positioning the mission's work in the field of racial science is the rather poor academic quality of most of the Almeidas' "Bushman" articles; they often showcase data without drawing broader conclusions or taking clear positions in contemporary scientific debates. With regard to racial science, António de Almeida did not display the intellectual and theoretical acuity of a Mendes Correia, as analyzed by Roque in this volume.

These reservations notwithstanding, their publications uncontestably reveal a great concern with classification and mapping (see map 8.1). In many of their writings, António and Maria Emília de Almeida were concerned with drawing as neat as possible distinctions between the "Bushmen," other non-Bantu groups, and "Bantu tribes" on the one hand and between the different "Bushmen" groups on the other hand. Adopting South African terminology, they classified the "Bushmen" in Angola in two different types: the "yellow Bushmen," who called themselves !Kung and were called either Mucuancalas or Vassekeles by neighboring Bantu-speaking people, depending on whether they lived west or east of the Cubango River; and the "black Bushmen" in distant southeastern Angola, who called themselves (Hu)kwè and were called either Cazamas or Cacuengos by their Bantu neighbors.[53] They also clearly distinguished the "Bushmen" from other assumedly non-Bantu people such as the fifty to one hundred surviving Kwadi ((Ova)kwepe or (Ova)kurokas), the Vatua, and the "Hottentots," whom they further subdivided in a few "real Hottentots" and the "hottentoid" Hai||om (Muquedes or Vakedes).[54]

The strong separation between "Hottentots" and "Bushmen" constituted an important difference with previous categorizations.[55] Accordingly, Almeida rarely used "Khoisan," a term coined in the 1920s to designate a common "Hottentot-Bushman" race and officially used in the Angolan censuses from 1940 onward.[56] But, overall, Almeida's classification, based on a mixture of somatic, cultural, and linguistic criteria, was not so different from earlier ones. This questions the role of his anthropobiological series. Indeed, it seems that he only used them in a second step to confirm his prima facie categorization by calculating statistical averages of his measurements, which then corresponded to "ideal types" of Mucuancala, Vassekele, or Cazama. Regardless of the great energy Almeida would spend on calculating averages and defining types until the early 1970s,[57] this kind of analysis differed from the typological approach that dominated physical anthropology in South Africa from the 1920s to the late 1950s. While Almeida was mainly interested in physically describing the actual types of "Bushmen," South African anthropologists like Raymond Dart, Robert Broom, and the early Tobias were more interested in finding and de-

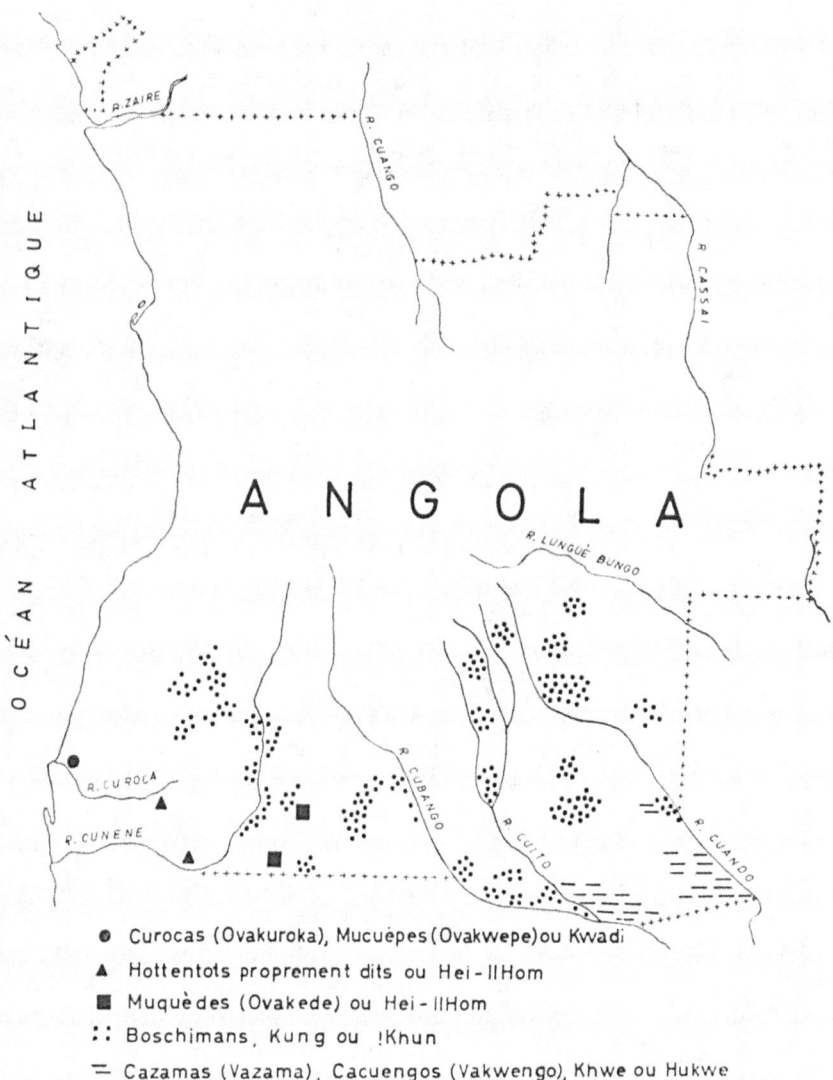

Map 8.1. Distribution of non-Bantu groups in Angola. Source: António de Almeida, "Sur les peuplades non-Bantoues de l'Angola," *Commentarii - Pontificia Academia Scientiarum* 1, no. 15 (1962): 11. Map courtesy of the Pontifical Academy of Sciences, Vatican City, www.pas.va.

fining the pure prehistorical racial types that, through admixture, had led to the actual physical types. Their typological assumptions were based not only on the measurements of living "Bushmen" populations but also on skulls and skeletons.[58] Despite Almeida's interest in the prehistory of the "Bushmen," he would not analyze any human fossils.[59]

This does not mean that Almeida completely dismissed or disdained the idea of typological races. In a 1956 article, for instance, in which he analyzed the phenotypical (ABO) and genetic (p, q, r) blood groups of the Mucuancalas, his results induced him to link these "Bushmen" to other "primitive races" of the Pacific American type such as the Mapuches in South America and the "aborigines" in Australia and to distance them from the Bantu people in Africa.[60] By doing this, he tapped into ideas of a global primitive race, which had been formulated since the late nineteenth century based on somatic (and sometimes cultural) similarities but which international blood research would ultimately dismiss.[61] In various articles, he also tried to find an answer to the long-standing question of whether the "Bushmen" derived, as some anthropologists had argued, from a "Mongoloid" root, and hence had their origins in Asia, or from a "Negroid."[62] As late as 1972, he repeated his support for the "Negroid" hypothesis by publishing a meticulous comparison between the "Bushman" "type" and the Chinese "type," which drew on his own descriptive, anthropometric, and physiological series from Angola and Macau.[63]

Almeida's support of the Negroid thesis was rather early. It undermined the idea of a proper "Bushman race," for which leading South African anthropologists had constructed a distinct and autochthonous genealogy going back to the so-called Boskop Man.[64] Only in the early 1960s would a consensus around the Negroid thesis emerge among them.[65] Almeida's doubts as to whether the "Bushmen" constituted a distinct race defined as "a group of individuals with certain physical features that are transmitted by heredity" can also gleaned from other parts of his writings.[66] He thus rejected various physical features that had drawn large attention since the nineteenth century and had long been held as racial characteristics of the "Bushmen" (and the "Khoisan" in general), such as steatopygia and macronymphia, as either not typical or not hereditary.[67] Steatopygia, a high degree of fat accumulation in and around the buttocks, only occurred in about 3 percent of the observed "Bushman" women in Angola, he argued, and was still rarer in "Bushman" men. Moreover, it also existed in other people.[68] Regarding macronymphia, the particularly large size of the labia minora, Almeida was utterly convinced that this *tablier* or *apron*, as it had often been called, was not an inherited trait but a feature that women had acquired through the deliberate elongation of the inner labia from childhood onward, with the purpose of increasing sexual pleasure and attraction. The same phenomenon, he stated, could be observed among many Bantu women in southern Angola and in other parts of Africa.[69] Almeida's ideas on these subjects were not singular—in both cases, he followed the opinions of local administrators who had been able to observe "Bushmen" people for many years[70]—but they were opposed to those of his South African colleagues. For them, both steatopygia and macronymphia were typical of the "Bushmen."[71]

Perhaps even more striking than his rebuttal of these sexualized stereotypes was that Almeida also questioned the small stature of the "Bushmen" as a racial marker. On the one hand, the mission's anthropometric series had revealed that, at least in Angola, the !Kung "Bushmen" were much taller than earlier anthropologists had assumed.[72] On the other hand, Almeida tended to believe that their stature was not a hereditary feature but rather the consequence of environmental conditions. "In the regions where economic conditions are more favorable," he stated in 1956, "their stature increases and the corpulence and nutritional status improve considerably, so that one can observe numerous natives [= !Kung Bushmen] who are as strong as most Negroes [*pretos*] of their region of origin."[73] Almeida was surely not the first or only one to establish a correlation between nutrition and stature. Yet, his assumption, often repeated but never substantiated, that better nutrition would perhaps even lead to a "normal" stature was at odds with not only old ideas of fixed typological races but also new ideas of genetic variation. Thus, Tobias argued that, after a generation of farm life with better conditions of nutrition, the Lake Chrissie "Bushmen" might perhaps have grown taller but were still the subgroup with the smallest stature. For Tobias, the general difference in stature between the (smaller) southern and the taller central and northern "Bushmen" was the result of neither different kinds of admixture nor of different nutrition and/or conditions of life but rather of genetic variation.[74]

Comparing Almeida's and Tobias's opinions on these matters reveals a crucial difference. Whereas Almeida mainly questioned the "Bushman" racial type by negating some of its salient features (and distinct origins) without dismissing the idea of typological races wholesale, Tobias questioned it in a more fundamental way. For Tobias, steatopygia, macronymphia, and small stature were no longer the expression of a fixed racial type, and exceptions or variations no longer the result of (the degree of) admixture with other races, but rather the outcome of genetic variation within African populations, which might have been promoted by natural and/or sexual selection.[75] Yet, both authors seem to have increasingly shared the basic idea that the physical and biological characteristics of the "Bushmen" were not stable and hereditary but rather the consequence of adaptation processes, either during life or over the course of generations. This shift conformed with broader developments in physical anthropology. As Michael Little has analyzed, human adaptability became a central issue in the "new physical anthropology" or "biological anthropology" from the 1950s onward, culminating in the human adaptability component of the International Biological Programme in the late 1960s and early 1970s.[76] Tobias's and Almeida's trajectories underscore the idea that this transition from a "typological and essentialist physical anthropology" to a population-based and evolutionary "biological anthropology," which has often been claimed to have occurred around 1950, was not an even and universal but instead a "slow, hesitant, piecemeal and very incomplete" process.⁷⁷

The slow and messy transition between both paradigms can also be gleaned from other studies into the biology of the Angolan "Bushmen" in the 1950s. Conducted in the trail of the Angola Anthropobiological Mission, some of them questioned but others still buttressed the notion of a racial type with distinct biological features. On the one hand, two nutritional studies presented at the Third Inter-African Nutrition Conference in Luanda in 1956 supported the idea of environmental adaptability. In the first, the medical doctor João Araújo de Freitas had examined the physical development of ten young adult "Bushmen" during their stay in a Luanda fishing company and concluded that, within less than a year, all of them had adapted well to their new diet and gained weight and sturdiness.⁷⁸ For the second study, a team of doctors from the Institute of Tropical Medicine in Lisbon had compared the diets and nutritional status of sixty-nine Mucuancalas and seventy-four Kwanyamas, south Angolan pastoralists. In both cases, they were surprised to find blood parameters that "were not so different from those considered normal in the white race," despite the chronic undernutrition of the "Bushmen" and the temporal deficiencies in the Kwanyama diet. To explain their data, they suggested that the "Bushmen" had experienced a "humoral adaptation to a condition of chronic hunger" and hence physiologically adapted to their environment.⁷⁹

On the other hand, a study suggesting the absence of the sickle cell trait in Angolan Vassekele "Bushmen," conducted by some of the same doctors from the Institute of Tropical Medicine a year earlier, in 1955, illustrates the persistence of racial biology.⁸⁰ Since its first description in 1910, sickle cell anemia (or drepanocytosis), a severe hereditary blood disorder occurring in people who have inherited abnormal copies of the haemoglobin gene (or the sickle cell trait) from both parents, had been widely interpreted as a racial disease affecting only black people or, if discovered in whites, people with black ancestry.⁸¹ Based on the idea that, similar to blood groups, the distribution of the sickle cell trait could shed light on the continent's racial history, research on different population groups in Africa boomed after World War II.⁸² Portuguese experts in tropical medicine eagerly participated in this trend. In the 1940s, several studies confirmed the high incidence of the sickle cell trait among the "Negro" populations in Angola, São Tomé, and Guiné and a much lower incidence among the pre-Bantu races in southern Angola.⁸³

Within this research logic, it was almost inevitable that, when Augusto Salazar Leite's research team from the Institute of Tropical Medicine found zero cases of the sickle cell trait in their sample of 249 "pure Bushmen," they did not consider environmental conditions but instead interpreted this as further proof for the racial character of the disease—and for the fundamental racial difference of the "Bushmen." This was still a common interpretation in the mid-1950s. South African researchers who had, around the same time, equally noted the absence of the sickle cell trait in their "Bushmen" samples from South West Africa had drawn the same conclusion.[84] In this case, the idea of biological adaptation was slow to gain ground. The hypothesis that the distribution of the sickle cell trait correlated with the incidence of falciparum malaria, against which the heterozygous trait offered a certain degree of protection, was put forward in 1954 but did not immediately gain unanimous acceptance.[85] Thus, in 1960, the Portuguese medical doctor J. H. Santos David, in his elaborate study on the sickle cell trait in northeastern Angola, still defended that the racial origins of a population—that is, their history of migration and admixture—and not the incidence of malaria and concomitant processes of selection and adaptation were decisive for the distribution of the trait. The study of the trait's distribution was, just like anthropometry and sero-anthropology, a means to study racial difference, he claimed.[86]

A Dying Race? From Extinction to Bantuization

While new anthropological and medical research cast doubt on the existence of a distinct "Bushman race," new demographic data also began to question the long-standing belief that the "Bushmen" were a dying race. In the late nineteenth and early twentieth centuries, the general belief in the "Bushmen's" imminent extinction had been based not on firm numerical evidence about demographic change but rather on the assumption that this was the inevitable outcome of a social Darwinist struggle between unequal races. Their small number and shattered distribution were seen as the provisional result of this ongoing process and, together with episodic evidence about sweeping epidemics and deadly violence against them, as unquestionable proof for the idea that they had been far more numerous in the past.[87]

However, the first quantitative evidence about demographic change among the Angolan "Bushmen," in the 1950s, pointed in a different direction. It suggested that the "Bushmen" population was increasing. Between the first comprehensive censuses of 1940 and 1950, the "Khoisan" population had risen from 5,882 to 7,049—and would further increase to 7,807 in 1960.[88] Certainly, the accuracy of these data is questionable, given the methods used, the vastness of the areas covered, and the mobility of the "Bushmen." Yet, Alexandre Sarmento, one of Portugal's foremost colonial demographers, accepted the numbers. While noting that the "Bushmen's" extinction had still been viewed as inevitable a few years before, he ascribed their demographic increase to the "revolutionary transformation process" they were going through with the gradual adoption of agriculture and a sedentary lifestyle.[89]

It is difficult to gauge the impact of these census figures. Almeida continued to cite rather low estimates of about four thousand "Bushmen."[90] The census numbers also stood in sharp contrast with the first administrative survey of the "Bushman" population in southern Angola in 1952 and 1953, which only accounted for 2,564 individuals.[91] Granted, observers in the 1950s suggested that the administrative authorities had only registered those people who had shown up to them and that the real number was much higher, some six thousand to eight thousand.[92] But, beyond the issue of registration, these contrasting figures also implicitly point at the underlying problem of definition: of defining who is (still) "Bushman" and who is not (or no longer).

A demographic study advanced by Tobias in the mid-1950s clearly illustrates this problem and, concomitantly, the shifting meaning of extinction. Drawing on new data, Tobias calculated the total number of "Bushmen" in southern Africa at about fifty-five thousand—a number much higher than had thus far been assumed.[93] In his opinion, these numbers "hitherto undreamed of and unexpected" indicated that the "Bushmen" were not yet extinct, but they did not contest demographic decline. They rather showed how many more "Bushmen" there must have lived in southern Africa before. Moreover, the biggest threat for the future, he added, was not physical extinction but disappearance as a race with its own physical and cultural characteristics through miscegenation with and cultural assimilation to the surrounding Bantu populations.

The Ambiguous Politics of Bantuization

Adaptation turned into the key category of analysis through which Portuguese observers came to view the "Bushmen" in southern Angola in the 1950s. Indeed, while the idea of biological adaptation and genetic malleability began to supersede the concept of the "Bushmen" as a fixed typological race defined by distinct morphological and biological features, debates on the cultural and socioeconomic adaptation of the "Bushmen," which had already emerged in the interwar years,[94] grew stronger as well. Arguably, both discourses were mutually reinforcing each other. Yet, more than anthropobiological test results and sophisticated scientific debates on race and genetics, Bantuization, as the cultural, socioeconomic, and—through racial mixing—even biological adaptation to the surrounding Bantu-speaking peoples was termed, was a concept that influenced colonial governance.[95] It was not only discussed by anthropologists but also increasingly used by administrative authorities—and with a different stance. While anthropologists viewed Bantuization as a threat, since it would do away with "Bushman" difference, administrative authorities welcomed Bantuization as the goal and in part already the consequence of their deliberate policies.

Indeed, after World War II, administrative policies toward the "Bushmen" in Angola slowly changed from outright neglect to more active intervention.

Various administrators now denied that the "Bushmen" were too primitive to be civilized. Praising their intelligence, they claimed that it was the task of the Portuguese authorities to help the "Bushmen" overcome their backwardness and adopt new ways of life similar to those of the surrounding Bantu peoples.[96] For them, Bantuization was both a civilizing mission and an ongoing process that various groups of "Bushmen" had initiated themselves, by sedentarizing and adopting agriculture or by engaging in contract labor, but for which they needed active support.

Accordingly, various administrators actively encouraged the sedentarization of "Bushmen" groups in new villages and their adoption of agriculture by providing them with plots of land, seeds, and hoes.[97] By doing so, they followed missionary policies in the region, as well as a more general Portuguese policy of villagization and agricultural development that had already started in the interwar years and was gaining traction in the 1950s.[98] But for administrators like Alberto Fernandes Geirinhas, the sedentarization and economic transformation of the "Bushmen" possessed a still greater urgency, as they considered it the only viable way to fight undernutrition and degeneration and hence to prevent their racial extinction.[99] Administrators also endorsed the growing incorporation of the "Bushmen" in the colonial economy: in the early 1950s, "Bushman" men had begun to accept migrant labor contracts for the fishing industries in Mossâmedes, Benguela, and even Luanda or for the coffee and sisal plantations farther north.[100] These policy changes not only rested on changing anthropological views but were also enabled by the expansion of administrative control in the areas where the "Bushmen" lived.

To a certain extent, they also mirrored growing interventionist policies on the other side of the colonial border toward those "Bushmen" who had thus far lived beyond direct government control. In Botswana, the British set up a successful though short-lived agricultural education program for "Bushmen" in the late 1930s.[101] And in Namibia, the South African government in the late 1940s hired "Bushman guards" to control and protect the "wild Bushmen" living outside the police zone and to teach them agricultural and animal husbandry techniques.[102] Other "Bushmen" from beyond the police zone, like the Khwe, were increasingly recruited for the South African mines.[103] A major difference between Angola and neighboring Namibia and Botswana, however, was that the Portuguese did not officially create reserves where "Bushmen" could pursue their "traditional" hunter-gatherer life, like the Etosha Game Reserve for the Hai‖om in Namibia until 1954 or the Central Kalahari Game Reserve in Botswana from 1963 onward.[104]

Overall, sedentarization and developmental policies in Angola were, like in Namibia and Botswana, riddled with contradictions: on the one hand, they were piecemeal and inconsistent, as they were the product of initiatives by local administrators rather than of a coordinated policy by the central government, and often not successful, as "Bushmen" sometimes returned to their nomadic life. On the other hand, they often triggered unintended effects and new social disruptions. Thus, one administrator complained that, instead of cultivating crops to sustain their life, the Vassekeles who had settled near his administrative post initially lived off the prostitution of their daughters.[105] But against cultural anthropologists like Manuel Viegas Guerreiro, who did ethnographic fieldwork among the !Kung "Bushmen" in southern Angola in the late 1950s and early 1960s and mourned the disruption of traditional "Bushman" society due to migrant labor, administrators agreed that social uplifting, even if it would take time, was the right and only path to follow.[106]

Perhaps even more fundamentally, some emphasized that, in order to succeed, it would be necessary to change the "Bushmen's" relationship with the surrounding Bantu peoples. In their opinion, most "Bushmen" were not autonomous hunter-gatherers but instead depended on the "Bantus," who controlled and despised them, to whom they had to provide meat, hides, fruit, and honey, and often their labor and that of their children, in turn for some cereals and other goods, so as not to starve.[107] In the eyes of the administrators, this was not an equal exchange but a state of servitude, which the "Bantus," as beneficiaries, would not want to change and which, hence, constituted the biggest obstacle to the "Bushmen's" socioeconomic advancement.[108] The administrative authorities were morally obliged to free the "Bushmen" from this bond. A good way to do this, administrators like Manuel Pereira Pontes Jr. and Carlos de Oliveira Santos argued, was by registering them and giving them labor contracts so that they would have to pay taxes and receive their identity card.[109] Liberating them from the "Bantus," in other words, meant to treat them like "Bantus": to end their "privileges" and to turn them into *indígenas* with the usual rights and duties.

This Bantuization policy only reached part of the "Bushman" population, particularly in southeast Angola, where Portuguese presence remained weak throughout the colonial period.[110] Yet, especially here, the idea that the "Bantus" oppressed them proved deadly influential. When, during the war of independence, Inspector of the Portuguese Secret Police (PIDE, from 1968 onward DGS) Óscar Cardoso constituted special anti-insurgent troops (*Flechas*) with "Bushmen" in southeastern Angola (1967–1974), he did not only want to make use of their famous tracking and hunting capacities.[111] Influenced by the ethnographic views of local administrators like Pontes, who would later write a very crude account of their enslavement for the DGS,[112] he also wanted to instrumentalize the "fear and hatred"[113] that the "Bushmen" allegedly nurtured toward the "Bantus."[114] Whether this was indeed the main reason why several hundreds of "Bushmen," mainly Khwe, joined the Portuguese armed forces, or whether it was the material and social benefits they gained from it, as Alyssa Battistoni and Julie Taylor have suggested, is open to debate. What is certain, however, is that after Portugal's withdrawal in 1974, most "Bushmen," including many !Kung, either were killed by victorious independence movements or fled to neighboring countries to escape retaliation.[115] There, ironically, the South African Defence Force in Namibia adopted a very similar policy, engaging many of them to fight the Namibian SWAPO independence movement and explaining the "Bushmen's" willingness to do so with their fears and primordial hatred toward the Bantu people.[116] Once again, colonial views on and policies toward the "Bushmen" in Angola and Namibia proved interwoven.

Conclusion

This chapter has demonstrated that notions of "Bushman" racial difference traveled across imperial boundaries but that exchanges did not happen on equal terms. Before World War II, there was hardly any research on the "Bushmen" in Angola, let alone by Portuguese scholars. The production of anthropological knowledge took place farther south, in Namibia and South Africa, and its interpretation occurred within a framework of racial categories that also built on the theoretical work of German, British, and French explorers and anthropologists. The resulting concepts of "Bushman" racial difference were subsequently adopted and, with minor adaptations, vulgarized in Portuguese writings. This setting (partly) changed in the 1950s, when the "Bushmen" in Angola became the object of various anthropological study missions and further medical and demographic research conducted by Portuguese scientists. While these scholars amassed a great deal of data, they were often reluctant to draw clear-cut conclusions from them and to explicitly intervene in broader debates about "Bushman" racial difference with scholars working on South Africa and Namibia.

Despite this hesitance, their findings dovetailed with larger shifts. Most of them, even if sometimes ambiguously, questioned the idea of the "Bushmen" as a fundamentally different, inferior, and dying race and explained the disappearance of physical and biological differences as the result of adaptation processes. To a certain extent, this shift ran parallel with a global, though also slow and messy, shift in racial sciences from typological races to population biology in the 1950s that can also be observed in the "Bushman" work of South African physical anthropologists like Philip Tobias. Yet, the Almeidas' "Bushman" work in the 1950s is much less sophisticated and often contradictory in this regard, since they do not explicitly abandon the general idea of categorizable racial (sub)types, which had been at the origin of their anthropological mission.

Changing anthropological views were entangled with novel administrative policies. After World War II, adaptation or Bantuization also became an administrative imperative. Administrators believed it was their civilizing mission to encourage this ongoing process, since, against prior beliefs, "Bushmen" showed capable of change and this was the only viable way to avoid racial extinction. Racial thinking, however, did not entirely disappear; during the war of decolonization, the Portuguese armed forces capitalized on what they perceived as still existing fundamental cultural, physical, and socioeconomic differences between "Bushmen" and "Bantus" to recruit the former as guerrilla troops.

Finally, this particular case study does not support the idea of important linkages in racial thinking and policies between both South Atlantic rims of the Lusophone world. For the few Portuguese scientists working on the "Bushmen" in Angola, Brazilian racial thought and/or anthropological fieldwork on Indigenous populations in Brazil were not important points of reference. Arguably, Brazilian ideas about whitening or miscegenation were hardly transposable to the "Bushman/Bantu" divide, as this divide did not include "white" colonizers and the figure of the *mestiço*. For Portuguese scholars and administrators, it was much easier and more intuitive to borrow and/or adapt concepts and practices from their germanophone and/or anglophone (colonial) neighbors trying to manage very similar populations.

SAMUËL COGHE is Visiting Professor and Interim Chair of African History at the Humboldt University in Berlin He received his PhD in history from the European University Institute in Florence in 2014 and has been Postdoctoral Fellow at the Max Planck Institute for the History of Science and the University of Giessen. His work focuses on the history of Portuguese colonialism in Africa, with special attention on the history of colonial medicine, demography, and anthropology. He is currently finishing a book on population politics in Portuguese Angola, and engaging with a new research project on cattle and capitalism in colonial Africa.

Notes

1. Although nowadays often considered derogatory in academic circles, I will follow Robert Gordon and use the colonial term "Bushmen" in this article. Not only has "Bushmen" become used as a self-designation, it also reveals much more clearly than the alternative, but also exogenous and often pejorative, term "San" (which is the word the cattle-herding Khoikhoi used for foragers, but at times also for vagabonds or bandits) the totalizing operation with which colonial observers, on the basis of linguistic, economic, or biological criteria, put different groups of people, which did not consider themselves linked, in a single racial category, thus differentiating them from other Africans. For a more extensive discussion of the problem of terminology, see Robert J. Gordon and Stuart Sholto-Douglas, *The Bushman Myth: The Making of a Namibian Underclass*, 2nd ed. (Boulder, CO, 2000), 4–8; Alan J. Barnard, *Anthropology and the Bushman* (Oxford, 2007), ix, 4–6.

2. See, most notably, Saul Dubow, *Scientific Racism in Modern South Africa* (Cambridge, 1995); Gordon and Sholto-Douglas, *Bushman Myth*; Barnard, *Anthropology*; Ute Dieckmann, *Haillom in the Etosha Region: A History of Colonial Settlement, Ethnicity and Nature Conservation* (Basel, 2007); Julie J. Taylor, *Naming the Land: San Identity and Community Conservation in Namibia's West Caprivi* (Basel, 2012).
3. See the introduction and Cláudia Castelo, this volume.
4. Bernardino José Brochado, "Descrição das terras do Humbe, Camba, Mulondo, Cuanhama e outros," *Annaes do Conselho Ultramarino* 1 (1854–1858): 194–97.
5. António Francisco Nogueira, *A raça negra sob o ponto de vista da civilização da África: Usos e costumes de alguns povos gentilicos do interior de Mossamedes e as colonias portuguezas* (Lisbon, 1880), 99–100; Serpa Pinto, *Como eu atravessei a África*, 2 vols. (London, 1881), 1:278–284; Hermenegildo Capello and Roberto Ivens, *De costa à contra-costa: Descripção de uma viagem atravez do continente africano*, 2 vols. (Lisbon, 1886), 1:206–8, 1:254–55; Francisco António Pinto, *Angola e Congo: Conferências* (Lisbon, 1888), 117–19.
6. Pinto, *Como eu atravessei*, 1:281. All translations are my own.
7. Dubow, *Scientific Racism*, 20–25.
8. Pinto, *Como eu atravessei*, 1:282.
9. See, e.g., Thomas Huxley, "On the Geographical Distribution of the Chief Modifications of Mankind," *Journal of the Ethnological Society of London* 2 (1870): 405–6; Paul Topinard, *L'anthropologie*, 3rd ed. (Paris, 1879), 502–10.
10. See Pinto, *Angola e Congo*, 116–26; José de Macedo, "As nossas riquezas coloniaes," *Boletim da Sociedade de Geografia de Lisboa* 18 (1900): 491–99.
11. Manuel Alves da Cunha, *Subsidiário etnográfico* (Luanda, 1913), 9–19; José de Oliveira Ferreira Diniz, *Populações indígenas de Angola* (Coimbra, 1918), 477–91. On the formation of this latter work, see Ricardo Roque, *Antropologia e império: Fonseca Cardoso e a expedição à Índia em 1895* (Lisbon, 2001), 298–301.
12. Cunha, *Subsidiário etnográfico*, 9–12, 21–23.
13. Gustav Fritsch, *Die eingeborenen Süd-Afrikas, ethnographisch und anatomisch beschrieben* (Breslau, 1872), 385–446, quote 395.
14. Gustav Fritsch, "Die afrikanischen Buschmänner als urrasse," *Zeitschrift für Ethnologie* 12 (1880): 300.
15. Dubow, *Scientific Racism*, 66–71.
16. Ibid., 66–72.
17. See also Johannes Fabian, *Time and the Other: How Anthropology Makes Its Object* (New York, 1983).
18. Patrick Brantlinger, *Dark Vanishings: Discourse on the Extinction of Primitive Races, 1800–1930* (Ithaca, NY, 2003).
19. Georg August Schweinfurth, *Im Herzen von Afrika* (Leipzig, 1874), 131–56.
20. Kairn A. Klieman, *"The Pygmies Were Our Compass": Bantu and Batwa in the History of West Central Africa, Early Times to c. 1900 C. E.* (Portsmouth, 2003), 14–15. For Portuguese support, see Conde de Ficalho, *Plantas úteis da África portuguesa* (Lisbon, 1884), 9–15; Ernesto Júlio de Carvalho Vasconcelos, *As colonias portuguezas: Geographia physica, politica e economica* (Lisbon, 1896), 163.
21. Wilhelm Bleek, *A Comparative Grammar of South African Languages*, 2 vols. (London, 1862–1869).
22. For a recent state of the art, see Koen Bostoen, "The Bantu Expansion," in *Oxford Research Encyclopedia of African History* (Oxford, 2018).
23. Jan Vansina, "Bantu in the Crystal Ball, I," *History in Africa* 6 (1979), 287–333, esp. 304–13; Jan Vansina, "Bantu in the Crystal Ball, II," *History in Africa* 7 (1980), 293–

325. See also Harry Johnston, *The Kilima-Njaro Expedition: A Record of Scientific Exploration in Eastern Equatorial Africa* (London, 1886), 478–88.
24. Vansina, "Bantu in the Crystal Ball, I," 295, 305.
25. See, e.g., Diniz, *Populações indígenas,* 473.
26. For South Africa, see Dubow, *Scientific Racism;* for German South West Africa, see, e.g., Siegfried Passarge, *Die Buschmänner der Kalahari* (Berlin, 1907); Felix von Luschan, "Pygmäen und Buschmänner," *Zeitschrift für Ethnologie* 46, no. 1 (1914): 154–73.
27. Ricardo Roque, "Antropologia colonial portuguesa (c. 1911–1950)," in *Estudos de Sociologia da Leitura em Portugal no Século XX,* ed. Diogo Ramada Curto (Lisbon, 2006), 789–822; Rui Pereira, "Antropologia aplicada na política colonial portuguesa: A missão de estudos das minorias étnicas do Ultramar português (1956–1961)" (MA thesis, Universidade Nova de Lisboa, 1986).
28. Francisco Venâncio da Silva, *Relatório do Serviço Permanente de Prevenção e Combate à Peste Bubónica no Sul de Angola, 1933* (Lisbon, 1936), 58–64; António Lebre, "Costumes gentílicos dos povos de além Cunéne," in *Trabalhos do 1.º Congresso Nacional de Antropologia Colonial, Porto, Setembro de 1934,* vol. 2 (Porto, 1934), 155–62; Dorothea Frances Bleek, "Bushmänner von Angola," *Archiv für Anthropologie* 21, nos. 1–2 (1927): 47–56; Dorothea Frances Bleek, "Bushmen of Central Angola," *Bantu Studies* 3, no. 1 (1928): 105–25; Carlos Estermann, "Les tribus bantoues du sud de l'Angola sont-elles fortement métissées avec la race bushman?" *Anthropos* 31 (1936): 572–76; Carlos Estermann, "Quelques observations sur les Bochimans !Kung de l'Angola méridionale," *Anthropos* 41–44 (1946–1949), 711–22.
29. Estermann, "Quelques observations," 717; Carlos Lopes Cardoso, "Contribuição para a bibliografia dos Bochimanes de Angola," *Boletim do Instituto de Angola* 14 (1960): 15. On the *indigenato* system in Angola, see Elizabeth Ceita Vera Cruz, *O estatuto do indigenato: Angola—A legalização da discriminação na colonização portuguesa* (Lisbon, 2005).
30. On population politics in colonial Angola more generally, see Samuël Coghe, "Population Politics in the Tropics: Demography, Health and Colonial Rule in Portuguese Angola, 1890s–1940s" (PhD diss., European University Institute, 2014).
31. António Coxito Granado, *Mucandas ou cartas de Angola: Vulgarização popular colonial Angolana* (Luanda, 1940), 66.
32. Julie J. Taylor, "Differentiating 'Bushmen' from 'Bantus': Identity-Building in West Caprivi, Namibia, 1930–89," *Journal of African History* 50, no. 3 (2009), 423–25.
33. Gordon and Sholto-Douglas, *Bushman Myth,* 57–85; Dieckmann, *Haillom,* 72–99.
34. Dieckmann, *Haillom,* 117–68.
35. I would like to thank Vítor Rosado Marques for granting me access to the collection of António de Almeida at the (now closed) Instituto de Investigação Ciêntífica Tropical (IICT) in Lisbon.
36. On Almeida, see Luís Frederico Dias Antunes, "António de Almeida (1900–1984): O Homem como património—Da biologia à etnografia," in *Viagens e missões científicas nos trópicos, 1883–2010,* ed. Ana Cristina Martins and Teresa Albino (Lisbon, 2010), 78–83.
37. António de Almeida, Relatório do Chefe da Equipa de Investigações Antropobiológicas de Angola, 15 October 1951, Fundo António de Almeida, IICT.
38. António de Almeida, *Bushmen and Other Non-Bantu Peoples of Angola: Three Lectures* (Johannesburg, 1965), xi.
39. See, e.g., António de Almeida, "Contribution à l'étude de l'ascendance des Bochimans !Khun [1972]," in *António de Almeida: Os Bosquímanos de Angola,* ed. Maria Cristina Neto and Maria Emília de Castro e Almeida (Lisbon 1994), 293–332.

40. António A. Mendes Correia, *Introducção à antropobiologia* (Coimbra, 1933); António A. Mendes Correia, "Da antropobiologia ultramarina," in *Introdução à antropologia tropical,* ed. Alfredo Athayde, Maria Emília de Castro e Almeida, and António A. Mendes Correia (Lisbon, 1962), 145–238.
41. Mendes Correia, *Introducção à antropobiologia*.
42. On Mendes Correia and his powerful position, see Patrícia Ferraz de Matos, "Mendes Correia e a Escola de Antropologia do Porto: Contribuição para o estudo das relações entre antropologia, nacionalismo e colonialismo (de finais do século XIX aos finais da década de 50 do século XX)" (PhD diss., Universidade de Lisboa, 2012); Roque, "Antropologia colonial," 804–6; Rui Pereira, "Raça, sangue e robustez: Os paradigmas da antropologia física colonial portuguesa," *Cadernos de Estudos Africanos* 7–8 (2004–2005), 213–216, 234.
43. On this wider program, see Ricardo Roque, this volume.
44. António Mendes Correia, Plano de Estudos Antropológicos Coloniais, 12 March 1941, Espólio das Missões Antropológicas, Processo 150, IICT. I would like to thank Ricardo Roque for drawing my attention to this source.
45. Vincent Bonnecase, "Avoir faim en Afrique Occidentale Française: Investigations et représentations coloniales (1920–1960)," *Revue d'Histoire des Sciences Humaines* 21 (2009): 162–67; Barbara Cooper, "The Gender of Nutrition in the AOF: Military Medicine, Intra-colonial Marginality, and Ethnos Theory in the Making of Malnutrition in Niger," in *Health and Difference: Rendering Human Variation in Colonial Engagements,* ed. Alexandra Widmer and Veronika Lipphardt (New York, 2016), 149–77.
46. Phillip V. Tobias, "Les Bochimans Auens et Naron de Ghanzi: Contribution à l'étude des 'Anciens Jaunes' Sud-Africains—Part I," *L'Anthropologie* 59 (1955): 235–252; 429–461; Phillip V. Tobias, "Les Bochimans Auens et Naron de Ghanzi: Contribution à l'étude des 'Anciens Jaunes' Sud-Africains—Part II," *L'Anthropologie* 60 (1956): 22–52, 268–289.
47. Phillip V. Tobias, "Fifteen Years of Study on the Kalahari Bushmen or San: A Brief History of the Kalahari Research Committee (1956–1973)," *South African Journal of Science* 71 (1975): 74–78.
48. Alan G. Morris, "Biological Anthropology at the Southern Tip of Africa: Carrying European Baggage in an African Context," *Current Anthropology* 53, no. S5 (2012): S158.
49. They were published only six years later. See Almeida, *Bushmen and Other Non-Bantu Peoples*; Phillip V. Tobias, "António de Almeida and the Bushmen of Angola: Introduction to the Re-edited Works of Professor Doctor António de Almeida on the Bushmen of Angola," in Neto and Castro e Almeida, *António de Almeida,* 10.
50. Phillip V. Tobias, "Preface," in Almeida, *Bushmen and Other Non-Bantu Peoples,* vii.
51. See, e.g., Maria Emília de Castro e Almeida, Maria Emília de Castro e, Luís Lopes, and Maria Cristina Neto, "Blood pressure in !Kung Bushmen and Cuanhamas of Southern Angola," *Garcia de Orta: Série de Antropobiologia* 9, no. 1 (1996): 23–30; Maria Emília de Castro e Almeida and Inês Maria Lapa-de-Passos, "The Nourishment of Angola Yellow Bushmen in the Fifties," *Garcia de Orta: Série de Antropobiologia* 9, no. 1 (1996): 31–38.
52. See, e.g., Alberto Carlos Germano da Silva Correia, "A necessidade do estudo antropológico das populações coloniais," in *Trabalhos do 1.º Congresso Nacional de Antropologia Colonial, Porto, Setembro de 1934,* vol. 1 (Porto, 1934), 157–83; António Vicente Ferreira, "A ciência e o empirismo na colonização moderna," *Economia e Finanças* 4 (1936): 147–65.
53. António de Almeida, "Alguns velhos e novos conceitos sobre os povos não-bantos de Angola [1964]," in Neto and Castro e Almeida, *António de Almeida,* 186; António de

Almeida, "Da morfologia dos Kung (Bosquímanos Amarelos) de Angola," *Memórias da Academia das Ciências de Lisboa: Classe de Ciências* 11 (1967): 67–80; António de Almeida, "Dos Cazamas ou Cacuengos de Angola," *Memórias da Academia das Ciências de Lisboa: Classe de Ciências* 11 (1967): 93–107.
54. See Almeida, "Alguns velhos," 183; António de Almeida, "Sobre os Hotentotes de Angola," *Memórias da Academia das Ciências de Lisboa: Classe de Ciências* 11 (1967): 81–92.
55. Cf. Carlos Estermann, "Notas etnográficas sobre os povos indígenas do distrito da Huíla," *Boletim Geral das Colónias* 11, no. 116 (1935): 41–44; Silva, *Relatório*, 58.
56. Isaac Schapera, *The Khoisan People of South Africa: Bushmen and Hottentots* (London, 1930), 5; Barnard, *Anthropology*, 5. See also Colónia de Angola—Repartição de Estatística Geral, ed., *Censo geral da população, 1940*, 12 vols. (Luanda, 1941–1947), 1:55, 9:222–29.
57. Many of the calculations were only made in the late 1960s and early 1970s. See Fundo António de Almeida, IICT.
58. Morris, "Biological Anthropology," 157–59; Dubow, *Scientific Racism*, 36–45.
59. Rita Juliana Poloni, "Expedições arqueológicas nos territórios de Ultramar: Uma visão da ciência e da sociedade portuguesa do período colonial (PhD diss., Universidade do Algarve, 2012), 157–62.
60. António de Almeida and Maria Emília de Castro e Almeida, "Contribuição para o estudo da sero-antropologia dos Bosquímanos de Angola (Mucuancalas) [1956]," in Neto and Castro e Almeida, *António de Almeida*, 385–93.
61. See, e.g., William C. Boyd, "Four Achievements of the Genetical Method in Physical Anthropology," *American Anthropologist* 65, no. 2 (1963): 243–52.
62. Almeida and Almeida, "Sero-antropologia"; Almeida, *Bushmen and Other Non-Bantu Peoples*, 4–5.
63. Almeida, "Contribution à l'étude de l'ascendance."
64. See, e.g., Phillip V. Tobias, "Bushmen of the Kalahari," *Man* 57 (1957): 37; Morris, "Biological Anthropology," 157–58.
65. See Tobias, "Fifteen Years," 76; Phillip V. Tobias, "Introduction to the Bushmen or San," in *The Bushmen: San Hunters and Herders of Southern Africa*, ed. Phillip V. Tobias (Cape Town, 1978), 9–10.
66. Almeida, "Da morfologia," 78.
67. See, e.g., Dubow, *Scientific Racism*, 23; for Angola, see Cunha, *Subsidiário etnográfico*, 13–14; José Nobre, "Esboço etnográfico," in *Generalidades sobre Angola: Para o 1.º cruzeiro de férias às colónias portuguesas*, ed. Fernando Mouta (Luanda, 1935), 37–40.
68. António de Almeida, "Sobre a esteatopigia dos Bosquímanos e Hotentotes de Angola [1959]," in Neto and Castro e Almeida, *António de Almeida*, 123.
69. António de Almeida, "La macronymphie chez les femmes indigènes de l'Angola [1956]," in Neto and Castro e Almeida, *António de Almeida*, 84–85.
70. See Manuel Pereira Pontes Jr., *Breves notas sobre os Vasekele do Cuando-Cubango: Monografia apresentada para o concurso de Administradores de Circunscrição* (Luanda, 1952), 34–35; Mário Henriques da Silva, "Subsídios para o estudo etnográfico da Circunscrição do Cuando" (thesis, Escola Superior Colonial), 1953–1954, 19; Carlos A. M. de Oliveira Santos, "Os Vassekele do Cuando: Contribuição para o seu estudo" (thesis, Universidade de Lisboa), 1958, 11–12.
71. Cf. Tobias, "Bushmen of the Kalahari," 34–35; Hertha de Villiers, "The Tablier and Steatopygia in Kalahari Bushwomen," *South African Journal of Science* 57 (1961): 223–27.

72. Almeida, "Alguns velhos," 189–90; cf. Maria Emília de Castro e Almeida, "Da estatura, peso e sua correlação em gentes nativas de Angola," *Garcia de Orta: Revista da Junta das Missões Geográficas e de Investigações do Ultramar* 4 (1956): 349–58.
73. Almeida and Almeida, "Sero-antropologia," 388–89.
74. Phillip V. Tobias, "On the Increasing Stature of the Bushmen," *Anthropos* 57 (1962): 801–10.
75. Cf. Tobias, "Bushmen of the Kalahari"; Tobias, "On the Increasing Stature"; Tobias, "Fifteen Years"; Tobias, "Introduction."
76. Michael A. Little, "Human Population Biology in the Second Half of the Twentieth Century," *Current Anthropology* 53, no. S5 (2012): S126–S38.
77. Nancy Leys Stepan, quoted in Veronika Lipphardt, "Isolates and Crosses in Human Population Genetics; or, A Contextualization of German Race Science," *Current Anthropology* 53, no. S5 (2012): S69. On this idea, see also Susan Lindee and Ricardo Ventura Santos, "The Biological Anthropology of Living Human Populations: World Histories, National Styles, and International Networks—An Introduction to Supplement 5," *Current Anthropology* 53, no. S5 (2012): S3–S16.
78. João Araújo de Freitas, "Resultado duma regular alimentação no Bochiman e a sua fácil adaptação a novas condições de vida," in *Conferência inter-africana de nutrição, 3. sessão (Luanda, Outubro 1956): Communicações*, vol. 2 (London, 1957), 519–31.
79. G. Jorge Janz, G. L. Pinto, Vítor Casaca, and A. Morais de Carvalho, "Estudo hematológico e bioquímico comparativo de dois grupos de africanos com hábitos alimentares diferentes. Mucancalas e Cuanhamas de Angola," in *Conferência inter-africana de nutrição, 3. sessão (Luanda, Outubro 1956): Communicações*, vol. 2 (London, 1957), 501–17.
80. Augusto Salazar Leite, G. Jorge Janz, A. F. Gândara, Luís Ré, Vítor Casaca, and A. Morais de Carvalho, "Relatório da missão do Instituto de Medicina Tropical a Angola (1954) em colaboração com a missão de prospecção de endémias em Angola," *Anais do Instituto de Medicina Tropical* 12, nos. 1–2 (1955): 219–23.
81. Ronald Singer, "The Sickle Cell Trait in Africa," *American Anthropologist* 55, no. 5 (1953): 634–37.
82. See, e.g., ibid., 637; Hermann Lehmann, "Distribution of the Sickle Cell Gene: A New Light on the Origin of the East Africans," *Eugenics Review* 46, no. 2 (1954): 101–21.
83. Alexandre Sarmento, "Contribuïção para o estudo da anemia de células falciformes nos negros de Angola," *Anais do Instituto de Medicina Tropical* 1, no. 2 (1944): 345–50; Waldemar Gomes Teixeira, "Hematias falciformes dos indígenas de Angola," *Anais do Instituto de Medicina Tropical* 1, no. 2 (1944): 365–74; Augusto Salazar Leite, J. V. Bastos da Luz, and Manuel T. V. de Meira, "Relatório da missão Médica do Instituto de Medicina Tropical a Angola, em 1945," *Anais do Instituto de Medicina Tropical* 4 (1947): 465–500. See also the overview in Carlos Pinto Trincão, "Anemia de celulas falciformes," *Anais do Instituto de Medicina Tropical* 5 (1948): 359.
84. Seaton Bythyl Griffiths, "Absence of the Sickle Cell Trait in the Bushmen of South-West Africa," *Nature* 171 (1953): 577–78; A. Zoutendyk, Ada C. Kopeć, and A. E. Mourant, "The Blood Groups of the Bushmen," *American Journal of Physical Anthropology* 11, no. 3 (1953): 361–68.
85. A. C. Allison, "The Distribution of the Sickle-Cell Trait in East Africa and Elsewhere, and Its Apparent Relationship to the Incidence of Subtertian Malaria," *Transactions of the Royal Society of Tropical Medicine and Hygiene* 48, no. 4 (1954): 312–18; Frank B. Livingstone, "Anthropological Implications of Sickle Cell Gene Distribution in West Africa," *American Anthropologist* 60, no. 3 (1958): 533–62.

86. J. H. Santos David, *Subsídios para o estudo da antropologia na Lunda: A drepanocitemia e a antropologia* (Lisbon, 1960), 49–58, 73–77.
87. See Schapera, *Khoisan People*, 3–4, 38–40.
88. Colónia de Angola, *Censo geral da população, 1940*, 9:25; Repartição Técnica de Estatística Geral da Província de Angola, ed., *II Recenseamento geral da população, 1950*, 5 vols. (Luanda, 1953–1956), 4: 115–17; Direcção dos Serviços de Estatística de Angola, ed., *III Recenseamento geral da população, 1960*, 5 vols. (Luanda, 1964–1969), 3: 84–93.
89. Alexandre Sarmento, "Subsídios para o estudo demográfico da população indígena de Angola," *Anais do Instituto de Medicina Tropical* 14, no. 3–4 (1957): 522–23.
90. Almeida, *Bushmen and Other Non-Bantu Peoples*, 1, 15.
91. Freitas, "Resultado," 525.
92. See Rui Mateus Pereira, "Conhecer para dominar: O desenvolvimento do conhecimento antropológico na política colonial portuguesa em Moçambique" (PhD diss., Universidade Nova de Lisboa, 2006), anexos, 254; Freitas, "Resultado," 525; Janz et al., "Estudo hematológico," 501.
93. Phillip V. Tobias, "On the Survival of the Bushmen: With an Estimate of the Problem facing Anthropologists," *Africa: Journal of the International African Institute* 26, no. 2 (1956): 174–86.
94. See Silva, *Relatório*, 58–59; Estermann, "Les tribus bantoues," 575–76; Bleek, "Bushmen," 106–7, 125.
95. On the usefulness of physical anthropology for colonial governance, see Emmanuelle Sibeud, "A Useless Colonial Science? Practicing Anthropology in the French Colonial Empire, circa 1880–1960," *Current Anthropology* 53, no. S5 (2012): S83–S94.
96. Pontes, *Breves notas*. 4–9; 71–74.
97. See, e.g., Lobato de Faria, "Povos do Baixo Cubango," *Mensário administrativo* 2, no. 13 (1948): 25–27; Augusto César de Castro Jr., "Os 'Va-kwa-n-kala' do Alto Cunene," *Mensário administrativo* 41–42 (1951): 21; Silva, "Subsídios," 20–21; Alberto Fernandes Geirinhas, "Contribuição para o estudo dos povos da Circunscrição dos Luchazes" (Thesis, Universidade de Lisboa, 1963-1964), 8, 262–304.
98. See Samuël Coghe, "Reordering Colonial Society: Model Villages and Social Planning in Rural Angola, 1920–1945," *Journal of Contemporary History* 52, no. 1 (2017): 16–44.
99. Geirinhas, "Contribuição," 8.
100. Ibid., 187–88; Manuel Viegas Guerreiro, *Bochimanes !KHU de Angola: Estudo etnográfico* (Lisbon, 1968), 142–45; Freitas, "Resultado."
101. Janet Hermans, "Official Policy towards the Bushmen of Botswana: A Review, Part I," *Botswana Notes and Records* 9 (1977): 65.
102. Gordon and Sholto-Douglas, *Bushman Myth*. 157–67.
103. Taylor, "Differentiating," 425–27.
104. Dieckmann, *Haillom*; Liz Wily, *Official Policy towards San (Bushmen) Hunter-Gatherers in Modern Botswana, 1966–1978* (Gabarone, 1979).
105. Santos, *Vassekele*, 17–18. See also Faria, "Povos"; Silva, "Subsídios," 20–21.
106. Guerreiro, *Bochimanes !KHU*. 144–145.
107. See, e.g., Faria, "Povos"; Silva, "Subsídios," 18; esp. Pontes, *Breves notas*. 4–8, 71–74.
108. In the late 1980s, the *historical* relation between "Bushmen" and surrounding peoples would give rise to the "Kalahari debate" among anthropologists. While "traditionalists" like Richard Lee defended that the "Bushmen" had always lived as isolated and independent hunter-gatherers, "revisionists" claimed that this ideal type of a foraging society had never existed and that the "Bushmen" had historically been part of a

greater Kalahari economy, in which they constituted an underclass. See, e.g., Barnard, *Anthropology,* 97–111.
109. Pontes, *Breves notas,* 73–74; Santos, *Vassekele,* 12, 99–100.
110. Alyssa K. Battistoni and Julie J. Taylor, "Indigenous Identities and Military Frontiers: Reflections on San and the Military in Namibia and Angola, 1960–2000," *Lusotopie* 16, no. 1 (2009): 116–18.
111. John Cann, *The Flechas: Insurgent Hunting in Eastern Angola, 1965–1974* (Solihull, 2013); Battistoni and Taylor, "Indigenous Identities."
112. Manuel Pereira Pontes Jr., *Apontamentos para a história dos bochimanes de Angola* (Luanda, 1970), esp. 32–39.
113. Santos, *Vassekele.* 12.
114. Cann, *The Flechas.* 30.
115. Battistoni and Taylor, "Indigenous Identities," 119–20; Maria Fisch, *The Mbukushu in Angola (1730-2002): A History of Migration, Flight and Royal Rainmaking* (Köln, 2005), 80–82.
116. Taylor, "Differentiating," 432–36; Battistoni and Taylor, "Indigenous Identities," 121–22.

Bibliography

Allison, A. C. "The Distribution of the Sickle-Cell Trait in East Africa and Elsewhere, and Its Apparent Relationship to the Incidence of Subtertian Malaria." *Transactions of the Royal Society of Tropical Medicine and Hygiene* 48, no. 4 (1954): 312–18.

Almeida, António de. "Alguns velhos e novos conceitos sobre os povos não-bantos de Angola [1964]." In Neto and Castro e Almeida, *António de Almeida,* 179–201.

———. *Bushmen and Other Non-Bantu Peoples of Angola: Three Lectures.* Johannesburg: Witwatersrand University Press, 1965.

———. "Contribution à l'étude de l'ascendance des Bochimans !Khun [1972]." In Neto and Castro e Almeida, *António de Almeida,* 293–332.

———. "Da morfologia dos Kung (Bosquímanos Amarelos) de Angola." *Memórias da Academia das Ciências de Lisboa: Classe de Ciências* 11 (1967): 67–80.

———. "Dos Cazamas ou Cacuengos de Angola." *Memórias da Academia das Ciências de Lisboa: Classe de Ciências* 11 (1967): 93–107.

———. "La macronymphie chez les femmes indigènes de l'Angola [1956]." In Neto and Castro e Almeida, *António de Almeida,* 68–86.

———. "Sobre a esteatopigia dos Bosquímanos e Hotentotes de Angola [1959]." In Neto and Castro e Almeida, *António de Almeida,* 117–30.

———. "Sobre os Hotentotes de Angola." *Memórias da Academia das Ciências de Lisboa: Classe de Ciências* 11 (1967): 81–92.

Almeida, António de, and Maria Emília de Castro e Almeida. "Contribuição para o estudo da sero-antropologia dos Bosquímanos de Angola (Mucuancalas) [1956]." In Neto and Castro e Almeida, *António de Almeida,* 385–93.

Almeida, Maria Emília de Castro e. "Da estatura, peso e sua correlação em gentes nativas de Angola." *Garcia de Orta: Revista da Junta das Missões Geográficas e de Investigações do Ultramar* 4 (1956): 349–58.

Almeida, Maria Emília de Castro e, and Inês Maria Lapa-de-Passos. "The Nourishment of Angola Yellow Bushmen in the Fifties." *Garcia de Orta: Série de Antropobiologia* 9, no. 1 (1996): 31–38.

Almeida, Maria Emília de Castro e, Luís Lopes, and Maria Cristina Neto. "Blood Pressure in !Kung Bushmen and Cuanhamas of Southern Angola." *Garcia de Orta: Série de Antropobiologia* 9, no. 1 (1996): 23-30.
Antunes, Luís Frederico Dias. "António de Almeida (1900-1984): O Homem como património—Da biologia à etnografia." In *Viagens e missões científicas nos trópicos, 1883-2010*, edited by Ana Cristina Martins and Teresa Albino, 78-83. Lisbon: Instituto de Investigação Científica Tropical, 2010.
Barnard, Alan J. *Anthropology and the Bushman*. Oxford: Berg, 2007.
Battistoni, Alyssa K., and Julie J. Taylor. "Indigenous Identities and Military Frontiers: Reflections on San and the Military in Namibia and Angola, 1960-2000." *Lusotopie* 16, no. 1 (2009): 113-31.
Bleek, Dorothea Frances. "Bushmänner von Angola." *Archiv für Anthropologie* 21, nos. 1-2 (1927): 47-56.
———. "Bushmen of Central Angola." *Bantu Studies* 3, no. 1 (1928): 105-25.
Bleek, Wilhelm. *A Comparative Grammar of South African Languages*. 2 vols. London: Trübner, 1862-1869.
Bonnecase, Vincent. "Avoir faim en Afrique Occidentale Française: Investigations et représentations coloniales (1920-1960)." *Revue d'Histoire des Sciences Humaines* 21 (2009): 151-74.
Bostoen, Koen. "The Bantu Expansion." In *Oxford Research Encyclopedia of African History*. Oxford: Oxford University Press, 2018.
Boyd, William C. "Four Achievements of the Genetical Method in Physical Anthropology." *American Anthropologist* 65, no. 2 (1963): 243-52.
Brantlinger, Patrick. *Dark Vanishings: Discourse on the Extinction of Primitive Races, 1800-1930*. Ithaca, NY: Cornell University Press, 2003.
Brochado, Bernardino José. "Descrição das terras do Humbe, Camba, Mulondo, Cuanhama e outros." *Annaes do Conselho Ultramarino* 1 (1854-1858): 187-97.
Cann, John. *The Flechas: Insurgent Hunting in Eastern Angola, 1965-1974*. Solihull: Helion & Company, 2013.
Capello, Hermenegildo, and Roberto Ivens. *De costa à contra-costa: Descripção de uma viagem atravez do continente africano*. 2 vols. Lisbon: Imprensa Nacional, 1886.
Cardoso, Carlos Lopes. "Contribuição para a bibliografia dos Bochimanes de Angola." *Boletim do Instituto de Angola* 14 (1960): 5-23.
Castro, Augusto César de, Jr. "Os 'Va-kwa-n-kala' do Alto Cunene." *Mensário Administrativo* 41-42 (1951): 11-27.
Coghe, Samuël. "Population Politics in the Tropics: Demography, Health and Colonial Rule in Portuguese Angola, 1890s-1940s." PhD diss., European University Institute, 2014.
———. "Reordering Colonial Society: Model Villages and Social Planning in Rural Angola, 1920-1945." *Journal of Contemporary History* 52, no. 1 (2017): 16-44.
Colónia de Angola—Repartição de Estatística Geral, ed. *Censo geral da população, 1940*. 12 vols. Luanda: Imprensa Nacional, 1941-1947.
Cooper, Barbara. "The Gender of Nutrition in the AOF: Military Medicine, Intra-colonial Marginality, and Ethnos Theory in the Making of Malnutrition in Niger." In *Health and Difference: Rendering Human Variation in Colonial Engagements*, edited by Alexandra Widmer and Veronika Lipphardt, 149-77. New York: Berghahn Books, 2016.
Cruz, Elizabeth Ceita Vera. *O estatuto do indigenato: Angola—A legalização da discriminação na colonização portuguesa*. Lisbon: Novo Imbondeiro, 2005.
Cunha, Manuel Alves da. *Subsidiário etnográfico*. Luanda: Imprensa Nacional, 1913.
David, J. H. Santos. *Subsidios para o estudo da antropologia na Lunda: A drepanocitemia e a antropologia*. Lisbon: Diamang, 1960.

Dieckmann, Ute. *Haillom in the Etosha Region: A History of Colonial Settlement, Ethnicity and Nature Conservation.* Basel: Basler Afrika Bibiographien, 2007.
Diniz, José de Oliveira Ferreira. *Populações indígenas de Angola.* Coimbra: Imprensa da Universidade, 1918.
Direcção dos Serviços de Estatística de Angola, ed. *III Recenseamento geral da população de Angola, 1960.* 5 vols. Luanda: DSEA, 1964–1969.
Dubow, Saul. *Scientific Racism in Modern South Africa.* Cambridge: Cambridge University Press, 1995.
Estermann, Carlos. "Les tribus bantoues du sud de l'Angola sont-elles fortement métissées avec la race bushman?" *Anthropos* 31 (1936): 572–76.
———. "Notas etnográficas sobre os povos indígenas do distrito da Huila." *Boletim Geral das Colónias* 11, no. 116 (1935): 41–69.
———. "Quelques observations sur les Bochimans !Kung de l'Angola méridionale." *Anthropos* 41–44 (1946–1949): 711–22.
Fabian, Johannes. *Time and the Other: How Anthropology Makes Its Object.* New York: Columbia University Press, 1983.
Faria, Lobato de. "Povos do Baixo Cubango." *Mensário Administrativo* 2, no. 13 (1948): 25–27.
Ferreira, António Vicente. "A ciência e o empirismo na colonização moderna." *Economia e Finanças* 4 (1936): 147–65.
Ficalho, Conde de. *Plantas úteis da África portuguesa.* Lisbon: Sociedade de Geografia de Lisboa, 1884.
Fisch, Maria. *The Mbukushu in Angola (1730–2002): A History of Migration, Flight and Royal Rainmaking.* Köln: Köppe, 2005.
Freitas, João Araújo de. "Resultado duma regular alimentação no Bochiman e a sua fácil adaptação a novas condições de vida." In *Conferência inter-africana de nutrição, 3. sessão (Luanda, Outubro 1956): Communicações,* vol. 2, 519–531. Luanda: Commission for Technical Co-operation in Africa, 1957.
Fritsch, Gustav. "Die afrikanischen Buschmänner als Urrasse." *Zeitschrift für Ethnologie* 12 (1880): 289–300.
———. *Die Eingeborenen Süd-Afrikas, ethnographisch und anatomisch beschrieben.* Breslau: Hirt, 1872.
Geirinhas, Alberto Fernandes. "Contribuição para o estudo dos povos da Circunscrição dos Luchazes." Thesis, Universidade de Lisboa, 1963–1964.
Gordon, Robert J., and Stuart Sholto-Douglas. *The Bushman Myth: The Making of a Namibian Underclass.* 2nd ed. Boulder, CO: Westview, 2000.
Granado, António Coxito. *Mucandas ou cartas de Angola: Vulgarização popular colonial Angolana.* Luanda: Imprensa Baroeth, 1940.
Griffiths, Seaton Bythyl. "Absence of the Sickle Cell Trait in the Bushmen of South-West Africa." *Nature* 171 (1953): 577–78.
Guerreiro, Manuel Viegas. *Bochimanes !KHU de Angola: Estudo etnográfico.* Lisbon: Instituto de Investigação Científica de Angola, 1968.
Hermans, Janet. "Official Policy towards the Bushmen of Botswana: A Review, Part I." *Botswana Notes and Records* 9 (1977): 55–67.
Huxley, Thomas. "On the Geographical Distribution of the Chief Modifications of Mankind." *Journal of the Ethnological Society of London* 2 (1870): 404–9.
Janz, G. Jorge, G. L. Pinto, Vítor Casaca, and A. Morais de Carvalho. "Estudo hematológico e bioquímico comparativo de dois grupos de africanos com hábitos alimentares diferentes: Mucancalas e Cuanhamas de Angola." In *Conferência inter-africana de nutrição, 3. sessão (Luanda, Outubro 1956): Communicações,* vol. 2, 501–17. Luanda: Commission for Technical Co-operation in Africa, 1957.

Johnston, Harry. *The Kilima-Njaro Expedition: A Record of Scientific Exploration in Eastern Equatorial Africa.* London: Kegan Paul, 1886.
Klieman, Kairn A. *"The Pygmies Were Our Compass": Bantu and Batwa in the History of West Central Africa, Early Times to c. 1900 C.E.* Portsmouth: Heinemann, 2003.
Lebre, António. "Costumes gentílicos dos povos de além Cunéne." In *Trabalhos do 1.º Congresso Nacional de Antropologia Colonial, Porto, Setembro de 1934*, vol. 2, 76–192. Porto: Edições da 1.ª Exposição Colonial Portuguesa, 1934.
Lehmann, Hermann. "Distribution of the Sickle Cell Gene: A New Light on the Origin of the East Africans." *Eugenics Review* 46, no. 2 (1954): 101–21.
Leite, Augusto Salazar, G. Jorge Janz, A. F. Gândara, Luís Ré, Vítor Casaca, and A. Morais de Carvalho. "Relatório da missão do Instituto de Medicina Tropical a Angola (1954) em colaboração com a missão de prospecção de endémias em Angola." *Anais do Instituto de Medicina Tropical* 12, nos. 1–2 (1955): 219–54.
Leite, Augusto Salazar, J. V. Bastos da Luz, and Manuel T. V. de Meira. "Relatório da missão médica do Instituto de Medicina Tropical a Angola, em 1945." *Anais do Instituto de Medicina Tropical* 4 (1947): 465–500.
Lindee, Susan, and Ricardo Ventura Santos. "The Biological Anthropology of Living Human Populations. World Histories, National Styles, and International Networks: An Introduction to Supplement 5." *Current Anthropology* 53, no. S5 (2012): S3–S16.
Lipphardt, Veronika. "Isolates and Crosses in Human Population Genetics; or, A Contextualization of German Race Science." *Current Anthropology* 53, no. S5 (2012): S69–S82.
Little, Michael A. "Human Population Biology in the Second Half of the Twentieth Century." *Current Anthropology* 53, no. S5 (2012): S126–38.
Livingstone, Frank B. "Anthropological Implications of Sickle Cell Gene Distribution in West Africa." *American Anthropologist* 60, no. 3 (1958): 533–62.
Luschan, Felix von. "Pygmäen und Buschmänner." *Zeitschrift für Ethnologie* 46, no. 1 (1914): 154–73.
Macedo, José de. "As nossas riquezas coloniaes." *Boletim da Sociedade de Geografia de Lisboa* 18 (1900): 411–609.
Matos, Patrícia Ferraz de. "Mendes Correia e a Escola de Antropologia do Porto: Contribuição para o estudo das relações entre antropologia, nacionalismo e colonialismo (de finais do século XIX aos finais da década de 50 do século XX)." PhD dissertation, Universidade de Lisboa, 2012.
Mendes Correia, António A. "Da antropobiologia ultramarina." In *Introdução à antropologia tropical*, edited by Alfredo Athayde, Maria Emília de Castro e Almeida, and António A. Mendes Correia, 145–238. Lisbon: Junta de Investigação do Ultramar, 1962.
———. *Introducção à antropobiologia*. Coimbra: Imprensa da Universidade, 1933.
Morris, Alan G. "Biological Anthropology at the Southern Tip of Africa: Carrying European Baggage in an African Context." *Current Anthropology* 53, no. S5 (2012): S152–60.
Neto, Maria Cristina, and Maria Emília de Castro e Almeida, eds. *António de Almeida: Os Bosquímanos de Angola*. Lisbon: Instituto de Investigação Científica Tropical, 1994.
Nobre, José. "Esboço etnográfico." In *Generalidades sobre Angola: Para o 1.º cruzeiro de férias às colónias portuguesas*, edited by Fernando Mouta, 37–40. Luanda: Imprensa Nacional, 1935.
Nogueira, António Francisco. *A raça negra sob o ponto de vista da civilização da África: Usos e costumes de alguns povos gentilicos do interior de Mossamedes e as colonias portuguezas*. Lisbon: Tipografia Nova Minerva, 1880.
Oliveira Santos, Carlos A. M. de. "Os Vassekele do Cuando: Contribuição para o seu estudo." Thesis, Universidade de Lisboa, 1958.
Passarge, Siegfried. *Die Buschmänner der Kalahari*. Berlin: Reimer, 1907.

Pereira, Rui Mateus. "Antropologia aplicada na política colonial portuguesa: A missão de estudos das minorias étnicas do Ultramar português (1956–1961)." MA thesis, Universidade Nova de Lisboa, 1986.

———. "Conhecer para dominar: O desenvolvimento do conhecimento antropológico na política colonial portuguesa em Moçambique." PhD disseration, Universidade Nova de Lisboa, 2006.

———. "Raça, Sangue e Robustez: Os paradigmas da Antropologia Física colonial portuguesa." *Cadernos de Estudos Africanos* 7–8 (2004–2005): 209–42.

Pinto, Francisco António. *Angola e Congo: Conferências.* Lisbon: Ferreira, 1888.

Pinto, Serpa. *Como eu atravessei a África.* 2 vols. London: Sampson Low, 1881.

Poloni, Rita Juliana. "Expedições arqueológicas nos territórios de Ultramar: Uma visão da ciência e da sociedade portuguesa do período colonial." PhD dissertation, Universidade do Algarve, 2012.

Pontes, Manuel Pereira, Jr. *Apontamentos para a história dos bochimanes de Angola.* Luanda: Direcção-Geral de Segurança, 1970.

———. *Breves notas sobre os Vasekele do Cuando-Cubango: Monografia apresentada para o concurso de Administradores de Circunscrição.* Luanda: Direcção-Geral de Segurança, 1952.

Repartição Técnica de Estatística Geral da Província de Angola, ed. *II Recenseamento Geral da População, 1950.* 5 vols. Luanda: Imprensa Nacional, 1953–1956.

Roque, Ricardo. "Antropologia colonial portuguesa (c. 1911–1950)." In *Estudos de Sociologia da Leitura em Portugal no Século XX,* edited by Diogo Ramada Curto, 789–822. Lisbon: Fundação Calouste Gulbenkian 2006.

———. *Antropologia e império: Fonseca Cardoso e a expedição à Índia em 1895.* Lisbon: Imprensa de Ciências Sociais, 2001.

Sarmento, Alexandre. "Contribuïção para o estudo da anemia de células falciformes nos negros de Angola." *Anais do Instituto de Medicina Tropical* 1, no. 2 (1944): 345–50.

———. "Subsídios para o estudo demográfico da população indígena de Angola." *Anais do Instituto de Medicina Tropical* 14, no. 3–4 (1957): 509–26.

Schapera, Isaac. *The Khoisan People of South Africa: Bushmen and Hottentots.* London: Routledge, 1930.

Schweinfurth, Georg August. *Im Herzen von Afrika.* Leipzig: Brockhaus, 1874.

Sibeud, Emmanuelle. "A Useless Colonial Science? Practicing Anthropology in the French Colonial Empire, circa 1880–1960." *Current Anthropology* 53, no. S5 (2012): S83–S94.

Silva, Francisco Venâncio da. *Relatório do Serviço Permanente de Prevenção e Combate à Peste Bubónica no Sul de Angola, 1933.* Lisbon: Agência Geral das Colónias, 1936.

Silva, Mário Henriques da. "Subsídios para o estudo etnográfico da Circunscrição do Cuando." Thesis, Escola Superior Colonial, 1953–1954.

Silva Correia, Alberto Carlos Germano da. "A necessidade do estudo antropológico das populações coloniais." In *Trabalhos do 1.° Congresso Nacional de Antropologia Colonial, Porto, Setembro de 1934,* vol. 1. Porto: Edições da 1.a Exposição Colonial Portuguesa, 1934, 157–83.

Singer, Ronald. "The Sickle Cell Trait in Africa." *American Anthropologist* 55, no. 5 (1953): 634–48.

Taylor, Julie J. "Differentiating 'Bushmen' from 'Bantus': Identity-Building in West Caprivi, Namibia, 1930–89." *Journal of African History* 50, no. 3 (2009): 417–39.

———. *Naming the Land: San Identity and Community Conservation in Namibia's West Caprivi.* Basel: Basler Afrika Bibiographien, 2012.

Teixeira, Waldemar Gomes. "Hematias falciformes dos indígenas de Angola." *Anais do Instituto de Medicina Tropical* 1, no. 2 (1944): 365–74.

Tobias, Phillip V. "António de Almeida and the Bushmen of Angola: Introduction to the Re-edited Works of Professor Doctor António de Almeida on the Bushmen of Angola." In Neto and Castro e Almeida, *António de Almeida*, 9–15.

———. "Bushmen of the Kalahari." *Man* 57 (1957): 33–40.

———. "Fifteen Years of Study on the Kalahari Bushmen or San: A Brief History of the Kalahari Research Committee (1956–1973)." *South African Journal of Science* 71 (1975): 74–78.

———. "Introduction to the Bushmen or San." In *The Bushmen: San Hunters and Herders of Southern Africa*, edited by Phillip V. Tobias, 1–15. Cape Town: Human & Rousseau, 1978.

———. "Les Bochimans Auens et Naron de Ghanzi: Contribution à l'étude des 'Anciens Jaunes' Sud-Africains—Part I." *L'anthropologie* 59 (1955): 235–52, 429–61.

———. "Les Bochimans Auens et Naron de Ghanzi: Contribution à l'étude des 'Anciens Jaunes' Sud-Africains—Part II." *L'anthropologie* 60 (1956): 22–52, 268–89.

———. "On the Increasing Stature of the Bushmen." *Anthropos* 57 (1962): 801–10.

———. "On the Survival of the Bushmen: With an Estimate of the Problem Facing Anthropologists." *Africa: Journal of the International African Institute* 26, no. 2 (1956): 174–86.

Topinard, Paul. *L'anthropologie*. 3rd ed. Paris: C. Reinwald & Cie, 1879.

Trincão, Carlos Pinto. "Anemia de celulas falciformes." *Anais do Instituto de Medicina Tropical* 5 (1948): 357–400.

Vansina, Jan. "Bantu in the Crystal Ball, I." *History in Africa* 6 (1979): 287–333

———. "Bantu in the Crystal Ball, II." *History in Africa* 7 (1980): 293–325.

Vasconcelos, Ernesto Júlio de Carvalho. *As colonias portuguezas: Geographia physica, politica e economica*. Lisbon: Typographia da Companhia Nacional Editora, 1896.

Villiers, Hertha de. "The Tablier and Steatopygia in Kalahari Bushwomen." *South African Journal of Science* 57 (1961): 223–227.

Wily, Liz. *Official Policy towards San (Bushmen) Hunter-Gatherers in Modern Botswana, 1966–1978*. Gabarone: University College of Botswana, 1979.

Zoutendyk, A., Ada C. Kopeć, and A. E. Mourant. "The Blood Groups of the Bushmen." *American Journal of Physical Anthropology* 11, no. 3 (1953): 361–68.

CHAPTER 9

"Anthrobiology," Racial Miscegenation, and Body Normality
Comparing Biotypological Studies in Brazil and Portugal, 1930–1940

Ana Carolina Vimieiro-Gomes

In 1934, the Portuguese anthropologist António Augusto Mendes Correia[1] from the University of Porto visited Brazil for the first time at the invitation of the dean of the University of Rio de Janeiro, Cândido de Oliveira Filho, for a series of lectures on the recently created Brazilian Institute of High Culture in Rio de Janeiro.[2] For the six months of his trip, Mendes Correia was able to visit not only Rio de Janeiro but also the cities of São Paulo, Santos, and Recife, as well as the state of Bahia. As an anthropologist, he said, "I was burning with desire to learn about this powerful ethnology lab that is this great country." As a Portuguese citizen, he sought "to contemplate the most brilliant pattern of colonization efforts by the Portuguese and to admire the current status of this magnificent endeavor."[3] These desires and interests were reflected in his scientific writings on Brazil and on the Brazilian people. This trip to Brazil generated publications and talks at conferences. His works included reports on his trip, such as the 1935 book *Cariocas e Paulistas*[4] (People from Rio de Janeiro and São Paulo), and scientific publications on his impressions regarding the makeup of the Brazilian population, including "A etnogenia brasílica," which was published in the 1935 *Anais da Faculdade de Ciências do Porto*.

On this trip, Mendes Correia visited a variety of cultural and medical-scientific institutions in São Paulo and Rio de Janeiro to establish exchange programs and academic relations with Brazilian scientists and intellectuals such as Pedro Calmon and Alfredo Ellis Júnior, as well as with physicians, anthropologists, and eugenicists such as Renato Kehl.[5] Mendes Correia then began to be involved in the enthusiastic debates in nationalist Brazil of the

1930s and on the formation of Brazil's population, often quoting reflections and publications from intellectuals such as Nina Rodrigues, Euclides da Cunha, and Oliveira Vianna. These debates mostly addressed immigration, assimilation, and the positive and negative effects of racial mixing (or miscegenation) among whites, blacks, and Indigenous peoples. Mendes Correia visited Brazil one year after the publication of Gilberto Freyre's *The Master and the Slave* (1933), in which the Brazilian sociologist "celebrated miscegenation" in Brazil, expressing his view on the distinction between race and culture and the equal contribution of black, Portuguese, and Indigenous on the formation of Brazilian cultural and racial identity.[6] Mendes Correia even met Freyre in person in one of these visits.[7] In the 1930s, however, Portuguese intellectuals, including Mendes Correia, were reticent about Freyre's positive conceptions on miscegenation, Portuguese colonial policy, and Portuguese adaptability to tropical colonial territories.[8] In his life of travels and conversations, Mendes Correia came across many studies on the anthropological types in the Brazilian population by the Brazilian National Museum anthropologist Edgard Roquette-Pinto.[9] He also found value in studies on Brazilian biotypes produced by biotypologists from the Rio de Janeiro School of Medicine (such as Isaac Brown), the School of Physical Education of the Army, and the Institute of Identification of Rio de Janeiro.[10]

In a historical context in which researchers sought to define the self-representation of the Portuguese nation,[11] the central concerns of the scientific agenda promoted by Mendes Correia and other medical anthropologists, eugenicists, and public intellectuals were to determine the origins of the Portuguese people and establish their racial quality, as well as to describe expansion of the Portuguese Empire.[12] Indeed, one of the main functions of European anthropology since the mid-nineteenth century has been to define and evaluate the civilizational stage of populations as mediated by racist and racialist concepts in order to justify imperial expansion into colonies.[13] Concepts of race, racial purity, and biological and cultural miscegenation in Portugal and the Portuguese colonies, as well as the development of racial and biological classification taxonomies and procedures, preoccupied this scientific agenda. The local historical realities and contexts reflect the differences in scientific agendas in Brazil and Portugal, but on theories, practices, fields of knowledge, and topics involving the biological and anthropological formation of the populations, the racial and biotypological science of the two countries had much in common.

Based on the evidence of circulations and intersections of scientific concepts regarding the biological and anthropological formation of populations, this study offers a comparative analysis of Brazil and Portugal, centered on the emergence of one of these fields of knowledge: biotypology. Two scientific communities are the focus of this comparative analysis. In the case of Brazil's scientific community, this study will explore 1930s publications on biotypology from the medical community around the Rocha Vaz Service, located at the discipline propaedeutic clinics in the Rio de Janeiro School of Medicine.[14] In the case of Portugal, the discussion will focus on the biotypological debates and investigations among the group of scientists (physicians and naturalists studying physical anthropology), and Mendes Correia in particular, who were part of the School of Anthropology in the Faculty of Sciences at the University of Porto. The analysis focuses on the differences between the two countries in their debates, scientific practices, and uses of racialist discourse on biotypology. This comparison between the ways in which biotypology emerged in the scientific communities in the two countries is expected to help reveal how theories and practices involving the ideas of race, miscegenation, and human biological diversity were formed, manifested, and engaged in different scientific subcultures.[15] Both communities had a relationship between constitutional types and racial typology, but the two countries arguably differed in their conceptions and uses of the idea of race in biotypology, and these differences led to unique perspectives and uses of biotypological concepts for classifying individuals.

In Brazil, hereditary and environmental aspects determined racialization, and in biotypology, this served as a foundation and central practice for giving meaning to the physically heterogeneous population of Brazil, formed by racial mixing. In the Porto School of Anthropology, individuals' "constitution," which Mendes Correia saw only on a phenotypical, and not a genetic, level, was considered complementary to race; that is to say, constitution was seen as another possible taxonomy for biological characterization in Porto's anthrobiological studies. Miscegenation, particularly in the colonies, was an important question for the Portuguese scientific community.[16] Those interested included Mendes Correia and other scientists such as those in the Portuguese Society of Eugenic Studies.[17] However, the Porto group did not consider miscegenation a central issue in the scientific agenda for biotypology. In fact, Mendes Correia's vision of Brazilian anthropological studies will be fundamental for exposing the similarities and differences in the two countries' scientific agendas for biotypology. Mendes Correia can therefore be considered one important agent in the circulation of knowledge from Brazil to Portugal. By comparing scientific subcultures in Brazil and Portugal, this study seeks to demonstrate how variations in the biotypological lexicon for classifying bodies into normal and abnormal were combined and modified to fit different racial and cultural ideologies.

Biotypology in Brazil and Portugal: Communities, Models, and Scientific Practices

Biotypology was formerly known as a type of constitutional medicine. It was reformed in the late nineteenth and early twentieth centuries, aiming for scientific credentials through the inclusion of practices such as statistical data collection and anthropometric measurement. The use of "biotypology" in constitutional medicine dates back to the first half of the twentieth century and has been attributed to Italian physician Nicola Pende. The term was mainly adopted in Latin countries such as France, Brazil, Argentina, and Mexico.[18] In the United States, meanwhile, these constitutional evaluations were referred to as "somatotyping," as proposed by the American physician William Herbert Sheldon (1898–1977).[19] In all its manifestations, it sought to map the biological factors that determined individual body types. In certain ways, constitution or biotypology also distanced itself from the notion of race, since it did not refer to common biological or geographic origins to determine similar anthropological features between individuals.[20] However, especially in Brazil and Portugal, biotypology was one of the faces of eugenics, because it proposed alternative methods for evaluating, monitoring, and intervening in individuals' health.[21] A medical practice based on the idea of constitution was seen as a way to correlate individuals' scientifically measurable biological traits with physical and psychological symptoms, physical capacity and aptitude for given occupations, predispositions for certain diseases, and even a tendency for criminal activities.[22] In practice, biotypology largely employed morphological measurements and/or observations (as seen with the naked eye), described with a specific lexicon that characterized individuals as normal or abnormal.

The definition of a "normal" individual physical profile may be considered the main scientific attribute of biotypology, and one that distinguished it from other classification-based sciences including anthropology and other racial sciences.[23] This taxonomy did, in fact, represent a hierarchy of types of humans, since its ultimate function was to determine which body types deviated from a supposed ideal of normal. Because of its distinctive taxonomy and praxis, biotypology offered an alternative to traditional racial typologies but was also often used to characterize individuals' and populations' biological identities and served as a medical and scientific reference for biopolitical agendas in many countries. In the scientific communities of both Brazil and Portugal, biotypological studies were involved in racialist practices and discourse, though they adhered to the peculiarities of each country's scientific cultures.

In the 1930s, the two countries each experienced a political transformation: both were under authoritarian regimes: Portugal's *Estado Novo* (1933–1974) and Brazil's Vargas Era (1930–1945).[24] These regimes were both marked by strong nationalist, populist, centralized political cultures; in the case of Portugal, the government also focused on corporatist and imperial policies. In Brazil, the regime was a reaction to the previous period, known as the First Brazilian Republic. The two governments were also similarly quasi-fascist—conservative, authoritarian regimes that were not entirely aligned with fascism. Each was, however, guided by its specific traditions, economic interests, and political cultures, including the association with Catholicism in Portugal and the economic, legislative, and cultural modernization desired and implemented by some groups within the Brazilian elite.

Amid these politics, science played a central role in promoting the political agenda and nationalist ideologies in both countries. Under the Vargas regime in Brazil, eugenic and racialist thought continued to influence debates on national racial identity and the ideal future for Brazil's people. This ideal was promoted in intellectual, medical, and scientific circles through debates on the value of Afro-Brazilian culture and foreign immigration restriction policies.[25] Under the Salazar dictatorship in Portugal, and because of the political balance in the *Estado Novo*, which was strongly influenced by the Catholic Church, scientific ideas regarding eugenics were not as widely accepted or implemented as in other Northern European countries such as Germany. Nevertheless, both eugenics and racial science maintained a constant presence in discourse and practices in various scientific institutions and events in Portugal. Examples include individual health care interventions, colonial policies, and debates on the anthropological makeup of the Portuguese Empire.[26] In the scientific communities of both countries, biotypology, which served to complement eugenics and offered an alternative language for racial discourse, was also promoted for analysis of the population, and medical or scientific control over it.

In Brazil, biotypology obtained significant visibility and academic acceptance in medical communities linked to criminology and legal medicine, clinical medicine, the military, physical education, and public education. The main center for Brazilian biotypological studies was in clinical medicine at the Rio de Janeiro School of Medicine, led by Juvenil Rocha Vaz. The group of physicians at what came to be known as the Rocha Vaz Service performed important research into the biotypological profile of Brazilians and produced the main publications on biotypology in Brazil.[27] Of course, other institutions such as offices of identification services, the army, and medical schools in Rio de Janeiro and around Brazil, including São Paulo and the northeastern region, contributed to the development of biotypological research, which also included analyses of regional data.[28] The scientific agenda for biotypology in Brazil had clear social implications. It influenced eugenics, debates on racial character, national identity, and the formation of the Brazilian population, as well as the ideal parameters of a "normal" Brazilian body. It even influenced which individuals were selected for certain occupations, as in the case of those drafted to the rubber soldiers program in the Amazon rain forest.[29]

As discussed by the historian Richard Cleminson, biotypology was also well received in Portuguese medicine, where it was conceived as a new science with practical implications for medicine and other scientific fields, including criminology.[30] At first glance, biotypology seemed to be a field in which the inconsistencies of eugenics would be revealed, particularly because it offered a focus on the individual rather than on hereditary reductionism. Biotypology was also seen, at least in theoretical terms, as an alternative to racial discourse and classifications. Though there were many enthusiasts and practicing experts (such as the University of Coimbra physician and biologist Luís Duarte Santos, the University of Lisbon psychiatrist Henrique Barahona Fernandes, and Mendes Correia, Luís de Pina, Alexandre Sarmento, and Alfredo Athayde from the Porto School of Anthropology), biotypology did not become as institutionalized in Portugal as it did in Italy (which had the Biotypological Orthogenetic Institute in Genoa) or as in Argentina (which had the Argentine Society of Biotypology, Eugenics, and Social Medicine). Furthermore, political initiatives involving public health focused on the use of biotypology also failed to be effective in any continuous or efficient way.[31] Nevertheless, biotypological studies in Portugal were maintained in a significant and visible way as a method for understanding the biological qualities of the Portuguese population and of the Portuguese Empire.

In Brazil and Portugal, biotypology was largely received through an appropriation of the models and practices based on the "Italian School." However, French biotypology theories (such as those of the physician Claude Sigaud) and Germany biotypology theories (such as those of Ernst Kretschmer) were consistent references among biotypologists in both Portugal and Brazil.[32] Each "school," or approach, proposed its own perspective, taxonomy, and biotypological lexicon. The most commonly debated and utilized Italian approaches in studies and publications were those of Giacinto Viola, who promoted a taxonomic model with an anthropometric perspective that classified bodies as longitype, brachytype, and normotype; others were from Pende, who discussed the role of hormones in determining individuals' constitutional types.[33] The Brazilian biotypologists from the Rocha Vaz Service were largely guided by Viola's method of anthropometrics. Meanwhile, the biotypology scholars at the Porto School of Anthropology took a more eclectic approach. In addition to the work by Viola and Pende, they also frequently relied on classification studies from Sigaud, who classified bodies into cerebral, muscular, respiratory, and digestive types. The Brazilian physician Waldemar Berardinelli cited Mendes Correia's use of Sigaud's, offering a harsh criticism of its limited applications and lack of a sufficient medical or scientific basis.[34]

Despite the wide circulation of foreign biotypological models in Brazil, Portugal, and many other countries from the Global North and South, each country's interpretations, agenda, and scientific practices were defined by local social, political, and cultural circumstances, as well as by local research groups and body features within the population. There was often a reappropriation of classification-based practices, whether to creatively address limitations in the local application of foreign theories and models, or to address operational issues in the classification of bodies.[35] Waldemar Berardinelli, a biotypologist and professor of the Rio de Janeiro School of Medicine, even proposed his own taxonomic model, known as the Barbára-Berardinelli model, which was, in fact, a local adaptation of the model by the Italian researcher Mario Barbára and an extension of Viola's method. It included new terminology and a new method for grouping normal biotypes in an attempt to offer new parameters of normality still within a deviant classification, as well as new terminology for deviants, "thus allowing for the classification of all individuals."[36] This classification served as a parameter in several studies on the biotypological profile of Brazilian populations, including Indigenous peoples such as Guaraní and the population of the Northeast.[37] Figure 1 shows examples of photographs of classified individuals taken from several studies according to Barbára-Berardinelli's biotypological lexicon. The representation indicates the various nomenclatures and representations used to describe normal and deviant bodies that he proposed.

In Portugal in the 1940s, the physician Luís de Pina (1901–1972) also tried to create his own classification method, which he referred to as a "biotypogram" or the "decal method." Although most individuals fit into a given biotypological classification, Pina asserted, "it is certain that some differ significantly in certain measurements of parts of their bodies." He identified this as a "vast" problem resulting in the imprecise classification of individuals. Citing Berardinelli and another Brazilian physician, Mario Roiter, Pina also argued that it was necessary to develop the means to classify the various deviant bodies, or those that did not fit the parameters and nomenclature of normality and abnormality according to the different classificatory models available.[38]

Pina's biotypogram was, in fact, a method for producing image-based records of bodies, though it was not a photograph. The use of images in biotypology, also a language and a classification-based procedure, was common practice among biotypologists. Such is the case of Sheldon, whose "somatotypes" were determined by anthropometric measurements carried out using photographs of men and women.[39] In Pina's case, the images were collected from the drawing of an outline of a body on transparent paper, "on the frosted glass of a large format camera with wide bellows." Markings of some main points of reference were made on the drawing, such as the contour of the head, the suprasternal notch, acromion, elbow, and the pubis. The drawings were then placed on standard checkered paper to measure body proportions. As seen in figure 2, the drawings of individuals of the same biotype, or "longitype," were then superimposed with the head, pubis, or feet matched up in order to find evidence of the deviant body parts such as the torso, limbs, or head.[40] Pina's proposal was therefore to examine the corporal proportionality of the Portuguese population. In search of a normal body standard on which to base deviations, Pina applied this method to hundreds of criminals from the Porto Institute of Criminology and concluded that there was a marked disproportion in the "lower limbs and particularly in the leg-foot segment."[41]

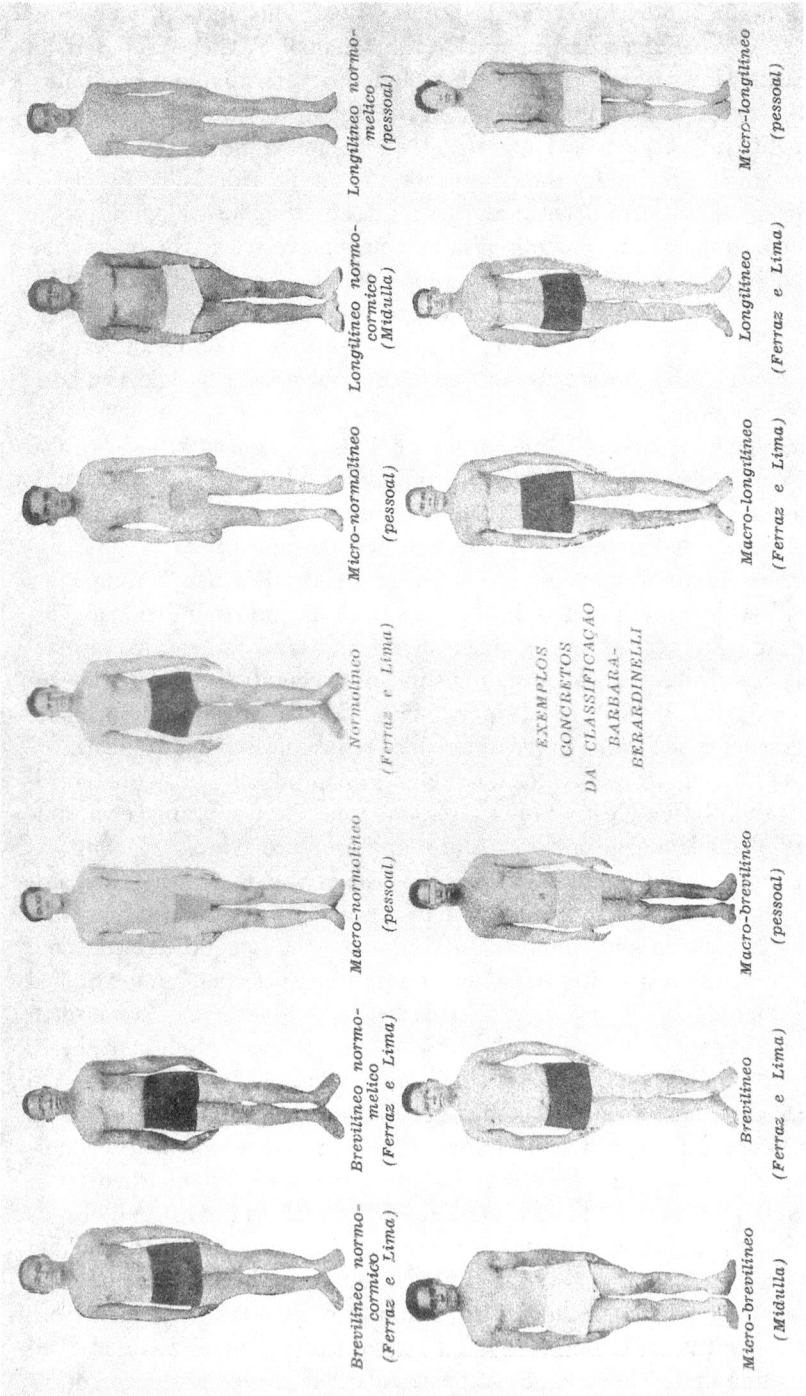

Figure 9.1. Examples of the Barbára-Berardinelli classification citing the biotypological studies from which the photographs were taken. *Top (left to right)*: brachytype normo-corms (torso), brachytype normo-melos (limber), macro-normotype, normotype, micro-normotype, longitype normo-corms, longitype normo-melos. *Bottom (left to right)*: micro-brachytype, brachytype, macro-brachytype, macro-longitype, longitype, micro-longitype. Source: Waldemar Berardinelli, *Tratado de biotipologia e patologia constitucional* (Rio de Janeiro: Francisco Alves, 1942).

"Anthropology," Racial Miscegenation, and Body Normality | 223

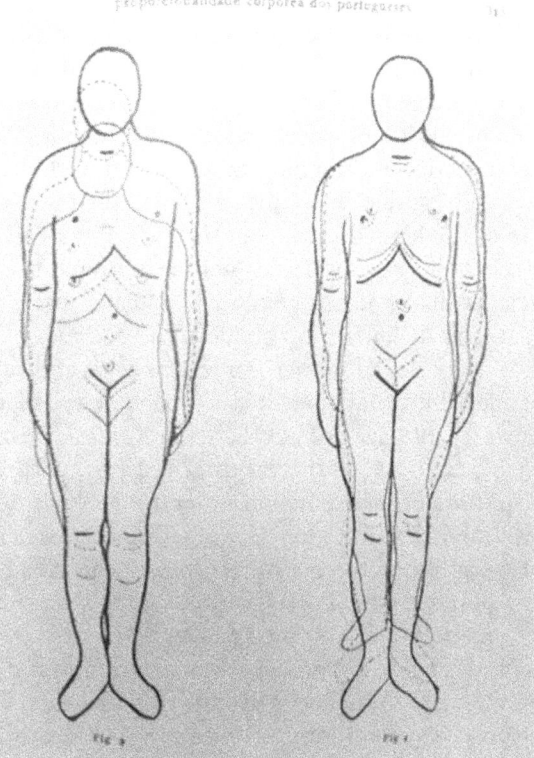

Figure 9.2. Biotypogram and the study of corporal proportionality in the Portuguese population. The image shows three overlapping "longitypes" of each side: with the pubis matched up (*left*) and with the head matched up (*right*). Source: Luís de Pina, "Acerca das proporções nos cânones biotipológicos portugueses," *Quarto Congresso da Associação Portuguesa para o Progresso das Ciências* 5 (1942): 541–42. Courtesy of University of Coimbra.

Despite some similarities between Brazilian and Portuguese researchers' biotypology practices, the differences in the racial debate between the two countries turned out to be a key factor in the theoretical concepts and scientific agendas associated with biotypology in each country: in Brazil, miscegenation and physical heterogeneity, while there was a conceptual difference between race and constitution in Portugal.

Biotypology in Anthrobiology: Constitution, Race, and Heredity

> Modern genetics teaches us that the product of crosses is more of a mosaic of characters from each parent than an average of hereditary traits. It is therefore difficult to presume the viability of a biological homogenization of the Brazilian population.[42]

Two of the most interesting parts of Mendes Correia's accounts of his travels to Brazil in the 1930s are his description of the studies and interpretations by scientists and intellectuals on the Brazilian population and his capacity to capture the racial debate in progress in Brazil, which was centered on the racially mixed nature of the Brazilian population.[43] Mendes Correia wrote of Brazilians' heterogeneous anthropological traits and of the unequal race relations in Brazil, arguing that Brazil did not have "the ingrained and absurd racial prejudices of the United States, but the cordiality of relations between whites and races of color certainly [did] not mean unquestioned blending."[44] Making his racialist bias evident, he always repeated in his writings about Brazil that he saw Rio de Janeiro in "an attractive selection of individuals of the same race," as "the rule."[45] In other words, he saw an anthropological affinity, with "white and white, mulatto and mulatto, black and black" couples; for him, these couples might have been explained by "social constraints" or "biopsychical mechanisms"—a view still far from Freyre's interpretation on Brazilian racial relations and miscegenation. Attentive to the Brazilian debate on miscegenation—whether it was seen as whitening or as heterogeneity—and based on genetic arguments, he questioned those who talked of progressive homogenization, of the assimilation of Europeans (as Vianna and Ellis Júnior did), or of the formation of "a new mixed race."[46] Mendes Correia shared the perception that Brazil's racial landscape was a complex and heterogeneous hereditary mosaic, made up of "very diverse racial elements."[47] His concept resembled that proposed by Roquette-Pinto and his idea of miscegenation as a "combination of hereditary factors" from the different anthropological types.[48]

The heterogeneity of the Brazilian population was, therefore, a central issue on the scientific agenda for biotypology in Brazil. Isaac Brown, at the Rocha Vaz Service, performed the most extensive study on the biotypological profile of the Brazilian population, *O normotipo brasileiro* (1934). The study sought to use the Italian classification-based models to define a normal (average) and ideal body type for different groups from different regions of Brazil and for different anthropological types: the population was classified as melanoderms (blacks), faioderms (white + black; biracial), and leucoderms (white) according to the anthropological types established by Roquette-Pinto and published in *Ensaios de antropologia brasiliana* (1933). The study eventually agreed with the idea that "there will be no single Brazilian type; there will be several Brazilian types," therefore assuming the corporal heterogeneity of the country's population.[49] Incidentally, Mendes Correia commented on a related limitation in Brown's study: the author's procedure was incapable of embracing the plurality of the Brazilian population. "In such a large country with so many ethnical elements," he wrote, "this discrimination is evidently insufficient; it is not possible to infer that some hinterlands regions of the country are represented in the series."⁵⁰ Brazilian biotypologists believed in the relationship between race and constitution and in the influence of the environment on the development of individual traits. With biotypology, they avoided the mere biological determinism associated with certain conceptions of heredity. Within this reasoning, biotypological studies in Brazil also maintained regional distinctions and specific regionalist discourses, such as those regarding the Northeast and São Paulo. Studies from both regions assumed that the constitution of the local populations differed from that of other regions as a result of the geographic, climatic, cultural, and social peculiarities of the respective regions.⁵¹

In the 1940s, in his presentation *As tendências bio-étnicas do Brasil contemporâneo* at the Fourth Portuguese-Spanish Conference in Porto, Mendes Correia returned his focus to the anthropological formation of the Brazilian population. He saw the country, because of its history of miscegenation, as "a natural anthropology laboratory."⁵² For this reason, he acknowledged local efforts involved in the difficult "study of the phenomena of racial mixing." However, based on arguments from Mendelian genetics, he stridently disagreed with the excessive emphasis that Brazilian scientists, "inspired by the studies by Franz Boas," placed on the idea that the "molding force of the environment" would be able to generate new human types. He also resumed his criticism of the Brazilian debate on the future standardization or homogenization of the population.⁵³ In this case, Mendes Correia seemed to be criticizing the positive perspectives surrounding racial mixing that were common among most contemporary Brazilian scientists and intellectuals, including Freyre. This perspective tended to value racial mixing, but in some cases, its proponents inconsistently valued whitening. Such a critical position was in line with the racialist perspective and Mendes Correia's opposition to racial crosses, as well as with his critical views on the full social and cultural assimilation of the peoples in the Portuguese colonies.⁵⁴

Nevertheless, racial miscegenation was also an important item on the scientific agenda and in the eugenic and anthropological debates on national identity during the *Estado Novo* in Portugal. In the 1930s, however, Portuguese identity was seldom self-represented as mixed. Miscegenation, while controlled, occasionally came up in discourses as a potential argument to support the renewal of the colonial populations and the geopolitical strengthening of Portugal in the world.⁵⁵ With the repeal of the Portuguese Colonial Act and the changes to colonial policies after 1951, the perspective on Portuguese miscegenation and identity was reversed (i.e., positivized) with the favorable reception and influence of the Luso-tropicalist ideology provided by Freyre.⁵⁶ Scholars such as the anthropologist Jorge Dias adopted Freyre's thought into the Portuguese colonial ideology and discourse. Luso-tropicalism became the official discourse of the *Estado Novo* in the 1950s, establishing itself as an intellectual and ideological foundation capable of reinforcing and justifying the peculiar Portuguese aptitudes for colonization, and thus sustaining foreign and imperialist policies. It was also used to combat resistance among colonized populations.[57]

Before World War II, however, concern over miscegenation, inspired by biological determinism and social Darwinism, was predominantly centered on the risks of Portuguese degeneration as a result of racial mixing with the peoples of the colonies. As observed by Cleminson, the Portuguese expansion "beyond the sea" and the control of the miscegenation between races in the colonies were both part of the nation- and empire-building project.[58] The view of "the Other" relative to the Portuguese colonies was actually a view of the empire itself. Moral and political discourse on colonialism and Portuguese identity often highlighted the negative effects of racial mixing (especially with the peoples of the colonies) on the integrity of the Portuguese population, arguments that reinforced the idea of miscegenation as a condemnable and disastrous practice.[59] Though distant from the Luso-tropicalist ideology, this discourse claimed that miscegenation was neither a colonial settlement policy nor a policy for improving humanity. The argument was supported by the eugenicist Eusébio Tamagnini from the University of Coimbra, who, in a clearly racist perspective based on genetic inheritance, defended the strategic presence of the Portuguese in the colonies but opposed social and biological miscegenation. He wrote of the supposed "racial purity" of the Portuguese population.[60] Though his discourse was more ambivalent, Mendes Correia partly shared this point of view. On the one hand, he admitted that some crosses, following eugenic principles, were advantageous, as in the case of areas of difficult acclimatization to the tropics or when there was a lack of colonizers. On the other hand, he stated: "Now we know that some nations with a relative anthropological personality such as ours, have completed an honorable and historic mission. Should miscegenation destroy our bioethnic continuity, exchanging the certainty of the effective pursuit of that mission for an unknown result?" In biological terms, Mendes Correia believed that uncontrolled and unregulated anthropological mixing could lead to the "destruction of the genetic patrimony" of the Portuguese.[61]

Despite its importance in the Portuguese scientific community, racial miscegenation did not represent a scientific issue in the biotypology practiced by the anthropologists from the Porto School of Anthropology as it did in biotypological studies of the corporal and anthropological heterogeneity the Brazilian population. As discussed earlier, a possible contextual explanation would be in the self-representation of the Portuguese population as unmixed or in the hostility to the notion of positive effects of racial mixing with the Indigenous peoples of the colonies. Another explanation could be the scientific practices as manifested in place of biotypology and the ideas of race, constitution, and heredity in the extensive scientific agenda of the anthropological studies of the Porto group. This research-based agenda was then termed anthrobiology.

Mendes Correia promoted "anthrobiology"[62] to validate the anthropological research program he had begun in Portugal and in the colonies in the years prior. In his view, "classic" anthropology, with its typologies and classifications of physical anthropology based on prehistoric or ethnographic studies, was unable to explain certain traits in populations. "Some traits are attributable to pure races, to crosses," he argued, and are influenced by ethnic factors, "individual variations," and the environment.[63] Meanwhile, the use of anthrobiology to study race was centered on projects on "the normal and pathological heredity in man, on eugenic studies, on the physiology of the races, on blood groups and other topics involving human biochemistry, on the constitutions and temperaments, and on the determination of the biological basis of the mentality and activity of the different races."[64] Thus, Mendes Correia held that the anthropological study of races based on the anthrobiology approach also had to be devoted to the "essential phenomena that constitute the manifestations of life."[65]

In this broader research program, constitution or biotypology was just one of several methods for corporal analysis aimed at determining the anthropological identity of the Portuguese people and of the population of the empire. The idea of constitution was understood as being "linked to the proportions of the body: not analytically or in detail, but rather as a synthesis or integration" of the individual, and linked to hereditary, physiological, and psychological qualities, as well as to predisposition to diseases."[66] Another understanding of constitution focused on its distinction from the concept of race. It was argued that classification into constitutional types did not take into account the complex variety of races. Citing the French anthropologist George Montandon and his treatise *La race, les races,* Mendes Correia attributed different genetic foundations to race and constitution.[67] Race referred to a common genealogical origin and "genetic makeup; to special genetic heritages." Therefore, each race presented its own genotype. Constitution, meanwhile, represented a much more "general human average" of physical features and traits. Constitutional types were therefore common among all races.[68] Mendes Correia distinguished his position from that of Berardinelli, for whom "constitution is phenotype"; in this definition, constitution is, above all, "the set of individual traits resulting from the action of the environment." Mendes Correia argued that, "according to Berardinelli's perspective, constitution is everything and nothing."[69] It is evident from this idea of constitution that the Porto School of Anthropology focused on the racial classification system. All anthrobiological traits evaluated, including constitutional type, were ultimately used to determine racial (genotypic and phenotypic) characteristics of the Portuguese and of the various population groups under the Portuguese Empire.

Several studies have demonstrated the pivotal role of the studies of the group of Porto anthropologists on colonial policies in the Portuguese Empire.

Evidence of their influence lies in their various topics of anthropological research, their involvement in Portuguese colonial exhibitions, the group's scientific publications, and the appointment of Mendes Correia as president of the Portuguese Board of Geographic Missions and Colonial Research in 1946.[70] In turn, their influence is evidence of the power afforded to science by European colonialism to address problems and to assist the imperial enterprise through methods such as mapping and incorporating colonial populations, territorial exploitation, and the optimization of modes of production.[71]

In the early 1930s, the First National Congress of Colonial Anthropology, held within the Portuguese Colonial Exhibition in Porto in 1934, was an opportunity for Mendes Correia and the other participants to argue for the role of science, and of anthropology in particular, in valuing and exploiting colonial peoples and territories. The conference, which was organized into three sessions, allowed for the presentation of papers on topics such as the classification of races (Guinea, Angola, and Mozambique), heredity, ethnic crosses and miscegenation, the psychosocial value of the "Indigenous people," human migration, and crime. During the colonial exposition, hundreds of Indigenous people (considered representatives of the local populations) underwent anthropometric assessments. These evaluations included blood tests, psychological tests, and biotypological studies, performed by Luís de Pina.

These scientific initiatives directed at colonial domination were performed by the Board of Geographic Missions and Colonial Research associated with the Portuguese Ministry of the Colonies, which, since 1936, had been the government entity in charge of coordinating scientific missions in the colonies and organizing colonial scientific institutions. The many "anthropological and ethnological missions," as they were called, occurred from 1936 to 1950 and were directed by anthropologists from the Porto School of Anthropology, such as Joaquim Santos Jr. in Mozambique, Amílcar Mateus in Guinea, and António de Almeida in Angola in Cape Verde, São Tomé and Príncipe, and Timor.[72] The colonial territories became field research sites where a substantial amount of anthropological information was recorded. Data on the geography, climate, diseases, and natural resources were also gathered and later sent to the "center of calculation" (Porto School of Anthropology) to be classified, organized, and interpreted.[73] These expeditions were part of the backbone of the Portuguese colonial administration and therefore, as in other European empires, part of the scientific contribution to the institutionalization and spread of colonial power.[74] Italy, for example, also sent expeditions organized by the Italian Committee for the Study of Population Problems to several regions of Libya in 1930 as part of the greater agenda for demographic and anthropologic studies on "primitive populations."[75] This agenda was put into practice during several Portuguese expeditions, allowing for the creation of a racial inventory of the peoples in the Portuguese Empire, as observed in Mendes Correia's extensive work *Raças do império* (1943), as well as in his reports on scientific expeditions such as the one to Portuguese Guinea.[76]

Biotypological studies were part of the program for the anthrobiological investigation of the empire, particularly in African countries. Important studies include those by Pina, Alexandre Sarmento (a physician in Angola's public health system and a member of the Portuguese Society for Anthropology and Ethnology), António Lis Ferreira (assistant professor in the Porto Institute of Anthropology and vice secretary of health care in Angónia District, Mozambique), and Alfredo Athayde (natural scientist and anthropologist from the Porto Faculty of Sciences). Mendes Correia also developed an anthropologic classification of the ethnic groups of Portuguese Guinea in 1946 during his "scientific journey" there, together with a description of morphological types.[77] Interestingly, none of the Portuguese scientists' investigations sought to establish parameters for biotypological body normality (or normotypes) for the population groups of the African colonies. This finding contrasted with contemporary studies on the Portuguese people, such as those by Duarte Santos, Pina, and Leopoldina Ferreira Paulo (assistant researcher in the Porto Faculty of Sciences), who were driven to establish an average biotypological profile for the Portuguese population, even including statistical analysis and regional distinctions.[78]

Luís de Pina was one of the main advocates for biotypology in Portugal. In addition to the study of the biotypogram and the biotypes of the Portuguese, he advocated the application of biotypology in criminology and its usefulness in the many domains of clinical medicine.[79] He also investigated "the constitutional types of black Africans." In his opinion, the knowledge on biotypology was meant to be applied to colonial medicine as a "medical basis for colonization or for professional orientation of the Indigenous people and colonists, etc." The study evaluated 225 individuals native to Angola, Guinea, and Mozambique. Some of them were showcased in the Portuguese Colonial Exhibition in Porto in 1934. Using Sigaud's model, Pina found a predominance of respiratory types (64.8 percent of the subjects), as well as muscular types (24.8 percent), digestive types (4.5 percent), and cerebral types (5.7 percent). Despite the coincidence in the predominance of respiratory types among the African and Portuguese subjects, the percentage was lower than that found by Mendes Correia in the Portuguese population (76.8 percent). A larger number of "longitype black" individuals was found when Viola's typology was applied. Pina cited and seemed to agree with Berardinelli regarding the predominance of certain constitutional types in specific races. The study's conclusion cited this theory, and linked the many existing models of biotypological classification: "70 percent of our blacks were longitypes, microsomics, microsplanics, linear, stenoplastic, leptosomic, stenotypes, etc."[80]

Alexandre Sarmento dedicated himself specifically to the study of the constitutional types of Angolan populations, and particularly of the "ethnic groups" of

Bié province and the town of Menongue: the Nganguela, Côkwe, and Nhemba. The main concern of these studies was ethnicity. Sarmento highlighted how medicine and anthropology sought to use biotypology to determine the "somatic and biopsychical traits" of the "many ethnic groups," and applied this knowledge to economic and social purposes such as making workforce allocations.[81] The results were consistent with those reported by Pina, which also focused on the predominance of the respiratory type and longitype individuals in the Angolan subjects studied.[82] The constitutional types found were then correlated with the Pignet index, a value that indicated the robustness or intensity of each type's physical capabilities (also referred to as constitution but categorized as poor, weak, average, and strong). Sarmento concluded the following about individuals from Bié: "respiratory types have, on average, weak constitution; muscular and digestive types have good constitution, and the cerebral constitution is poor."[83]

Alfredo Athayde, another Portuguese researcher, focused on the biotypological study of the Angolan peoples of Cuamatos, Cuanhamos and Evales. In his work, constitution was one of the range of aspects evaluated in the broader agenda of racial and anthropological classification, including also traits such as body size, nutrition, hair type, lips, face, skin color of the palms and of the body, anthropometric measurements, size and shape of fingers, and ethnic mutilation.[84]

António Lis Ferreira performed studies on the population of Mozambique that focused on medical aspects. Research on constitution, he argued, should "be based firstly on the study of hereditary diseases and possible causes for death." They should establish "the biological and social consequences of diseases such as tuberculosis, cancer, malaria, etc.," and "to what extent these diseases of the constitution would stop them from working in specific professions, cause early death or aging, etc."[85] Lis Ferreira correlated individual constitution with the color and texture of the skin, as well as with posture, morphological factors, and physiological functions. His main study focused on the incidence of several ailments and diseases, such as hernia, malaria, tuberculosis, and rheumatism, among members of each constitutional type observed in the Angone, Antumas, Chipeta, Matengo, and N'Dgena peoples (a total of 1,291 individuals studied) from Tete province in Mozambique.

Lis Ferreira's work contributed to another approach to anthropobiological research proposed by Mendes Correia: racial pathology, or the predisposition of specific "races" to the development of certain diseases.[86] This scientific reasoning was also associated with the alleged influence of hormones (endocrinological factors) on physical constitution and on individuals' psychological profiles. Mendes Correia summarized his general opinion on the constitutions of different ethnicities: "The people of the Mediterranean and the Arabs are longitypes, with active thyroids and underactive adrenal glands (that is to say, they present less vigor) (the adrenal glands are important for the physical vigor of individuals), etc. The excitability of the paleo-Negro and, perhaps, his hypogonadism (genital deficit) is also found in tall Hamitic Africans. It is important to remember that the Mongolian and Chinese present pathological mongoloidism with morphofunctional characteristics!"[87] By using a medical lexicon borrowed from endocrinology, Mendes Correia reinforced his scientific agenda: he pursued detailed ethnoracial classification, rather than bodily normalization.

Conclusion

This comparison of the receptiveness to biotypology in the scientific communities of Brazil and Portugal reveals the approximation of theoretical concepts and practices in the scientific subcultures of both countries. This includes their applications of biotypology to medicine, the development of particular methods and taxonomy, and their searches for a physical identity for the population (national and regional, and in the case of Portugal, with a view also to colonial populations). In both groups of researchers, the practice of biotypology has an evident social locus: it was engrained in the debates on race and national identities in both countries and was used as a base to formulate and confirm racialist, normalizing, and segregationist perspectives. Biotypology was thus used to create a hierarchy of human populations. This comparison has also revealed the transit of people, techniques, knowledge, and methods and has highlighted a wide network of scientific knowledge among biotypologist communities internationally, including in Brazil and Portugal. The historical connection between Portugal and Brazil, despite the differences in local contexts, seems to have contributed to the intersections between interpretations, scientific approaches, and debates on biotypology, national identity, and race.

The present comparative analysis, mediated by Mendes Correia's outlook on the population and local studies on the mixed racial composition of the Brazilian people, has helped also to reveal the differences between the two national scientific cultures in their notions of race and constitution and in their scientific agendas for biotypology. In Brazil, the practice of biotypology was closely connected to the debate on racial and national identity, as well as to the composition of the Brazilian population. Researchers sought to use their specialized biotypological taxonomy to establish ideal parameters for body normality and, above all, morphological normality for the Brazilian people. The Brazilian biotypology accepted the assumption that there was a relationship between race and constitution and that the environment (the individual's region of origin) also influenced physical constitution. For this reason, most Brazilian biotypological studies used racial classification (black, white,

Indigenous, and mixed race) as a parameter to categorize the population, and to establish a range of "Brazilian normotypes" rather than a single Brazilian normotype. Racial miscegenation and the heterogeneous profile of Brazilians were thus the broader context of the scientific agenda of biotypology in Brazil.

Anthrobiology, as proposed by Mendes Correia and followed by many scientists of the Porto School of Anthropology, focused on racial and ethnic classification and was based on biological determinism. Its scientific procedures were centered on the phenotypical and genotypical identification of different races, which itself focused on the Portuguese or on colonial populations of the Portuguese Empire. Although the matter of racial miscegenation was a central scientific question for the scientists of the University of Porto, and in Mendes Correia's writings specifically, it was not always present in their biotypological studies. Different meanings and objectives were attributed to race and constitution. Race was associated with the genetic and genealogical heritage of specific human groups, whereas constitution had a narrower meaning and was represented by the "racial phenotype." Constitution was a biomorphological manifestation and a classification to be generally applied to human beings as a whole. For this reason, the variety of biotypological taxonomy and terminology (as proposed by Sigaud, Viola, Kretschmer, Pende, et al.) could coexist with racial classifications. They were just a few of the many different measurements performed in the context of the general anthrobiological agenda.

This factor helps to explain the irrelevance of the normalizing vocabulary in the scientific agenda of the Porto researchers as applied to the colonial population. The continuous evaluation of constitutional types in anthrobiological studies reflects the exchange of theories, practices, and languages between different fields of knowledge: from constitutional medicine to anthropology, and from anthropology to constitutional medicine. The latter exchange is evident in the use of practices and terms from physical anthropology and ethnology in biotypological studies. In contrast to the more liberal perspective of cultural and racial miscegenation from the post-1950s Luso-tropicalism period, a question remains: was the scientific agenda of anthrobiology supported by the Porto School of Anthropology in fact a racialist, radical, and meticulous tool for biopolitical classification of human diversity, especially when applied to the Portuguese colonies?

The differences and similarities between the scientific cultures in the two countries in terms of their studies on race and biotypology reveal the interconnected way in which racialist, normalizing, and discriminatory perspectives had made themselves present in racial sciences. These factors have been reinforced over the course of Brazilian and Portuguese history as a language shared among different fields of science to give meaning to human biological diversity.[88] These perspectives were therefore much more than a simple system for classifying people as white, black, or mixed race.

ANA CAROLINA VIMIEIRO-GOMES has a PhD in History and is Professor of the History of Science at the Universidade Federal de Minas Gerais. Her main research interests include history of biomedical sciences and history of human biological diversity and medicine.

Notes

Research for this chapter was supported by the Conselho Nacional de Desenvolvimento Científico e Tecnológico (CNPq) and the Coordenação de Aperfeiçoamento de Pessoal de Nível Superior (CAPES), Brazil. All translations are my own unless otherwise indicated.
 1. Mendes Correia (1888–1960) worked as an anthropologist and archeologist in Porto's Faculty of Sciences and Faculty of Humanities. He was involved in creating the Portuguese Society of Anthropology and Ethnology in 1918 and helped found the Porto Institute of Anthropology. In addition to his scientific career, he was president of the Portuguese Board of Geographic Missions and Colonial Research from 1946 to 1959, and of the Lisbon Geographic Society in the 1950s. Patrícia Ferraz de Matos, "Mendes Correia e a Escola de Antropologia do Porto: Contribuição para o estudo das relações entre antropologia, nacionalismo e colonialismo (de finais do século XIX aos finais da década de 50 do século XX)" (PhD diss., Universidade de Lisboa, 2012), 23–29.
 2. Mendes Correia returned to Brazil in 1937 on a visit to the Royal Portuguese Cabinet of Reading in Rio de Janeiro to celebrate the institution's 170th anniversary. Patrícia Ferraz de Matos, "Um olhar sobre as relações entre Portugal e o Brasil a partir da obra de Mendes Correia: Desafios, pontes e interações," *População e Sociedade* 21 (2013): 53–70.
 3. António A. Mendes Correia, "A etnogenia brasílica," *Anais da Faculdade de Ciências do Porto* 19 (1935): 129–146.
 4. António A. Mendes Correia, *Cariocas e Paulistas: Impressões do Brasil* (Porto, 1935).
 5. The visited institutions included the Institute of Identification in Rio de Janeiro and the Service of Identification of São Paulo Police, the School of Physical Education of the Army, Beneficência Portuguesa Hospital, the Brazilian Institute of History and Geography, the National Library of Brazil, law schools and medical schools, the National Museum of Brazil, the School of Fine Arts of the Federal University of Rio de Janeiro, the Benjamim Baptista Institute of Anatomy, the Brazilian National School of Music, and the Royal Portuguese Cabinet of Reading. Matos, "Um olhar sobre as relações," 59, 56.
 6. Ricardo Benzaquén de Araújo, *Guerra e paz: Casa-grande e senzala e a obra de Gilberto Freyre nos anos 30* (São Paulo, 1994), 38.
 7. Matos, "Um olhar sobre as relações," 57.
 8. Cláudia Castelo, *"O modo português de estar no mundo": O luso-tropicalismo e a ideologia colonial portuguesa (1933–1961)* (Porto, 2011), 69.
 9. Mendes Correia refers to Edgard Roquette-Pinto, *Ensaios de antropologia brasiliana* (São Paulo, 1933).
10. António A. Mendes Correia, *Cariocas e Paulistas: Impressões do Brasil* (Porto, 1935), 271–302; Mendes Correia, "A etnogenia brasílica," 5–6.
11. Miguel Vale Almeida, "'Longing for Oneself': Hybridism and Miscegenation in Colonial and Postcolonial Portugal," *Etnográfica* 6, no. 1 (2002): 181–200.
12. Ricardo Roque, "Equivocal Connections: Fonseca Cardoso and the Origins of Portuguese Colonial Anthropology," *Portuguese Studies* 19 (2003): 80–109; Patrícia Ferraz de Matos, *As côres do império: Representações raciais no império colonial português*

(Lisbon, 2006); Richard Mark Cleminson, *Catholicism, Race and Empire: Eugenics in Portugal, 1900-1950* (Budapest, 2014).
13. Philippa Levine, "Anthropology, Colonialism, and Eugenics," in *The Oxford Handbook of the History of Eugenics,* ed. Alison Bashford and Philippa Levine (Oxford, 2010), 45.
14. Ana Carolina Vimieiro-Gomes, "Science, Constitutional Medicine and National Bodily Identity in Brazilian Biotypology during the 1930s," *Social History of Medicine* 30, no. 1 (2017): 137-57.
15. Warwick Anderson, "Racial Conceptions in the Global South," *Isis* 105, no. 4 (2014): 792.
16. Cleminson, *Catholicism, Race and Empire,* 203-45.
17. António A. Mendes Correia, "O mestiçamento nas colônias portuguesas: Estudo apresentado ao II Congresso da União Nacional," *Boletim Geral das Colônias* 21, no. 239 (1945) 177-81; Eusébio Tamagnini, "Os problemas da mestiçagem," in *Trabalhos do I Congresso Nacional de Antropologia Colonial,* vol. 1 (Porto, 1934), 39-63.
18. Francesco Cassata, *Building the New Man: Eugenics, Racial Science and Genetics in Twentieth-Century Italy* (Budapest, 2011); Gustavo Vallejo and Marisa Miranda, "Los saberes del poder: eugenesia y biotipología en la Argentina del siglo XX," *Revista de Indias* 64, no. 231 (2004): 425-44; Yolanda Eraso, "Towards a Taxonomy of Maternal Bodies: Biotypology, Eugenics and Argentine Nationalism (1930-1946)," *Clio Medica / The Wellcome Series in the History of Medicine* 92 (2013): 61-94; Alexandra M. Stern, "From Mestizophilia to Biotypology: Racialization and Science in Mexico, 1920-1960," in *Race and Nation in Modern Latin America,* ed. Nancy P Applebaum, Anne S. Macpherson, and Karin A. Rosemblatt (Chapel Hill, NC, 2003), 187-210; Marius Turda and Aaron Gillette, *Latin Eugenics in Comparative Perspective* (London, 2014).
19. Patricia Vertinsky, "Physique as Destiny: William H. Sheldon, Barbara Honeyman Heath and the Struggle for Hegemony in the Science of Somatotyping," *Canadian Bulletin of Medical History* 24, no. 2 (2007): 291-316.
20. António A. Mendes Correia, *Introdução à antropobiologia* (Coimbra, 1933), 45.
21. Cassata, *Building the New Man,* 210; Vimieiro-Gomes, "Science, Constitutional Medicine," 139; Cleminson, *Catholicism, Race and Empire,* 25.
22. Sarah W. Tracy, "George Draper and American Constitutional Medicine, 1916-1946: Reinventing the Sick Man," *Bulletin of the History of Medicine* 66, no. 1 (1992): 53-89; Olívia Maria Gomes Cunha, *Intenção e gesto: Pessoa, cor e a produção cotidiana da (in)diferença no Rio de Janeiro, 1927-1942* (Rio de Janeiro, 2002).
23. Vimieiro-Gomes, "Science, Constitutional Medicine," 138.
24. It is important to note that the Portuguese anti-republic military movement known as the 28 May 1926 coup d'état resulted in a dictatorship that, with the approval of the country's constitution in 1933, came to be referred to as the *Estado Novo* (New State).
25. Nancy L. Stepan, "Eugenics in Brazil, 1917-1940," in *The Wellborn Science: Eugenics in Germany, France, Brazil and Russia,* ed. Mark B. Adams (New York, 1990), 138-44; Anadelia Romo, *Brazil's Living Museum: Race, Reform, and Tradition in Bahia* (Chapel Hill, NC, 2010).
26. Cleminson, *Catholicism, Race and Empire,* 61-119; Matos, *As côres do império,* 53-68; Richard Mark Cleminson, "Between Germanic and Latin Eugenics: Portugal, 1930-1960," *História, Ciências, Saúde-Manguinhos* 23, no. S1 (2016): S73-S92.
27. Vimieiro-Gomes, "Science, Constitutional Medicine," 139.
28. Ana Carolina Vimieiro-Gomes, "Biotipologia, regionalismo e a construção de uma identidade corporal brasileira no plural, década de 1930," *História, Ciências, Saúde-Manguinhos* 23, no. S1 (2016): S111-S30.

29. Vimieiro-Gomes, "Science, Constitutional Medicine," 137.
30. Cleminson, *Catholicism, Race and Empire*, 87–91.
31. Ibid., 98.
32. Waldemar Berardinelli, *Tratado de biotipologia e patologia constitucional* (Rio de Janeiro, 1942); Luís Duarte Santos, *Biotipologia humana: Morfologia, temperamento, caráter, inteligência—Doutrinas, métodos, aplicações* (São Paulo, 1941); Mendes Correia, *Introdução à antropobiologia*, 43–49.
33. Pende was the most important physician in Italian constitutionalism during the fascist period. He was also a member of the party and involved in the Mussolini regime, which provided him with the means to create the Biotypological Orthogenetic Institute in Genoa in 1926. Cassata, *Building the New Man*, 193.
34. Berardinelli, *Tratado de biotipologia*, 38.
35. Another clear example of the efforts to adapt the biotypological models to the local medical practice is the "Tabela de equivalência aproximada dos tipos descritos por diversos autores," proposed by Duarte Santos in an attempt to organize the various classification models from constitutional schools of thought. Duarte Santos, *Biotipologia humana*, 72–73.
36. Berardinelli, *Tratado de biotipologia*, 130–35.
37. The study performed on the Guaraní Indigenous group analyzed their blood types and biotypological profiles. Leonídeo Ribeiro, Waldemar Berardinelli, and Mario Roiter, "Grupo Sanguíneo dos índios guaranys," *Archivos de Medicina Legal e de Identificação* 12 (1934): 1129–35. In his reports from his travels to Brazil in 1934, Mendes Correia commented on having knowledge of this study and highlighted the ability of this approach to complement the "work of traditional anthropology." Mendes Correia, "A etnogenia brasílica," 18.
38. Luís de Pina, "O biotipograma no estudo da proporcionalidade corpórea dos portugueses," *Arquivo de Anatomia e Antropologia* 26 (1949): 297–335.
39. For more on the controversy surrounding Sheldon's somatotype theory and his use of photographs of naked people—particularly of university students—to evaluate body types, see Vertinsky, "Physique as Destiny," 299–301.
40. Luís de Pina, "Acerca das proporções nos cânones biotipológicos portugueses," *Quarto Congresso da Associação Portuguesa para o Progresso das Ciências* 5 (1942): 541–43.
41. Pina, "O biotipograma," 334.
42. Mendes Correia, *Cariocas e Paulistas*, 282.
43. Mendes Correia, "A etnogenia brasílica," 7; António A. Mendes Correia, *As tendências bio-étnicas do Brasil contemporâneo* (Porto, 1944), 5–11.
44. Mendes Correia, "A etnogenia brasílica," 12.
45. Mendes Correia, *As tendências bio-étnicas*, 10.
46. Ibid., 5; Mendes Correia, "A etnogenia brasílica," 13.
47. Mendes Correia, *As tendências bio-étnicas*, 7.
48. Ricardo Ventura Santos, "Mestiçagem, degeneração e viabilidade de uma Nação: Debates em antropologia física no Brasil (1870–1930)," in *Raça como questão: História, ciência e identidades no Brasil,* ed. Ricardo V. Santos and Marcos Chor Maio (Rio de Janeiro, 2010), 83–108; Vanderlei Sebastião de Souza, *Em busca do Brasil: Edgard Roquette-Pinto e o retrato antropológico brasileiro, 1905–1935* (Rio de Janeiro, 2017).
49. Isaac Brown, *O normotipo brasileiro* (Rio de Janeiro, 1934), 90.
50. Mendes Correia, *As tendências bio-étnicas*, 11.
51. Vimieiro-Gomes, "Biotipologia, regionalismo," 125–26.
52. Mendes Correia, *As tendências bio-étnicas*, 5.

53. Ibid., 7–10. It is interesting to note that, contradictorily, in this same presentation, Mendes Correia provides a more positive view of miscegenation in Brazil. In a racist and segregationist perspective, he proposed whitening as the future of the Brazilian population through the "re-Portugueseation" (*reaportuguesamento*) of the country that, in his view, meant not necessarily a return to a past identity but rather "the re-integration of the Portuguese genetic influence," which would then be adjusted to the other races and the environment.
54. Cleminson, *Catholicism, Race and Empire*, 227.
55. Ibid., 230–31.
56. Freyrean Luso-tropicalism was the idea that the Portuguese were more adaptable to and fit for the tropics and, as a result, more prone to miscegenation, which was understood as racial and cultural mixing with the peoples of the colonies. Maria Lúcia Pallares-Burke and Peter Burke, *Repensando os trópicos: Um retrato intelectual de Gilberto Freyre* (São Paulo, 2009).
57. Castelo, *O modo português*, 69.
58. Cleminson, *Catholicism, Race and Empire*, 212.
59. Almeida, "Longing for Oneself," 189.
60. Tamagnini, "Os problemas da mestiçagem," 62.
61. Mendes Correia, "O mestiçamento nas colônias portuguesas," 8.
62. According to him, the German anthropologist Eugen Fischer coined this term. Mendes Correia, *Introdução à antropobiologia*, 17.
63. Ibid., 13. It is important to note that, according to the Porto anthropologists, the idea of ethnology was still focused on the study of races, with a bias toward biological or physical anthropology, as evidenced by their reference to the anthropology promoted by the French anthropologist Paul Broca.
64. Ibid., 18.
65. António A. Mendes Correia, "Da antropologia ultramarina," in *Introdução à antropologia tropical*, ed. Alfredo Athayde, Maria Emília Castro e Almeida, and António A. Mendes Correia (Lisbon, 1962), 148.
66. Ibid., 154.
67. Montandon was a Swiss ethnologist who had been based in Paris since 1925. In 1931, he became the chair of ethnology at the École d'Anthropologie and was known for his radically racist opinions compared to his contemporaries such as Paul Rivet (Musée de L'Homme) and Marcel Mauss. Montandon was a collaborator in the Nazi invasion of France. *La race, les races* was a compact version of previous publication *L'ologenèse humaine*, in which he developed a racial theory and proposed a description and ranking of the supposed races that composed humanity. Alice L. Conklin, *In the Museum of Man: Race, Anthropology and Empire in France, 1850–1950* (Ithaca, NY, 2013), 4, 176.
68. António A. Mendes Correia, "Conceitos genéticos de raça e constituição," *Boletim da Sociedade Portuguesa de Ciências Naturais* 13, no. S2 (1941): S27–S30.
69. Ibid., S28.
70. Matos, *As côres do império*, 192; Rui M. Pereira, "Raça, sangue e robustez: Os paradigmas da antropologia física colonial portuguesa," *Cadernos de Estudos Africanos* 7 (2005): 210–241.
71. Helen Tilley, *Africa as a Living Laboratory: Empire, Development, and the Problem of Scientific Knowledge, 1870–1950* (Chicago, 2011), 4–5.
72. Pereira, "Raça, sangue e robustez," 214.
73. Bruno Latour, *Ciência em ação: Como seguir cientistas e engenheiros sociedade afora* (São Paulo, 1998).

74. Tilley, *Africa as a Living Laboratory*, 15.
75. Luc André Berlivet, "A Laboratory for Latin Eugenics: The Italian Committee for the Study of Population Problems and the International Circulation of Eugenic Knowledge, 1920s–1940s," *História, Ciências, Saúde-Manguinhos* 23, no. S1 (2016): S51–S72.
76. António A. Mendes Correia, *Raças do império* (Porto, 1943); António A. Mendes Correia, *Uma jornada científica na Guiné portuguesa* (Lisbon, 1946).
77. Mendes Correia, *Uma jornada científica na Guiné portuguesa*, 163–64.
78. Luís de Pina, *Biotipologia e medicina* (Porto, 1935); Luís Duarte Santos, "O normotipo do homem da zona de Coimbra e o normotipo dos portugueses," *Arquivo de Anatomia e Antropologia* 21 (1941): 507–19; Leopoldina Ferreira Paulo, "Os tipos constitucionais nos portugueses," *Revista do Centro de Estudos Demográficos do Instituto Nacional da Estatística* 1 (1945): 15–38.
79. Pina, *Biotipologia e medicina*, 6; Luís de Pina, "A biotipologia na propedêutica criminal: Método de Viola-Barbára" (Porto, 1940).
80. Luís de Pina, "Tipos constitucionais nos negros africanos," in *Trabalhos do I Congresso Nacional de Antropologia Colonial*, vol. 1 (Porto, 1934), 363–64.
81. Alexandre Sarmento, "Sobre tipos constitucionais e robustez nos 'Bienos,'" *África Médica: Revista Mensal de Higiene e Medicina Tropical* 7, no. 1 (1941): 17.
82. Alexandre Sarmento, "Biotipologia angolana: Contribuição para o seu estudo," *Boletim Geral das Colónias* 16, no. 175 (1940): 31–34.
83. Sarmento, "Sobre tipos constitucionais," 22.
84. Alfredo Athayde, "Estudo bioanthropológico dos Cuamatos, Cuanhamas e Evales," *Memórias da Junta de Investigação do Ultramar* 55 (1968): 79–80.
85. António Lis Ferreira, "Observações sobre o tipo morfológico constitucional dos indígenas da Angònia-distrito de Tete," *Boletim da Sociedade de Estudos de Moçambique* 42 (1940): 29.
86. Mendes Correia, "Da antropologia ultramarina," 168.
87. Ibid., 190.
88. Francisco Bethencourt and Adrian Pearce, eds., *Racism and Ethnic Relations in the Portuguese-Speaking World* (Oxford, 2012).

Bibliography

Almeida, Miguel Vale. "'Longing for Oneself': Hybridism and Miscegenation in Colonial and Postcolonial Portugal." *Etnográfica* 6, no. 1 (2002): 181–200.

Anderson, Warwick. "Racial Conceptions in the Global South." *Isis* 105, no. 4 (2014): 782–92.

Araújo, Ricardo Benzaquén de. *Guerra e paz: Casa-grande e senzala e a obra de Gilberto Freyre nos anos 30*. São Paulo: Editora 34, 1994.

Athayde, Alfredo. "Estudo bioanthropológico dos Cuamatos, Cuanhamas e Evales." *Memórias da Junta de Investigação do Ultramar* 55 (1968): 75–108.

Berardinelli, Waldemar. *Tratado de biotipologia e patologia constitucional*. Rio de Janeiro: Francisco Alves, 1942.

Berlivet, Luc André. "A Laboratory for Latin Eugenics: The Italian Committee for the Study of Population Problems and the International Circulation of Eugenic Knowledge, 1920s–1940s." *História, Ciências, Saúde-Manguinhos* 23, no. S1 (2016): S51–S72.

Bethencourt, Francisco, and Adrian Pearce, eds. *Racism and Ethnic Relations in the Portuguese-Speaking World*. Oxford: British Oxford University Press, 2012.

Brown, Isaac. *O normotipo brasileiro*. Rio de Janeiro: Editora Guanabara, 1934.

Cassata, Francesco. *Building the New Man: Eugenics, Racial Science and Genetics in Twentieth-Century Italy*. Budapest: Central European University Press, 2011.

Castelo, Cláudia. *"O modo português de estar no mundo": O luso-tropicalismo e a ideologia colonial portuguesa (1933–1961)*. Porto: Afrontamento, 2011.

Cleminson, Richard Mark. "Between Germanic and Latin Eugenics: Portugal, 930–1960." *História, Ciências, Saúde-Manguinhos* 23, no. S1 (2016): S73–S92.

———. *Catholicism, Race and Empire: Eugenics in Portugal, 1900–1950*. Budapest: Central European University Press, 2014.

Conklin, Alice L. *In the Museum of Man: Race, Anthropology and Empire in France, 1850–1950*. Ithaca, NY: Cornell University Press, 2013.

Cunha, Olívia Maria Gomes. *Intenção e gesto: Pessoa, cor e a produção cotidiana da (in)diferença no Rio de Janeiro, 1927–1942*. Rio de Janeiro: Arquivo Nacional, 2002.

Duarte Santos, Luís. *Biotipologia humana: Morfologia, temperamento, caracter, inteligência—Doutrinas, métodos, aplicações*. São Paulo: Livraria Acadêmica Saraiva e Cia, 1941.

———. "O normotipo do homem da zona de Coimbra e o normotipo dos portugueses." *Arquivo de Anatomia e Antropologia* 21 (1941): 507–19.

Eraso, Yolanda. "Towards a Taxonomy of Maternal Bodies: Biotypology, Eugenics and Argentine Nationalism (1930–1946)." *Clio Medica / The Wellcome Series in the History of Medicine* 92 (2013): 61–94.

Latour, Bruno. *Ciência em ação: Como seguir cientistas e engenheiros sociedade afora*. São Paulo: Editora Unesp, 1998.

Levine, Philippa. "Anthropology, Colonialism, and Eugenics." In *The Oxford Handbook of the History of Eugenics*, edited by Alison Bashford and Philippa Levine, 43–61. Oxford: Oxford University Press, 2010

Lis Ferreira, António. "Observações sobre o tipo morfológico constitucional dos indígenas da Angònia-distrito de Tete." *Boletim da Sociedade de Estudos de Moçambique* 42 (1940): 25–38.

Matos, Patrícia Ferraz de. *As côres do império: representações raciais no império colonial português*. Lisbon: Imprensa das Ciências Sociais, 2006.

———. "Mendes Correia e a Escola de Antropologia do Porto: Contribuição para o estudo das relações entre antropologia, nacionalismo e colonialismo (de finais do século XIX aos finais da década de 50 do século XX)." PhD dissertation, Universidade de Lisboa, 2012.

———. "Um olhar sobre as relações entre Portugal e o Brasil a partir da obra de Mendes Correia: Desafios, pontes e interações." *População e Sociedade* 21 (2013): 53–70.

Mendes Correia, António A. "A etnogenia brasílica." *Anais da Faculdade de Ciências do Porto* 19 (1935): 129–46.

———. *As tendências bio-étnicas do Brasil contemporâneo*. Porto: Imprensa Portuguesa, 1944.

———. *Cariocas e Paulistas: Impressões do Brasil*. Porto: Fernando Machado, 1935.

———. "Da antropologia ultramarina." In *Introdução à antropologia tropical*, edited by Alfredo Athayde, Maria Emília Castro e Almeida, and António A. Mendes Correia, 145–236. Lisbon: Junta de Investigações do Ultramar, 1962.

———. "Conceitos genéticos de raça e constituição." *Boletim da Sociedade Portuguesa de Ciências Naturais* 13, no. S2 (1941): S27–S30.

———. *Introdução à antropobiologia*. Coimbra: Imprensa da Universidade, 1933.

———. "O mestiçamento nas colónias portuguesas: Estudo apresentado ao II Congresso da União Nacional." *Boletim Geral das Colónias* 21, no. 239 (1945) 177–81.

———. *Raças do império*. Porto: Portucalense Editora, 1943.

———. "Uma jornada científica na Guiné Portuguesa." Lisbon: Divisão de publicações e biblioteca da Agência Geral das Colónias, 1946.
Pallares-Burke, Maria Lúcia, and Peter Burke. *Repensando os trópicos: Um retrato intelectual de Gilberto Freyre*. São Paulo: Editora Unesp, 2009.
Paulo, Leopoldina Ferreira. "Os tipos constitucionais nos portugueses." *Revista do Centro de Estudos Demográficos do Instituto Nacional da Estatística* 1 (1945): 15–38.
Pereira, Rui M. "Raça, sangue e robustez: Os paradigmas da antropologia física colonial portuguesa." *Cadernos de Estudos Africanos* 7 (2005): 210–41.
Pina, Luís de. "A biotipologia na propedêutica criminal: Método de Viola-Barbára." Paper presented to the IV Congresso Nacional de Ciências da População, Porto, 1940.
———. "Acerca das proporções nos cânones biotipológicos portugueses." *Quarto Congresso da Associação Portuguesa para o Progresso das Ciências* 5 (1942): 541–50.
———. *Biotipologia e medicina*. Porto: Tipografia da Enciclopédia Portuguesa, 1935.
———. "O biotipograma no estudo da proporcionalidade corpórea dos portugueses." *Arquivo de Anatomia e Antropologia* 26 (1949): 297–335.
———. "Tipos constitucionais nos negros africanos." In *Trabalhos do I Congresso Nacional de Antropologia Colonial*, vol. 1, 361–65. Porto: Edições da Primeira Exposição Colonial Portuguesa, 1934.
Ribeiro, Leonídeo, Waldemar Berardinelli, and Mario Roiter. "Grupo Sanguıneo dos índios guaranys." *Archivos de Medicina Legal e de Identificação* 12 (1934): 1129–35.
Romo, Anadelia. *Brazil's Living Museum: Race, Reform, and Tradition in Bahia*. Chapel Hill: University of North Carolina Press, 2010.
Roque, Ricardo. "Equivocal Connections: Fonseca Cardoso and the Origins of Portuguese Colonial Anthropology." *Portuguese Studies* 19 (2003): 80–109.
Roquette-Pinto, Edgard. *Ensaios de antropologia brasiliana*. São Paulo: Companhia Editora Nacional, 1933.
Santos, Ricardo Ventura. "Mestiçagem, degeneração e viabilidade de uma Nação: Debates em antropologia física no Brasil (1870–1930)." In *Raça como questão: História, ciência e identidades no Brasil*, edited by Ricardo V. Santos and Marcos C. Maio, 83–108. Rio de Janeiro: Editora Fiocruz, 2010.
Sarmento, Alexandre. "Biotipologia angolana: Contribuição para o seu estudo." *Boletim Geral das Colónias* 16, no. 175 (1940): 31–34.
———. "Sobre tipos constitucionais e robustez nos 'Bienos.'" *África Médica: Revista Mensal de Higiene e Medicina Tropical* 7, no. 1 (1941): 17–22.
Souza, Vanderlei Sebastião de. *Em busca do Brasil: Edgard Roquette-Pinto e o retrato antropológico brasileiro, 1905–1935*. Rio de Janeiro: Editora da Fundação Getúlio Vargas, 2017.
Stepan, Nancy L. "Eugenics in Brazil, 1917–1940." In *The Wellborn Science: Eugenics in Germany, France, Brazil and Russia*, edited by Mark B. Adams, 138–44. New York: Oxford University Press, 1990.
Stern, Alexandra M. "From Mestizophilia to Biotypology: Racialization and Science in Mexico, 1920–1960." In *Race and Nation in Modern Latin America*, edited by Nancy P. Applebaum, Anne S. Macpherson, and Karin A. Rosemblatt, 187–210. Chapel Hill: University of North Carolina Press, 2003.
Tamagnini, Eusébio. "Os problemas da mestiçagem." In *Trabalhos do I Congresso Nacional de Antropologia Colonial*, vol. 1, 39–63. Porto: Edições da Primeira Exposição Colonial Portuguesa, 1934.
Tilley, Helen. *Africa as a Living Laboratory: Empire, Development, and the Problem of Scientific Knowledge, 1870–1950*. Chicago: University of Chicago Press, 2011.

Tracy, Sarah W. "George Draper and American Constitutional Medicine, 1916–1946: Reinventing the Sick Man." *Bulletin of the History of Medicine* 66, no. 1 (1992): 53–89.

Turda, Marius, and Aaron Gillette. *Latin Eugenics in Comparative Perspective.* London: Bloomsbury, 2014.

Vallejo, Gustavo, and Marisa Miranda. "Los saberes del poder: Eugenesia y biotipología en la Argentina del siglo XX." *Revista de Indias* 64, no. 231 (2004): 425–44.

Vertinsky, Patricia. "Physique as Destiny: William H. Sheldon, Barbara Honeyman Heath and the Struggle for Hegemony in the Science of Somatotyping." *Canadian Bulletin of Medical History* 24, no. 2 (2007): 291–316.

Vimieiro-Gomes, Ana Carolina. "Biotipologia, regionalismo e a construção de uma identidade corporal brasileira no plural, década de 1930." *História, Ciências, Saúde-Manguinhos* 23, no. S1 (2016): S111–S30.

———. "Science, Constitutional Medicine and National Bodily Identity in Brazilian Biotypology during the 1930s." *Social History of Medicine,* 30, no. 1 (2017): 137–57.

PART IV
Portugueseness in the Tropics

CHAPTER 10

Luso-tropicalism Debunked, Again
Race, Racism, and Racialism in Three Portuguese-Speaking Societies

Cristiana Bastos

Luso-tropicalism's Afterlife and the Need for Further Research

The term Luso-tropicalism was crafted in the 1950s by the Brazilian anthropologist and cultural historian Gilberto Freyre.[1] In his earlier works on colonial Brazil, Freyre suggested that the Portuguese colonizers had a special ability to adapt to the tropics by easily intermingling, intermarrying, and interchanging cultural elements with different peoples, given that they were themselves the result of multiple mixtures.[2] Two decades later, he expanded the idea into a concept suitable to all societies sharing Portuguese influence, whether colonial plantations, settler societies, or conquest territories.[3]

Before Luso-tropicalism could mature—or expire—as a theory, it was borrowed for political purposes by the Portuguese government and pasted into the official doctrine of the regime. The new doctrine, a combination of old imperial tropes and Freyre's novel ideas, was propagated in the 1960s and early 1970s. At its core was the assertion of a benign, humanistic, and nonracist distinctive Portuguese character as best shown in the tropics. From that assumption followed the claims about empire not being an empire but a unique multiracial nation across the continents, and colonies not being colonies but parts of a singular nation that extended from Minho in Northern Portugal to distant Timor in Southeast Asia. Those rhetorical devices were meant to dismiss the challenges to the Portuguese colonial rule that came from three fronts: internal political opponents, African nationalist movements, and the United Nations. Hardly convincing to the outside world, the ideas were internally imposed via propaganda and censorship. It is debatable whether

Freyre subscribed to the apologetic, indoctrinating, and nationalist tones of Luso-tropicalism's later version.

As the Portuguese authoritarian regime ended in 1974 and its colonial rule in Africa dissolved in 1975, one would expect Luso-tropicalism to be now a curiosity of the past. Yet, it keeps reappearing: in 2017, during an official visit to the island of Gorée, Senegal, a place where world leaders had formally apologized for the past involvement of their nations and institutions in the Atlantic slave trade, the president of Portugal evoked Luso-exceptionalism.[4] Back home, the episode ignited a public debate on the politics of reparation, the Portuguese role on the slave trade, and the effects of that involvement on the racialized inequalities of contemporary society.[5] Other examples illustrate the vitality of Luso-tropicalism's afterlife: in 2016 and 2017, when a mainstream newspaper published the double series "Racism in Portuguese" and "Racism, the Portuguese Way," which gave voice to the experience of nonwhite subjects living in Portugal, many accused the initiative of "reverse racism."[6] In 2017, when the European Social Survey revealed a high score of the subtle racism variable among the Portuguese, many in the public dismissed the conclusion because "everyone knew that the Portuguese were not racist."[7] And when activists and scholars suggested that the next population census, in 2020, should include ethnic/racial categories in order to better assess the social inequalities related to racial discrimination, they were blamed for opening a Pandora's box that would lead to racist havoc.[8]

The current debates in Portugal recall earlier episodes in Brazil. We know now that perhaps over half the Brazilian population descends from Africans forcedly brought into the plantations, before and after Brazil's independence from Portugal. Yet until recently that number was hard to estimate due to the reluctance to address race and to the strength of the belief in the advantages of national color blindness as an antidote to racism. In the 1950s, Florestan Fernandes and Roger Bastide were accused of creating a problem by candidly addressing racial relations in Brazil.[9] Decades later, Lilia Schwarcz would receive similar criticism for her work on racialist conceptions in historical Brazil.[10] In the 2000s, when anti-racist activists set the tone for affirmative action and some universities adopted quotas for student enrollment, they were accused of promoting racism by introducing foreign categories like "black" or "Afro-descendent."

Time and again, the tension between the political use of racial categories and the ideal of a society freed of racial categories—both of them presented as the best response against racist practices—emerges in Portuguese-speaking societies; then along come claims of color blindness, exceptionalism, and other tropes of Luso-tropicalism. Despite much debunking, and despite having lost their original function of supporting an anachronistic empire, Luso-tropicalist ideas persist and remain attached to claims of exceptionalism in racial matters.

And while exceptionalism is a common assertion of nations and empires, the use of miscegenation as a keyword to obfuscate racist practices and racialist beliefs is peculiar. It deserves further analysis, and hence this chapter: one more attempt to debunk Luso-tropicalism, to understand why it is there in the first place, and why it has persisted for so long.

My analysis diverges from existing scholarship on Luso-tropicalism in empirical references and in approach. I will briefly review the genealogy of the concept and correlated doctrine, but I will not engage directly with Freyre's writings or with the social contexts from where he drew his data—his origins in the Brazilian Northeast, and the places he visited in Africa and Asia. Nor will I look for signs of proto- or para-Luso-tropicalism in other writers. Instead, I will analyze practices and theorizations in Portuguese-speaking contexts that go in the opposite direction. I will examine three cases of racialized lives and racialist theorizations in Portuguese overseas communities external to Freyre's references: the community of early Portuguese settlers and their descendants in the southern Angola plateau, as seen by the physical anthropologist Alberto C. Germano da Silva Correia, who developed his own version of Luso-exceptionalism in the tropics;[11] the Portuguese in New England, as analyzed by the sociologist Donald Taft and as embodied in the local protests against him;[12] and the Portuguese in Hawai'i, as depicted in a variety of sources and ongoing research.[13]

From Concept to Doctrine: Rebranding Empire as Moral Miscegenation

Freyre was already famous for his books *Casa-grande & senzala* and *Sobrados e Mucambos* when he was invited to visit and write about the Portuguese colonies in Africa and Asia.[14] His earlier books had been innovative against the prevailing commonsense and the existing scholarship about colonial Brazil. Whereas the Portuguese were generally viewed in Brazil as predators and malign colonizers who should be blamed for the country's backwardness, or as parasitic and greedy shopkeepers, or yet as the fools in ethnic jokes, Freyre depicted them as imaginative, creative, even sexy colonizers who engaged in intimate relations with the Indigenous South Americans and displaced Africans. From that process had resulted the unique, beautiful, and cheerfully miscegenated Brazil.[15]

Freyre's style was too colorful for Salazar, the conservative, authoritarian, and austere prime minister of Portugal since 1932. Salazar promoted an ideal of modesty and religiosity that could not be further from Freyre's portrayal of the Portuguese as slick and sexy adventurers. Freyre's books were full of intercourse, romance, gestures, sounds, flavors, weaknesses, pleasures, interracial encounters and transactions—in sum, everything that the stiff historians and ideologues of Portuguese empire were not inclined to mention or celebrate. Yet, the modernist-oriented Portuguese propaganda director António Ferro foresaw the potential interest in coopting Freyre for modernizing the official discourse of the Portuguese state.[16] New symbols and a general rebranding were needed to replace the old imperial display and bold endorsement of racial hierarchies patent in the 1934 Portuguese Colonial Exhibition in Porto and the 1940 Exhibition of the "Portuguese World" in Lisbon.[17] Such need was proportional to the anachronism of Salazar's project.[18]

Ferro invited Freyre for a tour of the empire, but his schedule did not allow it. A new invitation was met with the same impossibility. A third attempt, now from the Head of the Overseas Ministry Morais Sarmento, was finally successful. Meanwhile, Salazar had to be persuaded into reading Freyre; we do not know if he actually did, but we know the two met in Lisbon in 1951. Freyre's charm and genuine Lusophilia convinced Salazar. Freyre reported the meeting with some esthetic distance. He also claimed not to accept constraints, and to write freely about what he observed.[19]

Freyre's reflective notes are compiled in the travelogue *Aventura e Rotina*. It allows us to follow the ways he processed his encounters. One deceptive moment occurred in Cape Verde, an archipelago whose population had grown from multiple unions of people of diverse African and European backgrounds. Cape Verdean intellectuals had found *Casa-grande & senzala* a most inspiring book to interpret their own society. Cape Verde could provide ground for further elaborations of Freyre's accounts and theories—or so they expected. But Freyre was not too impressed with the place or its people; he did not celebrate it as the epitome of miscegenation or show any particular interest for it—frustrating Cape Verdean colleagues' expectations. Also, he got to know Angola and Mozambique only superficially. He exulted, however, in Goa, which he found much similar to his homeland Brazil and where he first formulated the basis of Luso-tropicalism before an audience.[20]

The Luso-tropicalism doctrine was gradually adopted, and adapted, by the Portuguese regime. It was used in official documents and taught to colonial administrators, who learned to use the new vocabulary and repeat the mantra of nonracism, while also learning how to implement colonial authority and to represent the state in heavily racialized societies. In 1961, the government sponsored the publication of the institutional volume *The Portuguese and the Tropics* in several languages, which became the source and matrix for many supporting outlets—from textbooks to films and radio programs, from official memos to interventions in the UN.[21]

With no disavowal available, for the regime had a strong apparatus of censorship, many in Portugal and its colonies were fed the soothing idea that they were involved not in an anachronistic and racist imperial rule in Africa but in a sui generis civilizational mission of bringing together different peoples of the world under one nation and language. "Empire" and "colonial" were edited out of the official language and replaced with an imagery of a pluricontinental and multiracial nation cemented by benign interactions.[22] The fact that those ideas coexisted with daily racist practices speaks of the power of ideology to filter the perception of practices and make possible the persistence of the double-bind notion of a nonracist colonial rule.

Defeated Tales of Empire: The Racialism of Germano Correia

When Freyre was on the tour of Portuguese colonies that led to his Luso-tropicalist epiphany in Goa, another author, ironically a son of Goa, was finishing his six-volume racialist elegy, *The History of Portuguese Colonization in India*.[23] That author was Alberto Germano da Silva Correia, who in many instances stands for a symmetrical counterpart to Freyre.[24] Like Freyre, Correia claimed that the Portuguese had a special vocation to adapt, survive, and make a living in the tropics. But unlike Freyre, he believed that racial purity and strict endogamy were key to the success of the Portuguese in southern lands. Like Freyre, Correia wrote extensively, most often about the Portuguese in the tropics. Unlike Freyre, he never achieved notoriety beyond a small circle. The racialism that had guided him became obsolete and infamous after World War II. Yet, his work deserves analysis in what it reveals about miscegenation anxieties in Portuguese-speaking contexts.

Correia was born in 1888 as a *descendente*—the caste-like group of those born in India who traced their lineage exclusively to Portuguese ancestors. With the declining Portuguese influence in Goa in the nineteenth century, the past privilege and power of the *descendentes* were also in decline. They held to their prestige and dreaded being taken as mixed race—as did the other influential groups of Christian Brahmins and *Chardós*, whose ancestors had converted to Catholicism, accommodated to the Portuguese structures of power, and held aristocratic Portuguese names, but did not praise intermarrying.[25]

Correia transported his obsession about lineage purity to his writings, which combine empirical-based research with a constant appraisal of the Portuguese and a racialist framework. Although he worked on a variety of topics, much of his energy went into assessing the racial purity of the Portuguese descendants in India and Africa.[26] When serving in Angola as a physician in the 1920s, he met a group of descendants of Portuguese settlers from Madeira living in Huíla. Contrary to other Portuguese who had come to Angola, those settlers had not dissolved into the local population, disappeared from the sight of the state, or contributed massively to miscegenation. They had created, in

Correia's words, a successful Eurafrican population of Luso-Angolans. Based on that case, he argued that the Portuguese adaptation to the tropics resulted on an improvement of their race—not by mixing with the locals but by following strict endogamic practices.[27] He could not imagine that when, decades later, the government promoted a massive white settlement in Angola, the group he described would be racialized by the newcomers into a subaltern position ("chicoronhos," "second-class whites," "Madeirans," etc.) in a hierarchy that combined geographies, labor positions, and collective identifications.

The racialized reality of Huíla depicted by the racialist Correia was almost the opposite of Freyre's Luso-tropical dream of nonracialized interactions. Even though Freyre and Correia claimed to know of each other, it is unlikely that they truly read each other's works. Their work and lives went into opposite directions. Freyre's studies became famous; Correia's themes became infamous. He finished his life in obscurity and passed away in Lisbon in 1967, a few years after Goa became part of the Indian.

Figure 10.1. Portuguese settlers from Madeira at Chibia, Huíla Plateau, Angola, circa 1890. Lithography over original photograph by J. Cunha Moraes. Source: *As colónias portuguesas*, March 1891. Kindly reproduced from the journal by Fernando Ladeira, Lisbon Geographic Society.

Contested Whiteness: The Racialized Reception to Taft's Racialist *Two Portuguese Communities in New England*

The 1920s were a time of renewal in anthropology. And while Germano Correia was in Angola measuring the offspring of white settlers in order to expand his racialist theories, Freyre was in New York starting a journey into the opposite direction. Contrary to popular belief, he was not a doctoral student of Franz Boas at Columbia University. Freyre was there working on his Masters degree, and not under Boas supervision. The two met informally, however, and Boas's concepts visibly influenced Freyre's later works. Freyre would join the number of those who, like Boas and his celebrity students Ruth Benedict, Margaret Mead, and Alfred Kroeber, contributed to the shift from the centrality of biological race to that of culture in anthropology. The discipline was changing altogether, its social and cultural branch splitting from the physical-biological one. Whether endorsing the *Volksgeist*-inspired notion of culture as popularized in the United States, the structure-and-function approach to society used in Britain, or the attention to the mechanisms of solidarity and exchange proposed by Durkheim and Mauss in France, social scientists in the 1920s were ready to discard race and racialism.

Yet, some remained attached to the old paradigm, from Correia and his anthropometrics in Goa and Angola to many of the scholars at Columbia University. One example is Donald Taft and his 1923 doctoral dissertation, *Two Portuguese Communities in New England*. There is no evidence that the Massachusetts-born-and-bred Taft, then a mature doctoral student teaching elsewhere, met the young Brazilian graduate student Freyre—even though they might have been the only two on campus with an interest on things Portuguese. Their routes were very difference, and Taft's take on the Portuguese is eloquent about that.

Taft studied with meticulous detail two communities of Portuguese migrant laborers in southern New England: one in industrial Fall River, Massachusetts, and the other in rural Portsmouth, Rhode Island. Those were the empirical settings for his investigation on the social determinants of the high infant mortality rates in communities with many Portuguese migrants. His methods were state of the art: he used sophisticated statistical analysis, consulted multiple sources, engaged in local observation, interviewed with an interpreter, and analyzed the data with comments on the social and economic factors of distress behind poor health indicators. His account matched the purposes of social science. Yet, his conclusion blamed it all on race: the high infant mortality among the Portuguese was closer to that of black communities than of white communities because the Portuguese were mixed raced to begin with, their African blood bringing them closer to African Americans than to their white

Figure 10.2. Portuguese boys in Fall River, Massachusetts, circa 1910. Photograph by Lewis Wickes Hine. Courtesy of Library of Congress Prints and Photographs Division / LC-USZ62-108765.

counterparts. As the conclusion contradicts the analysis of the data provided in other chapters, one may speculate whether the racialist comments were endorsed in full by the author or imposed by his supervisor, Frank Giddings.[28]

The Portuguese who read or heard about the book rejected its racialized tone. Letters and articles against it appeared in the Portuguese press of Fall River, followed by that of New Bedford. Different from Fall River's homogenous community of recent Azorean migrants working the cotton mills' entry positions, New Bedford's was a diverse mix of Portuguese laborers, fishers, artisans, tailors, professionals, businesspeople, musicians, and more; together they kept several associations, clubs, and newspapers. They called for a meeting meant to prepare a written protest and were met with much success. The enthusiasm was such that the meeting became a demonstration of no less than six thousand people.[29] Six thousand people demonstrating in the streets against a book that hardly any of them had read was not about literary disapproval or academic disagreement, but about how they took offense. The demonstrators could not take lightly the epithet of miscegenation. In support of their point, they evoked history, ancestry, nobility, poets, warriors, genealogy—in sum, variations on racial purity. Like the author they so much repudiated, they endorsed racialism and disliked miscegenation, the core of Luso-tropicalism.

Taft left the subject of the Portuguese of New England and their health patterns behind and moved into other research interests like criminology and international migration.[30] Yet his book remained one of the few, if not the only one, about the Portuguese in America; despite the historical importance of the Portuguese in areas like New England, California, Hawai'i, and New Jersey, they remained a relatively unstudied and invisible community in the US.[31] When in the 1960s the *New York Times* published a series about the different ethnic groups and nationalities that made the United States, it was *Two Portuguese Communities* that was chosen to represent the group that had so disliked it decades before.

In and Out of the Plantation: The Portuguese in Hawai'i

There was, however, one place—a former Indigenous kingdom transformed into a US insular territory—where the Portuguese were quite visible and included in numerous social studies: Hawai'i.[32] From 1878, a Hawaiian kingdom–government-sponsored migration of Portuguese islanders began from the intersection of the Hawaiian government's putative interest to reverse population decline and sugar planters' interest in additional working hands.[33] Prior to that, a few hundred Portuguese, mainly single men, had already arrived in the islands as whalers and sailors who jumped ship and married native Hawaiians. That situation changed with the massive arrival of around twenty thousand Portuguese contract laborers between 1878 and 1913, who came mostly as families and married among themselves.[34] Many went to the plantations and established micro-communities, side by side with other groups of laborers: native Hawaiians, Chinese, and, later, Japanese, Filipinos, and others. Many also went to the city and worked in masonry, commerce, and services. Many in the sugar fields moved up to the position of *lunas*, the horse-riding intermediaries who supervised the work gang—although the head supervisors were mainly of Northern European descent.[35] Others became *paniolos* (ranch cowboys). Many moved out of the plantation and established businesses. Some moved to California. Many had residence and businesses in Punchbowl, a neighborhood of Honolulu that still holds some names of Portuguese resonance, like Madeira, Azores, or Lusitana streets.[36] In the year 1911, the Portuguese were 11.6 percent of the population in Hawai'i.[37]

Often considered the "last of the magic islands," society in Hawai'i contrasted with the continental United States in its race-based divisions; mainland visitors tended to see there a paradise of color blindness. This perception was reinforced by the existence of substantial intermarriage between native Hawaiian elites (*ali'i*) and *haole* (white, foreign) traders, missionaries, and planters from Great Britain and New England. Intergroup marriages also occurred

Figure 10.3. Portuguese girls and a boy working in a sugar field, Lahaina, Maui, Hawai'i, circa 1911. Photograph by Ray Jerome Baker. Courtesy of the Bishop Museum, Honolulu, Hawai'i, www.bishopmuseum.org.

among the laboring classes, except when they came in organized, sponsored contingents of families. That was the case with the Portuguese, whom, contrary to the stereotypes proposed by Freyre, stayed mostly within their group during their first few decades in Hawai'i.[38]

One can only speculate what Freyre would do—or not do, just like for Cape Verde—with the ubiquity of intermarriage and references to color blindness in Hawai'i, or with the fact that the English, not the Portuguese, married local. Perhaps he would find his stereotypical Portuguese in the whalers and sailors who had come earlier as single men and married locally, but so did all the others in those circumstances. In plantation life, however, most groups practiced endogamy. Later, and just like other groups, the Portuguese intermarried and contributed to the melting pot of Hawai'i; nowadays Hawai'i celebrates the multiple descents of most people, and descent is validated by genealogical research and, increasingly, by genetic testing.[39]

Up to their merging into mainstream whiteness in the 1940 census—a process fully implemented in the aftermath of World War II—the Portuguese were a distinct, racialized group in Hawaiian society. They appeared as a separate category in the census, among "other Caucasians." Although "race" was an ambiguous term, they were treated as a separate racial group in the team of the pioneering sociologist of racial relations in Hawai'i, Romanzo Adams. Adams came from Chicago in 1920 to begin the University of Hawai'i at Mānoa, followed by Andrew Lind shortly after. They trained students along the lines of their mentor Robert Park, who also came to Hawai'i as a visiting professor from 1931 to 1932.[40] For decades, the group mobilized students and community members into social research, much of it dedicated to racial issues. The archives of the Romanzo Adams Social Research Laboratory, stored at the University of Hawai'i's archival collections in Hamilton Library, keep many of the students' papers from the 1920s to 1950s on topics of race, hybrid families, interracial friendships, racial experiences at work, and so forth—revealing the involvement and the excitement of applying cutting-edge sociological concepts to one's own society, group, family, personal network.[41] In 1935, they began the publication of the yearly reference journal *Social Process in Hawai'i*.

Hawai'i was particularly attractive as a field to explore the sociological concepts of the day because its multiethnic society had been formed in a compressed historical time and was still in the process of change. The sugar economy developed rapidly in the second half of the nineteenth century and quickly attracted migrants from different nationalities—particularly Chinese, Portuguese, and Japanese, with Koreans, Puerto Ricans and Filipinos added to the mix in the early twentieth century—who intermingled and later intermarried with native Hawaiians, the haole class of missionaries and planters, and each other. Although none of those groups corresponded to a precise "race" in the terminology of the time, they were treated as racial categories for analytical purposes, with due distance from the biological definitions of race. Adams's classic 1937 *Interracial Marriage in Hawai'i* is punctuated with photographs of students of diverse backgrounds ("Native Hawaiian," "Korean-Hawaiian ancestry," "Portuguese ancestry," "English-Japanese-Hawaiian ancestry," etc.) that resemble those used by physical anthropologists to illustrate racial types—although, Adams notes, "they were selected to represent a social type rather than a racial type."[42]

Like their mentor Robert Park, Adams and colleagues used the dyad "accommodation" and "amalgamation" to study the interactions of the racialized groups. Still following Park's terminology, successful amalgamation would lead to assimilation. Along those lines also came "Social Placement of the Portuguese in Hawai'i as Indicated by Factors of Assimilation," Gerald Estep's master's thesis in sociology at the University of Southern California.[43] Estep addressed the Portuguese as one group among others, who came as laborers and followed the social processes of amalgamation. Although "racialized" into a social group, there was nothing exceptional about the Portuguese—not along the lines proposed by Freyre.

The sociologists James A. Geschwender, Rita Carroll-Seguin, and Howard Brill suggest that the Portuguese in Hawai'i provide a case to demonstrate the

Figure 10.4. Picture illustrating "Portuguese ancestry" in Romanzo Adams's *Interracial Marriage in Hawaii* (Macmillan, 1937). Photographer and model unknown. Someone has written *Pocho*—slang for Portuguese—in pencil.

universal dynamics of ethnicity—a classificatory "anomaly" in that they were of European extraction but considered local, not haole, because, contrary to the haole, who constituted a capitalist core, the Portuguese had come as labor.⁴⁴ And, like other groups of laborers, they were ethnically stereotyped—racialized as *portegee, pocho, poregee,* and so on. More recently, Moon-Kie Jung has suggested that "conceptualizing Portuguese, Japanese, Filipino and other migrants in racially disparate ways" was a way of keeping haole power and influence. The Portuguese in particular were left in "analytical ambiguity."⁴⁵

In one rare novel about the life of the early Portuguese settlers in the Hawaiian plantations, the Portuguese-American writer Elvira Osorio Roll establishes a narrative tension in which the protagonist, who is always distancing herself from the illiterate and backward *poregee* who work in the cane fields, explaining that she descends from Portuguese aristocracy and her father owns a business, ends up being stigmatized as *poregee* herself by the haole who disapprove of her romantic involvement with a young haole man. The way she finds to respond to the haole ladies who deprecate her Portugueseness is to exhibit tales of historical grandeur of her people.⁴⁶ The poetry of Manuel Coito, known as "the poet of Punchbowl," also often suggests topics of imperial grandeur as an ethnic pride motif.⁴⁷

By the mid-twentieth century, the Portuguese were no longer racialized but were acknowledged for their heritage, culture, and contribution to the making of modern Hawai'i. They were associated with iconic local foods like *malasadas* and Portuguese sausage, and the quintessential Hawaiian ukulele, ingeniously developed by Manuel Nunes, Augusto Dias, and José do Espírito Santo from their own *braguinha*.⁴⁸ On the 1978 centennial of the arrival of the *Priscilla*, the bark that first brought sponsored Madeiran islanders, a local committee of distinguished Portuguese marked the event with several celebrations and the construction of a marble *padrão* and Portuguese cobblestone pavement downtown.⁴⁹ A plaque in the monument pays homage to the Portuguese pioneers and notes their origin and dynamics of growth and upward mobility—their full integration in the island community. To this day, the number of Portuguese family names in Hawai'i is impressive, and although hardly anyone knows the language, there are festivals and associations that celebrate heritage and keep the flame of genealogy alight.⁵⁰

Race, Anxieties, and Double-Bind Responses: How Luso-tropicalism Became Handy and Persisted amid Racism

The three cases stand for different responses to racialized anxieties: the language of racial purity, as in Germano Correia; the idiom of racial pride, as in the response of Portuguese New Englanders to Taft; and the varying attitudes about ethnicized hierarchies, as in Hawai'i. Contrary to the main thesis of Luso-tropicalism, there is no evidence of more propensity toward miscegenation among these Portuguese groups than among other groups. Miscegenation/segregation, like amalgamation/accommodation for the Chicago sociologists, depend on a variety of circumstances and not on a presumed inner constitution, be it presented as biology or as culture.

The Madeiran settlers in Huíla had migrated in families and remained bounded within the community—separated from the local Africans and from the neighbor Boers, with the occasional crossover for romance, sex, or marriage, but largely self-contained, subject to a racialized life as a group. Their racial purity was acclaimed by anthropologist Germano Correia—only to be later discounted by the white newcomers from Portugal who arrived in the twentieth century. The Portuguese in New England were at odds with how they were described in the racial hierarchies of the moment. In order to claim a higher position in the hierarchy, they used the iconography of imperial pride. In Hawai'i, the Portuguese were one group among many on a complex social mosaic, separated from the haole whites, enduring racial prejudice associated with their labor positions, and eventually assimilating into the mainstream, occasionally having recourse to the language of imperial endeavor as a proxy for racial/national pride. On no occasion were the tropes of Luso-tropicalism ever evoked as distinctly Portuguese traits. In the often-precarious existences in fragile, racialized social positions, Portuguese would rather use a repertory of bravery and grandeur as identifiers. Thus, exceptionalism appears in very different terms from the miscegenation later celebrated by Luso-tropicalism and evoked by some Portuguese speakers today.

Given that the positive use of miscegenation as a Portuguese trait is not ubiquitous and can be traced to one source—Freyre and its use by the Portuguese government—the question of its pervasive afterlife remains. My attempt at an answer is that Luso-tropicalism's appraisal of miscegenation should be read less for what it says than for what it opposes. Miscegenation can be seen as an oppositional identity that stands as an inversion of the derogatory visions of Portuguese expressed by others—others who are also competitors. Freyre transformed the negative mixed-race, half-caste stereotypes about the Portuguese into something positive; where others saw vice, he proved virtue, as an *avant la lettre* mixed-race pride device against prejudice and abuse from competitors, rivals, and overseers.[51]

To support his views, Freyre selected examples of relationships, intercourse, and offspring between colonizers and colonized or enslaved individuals in the context of Portuguese colonial history. By treating them as distinctively Portuguese, he did not account for the fact that practices of violent or consensual interracial sex, romantic arrangements, and domestic partnerships had existed in other colonial empires, later removed from visibility by the adoption of stricter rules of segregation. Freyre wrote as a Brazilian shocked by the extreme segregation he found in the Southern United States. He framed the differences as contrasting, generic cultural patterns: agonistically racialized in the Anglophone world, mixed into nuances in the Iberian worlds.

It was as a major propaganda operation promoted by Salazar's regime that older imperial themes of grandeur—the pioneering colonial conquest, bravery in battles, conversion of the heathen—became combined with Freyre's glamorous miscegenation, which erased or obscured histories of colonial conquest, plantation violence, and slavery. The result of that combination was an oxymoron of sorts, a distorting mirror that provided the viewer a positive image while eclipsing from sight and cognition the harsh realities of racism and colonialism. One reason this cognitive duplicity was successful is that the two contrasting tropes could merge against a common adversary. Freyre had uplifted the Portuguese culture of mixing and mingling in opposition to an Anglophone culture of separating and accommodating. For Salazar's Portugal, the Anglophone world was the elephant in the room—figured as memories of the British competition for territories and commerce, the abolitionists criticizing labor practices in the Portuguese colonies, the UN challenging Portuguese rule in the 1960s, or in more diluted memories like the voice of English writers deprecating Portuguese "mongrelism."

Through Freyre, the stereotypes of the lowly, racially, and culturally mongrel *poregee, portygee,* or *portagee* were transformed into the imaginary Luso-trope of a mixed-race, ideal figure. The 1950s and 1960s ideological maneuver that grafted Freyre's appraisal of Portuguese miscegenation onto a residually racialist ideology of empire was an extraordinary success, in that its effects can be traced still now in the unsettled matters of racism in Portuguese-speaking contexts. Luso-tropicalism added an extra layer of exceptionalism to the theme of great early empire; it provided a positive image of glamorized miscegenation while eclipsing actual racist practices and formations. Furthermore, Luso-tropicalism not only has masked the harsh and bitter reality—past and present—it also continues to provide a language, an appealing evasion, that makes the speaker feel good and special.

CRISTIANA BASTOS is an anthropologist who also works in history, history of science, public health, colonialism, and migrations. She is currently leading the multitrack project "The Colour of Labour: The Racialized Lives of Migrants," funded by the European Research Council, with empirical research in New England mill towns, Hawaiian plantations, and Angolan settlements, among others. She is based at the Institute of Social Sciences at the University of Lisbon, where she heads the Identities, Cultures, Vulnerabilities research group, and has participated in a variety of programs and projects in Portugal,

Brazil, the United States, the United Kingdom, India, Mozambique, Germany, Spain, and Italy.

Notes

The original version of this chapter was presented in the Conference Racial Conceptions in the Global South, organized by Warwick Anderson, Ricardo Roque, and Ricardo Ventura Santos in Rio de Janeiro, April 2016. I am indebted to the organizers and all the participants who commented with wise insights on my early draft. The essay evolved into its current form with the agreement of the editors and due to my involvement with the European Research Council Advanced Grant "The Colour of Labour: The Racialized Lives of Migrants" (ERC-2015-AdG 695573), which allowed me to conduct empirical research on the Portuguese in Hawai'i. I also wish to thank the hosts and institutions who generously assisted the research in 2017: the East West Center Research Department; the University of Hawai'i at Mānoa, particularly at the Hawaiian and Pacific Collections at Hamilton Library; the Hawai'i State Archives; the Hawai'i Historical Society; the Bishop Museum; the Portuguese Genealogical and Historical Society at O'ahu; the Plantation Village; and the Maui Heritage Society—and an extensive number of people who kindly helped by sharing their memories, reflections, and expertise.

1. Gilberto Freyre, *Aventura e rotina: Sugestões de uma viagem à procura das constantes portuguesas de caráter e ação* (Rio de Janeiro, 1953).
2. Gilberto Freyre, *Casa-grande & senzala: Formação da família brasileira sob o regímen de economia patriarchal* (Rio de Janeiro, 1933); Gilberto Freyre, *Sobrados e Mucambos* (Rio de Janeiro, 1936).
3. Gilberto Freyre, *Integração portuguesa nos trópicos* (Lisbon, 1958); Gilberto Freyre, *O luso e o trópico: Sugestões em torno dos métodos portugueses de integração dos povos autóctones e de culturas diferentes da europeia num complexo novo de civilização, o luso tropical* (Lisbon, 1961).
4. The president referred to the pioneering act of outlawing slave ownership in Portugal in 1761. "Portugal reconheceu injustiça da escravatura quando a aboliu em 1761, diz Marcelo," *Público*, 13 April 2017, https://www.publico.pt/2017/04/13/politica/noticia/portugal-reconheceu-injustica-da-escravatura-quando-a-aboliu-em-1761-diz-marcelo-1768680. This is a much-repeated mantra, the problem with it being that slavery was outlawed in mainland Portugal and Goa to avoid competition with the colonies, and complete abolition in all territories only came in 1869; plus, the dual legal system separating "citizens" from "natives/Indigenous" made possible the existence of forced labor in Africa until 1961.
5. After social media buzz, the daily *Público* and others published op-eds on the politics of reparation and contemporary racism by historians, social scientists, activists, and critical theorists, with the conservative historians João Pedro Marques, Rui Ramos, João Paulo Oliveira e Costa, and others against apologizing for the past, and Paulo Pinto, Pedro Schacht, Elísio Macamo, Marta Araújo, Mamadou Ba, Joacyne Katar Moreira, and others arguing the need to address it in order to understand and act on the present.
6. Joana Gorjão Henriques, *Racismo em português* (Lisbon, 2016), and "Racismo à portuguesa," *Público*, 2017.
7. For a synthesis, see Joana Gorjão Henriques, "Portugal é dos países da Europa que mais manifestam racismo," interview with Jorge Vala, *Público*, 2 September 2017, https://www.publico.pt/2017/09/02/sociedade/noticia/portugal-e-dos-paises-da-europa-que-mais-manifesta-racismo-1783934/amp.

8. Rui Pena Pires, "Racismo e estatísticas: Não é possível combater o racismo e, em simultâneo, institucionalizar a classificação racial de todos os cidadãos," *Público*, 9 September 2017.
9. Roger Bastide and Florestan Fernandes, *Relações raciais entre negros e brancos em São Paulo* (São Paulo, 1955). See also Marcos Chor Maio, "Tempo controverso: Gilberto Freyre e o Projeto UNESCO," *Tempo Social* 11, no. 1 (1999): 111–36; Elide Rugai Bastos, "Um debate sobre a questão do negro no Brasil," *São Paulo em Perspectiva* 2, no. 2 (1988): 20–26; *Marcos Chor Maio and* Ricardo Ventura Santos, eds., *Raça como questão: História, ciência e identidades no Brasil* (Rio de Janeiro, 2010).
10. Lilia Moritz Schwarcz, *O espetáculo das raças: Cientistas, instituições e pensamento racial no Brasil—1870-1930* (São Paulo, 1993).
11. Alberto C. Germano da Silva Correia, *Os eurafricanos de Angola: Estudo antropológico* (Lisbon, 1925); Cristiana Bastos, "Race, Medicine and the Late Portuguese Empire," *Journal of Romance Studies* 5, no. 1 (2005): 23–35.
12. Donald R. Taft, *Two Portuguese Communities in New England* (New York, 1923); Cristiana Bastos, "Migrants, Inequalities and Social Research in the 1920s: The Story of Two Portuguese Communities in New England," *History and Anthropology* 29, no. 2 (2018): 163–83.
13. E.g., Romanzo Adams, *Interracial Marriage in Hawaii: A Study of the Mutually Conditioned Processes of Acculturation and Amalgamation* (New York, 1937); Andrew Lind, *An Island Community: Ecological Succession in Hawaii* (Chicago, 1938); Gerald Estep, "Social Placement of the Portuguese in Hawaii as Indicated by Factors in Assimilation" (MA thesis, University of Southern California, 1941); Edgar Knowlton Jr., "Portuguese in Hawaii," *Kentucky Foreign Language Quarterly* 7, no. 4 (1960): 212–18; Edgar Knowlton Jr., "The Portuguese Language Press of Hawaii," *Social Process in Hawaii* 24 (1960); Genevieve B. Correa and Edgar Knowlton Jr., "The Portuguese in Hawaii," *Social Process in Hawaii* 29 (1982), 55–61; Susana Caldeira, *Da Madeira para o Hawai'i: A emigração e o contributo cultural madeirense* (Funchal, 2010).
14. Freyre, *Aventura e rotina*.
15. Freyre, *Casa-grande & senzala*.
16. Cláudia Castelo, *"O modo português de estar no mundo": O Luso-tropicalismo e a ideologia colonial portuguesa (1933–1961)* (Porto, 1999); Cristiana Bastos, "Tristes trópicos e alegres Luso-tropicalismos: Das notas de viagem em Levi-Strauss e Gilberto Freyre," *Análise Social* 33, nos. 146–147 (1998): 415–32.
17. Patricia Ferraz de Matos, "Power and Identity: The Exhibition of Human Beings in the Portuguese Great Exhibitions," *Identities* 21, no. 2 (2013): 202–18.
18. Portuguese imperial biopolitics had a delayed start, and just when the former British and French colonies in Africa were on their path to become new nations, in the 1950s and 1960s, Angola and Mozambique were about to receive waves of Portuguese settlers and massive investment on infrastructures. Cláudia Castelo, *Passagens para África: O povoamento de Angola e Moçambique com naturais da metrópole (1920–1974)* (Porto, 2006).
19. Castelo, *O modo português*; Freyre, *Aventura e rotina*; Bastos, "Tristes."
20. Freyre, *Aventura e rotina*; Bastos, "Tristes."
21. Freyre, *O luso e o trópico*. 1961 was a threshold year for Portuguese colonialism: Goa was annexed to the Indian Union, anticolonial insurrection in Angola started, and so did governmental armed response.
22. The oxymoron of the sexy colonizers—sometimes in the sexist and chauvinistic reference to how Portuguese "contributed to the world by creating the beautiful mulattas"—appears often and spontaneously from otherwise progressive speakers, as was

the case in 2017, when a well-known biomedical scientist used those very words at a public event.
23. Alberto C. Germano da Silva Correia, *História da colonização portuguesa na Índia*, 6 vols. (Lisbon, 1948–1958).
24. Cristiana Bastos, "Um Luso-tropicalismo às avessas: Colonialismo científico, aclimação e pureza racial em Germano Correia," in *Fantasmas e fantasias imperiais no imaginário português contemporâneo*, ed. Margarida Calafate Ribeiro and Ana Paula Ferreira (Porto, 2003), 227–53.
25. Epithets of mixed race were commonly attributed to the Portuguese by the British and were extended to the Indo-Portuguese, who like to point out that just because their culture combines traditional elements from India and from Portugal does not mean they were mixed biologically. When the Portuguese government adopted Luso-tropicalist themes, the 16th-century marriages between Portuguese soldiers and local women in India became an emblem of Portuguese colonialism—and one that many like to distance themselves from based on class and caste.
26. Alberto C. Germano da Silva Correia, "Os 'luso-descendentes' da India," *Boletim eclesiático da Arquidiocese de Goa* 2 (1945–1946): 60–71, 177–85, 235–43, 283–89; Correia, *Os eurafricanos*; Alberto C. Germano da Silva Correia, "Os luso-descendentes de Angola: Contribuição para o seu estudo antropológico," *III Congresso Nacional Colonial: Actas das sessões e teses* (Lisbon, 1934).
27. Alberto C. Germano da Silva Correia, "Os eurafricanos," in *Trabalhos do I Congresso Nacional de Antropologia Colonial* (Porto, 1934); Cristiana Bastos, "Migrants, Settlers and Colonists: The Biopolitics of Displaced Bodies," *International Migration* 46, no. 5 (2008): 27–54.
28. The idiosyncratic Giddings (whom Freyre casually refers to) came to Columbia University to start sociology and taught and supervised hundreds of students but was unable to create a department or make the discipline highly influential—not in the sense that was achieved at the time by Chicago sociologists. See Bastos, "Migrants, Inequalities."
29. "Portuguese Government Asked by 6,000 to Answer to Dr. Taft," *New Bedford Evening Standard*, 24 March 1924; "6,000 Portugueses," *A Alvorada*, 24 March 1924; Bastos, "Inequalities."
30. Donald R. Taft, *Human Migration: A Study of International Movements* (New York, 1936); Donald R. Taft, *Criminology* (New York, 1942). From a teaching position held in Aurora, New York, Taft moved to the University of Illinois at Urbana-Champaign, where he had a full academic career.
31. Kimberly DaCosta Holton and Andrea Klimt, eds., *Community, Culture, and the Makings of Identity: Portuguese-Americans along the Eastern Seaboard* (North Dartmouth, 2009).
32. Far from Portugal and from its imperial routes, the Kingdom of Hawaiʻi—and later the US annexed territory—was a prime destination for Portuguese islanders in the late decades of the nineteenth and early twentieth centuries. Hawaiʻi's population decline, the fear of being engulfed by Asians, and the labor needs of the sugar economy led the government and planters to look for labor in distant places. The Portuguese were white enough to compensate for the "yellow peril" fears but not white enough to compete with the haole plantation owners.
33. Nicholas B. Miller, "Trading Sovereignty and Labour: Migration and the Consular Network of Nineteenth-Century Hawaiʻi," *International History Review* (forthcoming).
34. For a good synthesis on the planters and politicians' analysis of the advantages of the Portuguese as hardworking, peaceful laborers, and on the role played by William Hil-

lebrand in promoting Hawaiʻi in Madeira and the Portuguese in Hawaiʻi, see Ronald Takaki, *Pau Hana: Plantation Life and Labor in Hawaii 1835–1920* (Honolulu, 1983), 34–38. In a 1920s study of racial psychology in Hawaiʻi, the Portuguese deserve a chapter in which the authors synthesize the planters' choice as a result of knowing the disadvantages of having Oriental laborers while finding it difficult to attract Europeans, even the poorest, but a match was found in the islands of Madeira and Azores, "most part Portuguese but with a considerable mixture in some cases of negro or Morish blood." The authors also elaborate on that the Portuguese came out quite different than what the planters expected—higher salaries, larger families, the men bringing not only their wives but also their mothers and aunts—a fact that was mended with allowing children to work. Above all, they were not laborers to begin with, but often city artisans with other ambitions. Stanley David Porteus and Marjorie E. Babcock, *Temperament and Race* (Boston, 1926), 53, 54.

35. Jung, also referring to Lind, *An Island Community*, rightfully notes that *luna* was a "job category and inextricably racialized as Portuguese, although most Portuguese were not lunas and most lunas were not Portuguese." Moon-Kie Jung, *Reworking Race: The Making of Hawaii's Interracial Labor Movement* (New York, 2006), 76.
36. This important group was erased from the narrative of nation established later in Portugal. By the end of the nineteenth century, more Portuguese-born residents were in Hawaiʻi than in, for instance, Angola. The Lisbon Geographic Society bulletin published several articles on "Our Colony in Hawaii." But that "colony" of migrants was suppressed from collective memory through the selective twentieth-century self-image of the Portuguese Empire: while the African colonies were brought to the center, the Portuguese enclaves in other nations were eclipsed from the nation's official narrative. Hawaiʻi was not part of the traditional routes of empire, and the Portuguese who had sailed there were not discoverers and conquistadores but laborers. They went there not as navigators of Portuguese caravels but as passengers aboard English and German barks, schooners, clippers and steamers. They did not conquer the territories and subjugated the population but entered an economy and a society with a predefined role.
37. Lind, *An Island Community*, 47.
38. Adams, *Interracial Marriage*, 122.
39. For example, one must prove one-eighth native Hawaiian descent for Kamehame schools; for the Dolores Furtado scholarship at Punahou School, one must prove Portuguese descent.
40. The Department of Sociology at the University of Hawaiʻi at Mānoa still refers to its beginnings as an extension of the Chicago School. "Our History," accessed 11 October 2018, http://www.sociology.hawaii.edu/about/history.html.
41. Examples of students papers with keyword "Portuguese": Anonymous, "My Role in the Family"; J. F. Ptge., "Changing Times for a Plantation Family"; Margerie Fernandes, "Some Comments of the Stereotype of Racial Groups"; Margaret Fernandes, "My Experiences as a Hybrid" (Japanese-Portuguese); Mary Lou Gouveia, "Coffee Farmers in Kona"; "A Cultural Survival Among the Portuguese"; Bella Evans, "Successful Intermarriages: A Portuguese Family Intermarries"; Anne K. Kamau, "A Case of Racial Inter-marriage" (Negro-Portuguese); Roselyn Medeiros, "The Role Played by the Members of My Family."
42. Adams, *Interracial Marriage*, xvii.
43. Estep conducted research on-site, read the literature, interviewed scholars and key social actors, and attempted to test some sociological theories by using this understudied group as empirical reference. He eventually referred to Taft's *Two Portuguese Communities in New England* but did not use it as a model. For one, *Social Placement* has more

modest ambitions and scope. Second, Estep tested sociological models recurring to a sociological terminology and avoided Taft's use of racialist terminology.
44. James A. Geschwender, Rita Carroll-Seguin, and Howard Brill, "The Portuguese and Haoles of Hawaii: Implications for the Origin of Ethnicity," *American Sociological Review* 53, no. 4 (1988): 515–27.
45. Jung, *Reworking*, 61, 69.
46. Elvira Osório Roll, *Hawaiian Kohala Breezes* (New York, 1964); Timothy Paul Freitas, "From Captivity to Liberation: Literature of Madeiran Migration to Hawai'i" (PhD diss., Harvard University, 1979); Reinaldo Silva, "From the Top of the Racial Pyramid in Hawai'i: Demonizing the Hawaiian Portuguese in Elvira Osorio Roll's Fiction," *Interdisciplinary Journal of Portuguese Diaspora Studies* 2 (2013): 7–31.
47. Manuel de Jesus Coito, *Saudades das Ilhas: Madeirense*, bilingual ed., trans. Edgar C. Knowlton Jr., ed. Ana Isabel Spranger and Paul Chandler (Lisbon, forthcoming).
48. Jim Tranquada and John King, *The 'Ukulele: A History* (Honolulu, 2012).
49. John Henry Felix and Peter Senecal, eds., *The Portuguese in Hawaii* (Honolulu, 1978). Freitas, "From Captivity to Liberation," suggests that treating the *Priscilla* as the *Mayflower* of the Portuguese in Hawai'i implies a whitewashing of the migrants' suffering.
50. In November 2017, the "Festa" was held at the Plantation Village in Waipahu, O'ahu, in cooperation with the Puerto Rican community and their feat. In Maui, the heritage center joined efforts with the Puerto Ricans to have a center. On other islands, there are committees and societies dedicated to promoting Portuguese heritage. In O'ahu, the Portuguese Genealogical and Historical Society of Hawai'i serves a broad net of descendants in Hawai'i, California, and elsewhere seeking to know their genealogies and the names of their ancestors.
51. Maria Lúcia G. Pallares-Burke, *O triunfo do fracasso: Rüdiger Bilden, o amigo esquecido de Gilberto Freyre* (São Paulo, 2012). Pallares-Burke notes that, in his early works, Freyre shared much with his friend and classmate Bilden, who had explicitly depicted the Portuguese as mixed race; despite Freyre's assistance, Bilden never succeeded as a scholar, ending his life early and with a drinking problem. Freyre become a national star in Brazil, and Bilden's contribution was eventually edited out of Freyre's works.

Bibliography

Adams, Romanzo. *Interracial Marriage in Hawaii: A Study of the Mutually Conditioned Processes of Acculturation and Amalgamation*. New York: Macmillan, 1937.
Bastide, Roger, and Florestan Fernandes. *Relações raciais entre negros e brancos em São Paulo*. São Paulo: Anhembi, 1955.
Bastos, Cristiana. "Migrants, Inequalities and Social Research in the 1920s: The Story of Two Portuguese Communities in New England." *History and Anthropology* 29, no. 2 (2018): 163–83.
———. "Migrants, Settlers and Colonists: The Biopolitics of Displaced Bodies." *International Migration* 46, no. 5 (2008): 27–54.
———. "Race, Medicine and the Late Portuguese Empire: The Role of Goan Colonial Physicians." *Journal of Romance Studies* 5, no. 1 (2005): 23–35.
———. "Tristes trópicos e alegres Luso-tropicalismos: Das notas de viagem em Levi-Strauss e Gilberto Freyre." *Análise Social* 33, nos. 146–147 (1998): 415–32.
———. "Um Luso-tropicalismo às avessas: Colonialismo científico, aclimação e pureza racial em Germano Correia." In *Fantasmas e fantasias imperiais no imaginário português*

contemporâneo, edited by Margarida Calafate Ribeiro and Ana Paula Ferreira, 227–53. Porto: Campo das Letras, 2003.

Bastos, Elide Rugai. "Um debate sobre a questão do negro no Brasil." *São Paulo em Perspectiva* 2, no. 2 (1988): 20–26.

Caldeira, Susana. *Da Madeira para o Hawaii: A emigração e o contributo cultural madeirense*. Funchal: Centro de Estudos de História do Atlântico, 2010.

Castelo, Cláudia. *"O modo português de estar no mundo": O Luso-tropicalismo e a ideologia colonial portuguesa (1933–1961)*. Porto: Afrontamento, 1999.

———. *Passagens para África: o povoamento de Angola e Moçambique com naturais da metrópole (1920–1974)*. Porto: Afrontamento, 2006.

Coito, Manuel de Jesus. *Saudades das Ilhas: Madeirense*. Bilingual edition. Translated by Edgar C. Knowlton Jr. Edited by Ana Isabel Spranger and Paul Chandler. Lisbon: Faculdade de Letras da Universidade de Lisboa, forthcoming.

Correa, Genevieve B., and Edgar Knowlton. "The Portuguese in Hawaii." *Social Process in Hawai'i* 29 (1982): 55–61.

Correia, Alberto C. Germano da Silva. *História da colonização portuguesa na Índia*. 6 vols. Lisbon: Agência Geral das Colónias, 1948–1958.

———. "Os eurafricanos de Angola." In *Trabalhos do I Congresso Nacional de Antropologia Colonial*, vol. 1, 300–330. Porto: Editora da Primeira Exposição Colonial Portuguesa, 1934.

———. *Os eurafricanos de Angola: Estudo antropológico*. Lisbon, 1925.

———. "Os 'luso-descendentes' da India." *Boletim eclesiático da Arquidiocese de Goa* 2 (1945–1946): 60–71, 177–85, 235–43, 283–89.

———. "Os luso-descendentes de Angola: Contribuição para o seu estudo antropológico." In *III Congresso Nacional Colonial: Actas das sessões e teses,* 1–57. Lisbon: Sociedade de Geografia de Lisboa, 1934.

Estep, Gerald Allan. "Social Placement of the Portuguese in Hawaii as Indicated by Factors in Assimilation." MA thesis, University of Southern California, 1941.

Felix, John Henry, and Peter Senecal, eds. *The Portuguese in Hawaii*. Honolulu: Centennial Edition, 1978.

Freitas, Timothy Paul. "From Captivity to Liberation: Literature of Madeiran Migration to Hawaii." PhD dissertation, Harvard University, 1979.

Freyre, Gilberto. *Aventura e rotina: Sugestões de uma viagem à procura das constantes portuguesas de caráter e ação*. Rio de Janeiro: José Olympio, 1953.

———. *Casa-grande & senzala: Formação da família brasileira sob o regímen de economia patriarchal*. Rio de Janeiro: Editora Maia & Schmidt, 1933.

———. *Integração portuguesa nos trópicos*. Lisboa: Junta de Investigações do Ultramar, 1958.

———. *O luso e o trópico: sugestões em torno dos métodos portugueses de integração dos povos autóctones e de culturas diferentes da europeia num complexo novo de civilização, o luso tropical*. Lisbon: Comissão Executiva das Comemorações do V Centenário da Morte do Infante D. Henrique, 1961.

———. *Sobrados e Mucambos*. Rio de Janeiro: José Olympio, 1936.

Geschwender, James A., Rita Carroll-Seguin, and Howard Brill. "The Portuguese and Haoles of Hawaii: Implications for the Origin of Ethnicity." *American Sociological Review* 53, no. 4 (1988): 515–27.

Henriques, Joana Gorjão. *Racismo em português*. Lisbon: Tinta-da-China, 2016.

Holton, Kimberly DaCosta, and Andrea Klimt, eds., *Community, Culture and the Makings of Identity: Portuguese-Americans along the Eastern Seaboard*. North Dartmouth: Tagus Press, 2009.

Jung, Moon-Kie. *Reworking Race: The Making of Hawaii's Interracial Labor Movement.* New York: Columbia University Press, 2006.
Knowlton, Edgar, Jr. "Portuguese in Hawaii." *Kentucky Foreign Language Quarterly* 7, no. 4 (1960): 212–18.
——. "The Portuguese Language Press of Hawaii." *Social Process in Hawaii* 24 (1960).
Lind, Andrew. *An Island Community: Ecological Succession in Hawaii.* Chicago: University of Chicago Press, 1938.
Maio, Marcos Chor. "Tempo controverso: Gilberto Freyre e o Projeto UNESCO." *Tempo Social*, 11, no. 1 (1999): 111–36.
Maio, Marcos Chor, and Ricardo Ventura Santos, eds. *Raça como questão: história, ciência e identidades no Brasil.* Rio de Janeiro: Fiocruz, 2010.
Matos, Patricia Ferraz de. "Power and Identity: The Exhibition of Human Beings in the Portuguese Great Exhibitions." *Identities* 21, no. 2 (2013): 202–18.
Miller, Nicholas B. "Trading Sovereignty and Labour: Migration and the Consular Network of Nineteenth-Century Hawai'i." *International History Review* (forthcoming).
Pallares-Burke, Maria Lúcia G. *O triunfo do fracasso: Rüdiger Bilden, o amigo esquecido de Gilberto Freyre.* São Paulo: Editora Unesp, 2012.
Porteus, Stanley David, and Marjorie E. Babcock. *Temperament and Race.* Boston: R. G. Badger, 1926.
Roll, Elvira Osório. *Hawaiian Kohala Breezes.* New York: Exposition Press, 1964.
Schwarcz, Lilia Moritz. 1993. *O espetáculo das raças: Cientistas, instituições e pensamento racial no Brasil—1870–1930.* Sao Paulo: Companhia das Letras.
Silva, Reinaldo. "From the Top of the Racial Pyramid in Hawai'i: Demonizing the Hawai'ian Portuguese in Elvira Osorio Roll's Fiction." *Interdisciplinary Journal of Portuguese Diaspora Studies* 2 (2013): 7–31.
Taft, Donald R. *Criminology.* New York: Macmillan, 1942.
——. *Human Migration: A Study of International Movements.* New York: Ronald Press, 1936.
——. *Two Portuguese Communities in New England.* New York: Longman, Green & Co., 1923.
Takaki, Ronald. *Pau Hana: Plantation life and Labor in Hawaii 1835–1920.* Honolulu: University of Hawaii Press, 1983.
Tranquada, Jim, and John King. *The 'Ukulele: A History.* Honolulu: University of Hawaii Press, 2012.

CHAPTER 11

Being Goan (Modern) in Zanzibar
Mobility, Relationality, and the Stitching of Race

Pamila Gupta

This chapter addresses the interstitial spaces that diasporic Goans occupied in Zanzibar as a way to think through (and as a lens onto) ideas of Lusophone racial difference and race relations in an unexpected place, one that is less marked by a history of Portuguese colonialism. The writings of Engseng Ho and Thomas Metcalf on diaspora and webs of empire across the Indian Ocean form a starting point for tracing a very different history of itinerant Goans as operating within an "interimperial" world following the work of the historian Laura Doyle, one that connects Lusophone India and Zanzibar (a historic center of global trade, former British Protectorate and Omani Sultanate) in interesting ways through time and space, past and present. I next take lessons from Luso-tropicalism, suggesting that the Goan Zanzibari case works against Gilberto Freyre's exceptionalism and highlights several contradictions imbedded in his theories of nonracialism for the Portuguese colonial world. Rather, the category of "Goan" was always relational (considered under the umbrella of "Indian" alongside yet distinct from the diasporic Parsi and Gujarati) and was very much connected to an ability to harness Portugueseness (and Roman Catholicism) as signifiers of their community's civility and modernity. Being Goan in Zanzibar was also intimately tied to certain professions: tailoring, photography, retail, and baking. That mobile Goans were able to stitch race (to adopt a fitting metaphor of tailoring) in dynamic ways in cosmopolitan Stone Town (1950s to present) becomes the focus of my discussion, one that reads a visual archive ethnographically. Interestingly, these global Goans chose Zanzibar as a place to improve their lives and livelihoods precisely because it was *not* tied to their colonial pasts (a register of their discontent), yet at the same time, they actively self-fashioned their Portugueseness to do the work of adornment. This case study enables a perspective on Luso-tropicalism from the vantage point of its frayed seams.

Interimperiality in the Indian Ocean

> To grasp the conflicts of the national or transnational, we therefore need to study the legacies of this multiply inter-imperial history.[1]

Over the past ten years, there has been a shift toward studying minority diasporas caught within and between larger imperial networks; the focus is on horizontal mobilities within the Indian Ocean world rather than on vertical movements between colony and metropole. Here I briefly trace the writings of Ho, Metcalf, and Doyle in expanding this area of scholarship, opening up additional seams and folds that contribute to my understanding of the Goan Zanzibari community under analysis here.

In his innovative book *The Graves of Tarim* (2006), the anthropologist Engseng Ho has developed the concept of "local cosmopolitans" in relation to a lesser-known Hadrami diaspora, a group whose origins were in Yemen but were dispersed over many centuries across the Indian Ocean due to religion and politics. In the face of such mobility, they were able to maintain relations between the near and far over the *longue durée*.[2] Ho's case study splits open the binaries between homeland and host, local and global; he opens up the world of Indian Ocean diaspora to an exciting set of new research possibilities, wherein community members remain "itinerant across the oceanic space."[3] Moreover, "discourses of mobility" define them in their everyday diasporic lives, always mindful of those who left—"the society of the absent," as Ho describes them, even as they have chosen to stay behind.[4]

In his groundbreaking *Imperial Connections* (2007), historian Thomas Metcalf introduces the idea of imperial umbrellas, wherein diasporas operated within and across colonial territories that spanned continents. His case study, one that focuses on Indian diasporas caught between British India and British East Africa during the early twentieth century suggests that there was much horizontal movement within the Indian Ocean world, not only by those in power—a topic in itself that requires more study—but equally by colonial subjects who sought better colonial conditions for themselves, just as they took advantage of these "webs of empire" to do so. These Indian diasporas were able to fashion new identities for themselves in these new African contexts; they conceived of themselves less strictly as subjects of British colonial rule but rather as worldly "imperial citizens,"[5] the act of travel enabling and empowering them, in much the same way that Ho describes how discourses of mobility became part of the Hadrami way of seeing themselves. Metcalf's work adds yet another building block to imperial diaspora studies and helps position the working lives for a different set of diasporic mobilities that go beyond the scope of his study and point to far more complex historical patterns of migration. My focus here is on a diasporic case study that originates in

Portuguese India but then moves to British East Africa via imperial networks made available to them through Portuguese India's proximity and relationship to British India during the late nineteenth and early twentieth centuries. As we will come to see, this Catholic Goan diaspora very much perceived of themselves as imperial citizens, markers of their Portuguese past defining them in what was then a British protectorate and Omani Arab Sultanate.

With the particularities of the Goan Zanzibari case study in mind, Laura Doyle's intriguing study "Inter-imperiality: Dialectics in a Postcolonial World" (2014) proves most useful. She adds yet another (finishing) layer to the ideas of Ho and Metcalf. Here I offer it as the central framing device for looking more closely at this unusual Goan diasporic case. Doyle first defines inter-imperiality: "[it] names a political and historical set of conditions created by the violent histories of plural interacting empires and by interacting persons moving between and against empires." Adopting such a framework allows us to more fully understand the "dialectics of empires" that is at stake in writing new world histories. In other words, historians (and anthropologists alike, I would add) can no longer write the history (or ethnography) of one empire in isolation; rather, the entanglements through time and space of multiple empires should be gathered together to constitute this burgeoning field of study: "When we consider the "connected history" of states in all hemispheres (to use Sanjay Subrahmanyam's phrase), we begin to see more clearly the complex, multi-directional manoeuvres launched from above, from below and from beside, by imperialists, merchants, capitalists, labourers, wives and revolutionaries."[6] For Doyle, interimperiality is both theory and method, and one that I adopt here fully.[7] I do so to showcase a minority Indian community that historically crossed and sometimes even crisscrossed empires (Portuguese and British, in India and Africa), with a large portion of Goan Zanzibaris returning to Goa after the 1964 Zanzibar Revolution, which saw its integration alongside Tanganyika into the independent nation-state of Tanzania. Doyle's concept of interimperiality also proves useful for grasping the complex subjectivities of this group of Goans on the move, a diasporic group consisting not only of merchants, capitalists, laborers, and wives but also, and particular to the Zanzibar case, tailors, photographers, retailers, and bakers.

I argue, then, that the Goan imperial citizens examined here interpolate (and interpret) their "Goanness" in a variety of manners in this interimperial context, taking on a multitude of identities in the process: they are simultaneously Indian, African, Asian, East African, Zanzibari, Portuguese, British, and European, each embracing all, some, or none of these categories (both present and absent) of Goanness. Moreover, identity markers of race and class will be inflected in certain ways for this diasporic community, suggesting the elasticity of these markers in the act of travel, and the specific historical contexts to which they arrived and carved out lives and livelihoods.

Lessons from Luso-tropicalism

> It is as if in each tropical land peppered with even one drop of Portuguese blood or animated by a single splash of Portuguese culture there was a land predisposed to the blooming of that Lusotropical complex of civilization.[8]

Between August 1951 and February 1952, Gilberto Freyre traveled through Portugal, Cape Verde, Guinea, Angola, Mozambique, and Goa, after which he formulated his ideas on Luso-tropicalism.[9] The point of his worldly *tournée* was to look for himself at Portuguese colonialism in the making in a range of tropical settings in Asia and mostly Africa, confirming that it was indeed "good to think." Caio Simões de Araújo succinctly sums up Luso-tropicalism as "the idea that it was possible to generate, in the tropics, a civilization of European origin that nevertheless integrated and harmonized into itself cultures and peoples different from its own without compromising its modern outlook."[10] Freyre's theory would later be taken up by the Salazar's *Estado Novo* regime as a strategic means to an end, or rather a means to delaying the end of empire. My focus in this chapter is less on its history of ideas but rather to take three lessons from Luso-tropicalism, using the Goan Zanzibari case to do so. I first ask what happens when we apply Freyre's theory of Luso-tropicalism to other places and peoples: how do his ideas travel to different parts of the world, and in this case, to that of a Goan diaspora living outside a Portuguese colonial context? Next I point to what Cristiana Bastos has argued for Goa, that it was the "official cradle of formulation of Lusotropicalism,"[11] which makes this particular case of traveling Goans so interesting for exposing the fault lines of Luso-tropicalism.

Lesson 1

If Goa was at the epicenter of Freyre's imagined ideal of Luso-tropicalism, then why is there such a long history of Goans leaving Goa for elsewhere over the *longue durée*? Why would Catholic Goans choose to leave Goa not to live in another Portuguese colony (like Mozambique, for example, which in some ways confirms Freyre's ideas of Portuguese colonial exceptionalism) but rather to employ interimperial networks to first travel from Portuguese India to British India and then onto British East Africa? I suggest that these Goans chose a place like Zanzibar precisely because it was not Portuguese, which suggests that Goa was less than the harmonious utopia that Freyre visited and imagined. Freyre's idea of Portuguese colonialism as "good to think" did not translate easily into "good to live" for many Goans, which in turn suggests their racialization precisely within the bounds of Portuguese imperialism and their choice to live outside its confines.[12]

Lesson 2

I would argue that the Goan Zanzibaris took the "social plasticity" that Freyre applied strictly to Portuguese colonizers[13] as they traveled to new sites and fully embraced it in such a way to shape their livelihoods (and importantly, prosper) in a context outside Portuguese colonial influence. Could we argue that the "social plasticity" that he advocates for the Portuguese was instead taken up by the colonized, such as by certain middle-class Goans in surprising ways, so as to turn Freyre's theory on its head in practice? And to show up what the Portuguese had not anticipated for those under their colonial domination, that they would take this plasticity, or what we could also call adaptability, and make it their own (and use it agentively, we could say) and purposely in a context outside Portuguese colonial purview?

Lesson 3

Global Goans in Zanzibar were able to separate race and civilization from each other in dynamic ways that go beyond what Freyre had conceptualized for the Portuguese.[14] On the one hand, the act of travel across the Indian Ocean "unfixed" their racialization as "Goan" within a strict Portuguese colonial world.[15] Instead, they became "Indian" alongside other minority communities, the Parsi and the Gujarati, in a place as diverse as Zanzibar. On the other hand, they always maintained their distinctiveness by way of their Catholic Goanness and turned it into a relational category, one that did not prevent them from fashioning their Portugueseness as an adornment, a sign of their European modernity and civility that in turn shaped their professional lives. That all this took place in a British Protectorate and Omani Sultanate also shows how they rerouted Freyre's ideas to an Anglo-Saxon context and reinforces the ways in which they were able to take up categories of race and civilization and transform them into cultural traits.[16]

Goans on the Move to Zanzibar

> But the stories of these "in-between" [Goan] people remain to be told. Their "in-betweenness" took several forms—in-between the Portuguese and British (and sometimes the German) Empires; in-between Africans and Europeans; in-between Africa and Asia.[17]

More generally, Goan diasporas have remained understudied as a subject of historical and ethnographic research. My focus in this chapter is on Goan migrations that took place from the late 1800s onward, when they emigrated in larger numbers within Portuguese and British imperial umbrellas and for reasons of lifestyle choices of religion, culture, and language.[18] However, in this section, I briefly trace the longer history of their movements and migrations.

Goans have been moving to East Africa via the Indian Ocean since the sixteenth century, their in-between status being a defining feature of their diasporic lives. The few early studies of Catholic Goans living in British East Africa showcase them as minority communities operating within larger national(ist) histories. They were usually positioned together with other Asian and Indian migrants as "stranger communities"—or "the hyphen between Africans and Europeans," as the sociologist Jessica Kuper described them as early as 1979—despite the fact that they were a distinct religious group with their own cultural patterns of migration that were tied to Portuguese colonial efforts to convert them to Roman Catholicism. Kuper was the first to make a case for the uniqueness and separateness of the Goan community living in 1970s Uganda from other Indian diasporic communities who were most often Hindus or Muslims coming from British India. According to Kuper, these Ugandan Goans—largely working-class clerks, cooks. and tailors by profession—regarded themselves as "culturally European" rather than Indian, partly because of their inherited Portuguese Catholic pasts.[19] They also tended to see themselves as different from all other immigrant "Asians," kept to themselves within Ugandan society, and maintained stronger ties with their homeland of Goa than these other diasporic groups—a detail that reinforced their limited access and the difficulty of their study.

More recently, the multiple and diverse Goan diasporas of East Africa have become subjects of study in their own right. The sociologist Margret Frenz has completed an exhaustive overview of several Catholic Goan communities living in East Africa (Uganda, Kenya, Tanganyika, Zanzibar) that is to be commended for its breadth and scope. She tells the tale of their fascinating state of in-betweenness[20]—a story of migration that is generally characterized as involving what the anthropologist Marta Rosales calls the "better-positions groups."[21] These Goans tended to come from Goa's educated Catholic population, as opposed to its more oppressed Hindu population that was less likely (or able) to emigrate as colonial subjects under Portuguese rule. As Rochelle Pinto argues, and as we will come to see for this particular group, the Catholic Goans were often "placed to enjoy the social and political position of creole equivalents wherever they were located."[22]

According to data provided by Frenz in her fine-tuned study of global Goans, Goans constituted a startling 10 percent of the resident Indian population of East Africa after 1860. By the 1950s, approximately thirty thousand Goans were settled in East Africa and living between Kenya, Uganda, Zanzibar, and Tanganyika.[23] These figures suggest that Goan diasporas played decisive historical roles in East Africa, which in turn suggests a need for additional in-depth studies of localized Goan communities in order to trace the contours of their similarities and differences across these four countries. I also argue that ethnographic and cultural studies methods (specifically, a focus on the medium of photography, since many Goans in East Africa took up this trade) are useful for mapping these little-known littoral Indian Ocean zones and enrich diaspora studies more generally in the Global South—one that could gesture to the multiple Goan diasporas of Brazil that remain understudied and would offer a potentially interesting point of comparison.

The Goan Zanzibari diaspora that I explore in this chapter was purposely less interested in operating within a Portuguese world of language, religion, and culture such as the Goan Mozambican diaspora that I have extensively written about elsewhere and served as the impetus for sparking my interest in the study of such a markedly different Goan diaspora.[24] These Goans, as middle-class immigrants, chose Zanzibar precisely because it was *not* tied to their colonial pasts, even if they were largely (and inescapably) marked by their Portugueseness and Roman Catholicism, both operating as signs of their civility and modernity in a particularly multicultural setting. Relying on Indian Ocean circuits to live instead both as "local cosmopolitans" (following Ho) and British "imperial citizens" (following Metcalf), they looked to (British) India and East Africa as potential places for improving their lives and livelihoods, with Zanzibar being the most attractive place to stop and settle because of its cosmopolitanism, hybridity, and multitude of ethnic groups living easily side by side.[25] Frenz tells us that Zanzibar in particular was seen as a "magnet" for Indians (including Goans) more generally.[26] This group of "global Goans" took advantage of Zanzibaris' worldliness to make certain choices: they were largely business-minded, interested in a range of professions and in setting up shops for retail, tailoring, baking, and photography[27]—skills that they had acquired from their Portuguese colonizers and purposely took up and adapted in these new places when they saw the need for such specialty professions.

With regard to the case study here, I suggest that Frenz's excellent historical and sociological has been pioneering in putting the Goans of East Africa on the map of diaspora studies. However, the Goans of Zanzibar remain understudied because of their marginalization for a set of reasons having to do with their interimperial patterns of migration and Zanzibar itself. Included in this history is a pattern of multiple Indian diasporic communities (Parsi, Gujarati, and Goan) living side by side and a state revolution (1964) that foresaw the mass migration of many of these same minority Goans to mainland Tanzania, back to Goa, or onto Canada or the United Kingdom as the Omani Sultan was overthrown and Zanzibar became united with Tanganyika to become the nation-state of Tanzania. That the Goan community of Zanzibar has dwindled significantly in size since its apogee in the 1950s and 1960s—a shadow of what it once was—makes its history that much harder to access today. Here I suggest that adopting a visual and ethnographic lens offers a productive way to access experiences of diasporic living for a Goan Zanzibari community that is largely a "society of the absent."[28]

Six Goan Zanzibari Portraits

> When we begin to think inter-imperially, we . . . can glimpse the ways that literary and artistic forms have long mediated these struggles within a larger circuit of several empires, sounding intertextual notes to which we have been deaf.[29]

The Goans of Zanzibar tell an alternate diasporic story, one that I am very much attuned to by way of Doyle's call to think interimperially. I also take up her cue to look at artistic forms specifically as a way to access these "intertextual" subjectivities that we have yet to explore fully as historians and anthropologists. In this section, I fashion a set of portraits of Goan Zanzibaris, relying on the visual archive of Ranchhod Oza, a Gujarati immigrant to Zanzibar who opened his own photography studio in Stone Town in 1930 before adding my own two portraits by way of a concluding discussion. I purposely consider (the taking of) this first set of images by Oza as "acts of portraiture" even as they are of both people and things, which in my mind equally provide a landscape of Zanzibari Goanness. Fittingly named Capital Art Studio (CAS), Oza documented the worldliness of this dynamic community during the 1950s; it was very much part of his larger practice of running a busy photography studio and producing scenic postcards, activities that contributed to Zanzibar's position as a burgeoning center of Indian Ocean mobility and trade during this time period.[30]

It is also significant to note that when Oza arrived in the port of Zanzibar with a keen interest in photography, he entered a well-established Goan world of photographers. Oza's son, Rohit, tells me that his father's apprenticeship was with a Goan photographer named A. C. Gomes; it lasted for five years before he decided to open up his own studio. Gomes was just one of several photographers operating in and around Stone Town. Frenz also documents the history of Goan photography in Zanzibar, detailing that it was A. P. de Lord who was the first to set up shop, followed by E. C. Dias, Gomes, and finally the Coutinho brothers.[31] Interestingly, Gomes's studio in Zanzibar (established around 1868) was an offshoot of his first studio on the Kenyan coast.[32] This historical detail reflects three important aspects of this East African Goan diaspora: (1) members of this global community often traveled between or had strong ties (familial and or work related) to different port cities in the Indian Ocean; (2) middle-class Goans played a significant role in developing the first photography studios all along the East African littoral;[33] (3) the Goan diaspora has contributed a large archive of visual cultures, both of themselves and of daily life in different East African port cities.

With this rich history of Goan photographers serving as a backdrop, I now return to Ranchhod Oza's archive and his documentation of this same community. I discovered, however, that images of Goanness are not easily retrievable from this archive for reasons having to do with the son's relationship with the collection, and Zanzibar's particular history. First, (Ramesh) Rohit Oza has a complicated relationship with his father's photographic legacy. He took over running the studio in the early 1980s after his father's retirement, and more fully after his death in 1993. He still runs Capital Art Studio today and very much restricts access to his father's images, including which photographs to reprint, put on display, or even mention to researchers like me. Second, because of the tumultuous nature of the 1964 Zanzibar Revolution, the CAS collection is also not well preserved, precisely because negatives and images were lost, destroyed, or taken with as people hurriedly departed Stone Town for elsewhere.

When I first asked Rohit about the whereabouts of certain photographs of global Goans taken by his father, he said no section of Oza images was dedicated to this subject matter; rather, the subject is dispersed in much the same way that the Goan diaspora of Zanzibar is today. Even as his response made logical sense to me at the time, I could also see that Rohit was not interested in pursuing the topic on my behalf; again, his personal investments shaped what kinds of images he deemed worthy of discussion. I was fortunate in that a handful of Goan prints exist in the archive and I was able to gather a few myself, based on my two visits to CAS in 2012 and 2015. Thus, it was more by happenstance that I came across certain images of Goanness, which also reflects the serendipitous nature of ethnographic research. Lastly, the nature of my access to these (photographed) Goans is also reflective of the nature of their status and role within Stone Town itself, as an integrated but also atomized community within Zanzibari port city life.

Acts 1 and 2

A set of two images that I located in the Oza archives are of Stone Town's busy streets; both include placards of Goan businesses, the familiar CAS embossing in the lower edges of the photographs confirming that they were indeed taken by Oza. Rohit supplies additional information, telling me that his father most likely took them during the 1950s. The first image features the Goan (Portuguese) name Isidore I. Dias, the proprietor of a general store. The second features the Goan (Portuguese) name S. R. Faleiro, a specialist in "high-class tailoring and outfitting." I read these placards as standing in for Goanness for several reasons: their prominence on Stone Town's busiest streets suggests the importance and thriving nature of these Goan businesses. That numerous bicycles (markers of urbanity and modernity themselves) are propped up beneath both placards suggests the ease with which customers frequented these equally modern Goan shops either to buy something, perhaps a specialty Goan pastry, or get a new, fashionable dress made. That the streets beneath the placards show a diversity of persons (of religion, of dress, of generational difference) suggests

Figure 11.1. General stores of Isidore I. Dias, circa 1950s. Photograph by Ranchhod Oza. Courtesy of Capital Art Studio, Stone Town, Zanzibar.

how much these Goans shops permeated everyday life in Stone Town. Finally, that Oza sought to capture these placards of Goanness on film confirms them as acts of portraiture. These images contain what the anthropologist Liam Buckley considers moments of "grace" captured on film by Oza.[34]

Here I return to Frenz's study for filling in the backdrops to these images. She confirms Rohit's likely dating of these two photographs, noting that by

Figure 11.2. Tailoring and outfitting, S. R. Faleiro, circa 1950s. Photograph by Ranchhod Oza. Courtesy of Capital Art Studio, Stone Town, Zanzibar.

the 1950s some thirty to forty Goan tailors had established workshops along the main shopping roads of Zanzibar, "dotting" the landscape.[35] Specifically, these Goan tailors specialized in sewing outfits for ladies and gents,[36] just as Faleiro's placard states. Frenz also writes that while many of these traveling Goans "came from families with a tradition of certain activities [such as photography], others seem to have developed the necessary skills after they identified opportunities that opened up in a new location."[37] Hers is an important point for locating the Goan community specific to Zanzibar. The Goans filled particular niches in Zanzibari society (not only as photographers but, as we see in these two images, also as tailors and retailers) both because they saw an economic opportunity and because these professions were markers of them being modern, as arbiters or brokers of worldliness in the cosmopolitan place that was Zanzibar during the 1950s.[38] Interestingly, the Goans filled the ranks of these "specialty sectors of commerce" to such an extent that they came to be named "Goan" not only in Zanzibar but across East Africa more generally.[39] Lastly, I suggest that these two Zanzibari landscapes of things serve as portraits of Goanness in much the same way that individuals are able to.

Acts 3 and 4

I now turn to two images taken by Oza of this vibrant Goan diaspora that first made me think about Goanness in Zanzibar, past and present, and initially led me to pursue the topic more generally. That the Goans had their own distinct histories of migration and diasporic imaginaries meant that they too relied on culture, including its visual representation through photography to preserve their sense of self for themselves but also most likely for Goan members of the "society of the absent" located in Zanzibar, East Africa, and elsewhere.[40] I first glimpsed these rare images of resplendent Goanness by chance. During a moment when Rohit started to feel more comfortable with me and my many questions on the last day of that first visit to his studio in 2012, he finally let me wander into the back room, a space normally restricted from public view except for those who would have sat for a formal portrait, a practice that rarely took place during the studio days that I witnessed. These two images were located on a nondescript sidewall in the back room, a space that any customer would have normally overlooked in their haste to be seated in front of an all-encompassing backdrop. These portraits became emblazoned in my memory, but I had to wait until my second visit three years later to ask Rohit's permission to take my own photographs of his father's photographs on display. I took them rather nervously and hastily, both because I had been waiting so long in anticipation to take them and because I wanted to do so before he changed his mind.

Being Goan (Modern) in Zanzibar | 277

Figure 11.3. Newlyweds, Capital Art Studio, circa 1950s. Photograph by Ranchhod Oza. Courtesy of Capital Art Studio, Stone Town, Zanzibar.

These black-and-white photographs capture two different Goan wedding celebrations. The first one I see hanging on the wall is a portrait of a bride and groom, arms appropriately entwined; they are both smiling tentatively for the camera. He has a handkerchief tucked into a pocket. She wears a lacy veil and white gloves. A fancy purse is perched on her other (free) arm. Their sartorial styles suggest that it is the 1950s. I look at their shining eyes and wonder if they are about to be married or if they stopped by the studio after Catholic Mass to have Oza take their photograph. The portrait has been taken at CAS; I can confirm this detail from the familiar black-and-white checkered pattern of the backdrop flooring that I see in front of me now. The edges of the print on all sides are extremely frayed, which in turn suggests that the photograph has been hanging on that same spot on the wall for quite some time.

The second photograph is also of a Goan bride and groom—only in this image, the couple is surrounded by what look like family members in a classic wedding-party-style portrait. From their sartorial style, I estimate that Oza also took this photograph in the 1950s. I can confirm the location of the ceremony from a recognizable Greek statue in the backdrop: the front steps of St. Joseph's Cathedral in Stone Town, built during the late nineteenth century by

278 | Pamila Gupta

Figure 11.4. Wedding party, steps of St. Joseph's Cathedral, circa 1950s. Photograph by Ranchhod Oza. Courtesy of Capital Art Studio, Stone Town, Zanzibar.

French missionaries to Zanzibar and still in existence today. In the front row, I see three flower girls in flouncy dresses wearing simple crowns, surrounded by garlands of flowers. One such girl, who appears older than the other two, wears spectacles. The young ring bearer boy seems shy in front of Oza's camera lens.

While the bride and groom look stiff but happy on their special day, I home in on the expressions of the best man and maid of honor; they seem more at ease, proud to be there and to have witnessed this momentous event. I wonder what future this newlywed couple is contemplating together as their photograph is being taken. Like the first image, this second one is also worn thin, frayed at the edges with white spots eating away at the print. Yet, its lacy frame hints at its earlier pride of place. Now it looks poorly tacked on as a sample advertisement for wedding photographs, the label CAPITAL ART STUDIO featuring prominently above the wedding image with the following caption:

Proprietor R. T. Oza
Specialist PORTRAITURE & CHILDREN PHOTOGRAPHY INDOOR
AND OUTDOOR ZANZIBAR VIEW CARDS ETC.

It seems reasonable to suggest that Oza captured something in this image (that I was also drawn to) so much so that he used it at one point to draw other Zanzibaris to his studio to have their portraits taken. These two images of Goanness also show the vibrancy of a middle-class diaspora in their cultural practices. Specifically, these two acts of portraiture showcase two different Catholic Goan newlyweds; they also serve as fragments of a rich culture on display. Material markers such as the veil, gloves, and purse of the first bride, and the suits, ties, Greek statue, and flouncy dresses of the flower girls at the second couple's wedding, function as signs of this diaspora's civility and modernity that had come to be associated with and stand in for "Goan" in some sense, due to their inherited Portuguese European Catholic pasts.

Once again, Frenz fills in these wedding portraits with her study of global Goans, suggesting that social institutions such as the social club, church, and school had defining roles in constituting and reproducing a Goan diasporic community identity in East Africa, with the Goan Institute established in Zanzibar in 1904.[41] These few extant photographs also attest to the importance of social markers and gatherings in reproducing Goanness for generations to come. They also say so much about being Goan in Zanzibar—their middle-class position as local cosmopolitans (following Ho), arbiters of modernity and civility by way of their professions of tailoring and photography (and baking, which has not been featured in the photographs here); the role that Catholicism and ritual events (here, weddings) had in contributing to their sense of community and its successful reproduction; their ability to live as a minority Indian community alongside Parsi and Gujarati Hindus and Muslims as imperial citizens (following Metcalf) in a metropolitan place like Zanzibar; and finally, their ability to live as a dynamic diaspora that is attentive to cultural distinctiveness but that can also live comfortably in difference.

However, that there is little left in Zanzibar today of this once vibrant Goan community—in the aftermath of the Revolution, they were racialized as Indian (alongside the Parsi and Gujarati), as not having a defined place (and properties) in the new Afro-Shirazi state[42]—suggests the importance of these precious images. These two remaining photographs pinned on Oza's studio walls thus become markers of a meaningful and historically rich Goan past. I would like to think that reprints of these same images were not left behind but rather lovingly placed inside suitcases if and when these two sets of newlyweds left Zanzibar. I also contemplate their material futures and hope that they are well preserved in a photo album somewhere else (the United Kingdom, Canada, or perhaps back to Goa), and gazed upon frequently by future generations of Goans.

Acts 5 and 6

In a last act of portraiture, I would like gather up the seams of this dynamic diaspora by turning to two contemporary Goan Zanzibaris whom I met during my research visits in 2012 and 2015. I rely on their imaginaries of past and present in order fill in the spaces of rupture that took place with the Revolution and that left in its wake a very small but resilient community, its future generations continuing certain patterns of history. I also offer my own two (photographic) portraits of these two talented photographers.

John Da Silva is a Goan Zanzibari photographer, watercolor artist, and photo collector who grew up across the street from CAS. Several other Goans had told me I should meet him, so in 2012 I knocked on his door various times and was asked each time to come back later before I was finally able to sit down with the elderly man in his charming studio-cum-living-space for our interview. John proudly tells me that his father, a tailor, had been given the prestigious task of sewing the dress that Princess Margaret wore during an official British Royal visit to Zanzibar in 1956.[43] Growing up in Stone Town, John's passions were painting and photography, pursuing the latter as a career, first as photojournalist and then as an avid collector of Zanzibari postcards in the wake of the Revolution as a means for preserving Zanzibar's visual past.

I met Robin Batista on this same research visit to Zanzibar in 2012 and visited him again in 2015. He is a thirty-something Goan Zanzibari who studied photography in Goa before returning home to Stone Town to start his own business. His photography studio and shop is hard to miss, as it is located on a main road in the popular tourist circuit. Robin sells postcards of iconic Zanzibari views, as well as large prints (mostly black and white) of his own photographs of contemporary Zanzibar. We strike up a conversation while his elderly father, Miguel, sits next to him.[44] I learn that his father was also once a tailor, repeating the patterned history of father and son, tailor and photographer, that seems to circulate in Zanzibar. In an intriguing essay, Buckley has

Being Goan (Modern) in Zanzibar | 281

Figure 11.5. John Da Silva, 2012. Photograph by Pamila Gupta.

explored the relational quality of tailors and photographers, suggesting that they are of "the same category of adornment work." He points out that both professions practice "an aesthetic based on techniques aimed at appropriately presenting the surfaces and edges of the depicted person."[45] Buckley's analysis is equally fascinating (on its own) and fitting (here), for I see a similar occurrence in Zanzibar, but it is specifically generational in this case, one where the camera becomes the "scissors for seeing" by the son.[46]

In the wake of the Revolution, the Da Silvas and the Batistas are two of the few remaining Goan families who stayed after 1964, despite the fact that little space was left for Indian minority communities (not only the Goans but also the Parsi and Gujarati), many of whom would make difficult life choices (of race and class) to emigrate. I have purposely fashioned into a series of acts of portraiture these extant photographs (four in total) of people and things from the Oza collection that I was able to retrieve. Together, they stand in for Goan Zanzibariness precisely because Goans were either materially positioned as part of Zanzibar's landscape, as in the two street scene photographs, or centrally featured, as in the two wedding photographs I came across on the back walls of CAS. I would also like to suggest that "Goan" (as simultaneously Indian and European) was equally an important marker of Zanzibar's cosmopolitanism during the 1950s. Meanwhile, I have fashioned my own acts of portraiture of

Figure 11.6. Robin Batista, 2015. Photograph by Pamila Gupta.

two Goan photographers whom I met during the course of my research visits to Zanzibar in 2012 and 2015. John Da Silva and Robin Batista both carry a similar worldly sense of self but one that has added folds and layers—an ability to look outward to an Indian Ocean world in a manner similar to their ancestors but also now to a rapidly changing African Tanzanian society.

From the Frayed Seams of Luso-tropicalism

The Goan diasporic community of Zanzibar that is historically, visually, and ethnographically showcased here might be productively used to expose the increasingly frayed seams of Freyre's ideas of Luso-tropicalism. That global Goans have consistently been on the move from Goa, taking advantage of interimperial networks (Doyle) to live as imperial citizens (Metcalf) and local cosmopolitans (Ho) in a setting outside the confines of Portuguese colonialism first registers a sign of their discontent with Freyre's ideas that were perhaps less than ideal for living and working. That these Goans adopted the social plasticity assigned to their Portuguese colonizers and made it their own in a new setting such as Zanzibar also makes us rethink the applicability of Freyre in both time and space. Finally, that these Goans were able to unfix race and play up their civilizational qualities in the act of traveling across the Indian Ocean upends some of Freyre's rigid categories. Instead, they were simultaneously Indian and Portuguese, modern and European, and lived in worldly place that was Zanzibar.

The Goans profiled by the historian Margret Frenz, photographed by Ranchhod Oza during the 1950s, and interviewed by me—Da Silva and Batista—on my recent visits to Zanzibar together suggest an active middle-class community that was very much entrenched in daily port city. They historically fit in Zanzibar precisely because, as a British Protectorate and Omani Sultanate, it welcomed difference (and were seen simultaneously as European, because of their Portuguese pasts, and as Indian living easily alongside other similar minority groups). It also shows how race operated less significantly in this context; rather, their civilizational traits, as Portuguese, modern, and European, served and suited them better and became their professional markers (as tailors, bakers, retailers, and photographers) of being Goan Zanzibari. Yet, significantly and perhaps ironically, race as a marker of identity (as Indian or Asian, and *not* African) was placed onto them by newly elected Afro-Shirazi state officials and compelled many Goans to move from Zanzibar in the wake of the Revolution. Departing Goans from this setting would soon get caught up in alternative markers of race and class as they carved out spaces for themselves in other settings, and produced different subjectivities along the way, but that is another story of Luso-tropicalism and its discontents.

PAMILA GUPTA is Associate Professor at the Wits Institute for Social and Economic Research at the University of Witwatersrand. She holds a PhD in sociocultural anthropology from Columbia University. She writes about Lusophone India and Africa, Portuguese colonial and missionary history, decolonization, heritage tourism, visual cultures, and islands in the Indian Ocean. She has published in the *South African Historical Journal, African Studies*, the *Journal of Asian and African Studies, Ler História, Ecologie & Politique*, and *Public Culture*. She is the coeditor of *Eyes Across the Water: Navigating the Indian Ocean* (2010) and the author of *The Relic State: St. Francis Xavier and the Politics of Ritual in Portuguese India* (2014), and *Portuguese Decolonization in the Indian Ocean World: History and Ethnography* (2019).

Notes

The images featured in this chapter are reproduced with kind permission from (Ramesh) Rohit Oza, the current proprietor of Capital Art Studio, Stone Town, Zanzibar. My impressions of Ranchhod and Rohit Oza (father and son, the latter whom we met) and the history of Capital Art Studio are based on interviews and information gathered during two field trips to Stone Town with Meg Samuelson, 16–22 October 2012 and 14–21 July 2015. I thank John Da Silva for his generosity in sharing his life history and his insights on Zanzibar, showing us his impressive Zanzibar postcard collection that he amassed mostly overseas, and taking the time to meet with us at his home in Stone Town on 18 October 2012. He passed away in 2013.

1. Laura Doyle, "Inter-imperiality: Dialectics in a Postcolonial World," *Interventions* 16, no. 2 (2014): 161.
2. Engseng Ho, *The Graves of Tarim: Genealogy and Mobility Across the Indian Ocean* (Berkeley, 2006), 31.
3. Ibid., 189.
4. Ibid., 19.
5. Thomas Metcalf, *Imperial Connections: India in the Indian Ocean Arena, 1860–1920* (Berkeley, CA, 2007), 2. The shift from "colonial subject" to "imperial citizen" opened up a whole new world of possibilities, of different kinds of positionalities within rigid colonial hierarchies as with the Goan Zanzibari case discussed here.
6. Doyle, "Inter-imperiality," 160, 161, 163.
7. Ibid., 160–61.
8. Gilberto Freyre, *Um Brasileiro em terras portuguesas* (Rio de Janeiro: 1953), 182–83.
9. Caio Simões de Araújo, "Diplomacy of Blood and Fire: Portuguese Decolonization and the Race Question, ca. 1945–1968" (PhD diss., Graduate Institute International and Development Studies, 2017), 70.
10. Ibid., 77.
11. Cristiana Bastos, "Aventura e rotina: Um livro de meio de percurso revisitado," in *Gilberto Freyre: Novas Leituras do Outro Lado do Atlântico*, ed. Marcos Cardão and Cláudia Castelo (São Paulo: 2015), 41.
12. On the idea that Goans were primarily racialized through their circulation in the Portuguese empire, see Rochelle Pinto, *Between Empires: Print and Politics in Goa* (Oxford, 2007), 16–21.
13. Gilberto Freyre, *The Masters and the Slaves: A Study in the Development of Brazilian Civilization*, 2nd ed., trans. Samuel Putnam (Berkeley, CA, 1986), 14, first published as *Casa-grande & senzala: Formação da família brasileira sob o regímen de economia patriarchal* (Rio de Janeiro, 1933).
14. Ibid., 96.
15. Rochelle Pinto, "Race and Imperial Loss: Accounts of East Africa in Goa," *South African Historical Journal* 57, no. 1 (2007): 88.
16. Freyre, *The Masters and the Slaves*, 96. That these Goans managed to keep separate race and civilization in a place under British colonial influence (as a Protectorate) goes against Freyre's view that categories of race and civilization were imbricated in each other in strictly Anglo-Saxon colonial contexts (such as South Africa) while separate in Portuguese colonial contexts.
17. Margaret Frenz, *Community, Memory, and Migration in a Globalizing World: The Goan Experience, c. 1890–1980* (New Delhi, 2014), 2.
18. Ibid., 47–91.
19. Jessica Kuper, "'Goan' and 'Asian' in Uganda: An Analysis of Racial Identity and Cul-

tural Categories" in *Strangers in African Societies*, ed. William A. Shack and Elliott P. Skinner (Berkeley, CA, 1979), 243, 258.
20. Frenz, *Community, Memory, and Migration*, 1–46.
21. Marta Vilar Rosales, "'Our Lady of Carmo is the Patroness of our Family': Migration, Religion and Belonging of Portuguese-Goan Brahmans Converted to Catholicism," in *Migration and Religion in Europe: Comparative Perspectives on South Asian Experiences*, ed. Ester Gallo (London, 2014), 197.
22. Pinto, "Race and Imperial Loss," 88.
23. Margret Frenz, "Transimperial Connections: East African Goan Perspectives on 'Goa 1961,'" *Contemporary South Asia* 22, no. 3 (2014): 242.
24. See my writings on two distinct Goan communities in Mozambique. Pamila Gupta, "The Disquieting of History: Portuguese (De)colonization and Goan Migration in the Indian Ocean," *Journal of Asian and African Studies* 44, no. 1 (2009): 19–48; Pamila Gupta, "Some (Not So) Lost Aquatic Traditions: Goans Going Fishing in the Indian Ocean," *Interventions* 16, no. 6 (2014): 854–76.
25. Margret Frenz "Global Goans: Migration Movements and Identity in a Historical Perspective," *Lusotopie* 15, no. 1 (2008): 188.
26. Frenz, "Transimperial Connections" 242.
27. Frenz, *Community, Memory and Migration*, 98.
28. Ho, *The Graves of Tarim*, 19.
29. Doyle, "Inter-imperiality," 163.
30. See Abdul Sheriff, *Dhow Culture of the Indian Ocean: Cosmopolitanism, Commerce and Islam* (New York, 2010); William Bissell, *Urban Design, Chaos and Colonial Power* (Bloomington, IN, 2011).
31. Frenz, *Community, Memory and Migration*, 102–3.
32. Erin Haney, *Photography and Africa* (London: 2010), 49–51.
33. Frenz, *Community, Memory and Migration*, 102–3.
34. Liam Buckley, "Studio Photography and the Aesthetics of Citizenship in the Gambia, West Africa," in *Sensible Objects: Colonialism, Museums and Material Culture*, ed. Elizabeth Edwards, Chris Gosden, and Ruth Phillips (Oxford: 2006), 61–86.
35. Frenz, *Community, Memory and Migration*, 98, 100.
36. Frenz, "Global Goans," 189.
37. Frenz, *Community, Memory and Migration*, 102.
38. Frenz, "Transimperial Connections," 242. She provides a population estimate of seven hundred Goans living in Zanzibar for the year 1948 and states that these numbers increased greatly from the 1950s onward.
39. Frenz, *Community, Memory and Migration*, 109.
40. Ho, *The Graves of Tarim*, 19.
41. Frenz, "Global Goans," 191.
42. Abdul Sheriff, "Race and Class in the Politics of Zanzibar," *Africa Spectrum* 36, no. 3 (2002): 301–18.
43. Frenz, *Community, Memory and Migration*, 101. She interviewed one Goan Zanzibari named Stephen whose family members specialized in tailoring dresses for the royal family.
44. I thank Robin Batista and his father, Miguel Batista, for taking the time to meet and discuss with me their thoughts on the present-day Goan community of Zanzibar. Interviews in Stone Town, Zanzibar on 18 October 2012 and 15 July 2015.
45. Liam Buckley, "Self and Accessory in Gambian Studio Photography," *Visual Anthropology Review* 16, no. 2 (2000–2001): 81.
46. Ibid., 72.

Bibliography

Bastos, Cristiana, "Aventura e rotina: Um livro de meio de percurso revisitado." In *Gilberto Freyre: Novas Leituras do Outro Lado do Atlântico*, edited by Marcos Cardão and Cláudia Castelo, 35–48. São Paulo: Editora da Universidade de São Paulo, 2015.

Bissell, William. *Urban Design, Chaos and Colonial Power in Zanzibar.* Bloomington: Indiana University Press, 2011.

Buckley, Liam. "Self and Accessory in Gambian Studio Photography." *Visual Anthropology Review* 16, no. 2 (2000–2001): 71–91.

———. "Studio Photography and the Aesthetics of Citizenship in The Gambia, West Africa." In *Sensible Objects: Colonialism, Museums and Material Culture*, edited by Elizabeth Edwards, Chris Gosden, and Ruth Phillips, 61–86. Oxford: Berg, 2006.

Doyle, Laura. "Inter-imperiality: Dialectics in a Postcolonial World," *Interventions* 16, no. 2 (2014): 159–96.

Frenz, Margret. *Community, Memory, and Migration in a Globalizing World: The Goan Experience, c. 1890–1980.* Oxford: Oxford University Press, 2014.

———. "Global Goans: Migration Movements and Identity in a Historical Perspective," *Lusotopie* 15, no. 1 (2008): 183–202.

———. "Transimperial Connections: East African Goan Perspectives on "Goa 1961,"" *Contemporary South Asia* 22, no. 3 (2014): 240–54.

Freyre, Gilberto. *The Masters and the Slaves: A Study in the Development of Brazilian Civilization.* 2nd ed. Translated by Samuel Putnam. Berkeley: University of California Press, 1986. First published 1933 as *Casa-grande & senzala: Formação da família brasileira sob o regímen de economia patriarchal* by Editora Maia & Schmidt (Rio de Janeiro).

———. *Um Brasileiro em terras portuguesas.* Rio de Janeiro: José Olympio, 1953.

Gupta, Pamila. "Some (Not So) Lost Aquatic Traditions: Goans Going Fishing in the Indian Ocean." *Interventions* 16, no. 6 (2014): 854–76.

———. "The Disquieting of History: Portuguese (De)colonization and Goan Migration in the Indian Ocean." *Journal of Asian and African Studies* 44, no. 1 (2009): 19–48.

Haney, Erin. *Photography and Africa.* London: Reaktion Books, 2010.

Ho, Engseng. *The Graves of Tarim: Genealogy and Mobility Across the Indian Ocean.* Berkeley: University of California Press, 2006.

Kuper, Jessica. "'Goan' and 'Asian' in Uganda: An Analysis of Racial Identity and Cultural Categories." In *Strangers in African Societies*, edited by William A. Shack and Elliott P. Skinner, 234–59. Berkeley: University of California Press, 1979.

Metcalf, Thomas. 2007. *Imperial Connections: India in the Indian Ocean Arena, 1860–1920.* Berkeley: University of California Press.

Pinto, Rochelle. *Between Empires: Print and Politics in Goa.* Oxford: Oxford University Press, 2007.

———. "Race and Imperial Loss: Accounts of East Africa in Goa." *South African Historical Journal* 57, no. 1 (2007): 82–92.

Rosales, Marta Vilar. "'Our Lady of Carmo is the Patroness of our Family': Migration, Religion and Belonging of Portuguese-Goan Brahmans Converted to Catholicism." In *Migration and Religion in Europe: Comparative Perspectives on South Asian Experiences*, edited by Ester Gallo, 193–209. London: Routledge, 2014.

Sheriff, Abdul. *Dhow Culture of the Indian Ocean: Cosmopolitanism, Commerce and Islam.* New York: Columbia University Press, 2010.

———. "Race and Class in the Politics of Zanzibar." *Africa Spectrum* 36, no. 3 (2002): 301–18.

Simões de Araújo, Caio. "Diplomacy of Blood and Fire: Portuguese Decolonization and the Race Question, ca. 1945–1968." PhD dissertation, Graduate Institute of International and Development Studies, 2017.

Afterword I
Mixing the Global Color Palette

Nélia Dias

From the 2016 discussions among this book's contributors in Rio de Janeiro under the heading "Racial Conceptions in the Twentieth Century: Comparisons, Connections, and Circulations in the Portuguese-Speaking Global South" to the present book, *Luso-tropicalism and Its Discontents: The Making and the Unmaking of Racial Exceptionalism,* there is a discernable thematic continuity but also a rethinking of the theoretical framework. In Rio de Janeiro, a major concern of contributors was to address the distinctive nature and scope of Southern ideas about human variation. "Portuguese-speaking Global South" entailed somehow the existence of a transnational community as a place of knowledge making, sharing theories, concepts, research tools and practices, and hence a circulation of ideas and methodologies within this community. The eclectic array of authors being analyzed, the diverse disciplinary backgrounds (medicine, physical anthropology, psychiatry, genetics, and endocrinology), and the wide assortment of methodological practices precluded any attempt to grasp a community of practice or even a community of research. Because of the extreme variety of agents, epistemic practices, and methodologies, it was quite problematic to ascertain whence the "racial conceptions" stemmed: were they in medicine, in anthropology, in colonial policy, or in public culture? In addition, "Global South" was not without equivocation; as Warwick Anderson points out, it "is a productively ambiguous term; the true extent of it—what it encompasses—depends on historical legacies and patterns, on political dispensations and economic exploitation, not geographical pedantry."[1] Thus, the focus on "Luso-tropicalism" and on Gilberto Freyre's thought provided a common ground for analyzing the variety of racial conceptions and for highlighting comparisons, connections, and dissensions within the Portuguese-speaking world.

In this collection, Luso-tropicalism is envisioned as a concept, theory, and political project, although, in Freyre's thought, these three aspects emerged separately in distinctive historical periods (Castelo, this volume). "Luso-tropicalism" has never had a single meaning and has covered a range of subjects. Moreover, it is embedded in geographical and historical settings taken within the Lusophone world's distinct political and social configurations, as the chapters in this book have demonstrated. Though Freyre's theories are given, implicitly or explicitly, preeminence throughout the book, other ideas such as those expressed by António Augusto Mendes Correia, António de Almeida, Francisco M. Salzano, Alberto Germano da Silva Correia, and Renato Kehl, to name a few, are also discussed. Thus, writing an afterword entails raising the inevitable question aptly formulated by Vincent Crapanzano: "Whose words are these others' words? Those of the authors of the texts that precede the Afterword? Those of the authors of the texts ... they claim to represent ... paraphrase, comment on, elucidate, situate, or explain?"[2]

One may also wonder, which Freyre is being discussed throughout this book? Is it the author of *Casa-grande & senzala*, the advocate of Luso-tropicalism, or the source of inspiration for anti-racist UNESCO policies? As several chapters in this book point out, there were contrasting readings of Freyre's work throughout the 1950s; the authors have been setting forth findings that offer a less simple and less obviously ideological way of understanding the complexities of Freyre's thought, one that escapes the flaws shared by both "pro-" and "anti-Freyre." Far from being in contradiction, these divergent readings in the postwar period reveal the ways in which appreciation for Freyre's work was indebted to wider political discussions about national identity, cultural relativism, and the principle of unity of humankind. To add a layer to the complexities and intricacies of Freyre's work, let's turn to a non-Lusophone context, the French one.

The French translation of *Casa-grande & senzala* in 1952 under the title *Maîtres et esclaves* (similar to the English title), twenty years after the original publication and based on the fourth Brazilian edition, provides for three main reasons a good example of how a book's destiny is strongly dependent on national and intellectual contexts. First, the translator was the renowned French sociologist Roger Bastide, a specialist in Afro-Brazilian religions. Second, the famous French historian Lucien Febvre, cofounder of the journal *Annales: Économies, Sociétés, Civilisations,* wrote the preface.[3] Third, although Freyre's book was published by the distinguished Éditions Gallimard, it came out in a collection (*La Croix du sud*) devoted to Latin American literature, created in 1951 by the literary critic and sociologist Roger Caillois, cofounder of the Collège de Sociologie. Freyre's book was listed in the collection along with French translations of Jorge Amado, Jorge Luis Borges, Alejo Carpentier, and Ernesto Sabato. That three preeminent French intellectuals such as Bastide, Caillois, and Febvre were so deeply engaged with Freyre's book in the 1950s is far from being insignificant; it attests to the ways in which Freyre's ideas were appropriated, publicized, and disseminated in the French academy mostly among sociologists and historians.

The choice of Febvre to write the preface for *Maîtres et esclaves* was not random. As the French historian acknowledged, Freyre himself made this request. It is worth noting that Febvre was the coauthor along with a young historian, François Crouzet, of a small textbook, *Nous sommes des sang-mêlés: Manuel d'histoire de la civilisation française* (We are mixed-bloods: A manual on the history of French civilization),[4] presumably written in 1950; the book was commissioned by Otto Klineberg in the wake of several textbooks edited by UNESCO on race and racism but for unknown reasons never came out until 2012 (Maio, this volume).[5] In the "Notice to the Reader," the two authors point out that the book should serve as a model for how one could adapt history to the goals of "men of peace and goodwill who conceive humanity as a large family of united peoples" rather than "as a racial battlefield."[6] As the book's title clearly indicates, Febvre and Crouzet's goal was to demonstrate, on the one hand, that French civilization was the result of a historical process of mixing diverse civilizations and of mingling peoples. By pointing out the role played by miscegenation of *métissage* in French civilization, the authors made a distinction between nation and civilization: the latter was not and should not be exclusive to a single people. This assumption was undoubtedly a way of questioning the privilege allocated to Western civilization, considered the only one worthy of the name. On the other hand, Febvre and Crouzet emphasized that the French people developed through a long process of borrowing from other peoples and that, far from being a "pure race," were mixed and remixed products of thousands of years of heterogeneous alliances.[7] To sum up, French people were of mixed blood, and that constituted a real advantage.

In the light of this textbook, it is possible to understand why Febvre was a passionate if not an uncritical admirer of *Casa-grande & senzala*. Brazil represented for Febvre "a magnificent ethnic experience throughout history," and Brazilian history "a privileged experience of racial fusion and of exchanges of civilizations."[8] Febvre completely endorsed Freyre's perception of Brazil as a racially mixed country and of race mixture—more precisely, the "intimacy of the mixture" as expressed in the interracial sex—as a positive aspect.[9] Without denying the violence of the colonial encounter, the French historian praised Freyre's bravery addressing topics such as racism, sexuality, and slavery. Foremost, what interested Febvre in particular were the historical and sociological approaches of Brazilian history and the ways in which Freyre highlighted the "surprising accumulation of peoples, races, and civilizations."[10] In 1953, Febvre reiterated his admiration for *Casa-grande & senzala*, this time by writing a short book review for the *Annales*.[11] That he also wrote the book's preface did not seem, to the French historian, incompatible or to raise a potential conflict of interest.

Febvre's appraisal of *Casa-grande & senzala* and his positive perception of mixed-race Brazilian identity needs to be contextualized within the École des Annales movement on the one hand and the defense of humanistic universalism in the aftermath of World War II on the other.[12] In 1943, Fernand Braudel devoted a long and laudatory article to Freyre's books; by paying particular attention to the small details of everyday life and more specifically to material culture, Freyre was, according to Braudel, accomplishing a remarkable work of sociology and social history.[13] The use of "history" in Braudel's book review and in Febvre's preface, as well as their emphasis on Freyre's historical approach, is significant.[14] Freyre's literary vein, use of family anecdote, and vivid depictions did not detract from, according to the two French historians, the historical dimension of his work. What connected literature and history was precisely that they, to use Arnaldo Momigliano's words regarding Benedetto Croce, "expressed' individual facts."[15] Bastide also highlighted these literary qualities in his article on Caillois's Latin American literature collection at Gallimard; in this essay, published in the *Annales,* Bastide pointed out the close relationships between literature and sociology and the ways in which Freyre managed to introduce Proustian literary devices in sociology.[16] As for humanistic universalism, it was grounded on the assumption of the world as made up of different, but ostensibly equal, racial types and cultures. The commonality of humanity did not entail the acknowledgment of European civilization as the only one worthy of that name and thus as a necessary "common good for all peoples."[17] This defense of cultural relativism did not encompass the rejection of the very notion of race.

It has been common to present the decline of racial science in Europe and the United States in the aftermath of the World War II and the displacement of hierarchical conceptions of race in favor of more plural and cultural conceptions of difference. This "teleological narrative," based on the assumption that the culture concept came to officially replace or stand in for race, has been recently scrutinized and criticized; Anderson points out: "It should make us question, for example, whether the conventional explanation of the decline of racial thought in science in the 1940s and 1950s needs review and amendment."[18] A wealth of new studies, based on new sources and innovative approaches, has deepened our knowledge and understandings about the role of race in anthropology, notably in American anthropology characterized by the coexistence of racial essentialism and cultural relativism. Far from being in contradiction, "the somatic emphasis of racial anthropology," argues Tracy Teslow, "did not preclude anthropologists from also understanding race in cultural and historical terms."[19]

This same mixture of cultural, linguistic, and somatic criteria presided to the anthropobiological mission to Angola conducted by Almeida in the 1950s (Coghe, this volume). It is not irrelevant that Almeida, during his fieldwork in Angola, embraced the measurement techniques and the anthropometric instruments recommended by the French anthropologist Henri Vallois, an expert on the Bushmen and the author of "Les races de l'empire français" (1939–1940) and *Les races humaines* (1944).[20] Secretary of the Societé d'Anthropologie de Paris and editor of the journal *L'anthropologie* since 1938, Vallois replaced the anti-fascist Paul Rivet as director of the Paris Musée de l'Homme in 1941. Vallois appointed the colonial physician Léon Pales as deputy director of the Musée de l'Homme from 1943 to 1945, at the time when France was under the Pétain regime. As the head of health services in the colonial army, Pales conducted an anthropological mission in what was known as Afrique Occidentale Française, that is, French West Africa, from 1945 to 1947; he made more than seven hundred thousand measurements on ten thousand colonial subjects in order to set up a "comparative raciology of French West African populations."[21] That Pales's inquiries included topics such as alimentation, nutrition, muscular strength, and height is not surprising; these studies of the human body's constitution differentiated according to race had an obvious utility in the management and exploitation of colonial labor. It was important for colonial administrators to have precise knowledge of which groups were stronger, better nourished, or best suited for work or for the army, elements that informed national policies regarding Indigenous peoples. That the 1950s colonial anthropological missions pursued and reenacted "a nationalist and racialist tradition" in "an anti-racist and Luso-tropical era" (Roque, this volume) attests to the ways in which different and apparently contradictory theoretical approaches coexisted within the Portuguese-speaking world.

Contrasting views of miscegenation also appeared according to their sites of enunciation. Miscegenation, as it developed since the late nineteenth century as an analytic framework, was, far from being a homogeneous and monolithic body of knowledge, more open to pluralist interpretations. Freyre illustrates one facet of the miscegenation discourse, which reframes racial mixing as a positive thing (Castelo, this volume). The anthropological discourse on Bushmen as "the surviving remnants of a distinct, aboriginal, and dying race" (Coghe, this volume) exemplifies the other facet: that of miscegenation as equated with the disappearance of race and cultural assimilation. In addition, miscegenation was a crucial issue in the legal and administrative spheres.

Race was used as a category for counting people in censuses and for constructing policies and strategies to maintain forms of subordination—and thus for establishing discriminatory practices of regulation between governors and governed (Bastos, Coghe, this volume). As Ian Hacking notes, "classification of peoples by a category of race is an integral part of the control necessary to organize and maintain an empire, and it employs pollution rules."[22] The issue of miscegenation and the juridical, political, and scientific debates about the legal status of *mestiço* (Roque, this volume) reflected the anxieties about blurring the boundaries between Europeans and Indigenous peoples and the fear of interracial sex. The *mestiço* was a sensitive issue for colonial administration, scientists, and politicians because it embodied the continuous debates about the definition and diversity of legal categories (*assimilado* and *indígena*) and their constant shifts (Macagno, this volume); thus, the debates on *mestiçagem* highlight the contradictions of the colonial regime, namely a fundamental one, according to Ann Stoler—"a tension between a form of domination simultaneously predicated on both incorporation and distancing."[23]

The *mestiço* issue was also of the utmost importance for defining "whiteness" according to a wide range of criteria with physical features at the top. The one-drop rule epitomizes those anxieties so well depicted recently by Tony Morrison in her beautiful and poignant essay "The Color Fetish."[24] Along with race, skin color was a major criterion of difference deployed both for promoting racial mixture and for privileging whiteness; the racialization of skin color as expressed in the use of race-color terms perpetuated the practices of distinction making. In his preface to *Casa-grande & senzala,* Febvre referred to skin color—the white, the black, and the reddish brown—as an indicator of the three main races inhabiting Brazil.[25] The color palette going from reddish brown to pinkish white denoted not merely shades of skin color but also shades of soul (*nuances d'âme*). That this close relationship between skin color and psychological attributes conveyed racist undertones did not seem problematic to the French historian. Recent scholarly analysis shows that race-color issues have always been embedded within wider political discussions about economic inequality and social hierarchies.[26]

One of the arenas where the process of constituting racial difference conflated with the process of racialization of color was undoubtedly the museums and exhibition spaces. What was the role of exhibiting difference? How was race represented to the public? What was the place of racial science in professional and popular discourse? Why was the process of constituting racial difference associated with the ways in which it was visualized? Visual epistemic practices, notably visual displays of physical anthropology collections, were so central to racial theory that a history of race science should include a material history of scientific practices. It is not irrelevant that the anti-racist campaigns were also based on visual sources. *The Races of Mankind,* a thirty-one-page pamphlet published by Ruth Benedict and Gene Weltfish in 1943, was subsequently "translated" into visual forms, first as an exhibition—displayed at the Cranbrook Institute of Science (located in a suburb of Detroit) and as a traveling exhibition all around the United States, and then as a brief animated film and a short illustrated book.[27]

Understanding the role of race in the Portuguese-speaking world, which several of the chapters in this book have explored, must also take into account the reciprocal relations of anthropologies at home and away. Anthropologists such as Mendes Correia were concerned with the racial constitution of both the Portuguese metropolitan population and the colonial population; the technological devices for conducting anthropological measurements were applied to both groups, and the methodological precepts conceived for the study of non-European peoples provided the template for applying anthropology in the management of the metropolitan population. In other words, we must articulate the tasks of colonial administration and those of social management at home, and explore how anthropology, along with other scientific disciplines, is governmentally deployed to bring changes in the conduct of specific populations. How were *mestiços* perceived in Lisbon, and what was their legal status? How were color-line policies materialized in everyday metropolitan practices? To articulate the anthropology at home with the anthropology abroad may highlight the evasiveness and complexities of colonial discourses and practices, as well as the diversity of colonial situations.

The contributions in this volume aimed to question the assumption that racial mixing in former Portuguese colonies in particular and in Portuguese-speaking countries in general was unique, to the extent that it constituted an "exceptional" trait. They have demonstrated how the so-called specificity or exceptionality was a means of justifying the presumed benign aspects of Portuguese colonization. By exploring the "making and unmaking of racial exceptionalism," the chapters demonstrate there was hardly anything distinctive about Portuguese race mixing. Yet, Luso-tropicalism had a profound effect on race relations discernible in current racial disparities. Thinking about Luso-tropicalist legacies of racial domination in ways that are still evident today while avoiding the "fallacy of the leapfrogging legacy" constitutes a most demanding task.[28]

NÉLIA DIAS is Associate Professor in the Department of Anthropology at the Instituto Universitário de Lisboa and Researcher at Centro em Rede de Investigação em Antropologia. Her research concerns nineteenth-century history of French anthropology, ethnographic museums and collecting practices, cultural history, and epistemology. She is the author of *Le musée d'ethnographie du Trocadéro (1878–1908): Anthropologie et muséologie en France* (1991) and *La mesure des sens: Les anthropologues et le corps humain* (2004) and the co-editor of *Endangerment, Biodiversity and Culture* (2016) and *Collecting, Ordering, Governing: Anthropology, Museums and Liberal Government* (2017). Her articles have appeared in a wide range of periodicals including *History and Anthropology, Histoire de l'Art, Social Anthropology, Nuncius,* and *Museum and Society*. She received a PhD in modern and contemporary history from EHESS and a BA in anthropology from Paris V.

Notes

1. Warwick Anderson, "Racial Conceptions in the Global South," *Isis* 105, no. 4 (2014): 783.
2. Vincent Crapanzano, "Afterword," in *Modernist Anthropology: From Fieldwork to Text,* ed. Marc Manganaro (Princeton, NJ, 1990), 300.
3. Gilberto Freyre, *Maîtres et esclaves,* trans. Roger Bastide, preface by Lucien Febvre (Paris, 1952), first published as *Casa-grande & senzala: Formação da família brasileira sob o regímen de economia patriarchal* (Rio de Janeiro, 1933).
4. Lucien Febvre and François Crouzet, *Nous sommes des sang-mêlés: Manuel d'histoire de la civilisation française* (Paris, 2012).
5. Michele Brattain, "Race, Racism, and Antiracism: UNESCO and the Politics of Presenting Science to the Postwar Public," *American Historical Review* 112, no. 5 (2007): 1386–413.
6. Febvre and Crouzet, *Nous sommes des sang-mêlés,* 17–18. According to the "Notice to the Reader," Febvre wrote the first part of the book and supervised the entire volume.
7. Ibid., 42–44.
8. Lucien Febvre, "Préface: Brésil, terre d'histoire," in *Maîtres et esclaves* (Paris, 1952), 19.
9. Ibid., 15.
10. Ibid., 12.
11. Lucien Febvre, "Compte rendu: Gilberto Freyre, *Maîtres et esclaves,*" *Annales: Économies, Sociétés, Civilisations* 8, no. 3 (1953): 409–10.
12. Peter Burke, "Gilberto Freyre e a *nova história,*" *Tempo Social* 9, no. 2 (1997): 3–4
13. Fernand Braudel, "À travers un continent d'histoire: Le Brésil et l'oeuvre de Gilberto Freyre," *Mélanges d'Histoire Sociale* 4 (1943): 3–20.
14. Febvre deplored the French title, *Maîtres et esclaves,* more suitable as "a good title for a Russian novel of the 1900s." Febvre, "Préface," 9. *Casa-grande & senzala* would be republished by Gallimard in 1974 in the famous series "Bibliothèque des Histoires" with a new subtitle: *La formation de la société brésilienne.*
15. Arnaldo Momigliano, *Essays in Ancient and Modern Historiography* (Oxford, 1977), 356.
16. Roger Bastide, "Sous 'La Croix du Sud': L'Amérique latine dans le mirroir de sa littérature," *Annales: Économies, Sociétés, Civilisations* 13, no. 1 (1958): 40–41.
17. Febvre, "Préface," 18.
18. Anderson, "Racial Conceptions in the Global South," 791.
19. Tracy Teslow, *Constructing Race: The Science of Bodies and Cultures in American Anthropology* (New York, 2014), 4.
20. Henri Vallois, "Les races de l'empire français," *La Presse Médicale* (1939–1940); Henri Vallois, *Les races humaines* (Paris, 1944). *Les races humaines*—published in the famous series "Que sais-je?—was constantly reedited and went to its seventh edition in 1967.
21. On Léon Pales, see Denise Ferembach, "Léon Pales," *Bulletin et Mémoires de la Société d'Anthropologie de Paris* 5, no. 4 (1988): 297–300.
22. Ian Hacking, "Why Race Still Matters," *Daedalus* 134, no. 1 (2005): 115.
23. Ann Stoler, "Sexual Affronts and Racial Frontiers: European Identities and the Cultural Politics of Exclusion in Colonial Southeast Asia," *Comparative Studies in Society and History* 34, no. 3 (1992): 517.
24. Tony Morrison, "The Color Fetish," in *The Origin of Others* (Cambridge, MA, 2017), 41–54.
25. Febvre, "Préface," 12.

26. Christina A. Sue, *Land of the Cosmic Race: Race Mixture, Racism, and Blackness in Mexico* (New York, 2013).
27. Teslow, *Constructing Race*, 228–83.
28. Frederick Cooper, *Colonialism in Question: Theory, Knowledge, History* (Berkeley, CA, 2005), 17–18.

Bibliography

Anderson, Warwick. "Racial Conceptions in the Global South." *Isis* 105, no. 4 (2014): 782–92.
Bastide, Roger. "Sous 'La Croix du Sud': L'Amérique latine dans le mirroir de sa littérature." *Annales: Économies, Sociétés, Civilisations* 13, no. 1 (1958): 30–46
Brattain, Michele. "Race, Racism, and Antiracism: UNESCO and the Politics of Presenting Science to the Postwar Public." *American Historical Review* 112, no. 5 (2007): 1386–413.
Braudel, Fernand. "À travers un continent d'histoire: Le Brésil et l'oeuvre de Gilberto Freyre." *Mélanges d'Histoire Sociale* 4 (1943): 3–20.
Burke, Peter. "Gilberto Freyre e a *nova história*." *Tempo Social* 9, no. 2 (1997): 1–12.
Cooper, Frederick. *Colonialism in Question: Theory, Knowledge, History*. Berkeley: University of California Press, 2005.
Crapanzano, Vincent. "Afterword." In *Modernist Anthropology: From Fieldwork to Text*, edited by Marc Manganaro, 300–8. Princeton, NJ: Princeton University Press, 1990.
Febvre, Lucien. "Compte rendu: Gilberto Freyre, *Maîtres et esclaves*." *Annales: Économies, Sociétés, Civilisations* 8, no. 3 (1953): 409–10.
———. "Préface: Brésil, terre d'histoire." In Freyre, *Maîtres et Esclaves*, 9–21.
Febvre, Lucien, and François Crouzet. *Nous sommes des sang-mêlés: Manuel d'histoire de la civilisation française*. Paris: Éditions Albin Michel, 2012.
Ferembach, Denise. "Léon Pales." *Bulletin et Mémoires de la Société d'Anthropologie de Paris* 5, no. 4 (1988): 297–300.
Freyre, Gilberto. *Maîtres et esclaves*. Translated by Roger Bastide. Preface by Lucien Febvre. Paris: Éditions Gallimard, 1952. First published 1933 as *Casa-grande & senzala: Formação da família brasileira sob o regímen de economia patriarchal* by Editora Maia & Schmidt (Rio de Janeiro).
Hacking, Ian. "Why Race Still Matters." *Daedalus* 134, no. 1 (2005): 102–16.
Momigliano, Arnaldo. *Essays in Ancient and Modern Historiography*. Oxford: Blackwell, 1977.
Morrison, Tony. "The Color Fetish." In *The Origin of Others*, 41–54. Cambridge, MA: Harvard University Press, 2017.
Stoler, Ann. "Sexual Affronts and Racial Frontiers: European Identities and the Cultural Politics of Exclusion in Colonial Southeast Asia." *Comparative Studies in Society and History* 34, no. 3 (1992): 514–51.
Sue, Christina A. *Land of the Cosmic Race: Race Mixture, Racism, and Blackness in Mexico*. New York: Oxford University Press, 2013.
Teslow, Tracy. *Constructing Race: The Science of Bodies and Cultures in American Anthropology*. New York: Cambridge University Press, 2014.
Vallois, Henri Victor. "Les races de l'empire français." *La Presse Médicale* (1939–1940).
———. *Les races humaines*. Paris: Presses Universitaires de France, 1944.

Afterword II
Luso-tropicalism and Mixture in the Latin American Context

Peter Wade

Luso-tropicalism is based on the idea that Portuguese colonizers tended to adapt to their colonial habitats by mixing with the colonized women and that, "in all places where this kind of colonization dominated, racial prejudice appears as insignificant."[1] "Race mixture" is thus fundamental to Luso-tropicalism, and it is no surprise that the concept emerges from Brazil, where processes of mixture between Europeans, Africans, and Indigenous peoples led to *mestiços* forming a good third of the population during the late colonial period. As the chapters in this volume show, intellectuals and nation builders have made much of Brazilian *mestiçagem* as constituting a possible form of racial exceptionalism, conceivably extendable to other areas of the Lusophone world. Yet, it is worth bearing in mind the wider Latin American context, in which many similar claims and debates concerning *mestizaje* have been made: this helps to relativize claims about Brazil's exceptionalism (as does Coghe's argument that Lusophone science in and on Angola was more linked into transnational currents of scientific thought than into some national or imperial network).

The Duality of Mixture in Latin America

There is a long tradition of claims made about the democratic potential of *mestizaje*. In New Granada (today's Colombia) in 1861, the writer and political leader José María Samper claimed, "This marvelous work of the mixture of races . . . should produce a wholly democratic society, a race of republicans, representatives simultaneously of Europe, Africa, and Colombia, and which gives the New World its particular character."[2] Later, another Colombian politician and writer, Luis López de Mesa, in a book on the formation of the Colombian nation said that Colombians were "Africa, America, Asia, and Europe all at once, without grave spiritual perturbation" and that the country was no longer "the old democracy of equal citizenship only for a conquistador minority, but a complete one, without distinctions of class or lineage."[3] In a speech to a 1920 conference in Bogotá on the question of race in Colombia, one contributor, Jorge Bejarano, explicitly linked mixture and democracy: "What is the result of this variety of races? Politically [it is] the advent of a democracy, because it is proven that the promiscuity of races, in which the element socially considered inferior predominates, results in the reign of democracies."[4]

Better known than these Colombian intellectuals is the Mexican politician and intellectual José Vasconcelos and his ideas about *la raza cósmica,* a future world-dominating race, prefigured in the Ibero-American mestizo, who was heir to "the equality of all men by natural right [and] the social and civic equality of whites, blacks, and *indios,*" which had been declared by the leaders of the independent republics of Latin America. In so doing, they had, in Vasconcelos's view, initiated the "transcendental mission assigned to that region of the globe: the mission of uniting [all] people ethnically and spiritually."[5] Around the same time, Mexico's foreign ministry commented on a 1927 decree banning labor immigration from the Middle East, denying that this was evidence of "any racial or class prejudice, all the more because the great Mexican family comes from the crossing of distinct races."[6]

In more recent times, we can find a similar tendency to link mixture to democratic outcomes, specifically the erosion of racial hierarchy and racism—although it bears noting that the claims made above often include the erosion of class hierarchies too. For example, the mass immigration of Latin Americans (not to mention Asians) to the United States and the rise of a US-born Latino population is claimed to have led to the "browning" of the nation, unsettling the black-white binary that is held to underpin US racial hierarchies.[7] Over 40 percent of Hispanics ticked the "other race" box on recent census forms.[8] Famously, the poet and activist Gloria Anzaldúa associated *mestizaje* with the possibility of breaking down social hierarchies, and this link is explicit or implicit in much cultural theory about "hybridity."[9] At a more symbolic level, associations are commonly made between *latinidad* as a way of being and thinking, said to be typical of Latin American and Latino people, and a kind of cosmopolitan sensibility that welcomes diversity, openness, and tolerance—including of racial difference.[10] Finally, recent scientific data about the genetic mixture of Latin American national populations has, in some cases, been used to promote the idea of these nations as essentially mixed and thus more or less—or *potentially*—untroubled by racism, except perhaps at the margins, or at least unsuited to the introduction of policies that rely on clear racial identifications, such as race-based affirmative actions.[11]

The persistent association between mixture and the erosion of hierarchy, if not actual democracy, is somewhat perplexing in view of the equally persistent evidence that racism and racial hierarchy can easily coexist with claims about the democratic effects of mixture. Samper, while vaunting *mestizaje* in the abstract, characterized the black boatmen who transported him up and down the Magdalena River as only semi-human, despite being mixed—or rather, precisely because they were mixed; López de Mesa believed black and Indigenous Colombians had "impoverished blood and inferior cultures" and that their mixture was deleterious.[12] Vasconcelos notoriously said black people were a "lower type" of the species who would only be able to "redeem themselves ... through voluntary extinction, [as] the uglier breeds will gradually give way to the more beautiful."[13] All over Latin America, immigration officials routinely excluded black, Asian, and Jewish people, whether explicitly or in secret, all the while claiming to be nonracist.[14] While the United States may be browning to some extent, there is plenty of evidence that racialized appearance (e.g., skin tone) hierarchizes life chances among "brown" people.[15] Critiques are legion of dangers lurking behind the romanticization of hybridity.[16]

It is important to note at this point that racial mixture always figures as a biocultural process. While it may now be routinely assumed that discourse about "race" has, especially since World War II, shifted register from the biological to the cultural, Samper in the 1860s and López de Mesa and Vasconcelos in the 1920s and 1930s were all talking about biology and culture (or "civilization"), while Vimieiro-Gomes notes in this volume that biotypologists in the 1930s saw the environment as one element in the development of the biological body. In the same way, postwar invocations of *mestizaje* and *mestiçagem* (and hybridity), which cast them as cultural processes, are not at all free from ideas about bodies, blood, heredity, and even genes: sex and kinship remain, in an important sense, the model for thinking about culture—without this necessarily implying a kind of biological determinism or essentialism.[17]

This tension between claims about democratic mixing and those about racism may seem to be a conflict between ideology and reality, between the top-down imposition of an image or mask and the bottom-up experience of everyday life. Undoubtedly, many claims about the democratic effects of mixing are ideological. But why do they persist? I believe it is because mixture—in Latin America and doubtless elsewhere—is *partly* a reality, an everyday aspect of many people's lives and experiences. More than just a mask, it is a complex reality that can be read in different ways. It is made up of acts and meanings that can be articulated in different ways—in the double sense of articulation as expression and connection, which Stuart Hall highlights.[18] The same set of acts can be seen in contradictory ways, such that the same mixture can be seen as both reproducing hierarchy and overcoming it. A multiracial family is simultaneously a site in which racial difference is *both* undermined and blurred through acts of care and kinship between social equals *and* reproduced and reenacted through the differential valorization of lighter and darker family members, which obeys an ethic of whitening.[19]

In this sense, it is not accurate to counterpose "mixture" to "racism," because racism and nonracism are both immanent in mixture as a process. This is because, in *mestizaje*, the process of mixture does not entirely erase the origins, the ingredients, of the mix; the original "purities" are persistently there as a (symbolic) trace in the mixed outcome. It is thus always possible to reenact the hierarchies that ordered and still order those "original" ingredients. This is a particular instance of a broader tension between equality and inequality in liberal societies. Equality is proclaimed as an ideal, and some policies are enacted that tend in that direction by offering equality of opportunity. Meanwhile, the political economy's division of labor demands inequality, and the same policies institutionalize this by not fully addressing inequalities of outcome. Equality requires mixing and sharing between hierarchized elements (classes, genders, racialized groups, etc.), but every mixing or desegregation does not erase the origins of the elements being mixed, especially in the short term. Meanwhile, these origins are continuously reproduced in "pure" form by the divisions of labor required by the political economy.

Mixture and Duality in the Lusophone World

With this in mind, we can explore ideas of mixture in Lusophone thought, and especially Luso-tropicalism, as they appear in the chapters of this book. Bastos's contribution shows, among other things, that racial conceptions about the Portuguese themselves differed between Gilberto Freyre and Alberto Germano da Silva Correia. The former saw the Portuguese as mixed, in terms of contemporary racial understandings about Southern Europeans; Freyre built on this to underpin his ideas about the proclivity of Portuguese colonizers to mix, thus engendering (literally) less racial hierarchy. Correia seems opposed to Freyre, in his emphasis on hierarchy, endogamy, purity, and segregation. This is presented as a (contradictory) coexistence of mixture and racism, although this was inflected by a common challenge to Anglo-American views of the Portuguese as mixed and therefore inferior. Maio's chapter reinforces this sense of contradiction by demonstrating that, from the late 1940s, Freyre's work was criticized for overemphasizing mixture and its democratic effects. One critic wrote in 1947 that Freyre inclined too far toward favoring Brazil's black and brown people, presenting them as if they were the true Brazilian archetype; in fact, according to this critic, Brazil inclined more toward whiteness. Others criticized him for presenting Pernambuco as if it were typical of Brazil: the implied critique was that the supposed lack of racial prejudice that Freyre identified in his home region was not characteristic of other parts of the country. In different ways, these critics all highlighted the presence of racial hierarchy and thus seemed opposed to Freyre's position. However, as Dávila shows us in merciless detail, Freyre's own emphasis on mixture was *itself* structured by the same hierarchies invoked by Correia's and Freyre's critics—and implied by Anglo-American views. The "opposition" between Freyre and the others is an example of the way racism and nonracism are both immanent in mixture as a process.

The case of Goans in Zanzibar raises interesting questions. Gupta argues that this historical case challenges Freyre's Luso-tropicalism, insofar as the Goans were racialized in Goa, which was a key reason they chose to leave. She characterizes Freyre's ideas as theories of "nonracialism," but this seems misleading on two fronts. First, a theory about race mixture can never be nonracial, by definition, although it could claim to be nonracist. Second, and again invoking Dávila's analysis, Freyre's theory had elements that, in a conditional sense, challenged existing hierarchies of race while also reiterating them quite strongly: as I argued earlier, mixture entails both hierarchy and equality. So, that Goans in Goa felt themselves racialized in a hierarchical fashion is not surprising. This detail aside, it is still an intriguing idea that Goans, whether aspiring or already middle class, would choose to go to a British imperial setting, whether in India or Zanzibar (although many also went to Lusophone Mozambique, which raises the question of how important people's views of different racial formations were in shaping their migration choices). It may be that the type of "mixture" represented by a British imperial context—especially in a place like Zanzibar, which was intensely multicultural, to use an anachronistic term—offered a more attractive terrain for "interimperial" life trajectories and strategies, which juggled a whole host of modes of identification, belonging, and loyalty and thus potentially facilitated a greater sense of autonomy than the Lusophone setting with its more restricted version of mixture as *mestiçagem*.

The duality present in theories about biocultural mixture makes them inherently disposed toward multiple readings, as different perspectives establish varied relations among component elements of the assemblage. An example is the rather sudden change, analyzed by Castelo, in the reception in Portugal of Freyre's theories about Portuguese imperialism and mixture, which coincided with the 1951 change in the status of Portugal's colonies to that of "overseas provinces." In this context of global decolonization, it became important to emphasize the egalitarian dimensions of the mixture that was held to characterize the Portuguese style of managing colonial difference. Vastly different processes of mixture—Angola, Mozambique, Goa, Cape Verde, Brazil—were all part of the same complex (although this should be taken alongside Coghe's argument that, in the case of physical anthropological studies of Angolan populations, "Brazilian ideas about whitening or miscegenation were hardly transposable to the 'Bushman/Bantu' divide," as this divide did not include "white" colonizers and the figure of the *mestiço*). Before that time, Freyre's valorization of mixture was seen as a threat to white supremacy, even if it was actually quite compatible with it: the racial hierarchy present in ideas about racial mixture was not enough, Castelo shows, to satisfy someone like António Vicente Ferreira in the 1940s, especially if the mixture was proposed to have characterized the Portuguese themselves. However, intellectuals in colonies such as Cape Verde and Angola often embraced Freyre's theories, highlighting the "ethnic and cultural equilibrium" (Castelo) that *mestiçagem* was held to have established and appreciating what they saw as Freyre's valorization of African culture. This appropriation of Freyre's ideas—anti-racist in today's terms—was always inherently at risk from the very different and state-driven appropriation of the same ideas after 1951, when their anti-racist potential was reconfigured, building on the integral presence of hierarchy, into a neo-imperial discourse of governance.

A further factor multiplying the ways in which mixture can be interpreted and meanings of equality and hierarchy constructed and deployed is the biocultural character of the processes involved. This permits movement from biology to culture and back again, usually in the sense of deploying biological data to underwrite cultural or political statements but also in the sense that cultural values provide a rationale for certain directions and priorities in science, as well as suggesting certain categories with which to organize data (such as national, racial, and ethnic categories). For example, Castelo describes Almerindo Lessa's sero-anthropological missions to Cape Verde and Macao in the late 1950s and early 1960s to study what he called the "eugenic and civilizing possibilities of the Luso-tropical *mestiço*," a figure similar to the mestizo of Vasconcelos's *raza cósmica* in its supposed universalism. This was a clear attempt to collect biological data to sustain his conviction that the Portuguese people had made an "extremely original contribution . . . to the modern world." Although Castelo does not give us much detail of exactly how biological data were used to support this idea, she says that, in Cape Verde, Lessa found a population that he thought was homogeneous and in a state of "panmixia," and this clearly evokes an absence of racial hierarchy, even though Lessa is talking about biology and not social structure.

Dent and Santos trace a similar pattern, and although their frame is national rather than imperial, the same relationship between biology and culture or between scientific data and broader social concerns can be detected. Familiar narratives of what the Brazilian nation was and where it was going supplied the overall frame for the scientific endeavor to characterize Brazilians in biological terms; not surprisingly, race mixture occupied a central organizing role here, producing great biological heterogeneity, allied to racial harmony. Although Francisco Salzano and Newton Freire-Maia admitted "unfair prejudice against the Negro," this was not "poisoned by hate," which made Brazil very different from the "tragic situation" found in South Africa or the United States (Dent and Santos). Just as the cultural landscape had provided them with a narrative to organize their data, they found a way back down this road: biological data that demonstrated the "fallacious nature of racist theories" would be an important tool to ensure that Brazil did not end up like the United States.[20] This is indicative of a way in which the duality of hierarchy and equality in ideas about mixture can be temporarily resolved or suspended. Mixture necessarily involves a temporal dimension, and this can be given a teleological drive: mixing will lead to equality in the future, because this is its natural outcome, just as the tree grows from the seed. As we know, however, time is not teleological; human agency is. And human agency reproduces the hierarchy of which mixture cannot divest itself.

The examples of Lessa and Salzano and Freire-Maia could be taken to suggest a fairly simple relationship between "science" and "society." However, it is important not to artificially conceive of these as separate domains: they are interwoven, even if there is some institutional work of "purification" that tries to insulate the pursuit of scientific findings from the direct influence of social factors.[21] Wegner and Souza's chapter indicates the complexities of how science proceeds in its institutional setting. In many ways, Octávio Domingues and Salvador de Toledo Piza Júnior shared a common approach to eugenics and genetics, grounded in the transnational science of the 1920s and 1930s. Yet, the two men took diametrically opposite views of mixture (this was before the publication of *Casa-grande & senzala* in 1933). Domingues saw it as positive, producing normal and healthy individuals; he also decried racial hierarchy. Toledo Piza Júnior admitted that genetically miscegenation was not a problem, but he saw blacks and whites as biologically very different in terms of their endocrine systems, which made mixture between them undesirable. In this sense, the tension between equality and hierarchy in mixture is reflected in the very specific detail of scientific distinctions between genetic and endocrine systems.

A rather different relationship between biology and culture is evident in the work of António Augusto Mendes Correia and the mainly postwar expeditions of the Portuguese Board of Geographical Missions and Colonial Research, as analyzed by Roque. Mendes Correia was anti-Freyrean and anti-Luso-tropicalist: he saw mixing as problematic and preferred to think in terms of fairly rigid racial categories and hierarchies. Yet, as Roque shows, he believed in a spiritual and affective link between the racially inferior Timorese and the Portuguese, facilitated by the natural predilection of the latter for a life regulated by affectivity. This echoes the idea developed by Freyre and others that the Portuguese were naturally inclined to form unions with the women of their colonized populations. Roque highlights the religious, specifically Christian, connotations of Mendes Correia's discourse about spirit, but the notion also occupies an interesting position on the biology-culture continuum (mirrored perhaps by the status of affect, as conceived recently by theorists such as Gilles Deleuze and Manuel DeLanda, who see it as pre-discursive and thus not fully cultural, without its being simply biological). From a Romantic point of view—for example, for Johann Herder—the spirit (*Volksgeist*) was a deeply rooted national or ethnic sense of belonging or loyalty, which characterized whole peoples, shaped in part by their embodied relationship to the "soil." This resonates nicely with Roque's depiction of Mendes Correia's obviously intense nationalism, or imperial supranationalism, and raises the question in both cases of whether spirit in this sense is cultural, natural, or a natural-cultural assemblage. In any case, it is interesting that, while Mendes Correia emphasized hierarchy over equality, apparently rejecting (biological) mixture altogether, he embraced the idea of spiritual union, and, in this sense of mixture (which also fits comfortably into standard notions of *mestizaje/mestiçagem*), we can see the same dynamic of hierarchy and equality being played out. For Mendes Correia, the Timorese may have had spiritual affinities (note the kinship connotations of the word) with the Portuguese, but they were assigned a subaltern role in the relationship.

Conclusion

I have been concerned above all with race mixing. But it is clear that this phenomenon was being materialized through the circulation of many diverse elements: values, people, practices, ideas, theories, and so on. What it meant to "mix races" thus varied according to context, and to the theoretical and material resources in circulation. In New England, the idea of mixture was mediated by patterns of migration from Europe and the Azores. In Goa and Zanzibar, it was mediated by different imperial regimes, which thought about and regulated mixture in different ways. In Portugal, the idea of mixture was heavily mediated by changing imperial priorities in a decolonizing world—not just the value ascribed to mixing (as shown by Castelo) but also what mixing itself consisted of (as analyzed by Roque). Life science also supplied a multitude of cognitive and material resources for thinking about mixture: by definition, the focus here was on biology, but the data circulated more widely into ethical domains of value and social policy. Again, what mixture meant was constructed in particular ways: was it just about genetics, or was it the whole person, including the endocrine system (Wegner and Souza)? Should mixture be conceived as genetics and genealogy, or should it be seen also in terms of the biotypological constitution of the whole body (Vimieiro-Gomes)? In short, what constitutes race mixing cannot be taken for granted but must be traced through the materializations of race in specific cases.

PETER WADE is Professor of Social Anthropology at the University of Manchester and holds a British Academy Wolfson Research Professorship (2013–2016). His publications include *Blackness and Race Mixture* (1993), *Race and Ethnicity in Latin America* (2010), *Race, Nature and Culture: An Anthropological Perspective* (2002), *Race and Sex in Latin America* (2009), *Mestizo Genomics: Race Mixture, Nation, and Science in Latin America* (2014), and *Race: An Introduction* (2015). His most recent book is *Degrees of Mixture, Degrees of Freedom: Genomics, Multiculturalism and Race in Latin America* (2017). With Mónica Moreno Figueroa, he is currently codirecting the project "Latin American Antiracism in a 'Post-racial' Age."

Notes

1. Gilberto Freyre, *Conferencias na Europa* (Rio de Janeiro, 1938), 14, cited in Jerry Dávila, this volume.
2. José María Samper, *Ensayo sobre las revoluciones políticas y la condición social de las repúblicas Colombianas (Hispano-Americanas): Con un apéndice sobre la orografía y la población de la confederación granadina* (Paris, 1861), 299.
3. Luis López de Mesa, *De cómo se ha formado la nación Colombiana* (1934; repr., Medellín, 1970), 14, 7.
4. Catalina Muñoz Rojas, ed., *Los problemas de la raza en Colombia: Más allá del problema racial—El determinismo geográfico y las "dolencias sociales"* (Bogotá, 2011), 245.
5. José Vasconcelos, *The Cosmic Race / La raza cósmica*, trans. Didier T. Jaén (1925; repr., Baltimore, 1997), 59.
6. David Scott FitzGerald and David Cook-Martín, *Culling the Masses: The Democratic Origins of Racist Immigration Policy in the Americas* (Cambridge, MA, 2014), 236.
7. Richard Rodriguez, *Brown: The Last Discovery of America* (New York, 2002); Silvio Torres-Saillant, "Afro-Latinas/os and the Racial Wall," in *A Companion to Latina/o Studies*, ed. Juan Flores and Renato Rosaldo (Oxford, 2007), 376–75.
8. Clara E. Rodríguez, *Changing Race: Latinos, the Census, and the History of Ethnicity in the United States* (New York, 2000); Karen R. Humes, Nicholas A. Jones, and Roberto R. Ramirez, "Overview of Race and Hispanic Origin: 2010" (Washington, DC, 2010).
9. Gloria Anzaldúa, *Borderlands / La Frontera: The New Mestiza* (San Francisco, 1987); Peter Wade, "Images of Latin American Mestizaje and the Politics of Comparison," *Bulletin of Latin American Research* 23, no. 1 (2004): 355–66; Peter Wade, "Hybridity Theory and Kinship Thinking," *Cultural Studies* 19, no. 5 (2005): 602–21.
10. For some examples, see Peter Wade, *Degrees of Mixture, Degrees of Freedom: Genomics, Multiculturalism, and Race in Latin America* (Durham, NC, 2017), 261–62.
11. Peter Wade, Carlos López Beltrán, Eduardo Restrepo, and Ricardo Ventura Santos, eds., *Mestizo Genomics: Race Mixture, Nation, and Science in Latin America* (Durham, NC, 2014).
12. Samper, *Ensayo sobre las revoluciones políticas*, 88–94; Luis Antonio Restrepo, "El pensamiento social e histórico," in *Historia de Antioquia*, ed. Jorge Orlando Melo (Medellín, 1988), 380.
13. Vasconcelos, *The Cosmic Race*, 75.
14. FitzGerald and Cook-Martín, *Culling the Masses*.

15. See, e.g., Tanya Golash-Boza and William Darity, "Latino Racial Choices: The Effects of Skin Colour and Discrimination on Latinos' and Latinas' Racial Self-Identifications," *Ethnic and Racial Studies* 31, no. 5 (2008): 899–934.
16. Miriam Jiménez Román, "Looking at That Middle Ground: Racial Mixing as Panacea?" in Flores and Rosaldo, *A Companion to Latina/o Studies*, 325–36; Wade, "Images of Latin American Mestizaje"; Charles R. Hale, "Travel Warning: Elite Appropriations of Hybridity, Mestizaje, Antiracism, Equality, and Other Progressive-Sounding Discourses in Highland Guatemala," *Journal of American Folklore* 112, no. 445 (1999): 297–315.
17. Wade, "Hybridity Theory and Kinship Thinking."
18. Lawrence Grossberg, "On Postmodernism and Articulation: An Interview with Stuart Hall," *Journal of Communication Inquiry* 10, no. 2 (1986): 45–60.
19. Elizabeth Hordge-Freeman, *The Color of Love: Racial Features, Stigma, and Socialization in Black Brazilian Families* (Austin, TX, 2015); Mónica Moreno Figueroa, "'Linda Morenita': Skin Colour, Beauty and the Politics of Mestizaje in Mexico," in *Cultures of Colour: Visual, Material, Textual*, ed. Chris Horrocks (Oxford, 2012), 167–80; Mara Viveros Vigoya, "Más que una cuestión de piel: Determinantes sociales y orientaciones subjetivas en los encuentros y desencuentros heterosexuales entre mujeres y hombres negros y no negros en Bogotá," in *Raza, etnicidad y sexualidades: Ciudadanía y multiculturalismo en América latina*, ed. Peter Wade, Fernando Urrea Giraldo, and Mara Viveros Vigoya (Bogotá, 2008), 247–78; Elizabeth F. S. Roberts, *God's Laboratory: Assisted Reproduction in the Andes* (Berkeley, CA, 2012).
20. Francisco Mauro Salzano and Newton Freire-Maia, *Problems in Human Biology: A Study of Brazilian Populations* (Detroit, 1970), 61.
21. Bruno Latour, *We Have Never Been Modern*, trans. Catherine Porter (London, 1993).

Bibliography

Anzaldúa, Gloria. *Borderlands / La Frontera: The New Mestiza*. San Francisco: Aunt Lute Books, 1987.
FitzGerald, David Scott, and David Cook-Martín. *Culling the Masses: The Democratic Origins of Racist Immigration Policy in the Americas*. Cambridge, MA: Harvard University Press, 2014.
Flores, Juan, and Renato Rosaldo, eds. *A Companion to Latina/o Studies*. Oxford: Blackwell, 2007.
Freyre, Gilberto. *Conferencias na Europa*. Rio de Janeiro: Serviço Gráfico do Ministério da Educação e Saúde, 1938.
Golash-Boza, Tanya, and William Darity. "Latino Racial Choices: The Effects of Skin Colour and Discrimination on Latinos' and Latinas' Racial Self-Identifications." *Ethnic and Racial Studies* 31, no. 5 (2008): 899–934.
Grossberg, Lawrence. "On Postmodernism and Articulation: An Interview with Stuart Hall." *Journal of Communication Inquiry* 10, no. 2 (1986): 45–60.
Hale, Charles R. "Travel Warning: Elite Appropriations of Hybridity, Mestizaje, Antiracism, Equality, and Other Progressive-Sounding Discourses in Highland Guatemala." *Journal of American Folklore* 112, no. 445 (1999): 297–315.
Hordge-Freeman, Elizabeth. *The Color of Love: Racial Features, Stigma, and Socialization in Black Brazilian Families*. Austin: University of Texas Press, 2015.
Humes, Karen R., Nicholas A. Jones, and Roberto R. Ramirez. "Overview of Race and Hispanic Origin: 2010." Washington, DC: US Census Bureau, 2010.

Jiménez Román, Miriam. "Looking at That Middle Ground: Racial Mixing as Panacea?" In Flores and Rosaldo, *A Companion to Latina/O Studies*, 325–36.
Latour, Bruno, *We Have Never Been Modern*. Translated by Catherine Porter. London: Harvard University Press, 1993.
López de Mesa, Luis. *De cómo se ha formado la nación Colombiana*. Medellín: Editorial Bedout, 1970. First published 1934 by Librería Colombiana (Bogotá).
Moreno Figueroa, Mónica. "'Linda Morenita;: Skin Colour, Beauty and the Politics of Mestizaje in Mexico." In *Cultures of Colour: Visual, Material, Textual*, edited by Chris Horrocks, 167–80. Oxford: Berghahn Books, 2012.
Restrepo, Luis Antonio. "El pensamiento social e histórico." In *Historia de Antioquia*, edited by Jorge Orlando Melo, 373–82. Medellín: Suramericana de Seguros, 1988.
Roberts, Elizabeth F. S. *God's Laboratory: Assisted Reproduction in the Andes*. Berkeley: University of California Press, 2012.
Rodríguez, Clara E. *Changing Race: Latinos, the Census, and the History of Ethnicity in the United States*. New York: New York University Press, 2000.
Rodriguez, Richard. *Brown: The Last Discovery of America*. New York: Viking, 2002.
Rojas, Catalina Muñoz, ed. *Los problemas de la raza en Colombia: Más allá del problema racial—El determinismo geográfico y las "dolencias sociales."* Bogotá: Editorial Universidad del Rosario, 2011.
Salzano, Francisco Mauro, and Newton Freire-Maia. *Problems in Human Biology: A Study of Brazilian Populations*. Detroit: Wayne State University Press, 1970.
Samper, José María. *Ensayo Sobre las revoluciones políticas y la condición social de las repúblicas Colombianas (Hispano-Americanas): Con un apéndice sobre la orografía y la población de la confederación granadina*. Paris: Imprenta de E. Thunot y Cia, 1861.
Torres-Saillant, Silvio. "Afro-Latinas/os and the Racial Wall." In Flores and Rosaldo, *A Companion to Latina/o Studies*, 363–75.
Vasconcelos, José. *The Cosmic Race / La raza cósmica*. Translated by Didier T. Jaén. Baltimore: Johns Hopkins University Press, 1997. First published in Spanish 1925 by Agencia Mundial de Librería (Madrid).
Viveros Vigoya, Mara. "Más que una cuestión de piel: Determinantes sociales y orientaciones subjetivas en los encuentros y desencuentros heterosexuales entre mujeres y hombres negros y no negros en Bogotá." In *Raza, etnicidad y sexualidades: Ciudadanía y multiculturalismo en América latina*, edited by Peter Wade, Fernando Urrea Giraldo, and Mara Viveros Vigoya, 247–78. Bogotá: Universidad Nacional de Colombia, 2008.
Wade, Peter. *Degrees of Mixture, Degrees of Freedom: Genomics, Multiculturalism, and Race in Latin America*. Durham, NC: Duke University Press, 2017.
———. "Hybridity Theory and Kinship Thinking." *Cultural Studies* 19, no. 5 (2005): 602–21.
———. "Images of Latin American Mestizaje and the Politics of Comparison." *Bulletin of Latin American Research* 23, no. 1 (2004): 355–66.
Wade, Peter, Carlos López Beltrán, Eduardo Restrepo, and Ricardo Ventura Santos, eds. *Mestizo Genomics: Race Mixture, Nation, and Science in Latin America*. Durham, NC: Duke University Press, 2014.

Index

Adams, Romanzo, 252–253, 254fig
Afonso Arinos Law, 116, 149
African League, 75
afrocentrism, 61, 80
Afro-Shirazi state, 280, 283
Alcindor, John, 74
Allied forces, 172–173
Allport, Gordon, 115
Almeida, António de: about, 189–191; and Angolan "Bushmen" categories, 191–194, 193map; and Bantuization, 11, 198–201; and census research, 197–198; and evolutionary vs. biological anthropology, 196–197; and Mendes Correia, 36, 160, 165, 166fig; Negroid thesis, 194–195; and Porto School of Antrhopology, 228; racism of, 37
Almeida Jr., António Marques de, 190
Almeida, Maria Emília de Castro e, 189, 191
Alves da Cunha, Manuel, 186
amasiamento, 120
American Anthropologist, 72
American Board of Commissioners for Foreign Missions, 68, 70, 73, 74–75, 76, 77–78
American Sociological Review, 120
Anderson, Warwick, 14
Andrade, Mário Pinto de, 70
Angola Anthropobiological Mission, 11
Annales: Économies, Sociétés, Civilisations, 288
anti-racism, agenda, 8
A Província, 24
Araújo, Caio Simões de, 268
Araújo de Freitas, João, 196
Araújo, Ricardo Benzaquén de, 54
Argentina, 25, 113, 218, 220

Arinos de Melo Franco, Afonso, 116
Aryan supremacy, 96
assimilados, 69, 78–79, 292
Association of the Angola Natives, 30
As tendências bio-étnicas do Brasil contemporâneo, 225
Athayde, Alfredo, 220, 230
authoritarianism, 11, 57, 59, 218, 244, 245
Azevedo, Fernando de, 35
Azevedo, Thales de, 118, 122

Bahia, 52, 62, 112, 117–118, 119–120, 215
Bangham, Jenny, 137
Bantuization, 11, 198–201
Bantu-speaking peoples, 11, 187–188, 189, 191–194, 196, 198–202, 301
Barbára, Mario, 221
Barbosa, Ruy, 50
Barreto, Castro, 35
Bastide, Roger, 59, 112, 118, 288
Basto, Alberto Celestino Ferreira Pinto, 73
Batista, Miguel (Goan tailor), 280–282
Batista, Robin (Goan photographer), 280–282, 282fig
Battistoni, Alyssa, 200
Baylor University, 24, 47
Beira, 70, 73, 76, 78
Benedict, Ruth, 49, 120, 249, 292
Berardinelli, Waldemar, 220–221, 222fig, 227
Bicudo, Virginia Leone, 112, 122
Bilden, Rüdiger, 24, 25–26, 28, 49, 96
biotypogram, 221, 223fig, 229
biotypology, 9, 11, 216–217, 218–223, 224–227, 229–232
Black Experimental Theater (TEN), 116–117, 118
black identities, 59, 61–62

blackness, 62
Bleek, Dorothea Frances, 188
Bleek, Wilhelm, 187
Bleibtreu, Hermann, 139
blood studies, 34
Boas, Franz: at Columbia University, 5, 7; influence on Freyre, 47, 49–52, 104, 114, 249; influence on Simango, 5–7, 68, 69–72; influences on Luso-tropicalism, 24–28, 79–81; neo-Lamarckianism of, 93–94; patronage of Simango, 73–77; race and nature-nurture (culture) discussions, 51–55, 114, 225; and race vs. culture, 114; and Roquette-Pinto, 96, 104
Boletim de Eugenia, 97, 99, 100–101
Bonnevie, Kristine, 102
Boskop Man, 194
Botswana, 184, 191, 199
Boxer, Charles R., 4
brancos, 137, 138, 140
Brantlinger, Patrick, 187
brasileiras: Aspectos demográficos, genéticos e antropológicos
Brasília, Universidade de, 146
Brill, Howard, 253
Broom, Robert, 198
Brown, Isaac, 224–225
Bryce, James, 25
Buarque de Holanda, Sérgio, 123–124
Bunker, Fred, 70, 73
"Bushmen," 9–11, 163, 184–189, 190–198, 199–202, 291. *See also* Khoisan

Caliban, 90–91, 102, 105
Calmon, Pedro, 215
Camacho, António de Brito, 74
Camões, Luís de, 27
Cândido, Antonio, 123
Cantril, Hadley, 115
Canudos, 52
Cape Verde, 3, 6, 28–29, 34–37, 105, 161–162, 228, 246, 252, 268, 300–301
Capital Art Studio (CAS), 273, 277, 279, 280, 281
Cardoso, Fernando Henrique, 8, 47, 138
Cardoso, Artur da Fonseca, 167
Cardoso, Óscar, 200
Carnation Revolution, 60
Carneiro, Edison, 48, 56

Carneiro, Edson, 112
Carneiro, Paulo Estevão de Berredo, 117
Carney, Mabel, 71
Carrara, Sérgio, 92
Carroll-Seguin, Rita, 253
Casa-grande & senzala: American/Lusophone juxtaposition, 1; Boas's conversation with Herskovits, 79; Brazilian literacy and, 47; Cape Verdean intellectuals and, 246; citations, 26; colonizer portrayed in, 91; contrasted with Roquette-Pinto and Kehl, 90; criticisms of, 32, 56; cultures, 53–54, 58; English translation, 123; Febvre's admiration, 289–290; foreword, 93, 104; Freyre's criticism of Viana, 123; imperial grammar, 68; lack of quantitative data, 138; Luso-tropicalism, 27, 105, 288; miscegenation, 245; Northeastern Brazil, 124; particularities of Portuguese colonialism, 135; preface, 25, 49, 54, 289, 292; publication, 46, 48, 50, 56, 58, 93, 94, 96, 114, 288, 302; race relations, 93, 113–114, 115, 121, 125; redemption allegory, 52; research, 24; reverence for, 29–30; slavery, 27; social visions for Brazil, 143; success of, 8, 97; symbolism of sailors, 56; terminology, 62
Casely-Hayford, Adelaide, 73
Catholicism, 13, 119, 121, 126, 169, 174, 218, 247, 265, 270–271, 279
Caucasians, 34, 144, 162, 252
Cele, Madikane, 80
Center for Political and Social Studies (Centro de Estudos Políticos e Sociais, CEPS), 33, 34, 37
Cerejeira, Cardinal of Lisbon, 79
Certeau, Michel de, 81
Chadarevian, Soraya de, 137
Chardin, Pierre Teilhard de, 37
Chesterton, G. K., 25
Christian Reconquest, 32
Claridade, 29
Cleminson, Richard, 219, 226
Coaracy, Vivaldo, 123
Coelho, Ruy, 114, 118
Coimbra, University of, 30, 220, 226
Coito, Manuel, 255
Columbia University: author's research at, 70; Boas at, 5, 7, 47, 50, 68, 71–72,

77, 79, 114, 249; Freyre at, 1, 24–25, 47, 49–50, 79, 114, 249; Joaquim Nabuco Institute staff trained at, 124; joint project with Bahia, 118; Simango at, 7, 68, 71–72, 77, 79; Wagley at, 118, 139
commissioned books, 58
communism, 60, 142
Congresso do Mundo Português, 31
Conniff, Michael, 46
Correia, Germano. *See* Germano da Silva Correia, Alberto
Correia, Mendes. *See* Mendes Correia, António Augusto
Corte-Real, Aleixo (Dom), 164, 174–175
Costa, Carrington da, 36
Costa e Silva, Valéria, 55
Costa Pinto, Luiz de Aguiar, 112, 118, 122, 123, 124
Coussey, Christine Mary, 76, 80
Cranbrook Institute of Science, 292
Crapanzano, Vincent, 288
Croce, Benedetto, 290
Crouzet, François, 289
Cruzeiro, 58
Cunha, Euclides da, 52, 216
Curtis, Natalie, 68, 70, 71, 80

Dart, Raymond, 192
Da Silva, John, 280–282, 281fig, 283
Davenport, Charles B., 96, 100, 101
David, J. H. Santos, 197
decal method, 221
descendente, 12, 161, 247
Dessai, Mortó, 34
Diário de Pernambuco, 58
Dias, Augusto, 255
Dias, E. C. (Goan photographer), 272
Dias, Isidore I. (Goan store owner), 273, 274fig
Dias, Jorge, 33–34, 35, 36, 37, 225
Dili, 165, 166fig, 167, 170
Diniz, José de Oliveira Ferreira, 186
discrimination: across social institutions, 143; Brown's study and, 224; Dunham incident of, 116; Freyre's criticism of protests against, 59–61; lack of, 4, 35; in Lusophone colonial history, 3; racial, 3–4, 30, 78, 115, 122, 125, 127, 143–144, 149, 175, 244; wage, 78
Dobzhansky, Theodosius, 144

Doke, Clement Martyn, 77
Domingues, Octávio, 90, 94, 98–99, 102–103, 104
Doyle, Laura, 265, 266, 267, 272, 283
Duarte, Paulo, 122–123
Duarte Santos, Luís, 220, 221
Du Bois, W.E.B, 7, 26, 47, 68, 74, 75
Durham, Katherine, 116
Durkheim, Émile, 178, 249

Earthy, Dora, 72
Easmon, John Farrell, 73
Easmon, Kathleen, 72–73, 74, 75, 80
Ecos do Atlântico Sul, 105
Ellis Júnior, Alfredo, 215, 224
endocrinology, 100–102
endogamy, 247, 252, 299
England, 76, 113
Espírito Santo, José do, 255
Estep, Gerald, 253
Estermann, Charles, 188
ethnography: account on the "Bushmen", 185–186, 188, 189–190, 200; Boas and Simango's works, 7, 72, 76–77, 80–81; Boas's work, 69; of empires, 267; focus of Boas's students, 49; of Goans, 269, 271, 272, 273, 282; Mendes Correia's views on, 227; Ramos' criticism of Freyre, 48; research, 269, 271, 273; Ribeiro's thesis, 120, 122, 125; Simango's interest in, 71; studies of photography, 13, 265, 271, 272
European colonial empires, 23
exceptionalism: Brazilian, 7, 136, 148, 296; colonial, 9–10, 159, 162, 175, 268; Iberian, 126; Lusophone, 1–2, 9; Luso-tropical, 12, 161; nation-states and, 2–3; racial, 1–3, 4, 12, 79, 159, 161, 162, 293, 296

Faleiro, S. R. (Goan tailor), 274, 275fig, 276
Febvre, Lucien, 288, 289–290, 292
Federal do Rio Grande do Sul, Universidade, 146
Fernandes, Florestan, 8, 60, 112, 122, 123, 124, 138
Fernandes, Henrique Barahona, 220
Fernández Retamar, Roberto, 90
Ferreira, António Vicente, 32
Ferreira, Lis, 230–231

First Brazilian Republic, 218
First National Congress of Colonial Anthropology, 30, 228
Fischer, Eugen, 96, 101
Frazier, Franklin, 117, 119–121
Frazier, Franz, 28
Free School of Sociology and Politics, 123–124
Freire-Maia, Newton: and Brazilian genetics research, 8, 9, 135–137, 145–148; career trajectory of, 144–145; genetics-sociology synthesis, 137–139; on race and the nation, 141–144, 148–149; racism of, 301; "tri-hybrid" race theory of, 136, 140–141
Frenz, Margret, 270–271, 272, 275–276, 279, 283
Freud, Sigmund, 3, 51
Freyre, ideology of colonialism, 60, 62
Freyre, Fernando de Mello, 49
Fritsch, Gustav, 186
Fróes da Fonseca, Alvaro, 104
Fundação Joaquim Nabuco, 49

Gamio, Manuel, 49
Garvey, Marcus, 73, 74
Gates, Reginald Ruggles, 99
Geirinhas, Alberto Fernandes, 199
genetics: blood groups, 194; of Brazil, 7–9, 52, 90–91, 94, 95–96, 98, 103, 135–149; of Cape Verde, 34–35; crosses, 223; differentiated from race, 52; endocrine systems and, 302, 303; eugenics and, 302; human population, 7, 8; investigation of, 8, 14; of Macau, 34; malleability, 185, 198; Mendelian, 93–97, 99, 100, 101, 102, 103, 225; miscegenation and, 224, 226, 302; mutationism, 161, 168–170, 175; phenotypes and, 194, 217, 227, 232; racism and, 37, 297; relationships, 25, 114; research, 187, 287; testing, 252; variation, 195
genomics, 3, 136, 149
Germano da Silva Correia (Germano Correia), Alberto, 12–13, 30–31, 105, 161, 249, 255–256
Germany, 23, 32, 61, 94, 97–98, 219–220, 258
Geschwender, James A., 253

Ghana, 73, 76, 78
Giddings, Frank, 250
Giddings, Franklin, 25
Gil-Riaño, Sebastián, 148
Ginsberg, Aniela, 112
Global South, 1–3, 23, 258, 271, 287
Goa, 3, 6, 161, 246–249, 267, 270, 280, 282, 300, 303
Godinho, Fernando, 36
Gogoi (Gogoyo), 73, 76–77
Gomes, A. C. (Goan photographer), 272
Goulart, João, 143, 146
Graves of Tarim, The, 266
Guerreiro, Manuel Viegas, 200
Guerreiro Ramos, Alberto, 28, 35, 48, 118, 124
Guimarães, Antonio Sérgio, 59
Guinea, 178, 228–229, 268
Guinea-Bissau, 3, 60, 79, 160
Gurvitch, George, 115

Hacking, Ian, 291
Hampton Institute, 68, 71, 73
Harlem Renaissance, 80
Harris, Marvin, 112
Hawai'i, 251–253, 255–256, 260n32, 261n34, 262n50
Hawai'i, University of, 253
Hayes, Carlton, 50
Hayes, Roland, 80
Hearn, Lafcadio, 25
hematology, 34, 36
Henrique of Portugal, Infante D., 125
Herskovits, Melville, 28, 49, 53, 72, 79, 117, 119–120
Hindus, 270, 279
Hispanic American Historical Review, 49
Ho, Engseng, 265, 266, 279, 283
Holocaust, 112, 115
Horkheimer, Max, 115
Hottentots, 186–187, 192
Howard University, 120
Hunt, George, 81
Hunt, Ida Alexander Gibbs, 74
Hurston, Zora Neale, 48, 49

Ianni, Octavio, 8, 138
immigration, 51, 53, 56, 91–92, 97, 104, 139, 142, 216, 219, 297–298
Imperial Connections, 266

Indian Ocean, 265, 266, 269, 270–272, 282, 283
indígenas, 10, 78, 171, 176, 200, 292
Indigenato regime, 79, 171, 188
índios, 137, 138, 140, 297
Institute for the Study of Man, 191
Institute of Social Anthropology, 119
interimperiality, 267, 272
Interracial Marriage in Hawai'i, 253
Italy, 220, 228, 258

James, William, 14
Jeca Tatú (fictional character), 51–52
Jewish peoples, 27, 32, 33, 53, 298
Joaquim Nabuco Institute, 116, 119, 120–121, 124
Johannesburg, 191
Johnston, Sir Henry (Harry), 25, 187–188
Jung, Moon-Kie, 255
Junod, Henri-Alexandre, 72, 77, 81
Junod, Henri-Philippe, 72
Junqueira, Clóvis, 36
Junta das Missões Geográficas e de Investigações Coloniais (JMGIC), 160, 166–167, 190. *See also* Portuguese Board of Geographic Missions and Colonial Research
Junta de Investigações do Ultramar (JIU), 33, 34–36, 160, 166–167. *See also* Overseas Research Board

Kalahari Research Committee (KRC), 191
Kehl, Renato, 90, 94, 97–100, 101, 102, 104, 215
Kenya, 270, 272
Khoisan, 9, 192, 194, 197. *See also* "Bushmen"
Klineberg, Otto, 28, 115, 118, 123, 289
Kofi Amoah III, Chief, 74
Kretschmer, Ernst, 220
Kroeber, Alfred, 249
Kuper, Jessica, 270

La Croix du sud, 288
Landes, Ruth, 28, 53
L'anthropologie, 291
Lapps, 101–102
La race, les races, 227
la raza cósmica, 297, 301
Laski, Harold, 74

latinidad, 297
Leão, Carneiro, 35
Lebre, António, 188
"Les races de l'empire français", 291
Les races humaines, 291
Lessa, Almerindo, 24, 34–36, 37, 162
Lévi-Strauss, Claude, 69
Lewis, David Levering, 75
Lições de eugenia, 97–98, 104
Lind, Andrew, 253
Lins do Rego, José, 123
Lipphardt, Veronika, 149
Lisbon, 31, 34, 74–75, 76–77, 79, 165, 189, 196, 246, 248, 293
literacy, 47–48
Little, Michael, 195
liurai, 174–175
Lobato, José Bento Monteiro. *See* Monteiro Lobato, José Bento
London, 73, 74–75, 76, 79, 93
Lopes da Silva, Baltasar, 105
Lord, A. P. de (Goan photographer), 272
Lowie, Robert Harry, 27
Luso-colonial racial science, 159
Luso-tropicalismo, 1, 4, 7, 9, 136–139, 162–163
Lusotropicology, 57

Macau, 3, 161–162, 163, 194
macronymphia, 194–195
Magalhães, José de, 74, 75
Magalhães, Lieutenant Colonel Leite de, 172
Malayan race, 167–168
Malay Archipelago, 167–169
Manchete, 59
Mansions and the Shanties, The, 114, 125
Martin, Percy Alvin, 24
Mateus, Amílcar, 228
Maurras, Charles, 125
Mauss, Marcel, 69, 82n4, 236n67, 249
Mayor, Leopoldo, 36
Mead, Margaret, 49, 120, 249
Melanesia, 168
Mendel, Gregor, 8, 52, 93–94, 100
Mendelism, 8, 52, 90, 93–97, 99–103, 225
Mendes Correia, António Augusto: about, 159–161, 215–217; affective patriotic primitivism, 10, 171–172, 178; and António de Almeida, 190; and Brazilian

vs. Portuguese biotypology, 217–223; and colonialism, 9, 165–167, 166fig, 173–176, 176fig, 228–231; critique of Boas and Freyre, 225–226; dualistic racial primitivism of, 161–164, 177; mutationist theory of, 167–171; and the Porto School of Anthropology, 228–232; and "racial purity", 31–32, 105, 169, 216, 226–227, 247; racism of, 37; and Roquette-Pinto, 224
mestiçagem, 7, 9, 135–137, 169, 292, 296, 298, 300, 301, 303
mestiços, 24, 29–31, 34–36, 92, 95–96, 104, 140, 162–163, 202, 292–293, 296, 301
mestizaje, 296, 297, 298, 299, 303
mestizos, 28, 30–32, 34, 35–36, 52, 75, 140, 160, 169, 297, 301
Metcalf, Thomas, 265, 266, 266–267, 283
Métraux, Alfred, 114, 118, 119, 121, 124–126, 144
Mexico, 49, 61, 218, 297
Michigan, University of, 145
military, 32, 48, 60, 136–138, 146, 172–173, 219
Milliet, Sergio, 123
Missão Antropológica de Timor, 160–161, 164, 167. *See also* Timor Anthropological Mission
missionaries, 5, 7, 24, 47, 68–69, 70–72, 73–78, 80–81, 188, 199, 251, 253, 278
Mjöen, Jon Alfred, 100–102
Mohr, Otto Lous, 101–102
Momigliano, Arnaldo, 290
Monteiro Lobato, José Bento, 51–52, 53
Moors, 27, 32, 33
Moreira, Adriano, 33, 34–35, 37
Morgado, José, 30
Morrison, Tony, 292
Morton, Newton, 139
Mota, Carlos Guilherme, 57
Mucassequeres, 185
Mucuancalas, 192, 194. *See also* Vassekeles
mulattoes, 25, 29–30, 32–33, 48, 50–51, 54, 138–140, 224
Musée de l'Homme, 291
Muslims, 27–28, 53, 169, 270, 279
mutationism, 161, 168, 170, 176

Nabuco, Fundação Joaquim, 49, 50
Namibia, 9–10, 184, 188–189, 191, 199, 201
Nascimento, Abdias do, 48, 61, 62, 116
Nash, Roy, 26, 27
National Association for the Advancement of Colored People (NAACP), 26
national identity, 26, 47, 54, 56, 57, 62, 92, 113, 122, 138, 219, 225, 231, 288
nationalism, 2–3, 31, 46, 57, 68, 69–70, 177, 303
nationalistic optimism, 57
nature-nurture debate, 53
Navy, 55
Nazism, 23, 32, 92, 97, 148
Ndau peoples, 69–70, 80–81
Neel, James V., 145
negros, 137, 138, 140
"Negros do Brasil", 122
neo-Lamarckism, 8, 90, 91, 93–94, 97
New England, 12–13, 245, 249, 251, 255–256, 303
New Guinea, 168
Nogueira, Oracy, 112
Nordics, 101–102
Northwestern University, 119–120, 124
Nous sommes des sang-mêlés: Manuel d'histoire de la civilisation française, 289
Nunes, Manuel, 255

O Estado de S. Paulo, 122
Oliveira, José Osório de. *See* Osório de Oliveira, José
Oliveira, Lieutenant Colonel Luna de, 174
Olivier, Sir Sidney, 74
O negro brasileiro, 53
O normotipo brasileiro, 224
Ordem e progresso, 51, 58
Osório de Oliveira, José, 28–29, 105
Osorio Roll, Elvira, 255
Os sertões, 52
Overseas Research Board, 33, 34, 35, 36, 160, 165. *See also* Junta de Investigações do Ultramar (JIU)
Oza, Ranchhod, 272–273, 274fig, 275fig, 276–280, 277fig, 278fig, 283
Oza, Rohit, 272, 273

Palès, Léon, 178, 291
Pallares-Burke, Maria Lúcia, 25, 49, 79
Papuan race, 167–168
Paris, 36, 74, 119, 124, 125, 291
Park, Robert E., 28, 253

Passos, José Luiz, 55
patriarchalism, 1, 24, 26, 28, 90, 120–121, 124, 126
patriotism, 10, 92, 159–160, 163–164, 170, 171–172, 173–175, 176–177
Paulo, Leopoldina Ferreira, 229
Peabody, George Foster, 70, 71, 72
Pende, Nicola, 218
Pereira, José Maria, 60
Pernambuco, 6, 8, 24, 47, 112, 116, 120, 124–125, 299
phenotype, 227, 232
Picasso, Pablo, 51
Pierson, Donald, 28, 123, 124
Pignet index, 230
Pina, Luís de, 220, 221, 223fig, 228, 229
Pinto, Luiz Costa, 36
Pinto, Rochelle, 270
Pinto, Serpa, 185
Pires de Lima, Joaquim Alberto, 31
polygamy, 120
Pontes Jr., Manuel Pereira, 200
Populações brasileiras: Aspectos demográficos, genéticos e antropológicos, 9, 135–138, 142, 145–146, 148. *See also Problems in Human Biology: A Study of Brazilian Populations*
Populações indígenas de Angola, 186
populism, 46, 56, 57, 62, 122
Porto School of Anthropology, 228
Porto, University of, 11, 31, 161, 165, 190, 215, 217, 232
Portugal: 1920s, 68; anthropology in, 188, 190, 192, 197; and Brazil, 215–2223, 224–232, 244; *Casa-grande & senzala,* 93, 105; colonial racism in, 5; empire-nation, 172, 243; ethnology in, 172; forced labor in Africa, 74, 258n4; Freyre's exile in, 24; Freyre's lectures in, 46, 113; Freyre's thinking received in, 79, 105, 138, 300; Hawaiian migrants, 256, 260n32, 261n36; history of, 139; imperial power, 45; Latin eugenic movement in, 34; Lusophone scope, 3, 6, 11, 13; Luso-tropicalism in, 12, 14, 37, 105, 113, 169, 178, 244, 246, 268; *Luso-tropicalismo,* 138; miscegenation, 6, 23, 37, 216; "multi-continental nation," 33; Nash's summer in, 26; racialization, 1, 4–5, 9, 11, 12, 28–29, 36, 161, 163, 169, 185, 216, 256, 260n25, 303; Republic of, 73; Salazar dictatorship, 5, 57–59, 138, 245, 257; Simango and, 6, 77; and Timor, 164, 169, 172–176
Portuguese and the Tropics, The, 246
Portuguese Board of Geographic Missions and Colonial Research, 228. *See also* Junta das Missões Geográficas e de Investigações Coloniais
Portuguese colonial anthropology: in Angola, 160, 184–189, 190–198, 202, 291; in Brazil, 215–217, 218–221, 222–226, 231–232; in Timor-Leste, 159–164, 165–170, 171–172, 174–179
Portuguese Colonial Exhibition, 228–229, 246
Portuguese colonialism: in Africa, 45, 46, 57–58, 60; and the African League, 75; criticism of, 74; exploitative, 2; Freyre's thinking and, 4, 30, 60, 243, 283; genetics of, 135, 139, 149; Pan-Africanist critique of, 7; racial conceptions beyond Luso-tropicalism, 159; racial democracy, 1, 4; and Salazar's dictatorship, 58, 257; in South Asia, 45; violence of, 289
Portuguese colonies: in Africa, 68, 73, 160; African voices in, 6, 45–46; anthropology in, 227–231; in Brazil, 90, 91, 105, 114, 121, 137; "Bushmen" in, 184–189, 190–198, 199–202; "Bushmen" (Khoisan) in, 184–189, 190–198, 199–202; Cape Verde, 29; and Carnation Revolution, 60; defense of, 59; forced labor in, 74, 257, 291; former, 70; Freyre's thinking received in, 23, 105, 247, 300–301; Freyre's travel to, 59; geography, 12, 13; in Goan Zanzibar, 265, 266–267, 268–272, 283; governance, 10–11; heritage of, 14–15; history, 3, 256, 265; leaders of, 60; Luso-tropicalism, 33, 105, 113, 243–246, 247; miscegenation in, 23, 27–28, 30–32, 33–34, 37, 137; multi-continental nation, 33, 243, 247; nonracist trope, 4, 12, 247; overseas provinces, 300; policy, 31–33, 79, 199–201, 287, 291; populations, 9, 11, 293, 302; race relations, 265, 293, 296; racializing of, 9–10; São Tomé, 75;

scope, 3, 243; Simango in Mozambique, 76–78; subordination of Africans, 62; Timor-Leste, 10, 159–164, 165–170, 171–176. *See also* Portuguese colonial anthropology

Portuguese Constitution, 171–172

Portuguese exceptionalism: in Angola, 9, 178, 184–186, 189–191, 192–197, 198–202; colonialism, 268; Luso-tropicalism, 79, 159, 162, 244–245, 256–257, 265; miscegenation, 162, 256–257; racializing the "Bushmen", 185–189; in Timor, 9–10, 164, 175, 178

Portugueseness, 9, 11, 13, 174, 255, 265, 269, 271

Príncipe, 74

Problems in Human Biology: A Study of Brazilian Populations, 135–136, 141, 142, 145–147, 148. *See also Populações brasileiras: Aspectos demográficos, genéticos e antropológicos*

Prospero, 90–91, 102, 105

Protestantism, 7, 69–70, 73, 75, 119

Provine, William, 99

psychiatry, 52–53, 120, 287

"pure races", 102, 161, 227, 289

Quadros, Jânio, 143

Queiroz, Rachel de, 123

Quilombo, 48

Quirino, Manoel, 117

Raças do império, 229

race mixing: Brazilian heterogeneity, 141; Correia's abhorrence of, 169; Correia's research omission, 161; degeneration of, 30; eugenic skepticism toward, 178; Freyre's views of, 4, 14, 28, 162–163; Luso-tropicalism, 12, 14, 293; *Luso-tropicalismo,* 4; mestiçagem, 9, 136, 303; miscegenation, 37, 137; North American studies of, 23, 28; obscured histories and, 149; Portuguese, 10; preoccupation with, 14; racial difference and, 191; racialization beyond the trope of, 1; rethinking, 13; secondary to biotypology, 11; theories about the powers of, 170; theory beyond, 161; Timorese, 168–170; valorization of, 12, 136

racial democracy, 1, 7, 14, 45, 54, 59–60, 62, 93, 103, 113–114, 125, 127, 143

Racial Differences, 123

racial exceptionalism, 1–3, 4, 12, 79, 159, 161, 162, 293, 296

racial heterogeneity, 11, 13, 33, 138, 141, 147–148, 168, 217, 223–224, 226, 232, 289, 301

racial laboratory, 7, 9

racial populism, 46, 56, 57, 62

Ramos, Artur (Arthur), 28, 29, 35, 52–53, 56, 59, 117

Ramos, Guerreiro. *See* Guerreiro Ramos, Alberto

Recife, 8, 24, 48, 56, 113, 116, 118–121, 124–125, 127, 215

Reconquista (Christian Reconquest), 32

Religião e relações raciais, 124, 126

Rennie, John Keith, 70

Revolution of, 1930, 24

Reyes, Rudolfo, 35

Ribeiro, Darcy, 138

Ribeiro, René, 8, 112, 113, 119, 120–122, 124, 126–127

Rio de Janeiro, 24–25, 29, 34–35, 55, 59, 61, 95, 98–99, 112, 118, 124, 215–216, 219, 224, 258, 287

Rio de Janeiro School of Medicine, 216–217, 219, 220

Robeson, Paul, 80

Rocha Vaz, Juvenil, 219

Rockefeller Foundation, 144–145, 147

Rodó, José Enrique, 90

Rodrigues, Nina, 117, 216

Roiter, Mario, 221

Roll-Hansen, Nils, 101–102

Romanzo Adams Social Research Laboratory, 253

Roquette-Pinto, Edgard: and biotypes, 216; and eugenics, 52–53, 55–57, 90, 104; on Kehl, 99–100; and Luso-tropicalism, 25, 28, 31; and Mendelian genetics, 96–97; on miscegenation, 31, 102–103, 104, 224

Rosa, César Serpa, 166fig

Rosales, Marta, 270

Ross, Edward Alsworth, 74

Ruas, Óscar, 173

Ruffié, Jacques, 34, 36

sailors, 55–56
Salazar, António de Oliveira, 58, 59, 138, 164, 173, 219, 245, 257
Salzano, Francisco M.: background and career, 135–137, 144–145; and Brazilian genetics research, 9, 145–148; genetics-sociology synthesis, 8, 137–139; on race and the nation, 141–144, 148–149; "tri-hybrid" race theory of, 136, 140–141
Santos Jr., Joaquim, 228
São Francisco River, 119
São Paulo, 35, 55, 98, 112, 116, 118, 122–124, 215, 219, 225
São Paulo, University of, 60, 122–124, 138, 144
São Tomé, 3, 74–75, 196
Sarmento, Alexandre, 197, 220, 229–230
Sarmento Rodrigues, Manuel Maria, 164, 165
Schreiner, Kristian, 102
Schumaker, Lyn, 81
Schweinfurth, Georges, 187
scientific racism, 23, 51, 52, 96, 97, 103, 159, 161, 163, 184, 187
Seigel, Micol, 148
Sexo e civilização: Aparas eugênicas, 97
Shakespeare, 90–91
Shakespeare, William, 89, 90–91
Sheldon, William Herbert, 218, 221
Shepherd, William R., 24, 49
sickle cell trait, 196–197
Sigaud, Claude, 220, 229
Silva, Francisco Venâncio, 188
Simango, Kamba: and assimilationism, 78–81; and Boas and Freyre, 5–7, 68–70, 72, 75, 77–78; Ndau study, 70–72; pan-Africanism of, 72–76
Simkins, Francis Butler, 24, 49
slavery, 24–28, 37, 50, 55–56, 60, 92, 120–122, 126, 135, 143, 257, 289
Sobrados e Mucambos, 30, 58, 138, 245
social plasticity, 269, 283
Social Process in Hawai'i, 253
Societé d'Anthropologie de Paris, 291
Sociologia, 123
somatotypes, 221
Sousa, Henrique Teixeira de, 29
Southern California, University of, 253
Special Public Health Service, 119
Spencer, Herbert, 25

Spingarn, Joel Elias, 26
spirituality, 10, 61, 78, 90, 159–161, 163–164, 169–172, 173–177, 297, 302–303
Spitzer, Leo, 81
Stanford University, 24
steatopygia, 194–195
Stepan, Nancy, 23, 91, 93, 103
Stocking, George, 93
Stoler, Ann, 292
Stow, George, 186
Subrahmanyam, Sanjay, 267

Taft, Donald, 12, 13, 249–251, 255
tailors, 250, 265, 267, 270–271, 273, 275fig, 276, 279, 280–281, 283
Tamagnini, Eusébio, 30, 32, 226
Tanganyika (Tanzania), 267, 270, 271
Tannenbaum, Frank, 58
Tatú, Jeca (fictional character), 51–52
Taylor, Julie, 200
Teixeira, Anísio, 118
Tempest, The, 90
Tensions Affecting International Understanding: A Survey of Research, 115
Theal, George, 186
The Races of Mankind, 292
Thomaz, Omar Ribeiro, 105
Timor Anthropological Mission, 160, 165, 166fig, 167, 168, 176fig. *See also* Missão Antropológica de Timor
Timor português, 168, 171, 174
Tobias, Phillip, 190–191, 193, 195, 201
Toledo Piza Júnior, Salvador de, 90, 94, 99, 100–102
Torres, Alberto, 51, 56
Torres Bodet, Jaime, 117
Two Portuguese Communities in New England, 249, 251

Uganda, 270
UNESCO, 8, 33, 112–113, 114, 115–117, 118–119, 121–122, 124–126, 140, 288–289
União Nacional dos Estudantes, 146
United Nations, 32, 243, 32, 243

Vallois, Henri, 291
Vargas Era, 57, 218–219
Vargas, Getúlio, 57, 92, 218, 219

Vasconcelos, José Leite de, 75
Vassekeles, 192, 200. *See also* Mucuancalas
Viana (Vianna), Oliveira, 122–123, 216, 224
Viola, Giacinto, 220, 221, 229
Virchow, Rudolf, 94
Volksgeist, 249, 303

Wagley, Charles, 112, 118, 123–124, 139
Wallace, Alfred Russel, 167–168, 170
Washington, Booker T., 47
Weltfish, Gene, 292

whiteness, 2, 12–14, 162–163, 252, 292, 299
whitening, 12, 14, 25, 27, 51, 103, 122, 202, 224, 225, 299, 300
Wilberforce, William, 50
Witwatersrand, University of, 191
Woodson, Carter, 47
World Health Organization, 147

Zanzibar, 12–13, 265–269, 270, 271–275, 276–279, 280–283, 300, 303
Zanzibar Revolution, 267, 273, 283
Zimmern, Alfred, 25

www.ingramcontent.com/pod-product-compliance
Lightning Source LLC
Chambersburg PA
CBHW072144100526
44589CB00015B/2088